COLONIAL NORTH
CAROLINA
IN THE EIGHTEENTH
CENTURY

COLONIAL NORTH CAROLINA IN THE EIGHTEENTH CENTURY

A STUDY IN HISTORICAL GEOGRAPHY

*BY
HARRY ROY MERRENS*

THE UNIVERSITY OF NORTH CAROLINA PRESS · CHAPEL HILL

Copyright © 1964 by
The University of North Carolina Press

Library of Congress Catalog Card Number
64-13555

to Sheila and Mark

PREFACE

This monograph surveys the changing geography of colonial North Carolina, and may be described as a study in the field of historical geography. The approach used illustrates a current emphasis within that field on the analysis of changing geographies and of forces contributing to change. Recent discussions of the nature of historical geography have helped to dispel earlier confusion and there is no need to redefine the scope and purpose of the field here.

More specifically, the work is intended as a contribution to the understanding of the colonial geography of the Atlantic Seaboard, a large but much neglected subject. What is presented in the following pages represents an attempt to begin the study of the colonial Seaboard by analyzing a segment of it.

During the eighteenth century a large and rapid increase of population took place in North Carolina as settlers spread over much of the land between the coast and the Appalachians. The period emphasized in this work runs from about the middle of the century to the Revolution. The use of a vague phrase to indicate the starting point is deliberate. Rather than fix upon any one year it was decided to adopt a fairly flexible date line and to begin the analysis of particular topics at whatever point in time seemed most appropriate. The outbreak of the Revolutionary War in 1775 provided a convenient and conventional stopping point.

During the time that has elapsed since I first began working on the geography of the colonial Seaboard I have imposed upon the kindness of many persons. I am especially indebted to certain individuals in North Carolina, and among those who helped me with their particular knowledge and made my research and travels in that state one of the most enjoyable phases of the work were the following: Dr. C. C. Crittenden, Mr. D. L. Corbitt, Mr. H. G. Jones, Mr. W. S. Tarlton, and Mrs. Mary Rogers of the North Carolina State Department of Archives and History; Professor Louise Hall of Duke University, and Miss Florence Blakeley, at Duke University Library; the staff of the Moravian Archives in Winston-Salem; Dr. Frank P. Albright (who made my visit to Old Salem enjoyable and instructive); Miss Georgia Faison, at the North Carolina State Library; Professor E. F. Goldston, of North Carolina State of The University of North Carolina at Raleigh; Professor H. T. Lefler, of the University of North Carolina at Chapel Hill; and Professor William P. Cumming of Davidson College. Mr. William S. Powell of the University Library at Chapel Hill, provided continuing assistance in innumerable ways and I gained much from his advice and help. Archival research and field work in North Carolina were facilitated through funds granted by the University of Wisconsin, in the form of a Kemper K. Knapp Graduate Fellowship, and a Travel Award from the Department of Geography.

While I was at the University of Wisconsin, first as a graduate student and then later as a faculty member, I received valuable criticism from members of the Geography and History Departments. Professor Clarence W. Olmstead offered advice and raised pertinent questions during the early phases of the research. To Professor Merrill Jensen I owe a special statement of thanks for his aid on many occasions. Professor Richard Hartshorne generously accepted an extra responsibility and I benefited as a result. Professor Andrew H. Clark was the one upon whom I imposed in the greatest variety of ways; even a protracted transatlantic correspondence did not affect his ability to stimulate and to furnish provocative criticism. I have learned much from him.

Friends and colleagues elsewhere, and especially those at San Fernando Valley State College, have helped in various ways. Most of all, I am indebted to Professor Joseph A. Ernst, for willingly undertaking the laborious task of reading the first and roughest draft and for his perceptive criticism on many subsequent occasions. Professor William Pattison has had much to do with my commitment to American studies; I am grateful for his critical interest, expressed initially as a tutor (at University College London) and subsequently as a colleague and friend in the Department of Geography at San Fernando Valley State College. Another friend with an enthusiastic and critical interest in the geography of colonial America, Mr. James Lemon, made helpful suggestions after reading an early version of the manuscript.

Several cartographers and typists have assisted me with their special skills. Most of the original maps were drawn by Miss Phyllis Graebel and Mr. Paul E. Sisco, Jr., and their conscientious help was invaluable. I am also very grateful to Miss Jerrilyn Schnepple, who competently disposed of the final typing and proofreading. Finally, in preparing the manuscript for publication I have enjoyed working with the patient and experienced staff of the University of North Carolina Press. For those errors that survive, despite the careful help of readers, cartographers, and typists, I alone am responsible.

My wife Gerda died a few weeks after the manuscript for this book was completed. I am grateful for what she invested in my work.

Northridge, California
February 1, 1964

Harry Roy Merrens

CONTENTS

Preface vii

Part I · THE COLONIAL SETTING

I. A SUMMARY VIEW OF THE EASTERN SEABOARD IN 1750   3
II. REVIEW OF SETTLEMENT IN THE PROPRIETARY PERIOD, AND THE AREAL ORGANIZATION OF THE ROYAL COLONY OF NORTH CAROLINA   18
III. THE LAND—IMAGE AND REALITY   32

Part II · THE PEOPLE

IV. THE INFLUX OF SETTLERS AND DEMOGRAPHIC CHANGES   53

Part III · THE CHANGING ECONOMIC GEOGRAPHY

V. UTILIZATION OF THE FORESTS   85
VI. COMMERCIAL FARMING: CROPS, PLANTATIONS, AND LIVESTOCK   108
VII. URBAN SETTLEMENTS AND DECENTRALIZED TRADE   142
VIII. CONCLUSION   173

APPENDICES

I. FIRE AND OPEN LAND   185
II. DATA: TECHNIQUES AND SOURCES   194

Abbreviations   205
Notes   207
Bibliography   266
Index   289

ILLUSTRATIONS

Figure

1.	SETTLED AREAS OF THE SEABOARD, 1740 AND 1760	4
2.	COLONY OF CAROLINA, 1663	19
3.	LOCATIONS OF MAJOR RIVERS, LAKES, AND SOUNDS	20
4.	NORTH CAROLINA SETTLEMENTS *ca.* 1730	23
5.	NORTH CAROLINA COUNTIES, 1740	28
6.	NORTH CAROLINA COUNTIES, 1775	28
7.	COUNTIES ESTABLISHED, 1750-1775	29
8.	BOUNDARIES OF COLONIAL NORTH CAROLINA	30
9.	GENERALIZED TERRAIN REGIONS IN NORTH CAROLINA	37
10.	DISTRIBUTION OF PEAT SOILS IN EASTERN NORTH CAROLINA	38
11.	LITHOLOGIC BOUNDARY BETWEEN COASTAL PLAIN AND PIEDMONT	40
12.	SOME VARIATIONS IN TERRAIN CONDITIONS IN NORTH CAROLINA	41
13.	DISTRIBUTION OF LARGE CAROLINA BAYS	42
14.	AVERAGE ANNUAL PRECIPITATION	43
15.	AVERAGE ANNUAL TEMPERATURE	44
16.	AVERAGE LENGTH OF FREEZE-FREE SEASON	45
17.	GENERALIZED FOREST REGIONS	46
18.	TWO NORTH CAROLINA COUNTIES—POPULATION GROWTH, 1754-1770	55
19.	DISTRIBUTION OF SCOTCH-IRISH, 1750-1775	56
20.	DISTRIBUTION OF SCOTTISH HIGHLANDERS, 1750-1775	58
21.	DISTRIBUTION OF GERMANS, 1750-1775	60
22.	THE INFLUX OF IMMIGRANTS, 1750-1775	66
23.	DISTRIBUTION OF SETTLERS, 1750-1775	68

24.	DISTRIBUTION OF TAXABLES, 1753	69
25.	DISTRIBUTION OF TAXABLES, 1761	70
26.	DISTRIBUTION OF TAXABLES, 1769	71
27.	NORTH CAROLINA COUNTIES, 1753	72
28.	NORTH CAROLINA COUNTIES, 1761	72
29.	NORTH CAROLINA COUNTIES, 1769	73
30.	NEGRO TAXABLES, 1755	78
31.	NEGRO TAXABLES, 1767	79
32.	LONGLEAF PINE FOREST, 1700-1900	86
33.	PORTS OF COLONIAL NORTH CAROLINA	87
34.	EXPORTS OF NAVAL STORES FROM NORTH CAROLINA PORTS, 1768-1771	88
35.	VOYAGE OF THE BRIG "JOANNAH," 1768	92
36.	NORTH CAROLINA EXPORTS OF WOOD PRODUCTS—RELATIVE IMPORTANCE OF PORTS OF ORIGIN, 1768-1772	97
37.	BOTTOMLAND AND SWAMP HARDWOODS IN EASTERN NORTH CAROLINA *ca.* 1940	103
38.	DISTRIBUTION OF COMMERCIAL WHEAT GROWING *ca.* 1765-1775	114
39.	PUBLIC WAREHOUSES FOR TOBACCO INSPECTION IN NORTH CAROLINA, 1754 AND 1767	122
40.	LOWER CAPE FEAR COUNTIES *ca.* 1770	128
41.	ROADS AND TOWNS IN NORTH CAROLINA, 1775	144
42.	ORIGINAL SITES OF CROSS CREEK AND CAMPBELLTOWN	158
43.	LOCATION OF SOME UPLAND GRASS-SEDGE BOGS *ca.* 1928	187
44.	POND PINE-POCOSIN IN EASTERN NORTH CAROLINA *ca.* 1940	191

TABLES

Table

1. SLAVEHOLDING IN SELECTED AREAS OF NORTH CAROLINA, 1755-1774 — 76-77
2. SLAVEHOLDING IN NEW HANOVER COUNTY, 1755-1767/69 — 80-81
3. EXPORTS OF NAVAL STORES FROM NORTH CAROLINA PORTS, 1768-1772 — 90-91
4. EXPORTS OF WOOD PRODUCTS FROM NORTH CAROLINA PORTS, 1768 — 94
5. EXPORTS OF WOOD PRODUCTS FROM NORTH CAROLINA PORTS, 1769 — 94
6. EXPORTS OF WOOD PRODUCTS FROM NORTH CAROLINA PORTS, 1770 — 95
7. EXPORTS OF WOOD PRODUCTS FROM NORTH CAROLINA PORTS, 1771 — 95
8. EXPORTS OF WOOD PRODUCTS FROM NORTH CAROLINA PORTS, 1772 — 96
9. NORTH CAROLINA EXPORTS OF WOOD PRODUCTS: RELATIVE IMPORTANCE OF PORTS, 1768-1772 — 96
10. INDIAN CORN EXPORTED FROM NORTH CAROLINA — 109
11. TOBACCO EXPORTED FROM NORTH CAROLINA PORTS — 120
12. RICE EXPORTED FROM NORTH AND SOUTH CAROLINA — 126
13. INDIGO EXPORTED FROM SOUTHERN COLONIES — 127
14. LIVESTOCK PRODUCTS EXPORTED FROM NORTH CAROLINA — 135

PART I
THE COLONIAL SETTING

CHAPTER I · A SUMMARY VIEW OF THE EASTERN SEABOARD IN 1750

The first permanent English settlement on the Atlantic Seaboard was begun in 1607. During the following century and a half the process of colonization resulted in the emergence of the thirteen colonies that were subsequently to join together to form the United States. What had begun as a handful of settlers insecurely seated on a forbidding neck of land had become, by 1750, a more or less continuous belt of settlement stretching for a distance of over 1,000 miles, and containing about 1,171,000 inhabitants.[1]

Each one of the thirteen colonies developed its own marked individuality and its own internal diversity. The distinctiveness of the colony of North Carolina is the chief subject of the chapters that follow. To place its unique qualities in an appropriate perspective it is necessary first to survey the geography of the other twelve colonies at the middle of the eighteenth century. Traditionally, historians have distinguished between the New England, Middle, and Southern colonies, a division which will serve as a suitable framework for this introductory survey of the geography of the colonial scene in 1750. Fig. 1 is a guide to the distribution of the areas settled and illustrates the expansion that was taking place around the middle of the century.[2]

NEW ENGLAND COLONIES

New England in 1750 contained about a third of the total population of the mainland colonies. The proportion of Negroes in this population was small, since slavery was practiced on a

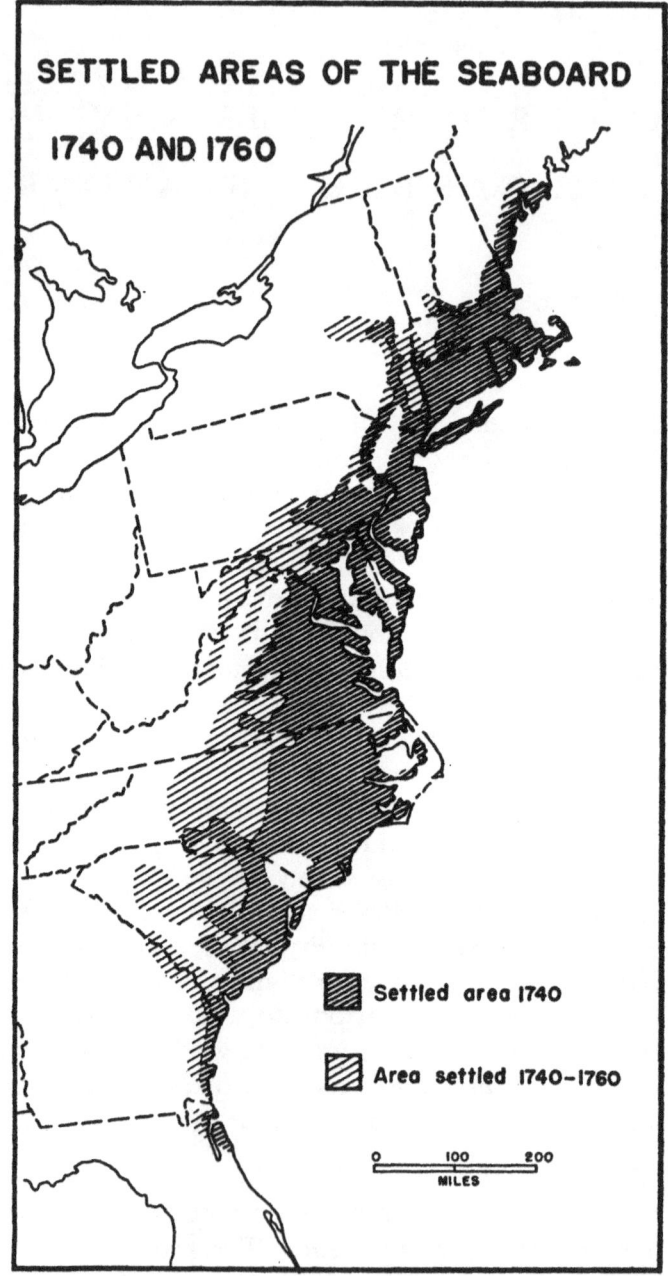

Fig. 1

much smaller scale than in the Southern colonies. The prevalence of townships in the region contributed much to its individuality. The township system was used as a method of survey, as the basis of land granting, and as a form of local government; it gave rise to distinctive settlement patterns that still persist as a feature of the area.

Most of the inhabitants of New England's townships were small farmers. They grew a variety of crops and produced quantities of beef, pork, and livestock for export, as well as food and provisions for local villages and towns. Other New Englanders earned a living by engaging in commerce, or shipbuilding, or manufacturing, or fishing, or by exploiting the forest resources, or by combining two or more of these occupations. Occupational diversity was perhaps more common here than elsewhere along the Eastern Seaboard. But in this, as in other respects, there were considerable differences among the four New England colonies.

In Massachusetts, by 1750, settlement had spread far from the original coastal centers, both to the west and north. Settlements in the form of single dispersed farms had increased and it would be difficult to say whether these or the compact farm villages were the more typical form of settlement. Not all of the inhabitants were rural folk, and among the urban settlements in the colony Boston was pre-eminent.

The metropolis of Boston had a population of about fifteen thousand by the middle of the century. It was still of major importance as a commercial and shipping center of the overseas British Empire and the city's merchants carried on trade with many ports on both sides of the Atlantic. It was also the focus of the political, economic, and cultural life of Massachusetts. Many of the products of Massachusetts' fields and forests were exported from Boston, as were the products of its distilleries, iron works, and shipyards; the population of the city furnished an important consuming market for its agricultural hinterland, and additional grain was imported from other colonies to augment the food supply. Salem, too, was an important urban center in Massachusetts; founded earlier than Boston, it remained primarily a seafaring community, whose members were chiefly concerned with shipbuilding, fishing, and maritime trade.

New Hampshire, by contrast, did not have any large or important urban center. The total population was less than twice as large as Boston, and it was the least populous of the New England colonies. The utilization of forest resources was of special significance in New Hampshire, where the drastic harvesting of the magnificent stands of white pine was underway and constituted the basis of an important trade in ship timber. Most of the people, however, were farmers. The undramatic but steady process of extending the settled area absorbed much of their time and labor, and gradually transformed the landscape.

In Connecticut, signs of the dualism that still characterizes this area today were already evident by the middle of the eighteenth century. While eastern parts of the colony looked to Boston, western parts of the colony found New York best equipped to serve their commercial and cultural needs. There were, furthermore, within Connecticut itself a number of growing urban centers, both on the coast and inland, including Middletown, New Haven, New London, Norwich, and Wallingford. Here as elsewhere in New England by the middle of the eighteenth century both group settlements and single dispersed farms were widespread. Though commerce was important, here again more people were concerned with raising crops and livestock.

Within the small area of Rhode Island there was a considerable amount of diversity. The flourishing town of Newport was both a cultural and commercial center, producing, among other things, nails, rum, sugar, candles, and ships. Foreign trade with many ports on both sides of the Atlantic, in the Boston pattern, was important. While there were many small farms in Rhode Island, there was also a group of "gentlemen farmers," with substantial holdings of both land and slaves. It was these latter, the Narragansett planters, who were making of the Narragansett country a specialized commercial agricultural area; they produced milk, cheese, butter, pork, beef, and livestock for sale, and based the agricultural economy upon the use of hay and pasture land.

MIDDLE COLONIES

While the New England colonies had a total population of about 360,000, the Middle colonies, comprising New York, New

Jersey, Pennsylvania, and Delaware, had about one-fifth fewer (296,000), or somewhat less than a third of the total population of all the mainland colonies. In some ways the Middle colonies were unlike both New England and the colonies to the south. Whereas settlement in New England initially was on a community basis, in compact groups, in the Middle colonies single farmsteads were a more common form of settlement; and the single units of settlement in the Southern colonies were often large, cultivated through the use of slave labor, whereas in the Middle colonies the individual family farm predominated, and was cultivated and run by the family who owned and resided on the farm. One aspect of the regional distinctiveness of the four Middle colonies is implicit in the alternative name bestowed upon them by contemporaries: they were called "Bread colonies" because their inhabitants produced and sold large quantities of Indian corn, wheat, flour, and breadstuffs.

In New York, the settled area in 1750 was still largely restricted to the Hudson Valley and the small islands at the mouth of the river, although settlers were beginning to move into the Mohawk Valley. The British government continued the early Dutch practice of granting large estates, so that by 1750 large amounts of land were concentrated in the hands of a small number of people. This practice reduced the appeal of the area for incoming settlers and the colony gained relatively few of the many arriving from overseas. The large estates along and to the east of the Hudson were farmed if at all on a tenant basis, or through the use of slave, indentured, or hired labor. The existence of such manorial domains, often equipped with the barns, mills, granaries, outhouses, and other features associated with large-scale production, gave New York something in common with sections of the Southern colonies. The decline in the fur trade and the emphasis on a staple crop for export accentuated the similarity.

At one end of one of the small islands at the mouth of the Hudson River was the metropolis of New York. It functioned not only as the commercial, political, and social center of the province, but also as the trading center for parts of eastern New Jersey and western Connecticut. Although the city was still not as populous as Philadelphia, and possibly not even as large as

Boston, the inhabitants formed an important center of consumption. Captain Tibout, for example, was a farmer on the outskirts of New York; in 1757, he obtained three-quarters of his farm income from the sale of cabbages, turnips, and other "Garden truck" to New Yorkers, and manured his land with the mud, dirt, and dung that he carted back from New York each day.[8]

Pennsylvania was the most popular destination for eighteenth-century immigrants. The province reaped the fruits of William Penn's early publicity campaign in Europe, and among the many first setting foot in America on Pennsylvania soil Germans and Ulster Scotch-Irish were particularly well-represented. In 1750, for example, over four thousand Germans landed in Philadelphia, and the German influx was at its peak between 1749 and 1754.[4]

Not all of the immigrants stayed in Pennsylvania. Some of the Scotch-Irish and Germans only stayed long enough to work off their indentures or to earn a little capital before moving south to less crowded areas where land was cheap and easier to obtain. Less than ten years after their arrival in the early 1740's, the Moravians sent some of their members to North Carolina, there to begin again the laborious work of planned pioneering. But enough of the new arrivals stayed in the colony to make it the most populous of the Middle colonies and to set their distinctive imprint upon it.

One of the first views of America that many of the new arrivals saw was the port city of Philadelphia. From the deck of the ship on which they arrived, exhausted immigrants probably saw little more than the wharves of the city and the crowds gathered there, either to greet them or else to carry them off to servitude of one kind or another. But there was much more to Philadelphia than the port facilities. With a population of about seventeen thousand in 1750, it was the largest city in the colonies, a leading cultural metropolis, and an important retail and wholesale trading center. The large urban population constituted a market for some of the farm produce of the interior and an outlet for shipment of the rest to other colonies or to ports across the Atlantic. The growth and size of the city was reflected in the use of land immediately outside it; so much of the forest in the vicinity of the city was cut, that there was already a shortage of wood in the area, and the land around Philadelphia was of such value that it was cultivated more intensively than elsewhere.[5]

The growth of Philadelphia was partly a consequence of the agricultural productivity of the colony. A usable road network within the province enabled wagons to transport a variety of farm products to the city. One writer ventured an estimate of the volume of this overland trade: "There may be from 7000 to 8000 Dutch Waggons with four Horses each, that from Time to Time bring their Produce and Traffick to Philadelphia, from 10 to 100 Miles Distance."[6] Wheat, flour, bread, Indian corn, beef, and pork were all exported in considerable amounts; agricultural products such as these furnished the basis of the export trade carried on by the five hundred ships annually entering and clearing the port of Philadelphia in the 1750's.[7] Nonagricultural exports included skins and furs, ships and wood products, as well as much of the iron produced by ironmasters in the province.

Western New Jersey and the Delaware counties felt the effects of their proximity to the large collecting and distributing center of Philadelphia. Most of the settlers of the Jerseys, which by mid-century had a population of about 65,000, were so located that they had easy access to either New York or Philadelphia, whence they exported surplus amounts of grain, beef, pork, and forest products to the West Indies and Europe. The alteration of some of the forest land was so effective that by this time much of the white cedar had disappeared from the southeastern swamp lands.[8]

Confusion concerning titles to land plagued officialdom in the Jersey's. This was partly because the two proprietary groups retained interest in land even after New Jersey became a royal province, and partly because of the existence of disputed territory in the area adjoining New York. But disputes about land titles did not prevent squatters from moving onto lands in real or feigned ignorance of legal niceties.

On the other side of Delaware Bay from New Jersey were the three counties that constituted the sum total of the colony of Delaware. The area was small, the population was less than thirty thousand, and the colony was chiefly remarkable for its anomalous political status. A traveler who passed through its capital, Newcastle, wrote of the town in slighting terms: "It is . . . a place of very little consideration; there are scarcely more than a hundred houses in it, and no public buildings that deserve to be taken notice of. The church, presbyterian and quaker's meeting-houses, court-house, and market-house, are almost equally bad, and undeserving of attention."[9] But Newcastle did have some of the essential attributes of an urban settlement and was also probably of some importance as a port of disembarkation for many of the immigrants to the colonies.

SOUTHERN COLONIES

Adjacent to the Middle colonies was Maryland. Sometimes assigned to them, at other times referred to as one of the Southern colonies, in reality mid-eighteenth-century Maryland fits neither category very well. It is perhaps more appropriately regarded as a transitional area. In the predominance of white rather than Negro labor, in the importance of bar iron and pig iron production, in the increasing emphasis upon wheat, in the variety of crops produced, in the growth of a port city flourishing on the basis of an increasingly widespread use of wagons for carriage to and from the interior—in all these respects conditions in Maryland resembled those in Pennsylvania. The changes that were going on in the early 1740's caught the eye of one traveler, who remarked upon a development in Maryland that was accentuating its similarity to the Middle colonies: "The Planters in Maryland have been so used by the Merchants, and so great a Property has been made of them in their Tobacco Contracts, that a new Face seems to be overspreading the Country; and, like their more Northern Neighbours, they in great Numbers have turned themselves to the raising of Grain and live Stock of which they now begin to send great Quantities to the West Indies."[10] Tobacco, however, continued to play an important role as an export staple in Maryland, and this with the large number of tidewater plantations and the presence of a political aristocracy were features more characteristic of Maryland's southern neighbors.

There were about 140,000 people in Maryland in 1750 and urban settlements played an important role in the colony. Frederick, Georgetown, and Hagerstown were incorporated about this time. The increased use of overland trade and transportation bolstered their growth, for they were essentially trading centers. Their beginnings were modest, but their population and size, and the range of services they offered, multiplied rapidly; by 1771, Frederick was said to offer "all conveniences, and many superfluities" and was an important link in trade between the interior and Baltimore.[11] The rise of Baltimore was spectacular. The boom that began in the 1740's was a consequence of the increasing density of settlement in the western and northern parts of Maryland, the greater use of road transportation, and the export trade in farm crops, particularly wheat. In its commercial importance Baltimore soon overshadowed Annapolis, although the latter continued to serve as the cultural and political center of the colony. The inhabitants of Annapolis lived in what was one of the most remarkable of all colonial centers. Builders of the nineteenth and twentieth centuries have not entirely submerged its distinctive layout and distinguished architecture.

The Potomac River was the southern boundary of Maryland and beyond this river were the Southern colonies proper, comprising Virginia, North Carolina, South Carolina, and Georgia. Despite differences in area, population, and length of settlement, they all exhibited certain similarities. They contained about 375,000 people, or roughly a third of the total population of the mainland colonies, and Negroes made up a considerable proportion of the population in all of them. There was in each of the Southern colonies a segment of society that constituted something approaching an aristocracy, possessed of large holdings of land and slaves, residing often on riverside or coastal plantations; on the lands of this group staple export crops were produced, notably tobacco in Virginia and rice and indigo in South Carolina. Livestock raising was a feature of parts of all of the Southern colonies. In the middle of the eighteenth century all of them felt the effects of the arrival of many new settlers, some coming south from the Middle colonies, others coming directly from Europe. Many towns were being founded in the interior regions, and some of them grew rapidly. The inland margin of the settled area was reaching the line of the Blue Ridge, and in Virginia at least it had gone beyond into the Great Valley.

Virginia in 1750, with a total population of about 230,000, was by far the most populous of the Southern colonies, and, indeed, of all the colonies on the Atlantic Seaboard. A network of trading facilities, in the form of roads, rivers, ports, inland villages and towns, warehouses and stores, catered for the increasing volume of commercial production. Although all the towns and villages had in common the fact that they functioned as trading centers, in other respects they were often dissimilar, as were, say, Williamsburg, Norfolk, Winchester, and Fredericksburg.

East of the Appalachians, tobacco was in many areas still the chief export crop; but the amount exported fluctuated considerably from year to year, and wheat was becoming an important export crop. A variety of other products, including provisions, naval stores, and shingles, were locally important items for the export trade. In the Valley of Virginia, beyond the Blue Ridge, large numbers of settlers had arrived by 1750. Scotch-Irish and Germans were particularly numerous there, having come in from the north; they engaged in general farming and livestock raising, and took advantage of the developing network of roads and towns to establish trading ties with markets outside the valley. The valley itself was a major thoroughfare for many of the immigrants moving southwards from the Middle colonies. Between 1750 and 1775 successive editions of the Fry and Jefferson map of Virginia show more and more of "The Great Road from the Yadkin River thro' Virginia to Philadelphia distant 435 miles," and it is not unlikely that these successive extensions of the road on the maps were but belated recognitions of the increasing importance of the routeway.[12]

Colonial conditions in the Valley of Virginia have attracted much attention and have often been contrasted with conditions in the rest of Virginia. There were also marked regional variations within Virginia east of the Appalachians in the mid-eighteenth century, though no clear picture of these has ever been presented. The characterization of any part of eastern Virginia in terms of a typical unit of occupancy can be misleading; in one particular tidewater county, for example, tobacco plantations in the 1740's varied from a small family farm of a few acres to an estate of many acres employing scores of slaves.[13] And variations such as these also existed in the non-tidewater portion of eastern Virginia.

North Carolina can be omitted from this introductory survey and attention turned next to the South Carolina of 1750. The total population of South Carolina was then about 65,000, not very different from that of its neighbor to the north. But neither North Carolina nor any other Southern colony could boast of a city to rival Charleston. One of the four major colonial metropolitan centers, Charleston served as the political and cultural capital of South Carolina. Its economic importance was also great, the trade area of the city including parts of Georgia and North Carolina as well as most of the settled area of South Carolina, which had spread a considerable way into the interior by the middle of the century. The city shared with the colony a widespread reputation for being afflicted with an extremely unhealthy climate, especially during the "sickly season," which lasted for several months of each year. An unusually large number of renowned physicians resided in Charleston, but this was apparently not an effect of the prevalent ill-health.

There was a higher proportion of slaves in the population of South Carolina than in that of any other colony, and their labor helped to make rice the colony's chief export staple. In the 1740's indigo also became an important export item, and naval stores, lumber products, skins, and furs continued to play a role in the export trade. The surplus production from the interior regions was marketed mainly in Charleston, arriving there by wagon, boat, and even sledge. By the middle of the century, farmers in the interior were beginning to furnish the city with foodstuffs and supplies that earlier had been imported from the Middle colonies; describing the situation around 1750, Governor Glen of South Carolina noted that the colonies of New York and Pennsylvania "used to drain us of all the little Money and Bills we could Gain upon our Trade with other Places, in Payment for the great Quantities of Bread, Flour, Beer, Hams, Bacon, and other Commodities of their Produce wherewith they then supplied us: all which, excepting Beer, our new Townships, inhabited by Germans, begin to supply us with."[14] But the beer problem was soon solved to the satisfaction of all. By 1774, according to a report in the provincial newspaper, Mr. Egan's new brewery in Charleston was "in such a State, as to rival our Northern Neighbours, and retain in this Province near 20,000 l. a Year."[15] And a visitor to the city in the same year noted that "People of Property," who preferred imported beer, were getting their bottles of porter directly from England.[16]

The townships of South Carolina mentioned by Governor Glen were to be found nowhere else in the Southern colonies. The results of a scheme to attract settlers to interior portions of the colony, the townships were tracts of land set aside for newcomers in a conscious imitation of New England precedents. But in singling out the Germans for attention, Governor Glen was invidiously ignoring the Scotch-Irish, Welsh, and others who had also occupied township lands. Furthermore, although the frequency of contemporary references to the townships and their inhabitants is significant, it obscures the ubiquitous influx of English settlers. The number of English in the colony steadily increased, and they moved into all sections of the territory; but, as always, they failed to attract much attention, whether they came in individually or in groups.

Last, and most exceptional, was the colony of Georgia. In the 1740's the ban on slavery was lifted, earlier restrictions on the disposal of land were abolished, and some of the more fruitless experimental ventures were abandoned. Georgia, nevertheless, remained unlike the other Southern colonies in some important respects. The population numbered at most a few thousand and only a very small portion even of the area east of the Appalachians was actually settled by 1750. While lumber products, tar, rice, indigo, horses, and skins were exported, the total volume of the trade was very small.

In some other ways, however, conditions in Georgia were not unlike those farther north. Included among the population were groups of Germans, Scottish Highlanders, and Scotch-Irish. The total number of colonists was small, but as in the other Southern colonies it was increasing rapidly through immigration. In 1750, some settlers even felt that they were being crowded out by the arrival of "great 500 acre Gentlemen late of Carolina."[17] Livestock raising remained important, even though the abandonment

A SUMMARY VIEW OF THE EASTERN SEABOARD IN 1750   15

of the Trustees' Cowpen put an end to an early experiment in large-scale ranching. The roads of Georgia converged on Savannah, which began to grow rapidly after a slow start, so rapidly in fact that one observer commented upon the suburban growth around the town.[18]

THE COLONIES AS A WHOLE

The thirteen colonies exhibited varying degrees of distinctiveness, and possibly a strong case could be made for regarding Georgia as the most distinctive of all. But neither Georgia nor any one of the other colonies was unique. The thirteen shared some features in common, and some of the same forces were at work making for change in all of them.

In every one of the colonies population was increasing. New areas were being settled and the density of population was increasing in some of the areas settled earlier. Along the Seaboard, the replacement of the indigenous population by a heterogeneous collection of Europeans was all but complete.

Numerically, the least important segment of the new population was the very small urban minority. But even if the towns and cities were neither numerous nor very large, their inhabitants were precipitating changes in rural areas. The merchants residing in the urban places fostered the trade in agricultural products, which in turn hastened the commercialization of agriculture and led to the beginnings of regional specialization in the production of crops and livestock. Towns and cities served as collection and distribution points for the surrounding agricultural areas, the single most important function in all of them being trade. Through them passed the manufactured goods that were being imported, and the products of fields and forests that were destined for export. The larger towns also provided some services, carried on a little manufacturing, and consumed some of the local produce.

Most of the colonists were farmers. To call them subsistence farmers is misleading, for there were probably few of them who did not plan their yearly activities with a view to selling at least part of their produce. Writing during or shortly after the Revolution, St. John de Crèvecouer referred to the American farmer as "a universal fabricator like Crusoe";[19] but even before the Revolution the development of trade and transportation, markets and communications was sufficiently advanced as to render superfluous the cultivation of those qualities of Crusoe that enabled him to subsist in an isolated wilderness.

Agriculture in the colonies, whether oriented around the production of an export staple, or in the form of diversified farming with the sale of only one or two items off the farm, did show certain nearly universal features. Corn was grown almost everywhere and its ubiquity was an indication of its great usefulness. There was as yet no shortage of farmland, although the relative ease with which it could be acquired was diminished in some localities by the effects of land speculation. Because land was fairly plentiful, and holdings rarely very small, intensive cultivation was the exception rather than the rule. The lack of any widespread evidence of the husbanding of soil and forest resources led many visitors from Europe, where land was in shorter supply and labor more abundant, to decry the wastefulness of American agriculture. The variety of crops being tried in some places also struck travelers; but optimism and hopes for quick profits rather than reason or the spirit of scientific improvement generally prompted such experimental ventures.

Experiments with new crops, or with old crops in new places, were only one of the many aspects of land utilization that were transforming the landscape of the Atlantic Seaboard. The exploitation of certain tree species, the grazing of livestock, the use of fire, the mining of soil fertility, the organizing of farms and plantations, the building of roads and settlements—these and other processes were all playing a part in changing the scene. The single most widespread alteration of the Seaboard was the clearing of the forest. During uncertain early days on a forested neck of land in Virginia, Captain John Smith had urgently requested that there be sent from England more men well qualified as "diggers up of trees' roots."[20] But his request was superfluous, since colonists soon learned how to do the job for themselves. So successful were the subsequent labors of grubbers and axmen that woodland was already at a premium in some places even before the end of the colonial period.

It is almost impossible to generalize about the effects of the various processes causing changes along the Seaboard. The new landscape being created did not emerge with any neat uniformity or simultaneity. Changes were going on from place to place at different rates and in different directions. Perhaps the best way of gaining an understanding of the nature of these changes is to consider what happened to the geography of one portion of the Eastern Seaboard during the eighteenth century.

CHAPTER II · REVIEW OF SETTLEMENT IN THE PROPRIETARY PERIOD, AND THE AREAL ORGANIZATION OF THE ROYAL COLONY OF NORTH CAROLINA

The Charter of 1663 officially established the colony of Carolina by granting to eight Lords Proprietors all the land between 36° and 31°N. (see Fig. 2).[1] During the next half century the colony was divided into North Carolina and South Carolina. The appointment of a deputy governor for the northern portion of Carolina in 1691 was a tacit recognition of the problem of governing as one unit two clusters of population, one in the north and one in the south, separated by a broad wilderness and by Indians. The appointment of a separate governor in 1712 symbolized the emergence of North Carolina as a distinct political unit. The new entity did not survive long as a proprietary colony. In 1729, a series of negotiations between the proprietors and the Crown was completed, the proprietors surrendered the charter, and the colony came under direct royal control. The arrival of George Burrington from England in 1731 as the first governor under the Crown completed the transformation of North Carolina into a royal colony.

The chief object of attention in this study of the changing geography of colonial North Carolina is the events of the period following the establishment of royal control. This chapter includes a review of the course of settlement in the proprietary period and a brief account of the organizational framework

THE PROPRIETARY PERIOD AND AREAL ORGANIZATION 19

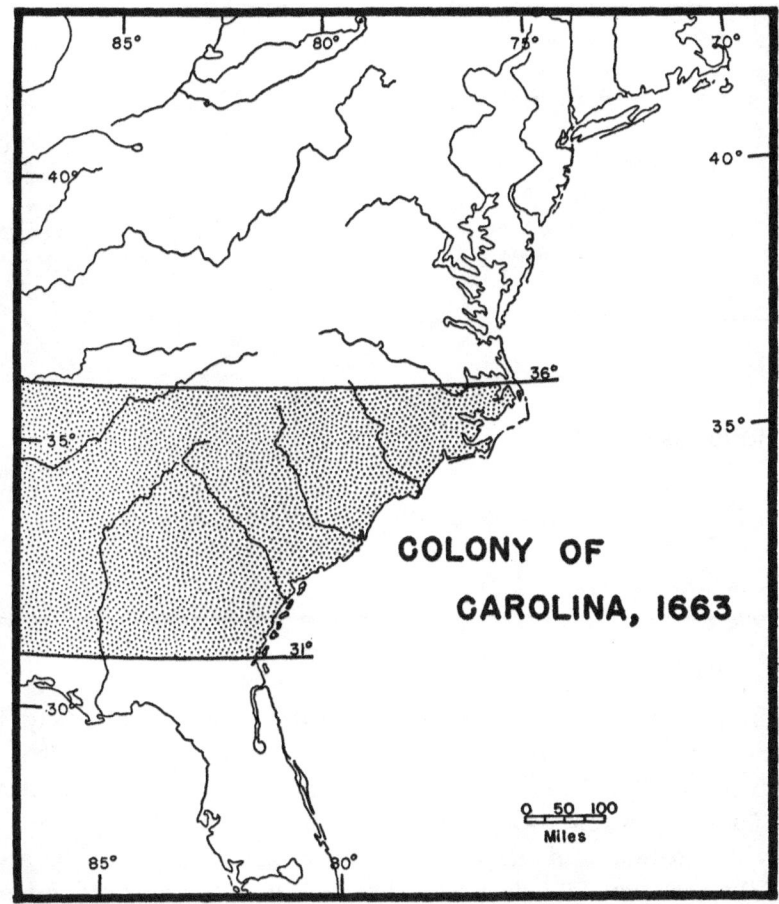

Fig. 2

(political, administrative, and cadastral) of the area of the royal colony.[2]

SETTLEMENT IN THE PROPRIETARY PERIOD

The first permanent white settlers within the area that was subsequently to become North Carolina territory probably came from Virginia and moved onto the lands north of Albemarle Sound (see Fig. 3)[3] some years after the Jamestown colony re-

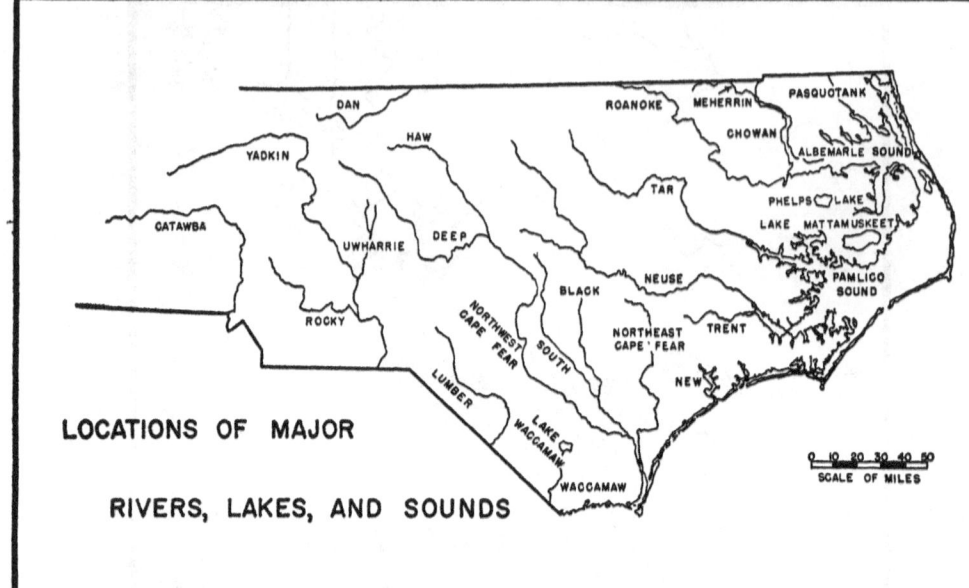

Fig. 3

covered from its early troubles. While population slowly increased in the Albemarle area, efforts made in the 1660's to establish a colony along the Cape Fear estuary came to nothing. In 1690, only a few thousand[4] settlers lived within the bounds of North Carolina and all of them were in the Albemarle area. Within the next few decades other settlements appeared farther south, along and between the rivers Roanoke, Tar, Neuse, and Trent. Political and religious troubles, as well as Indian wars, retarded the development and settlement of the colony as a whole, but a couple of years after North Carolina became a royal colony its population amounted to about 36,000.[5]

The inhabitants of the newly established royal province were mainly of European origin, although there were some Indians and Negroes. Numerically, the Indians were the smallest group; by the early 1730's there were probably no more than a thousand[6] of them left east of the Blue Ridge. The Negroes were not much more numerous. Governor Burrington reported that there were only 6,000 Negroes in the total population of 36,000.[7]

The 30,000 whites in the province were a mixed group. English settlers formed the majority, but scattered here and there about the province were a few clusters of non-English colonists. The minority groups included Welsh, French, German Palatines, and Scotch-Irish.

Almost all the information bearing upon the Welsh stems from the dissolution, in 1730, of a Philadelphia printing partnership between Benjamin Franklin and a Welsh Pennsylvanian, Hugh Meredith.[8] When Franklin dissolved the partnership, Meredith announced his intention of joining his Welsh countrymen, who were settling in North Carolina because of the cheapness of land there. After his arrival in the province Meredith wrote a detailed account of his travels in the Cape Fear area; in his account he mentions a David Evans,[9] who had come to the Northeast Cape Fear River from Delaware and whose name suggests a Welsh origin. In the same general area there was a "Welsh Tract" (an administrative subdivision in the 1730's and later), a "Welches Bluff," and a "Welsh's Creek."[10] There is no further information on Welsh settlers in the colony, which suggests that they could not have been very numerous. With no villages to provide the focal point of community life and organization, and with farms spread thinly over a fairly large area into which other and more numerous settlers soon came, Welsh settlements probably quickly lost whatever distinctiveness they may have possessed at the outset.[11]

The few French who came to the colony during the proprietary period are even more shrouded in anonymity. Some French Huguenots from Virginia settled in North Carolina before the Welsh arrived. One group supposedly came to the area near the head of Pamlico Sound in 1690 or 1691. Another group came a little later to the Trent River, and when visited in 1708 were said to be very industrious; they were then growing hemp and flax, manufacturing linen, experimenting with grape growing, and engaging in some local trade.[12] There appears to be a complete lack of information bearing upon the subsequent form of their settlements.

Only one of the early colonization ventures of a minority group is well documented. In 1710, several hundred German-speaking Protestants from the Swiss town of Bern and from the Rhine Palatinate established a colony around the confluence of the Neuse and Trent rivers.¹³ This settlement of Swiss and Palatines, one of the most fully organized of all the early colonizing projects in proprietary North Carolina, did not achieve the unity and cohesion that its leaders envisaged. For about a year after its establishment the venture prospered, but subsequent political and economic troubles, and an Indian massacre, were severe blows to the planned community. The few survivors seem to have dispersed and settled not far from the original site of their colony, so intermingled among other settlers and apparently so completely assimilated with their neighbors that they became indistinguishable from them.¹⁴ But the town of New Bern, which had been founded by the Swiss leader of the settlement, Christoph von Graffenried, was later resuscitated and became one of the major towns in the colony.

Some Scotch-Irish settled in North Carolina before it became a royal province but they were probably not very numerous. Most of what little is known about them derives from an investigation made by the Irish House of Commons into the means used to transport Irish Protestants to North Carolina. In March, 1736, a committee of the House presented a report dealing with an attempt to persuade numbers of these people to emigrate to the colony. The report revealed that one of the schemes was organized by a Dublin shipmaster and his relatives; the organizers publicized in various parts of Ireland the virtues of the promised land of North Carolina, and then began to starve and tyrannize their shipload of prospective indentured servants even before the vessel had left Dublin harbor. The main theme of the report is the mistreatment of the passengers. It also indicates that traffic of this kind had been going on for some time, certainly to North America, and possibly to North Carolina. There are no indications of where in North Carolina their forerunners, if any, went.¹⁵

All these settlers, Welsh, French, Palatines, and Scotch-Irish, were minor elements in the population. If some had initially formed distinctive settlements, by the early 1730's they were submerged by the predominant strain of settlers, the English. About five out of every six of the thirty thousand whites were probably

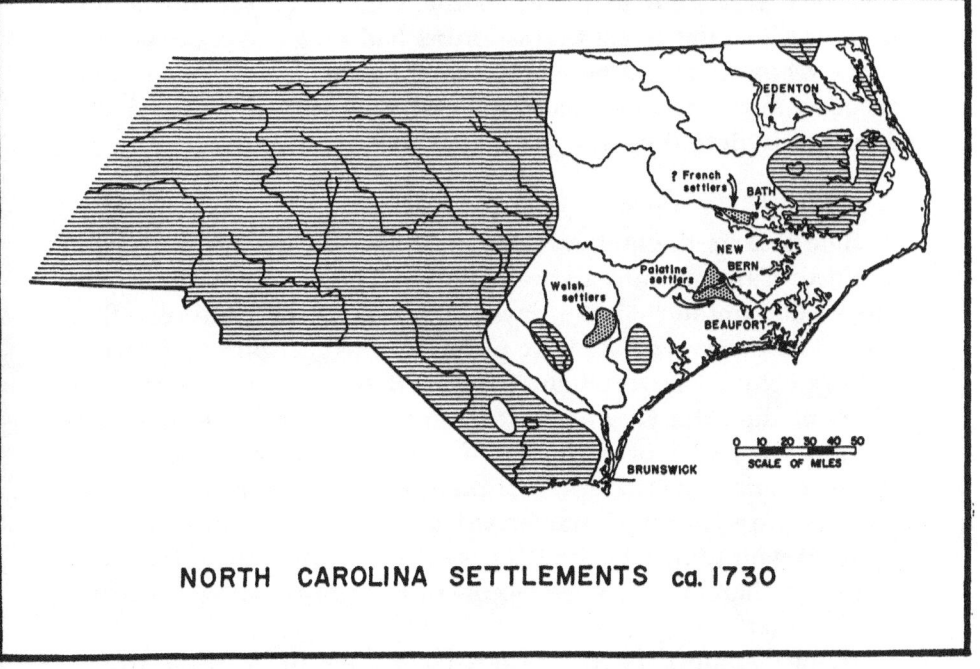

Fig. 4

The shaded area (horizontal lines) shows the probable extent of the portion of North Carolina not inhabited by colonists as of about 1730.

English. They had come into North Carolina either directly, or by way of other North American colonies, and particularly New England, Virginia, South Carolina, and the West Indies. Their infiltration was slow and unspectacular, and rarely attracted attention. After their arrival they began to clear farms, to found a few towns, and to go about the labors of colonization.

Fig. 4[16] shows the extent of the settled area as of about 1730, together with the location of the towns that had been established by then. The map gives no impression of variations in population density, because there is no way of establishing the variations with any degree of precision. Densities were probably greatest in the oldest settled region, north of Albemarle Sound,[17] and lowest in the vicinity of the Cape Fear River, which was just beginning to be settled around 1730. Elsewhere there were probably relatively high densities in the vicinity of the towns and along some of the rivers that colonists had sought out on account of their bottomlands, their fish, and their facilities for communications and trade. Portions of the east were still unoccupied, and these are indicated on the map.

AREAL ORGANIZATION OF THE ROYAL COLONY

The settlers themselves were little affected by the conversion of North Carolina into a royal colony. The change, here as elsewhere, left untouched the day-to-day routine of administration. While the Crown replaced the proprietors as the source of authority, the colonial government continued to regulate the internal affairs of the colony. There were no jurisdictional limits clearly defining the realm of authority of the British as opposed to that of the colonial government. Disputes between the royal governor and the lower house characterized the politics of the colony up to the Revolution, revealing the weakening of royal government on the one hand and the development of colonial self-government on the other.

In one administrative matter, conditions in North Carolina were somewhat unusual. One of the eight Lords Proprietors of Carolina, John Lord Carteret, later Earl of Granville, did not sell his proprietary rights when the other seven sold theirs. He retained property rights over one-eighth of the area earlier granted to the proprietors. This large tract of land comprised approximately the northern half of North Carolina, which came to be known as the Granville District. It was formally granted to him in 1744 and demarcated between 1743 and 1774 so as to include all of the area between the Virginia line on the north and latitude 35°34'N. on the south, from the coast to the Blue Ridge. The Earl of Granville granted land within this area, neither the Crown nor the colony having any say in its disposal.[18]

The existence of two different sources of land disposal within the one colony had little influence on the course of settlement, for several reasons. There was as yet no shortage of land in either half; as Governor Burrington pointed out, "land is not wanting for men in Carolina, but men for land."[19] In both areas, when methods of land disposal threatened to obstruct settlers they generally moved on to the land and left to a future date the resolution of legal niceties.[20] And in neither half of the colony was the system of making land grants a very orderly one.

On paper, the process of partitioning up the land into individual grants was well regulated. As land was officially taken up, it was to be surveyed by marking out the grant on the ground and officially registering a description and map of the area surveyed. Surveyors had detailed instructions on how to go about their job. It was their duty to make sure that the bounds of tracts touching upon rivers extended four times as far back from the river as they lay along it. Elsewhere surveyors were to lay out lands in the form of squares, the sides of which were to be oriented according to the cardinal compass points. From their field notes surveyors had to compile maps of each survey, in triplicate, to insure that titles to land would be securely held.[21]

No orderly system came into being. The defects inherent in the system of surveying according to metes and bounds were aggravated by ambiguous references to poorly defined physical features, inaccurate measurements of distances, and by the use of markers such as saplings, cowpens, tar kilns, and stakes in marshes. Moreover, surveyors often failed to follow their instructions. Governor Dobbs asserted that some simply found out what kind of timber grew upon the land, ". . . and at the fire side laid down their plan, if not joined to any neighbouring Plantation then named an imaginery Tree, a pine red white or black oak or hiccory etc and so enter beginning at a hiccory and so name imaginery Trees at any angle and conclude as usual so on to the first station. . . . You may judge what confusion that has & does create. . . ."[22] The result was the laying out on the land of a fairly haphazard pattern of variously shaped grants.[23]

The sizes of grants were more uniform than were their shapes. Under the headright system, the head of a family could claim fifty or one hundred acres for himself,[24] and fifty acres for each person he brought in, whether a member of his family or a servant. Grants were generally small. Most of them were for amounts of less than six hundred acres, and grants of between one hundred and three hundred acres seem to have been common.[25] A few persons did manage to obtain large quantities of land, to use either for speculative purposes or for building up large estates. Extensive holdings of land were so rare that neither practice was common, but there are instances of both and their effects were evidently quite different.

The practice of using land for speculation had little effect on the progress of settlement. Not only did squatters tend to ignore, and even resist, the protestations of speculators, but the speculators themselves were concerned to sell their properties in small parcels as quickly as possible. Henry McCulloh was the unrivalled leading speculator in North Carolina. In the 1730's and 1740's he and some associates obtained about 1,200,000 acres of land in several large blocks scattered about North Carolina. McCulloh was subsequently reported to be "hawking it about in small quantities thro' all the back parts of the Province and quite thro' America even to Boston"; and the survey book of his son clearly shows that the land was sold in small parcels, generally of less than two hundred or three hundred acres.[26]

McCulloh and his associates were exceptional and there are no other instances of land speculation on anything like this scale. Most of the speculation that went on in the colony involved much smaller amounts, such as pieces of farmland and lots in towns, both of which commonly changed hands several times. One merchant-planter who went to North Carolina in the 1730's complained that those who knew where vacant land was to be found would patent it "and then screw as much as they can from a stranger for it, who in his turn serves others the same way."[27] Regardless of the scale at which it was carried on, the net effect of all land speculation was simply to raise the price of land. It did not prevent the land from being used.

The other practice associated with extensive land grants, the building up of large private estates, was restricted to a few men prominent in public affairs. Edward Moseley, a leading political figure in North Carolina during the first half of the eighteenth century, bequeathed more than 25,000 acres of land on his death.[28] Thomas Pollock, a president of the council for a short period early in the century, left an estate of fifty thousand acres in 1722.[29] In general, large domains of this kind were held in scattered pieces rather than in one block and were in any case rare.

THE PROPRIETARY PERIOD AND AREAL ORGANIZATION 27

Only along the lower Cape Fear River did large holdings become a significant feature. This area was officially closed to settlement during most of the proprietary period, but between about 1725 and 1730 a few men were somehow able to take possession of large amounts of the land. By 1731, there were twenty-eight patentees in this area. At least half of them were related to one family, the Moores, who then held 83,000 out of the 105,000 acres patented.[30] Comparatively large landholdings remained characteristic of this area throughout the colonial period. In the 1780's, in the two counties on either side of the mouth of the Cape Fear River (Brunswick County and New Hanover County), the average size of landholdings was larger than elsewhere in North Carolina; and these two counties also contained the highest proportion of large holdings.[31] But even though large holdings were a distinctive feature in the lower Cape Fear, there was room enough for small landholders to move in.[32]

Property lines were only one of several forms of land subdivision within North Carolina. The county boundaries were in some respects the most important of all, for the county was the basic unit of local government.[33] It was organized around the county court, which met regularly in the local courthouse and exercised judicial and administrative powers. The court supervised many of the civil affairs of the county, such as the maintenance and construction of roads, the listing of taxables, the registration of the brands and marks of livestock, and the granting of licenses to build mills and operate taverns.

County boundaries were altered frequently in the royal period and the changes illustrate, in a rough way, the increases in population density and numbers in various parts of the colony. New counties were created at a particularly rapid rate towards the end of the period (see Figs. 5, 6, and 7).[34] As more and more of the western and central portions were settled, new counties were set up to provide rudimentary administration for these areas: Anson County was established in 1750; Orange, in 1752; Rowan, in 1753; Cumberland, in 1754; Dobbs, in 1758; Mecklenburg, in 1762; Bute, in 1764; Tryon, in 1768; and in 1770, Surry, Chatham, Guilford, and Wake were all established. In the east, new counties were set up by subdividing counties that had become

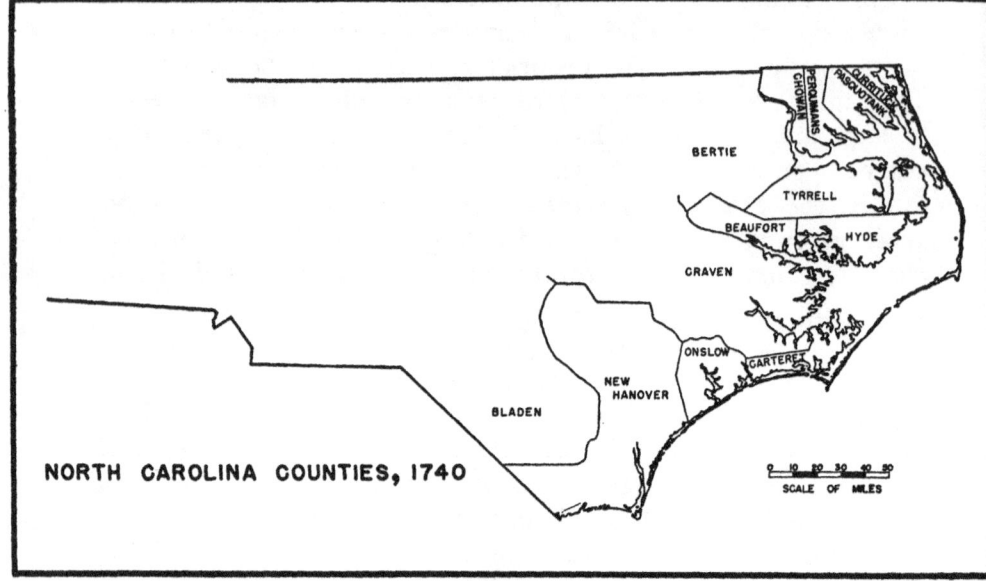

Fig. 5

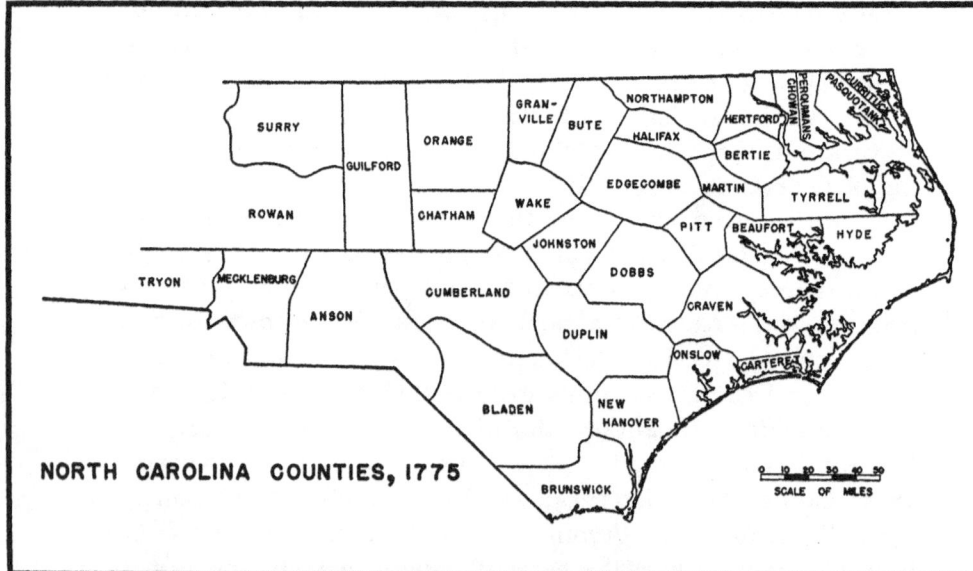

Fig. 6

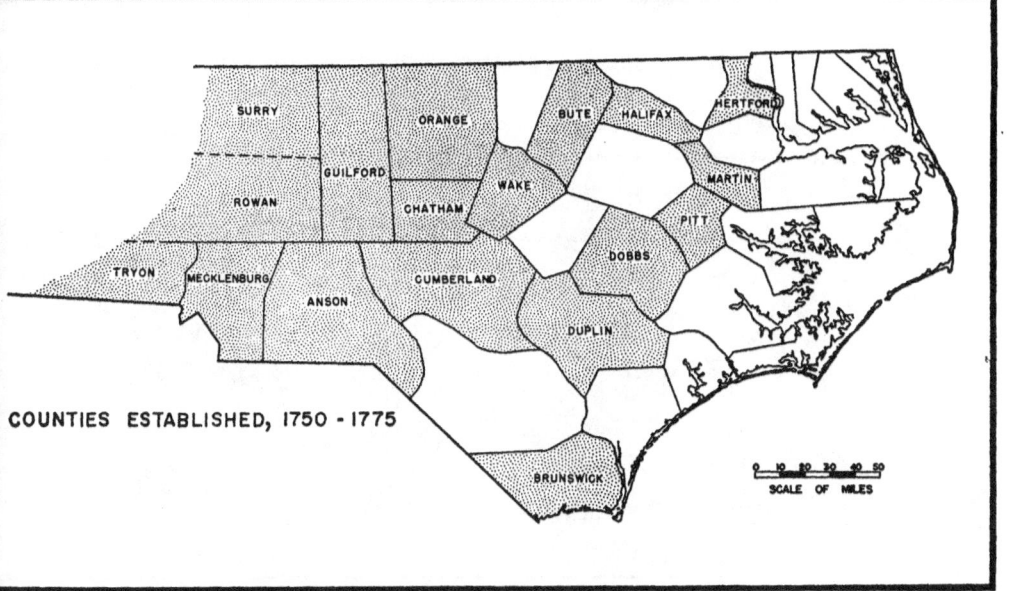

FIG. 7

All county boundaries shown are those of 1775; the counties shaded and named are those established 1750-1775.

too populous for efficient administration. This consideration was at least partly responsible for the creation of Duplin in 1750; Halifax, in 1758; Hertford, in 1759; Pitt, in 1760; Brunswick, in 1764; and Martin in 1774, with the result that the number of counties in the east had doubled by 1775. Since the process of creating new counties was governed by political expediency as well as by administrative needs, and since sectional hostility was of some significance in determining when and where new ones were set up, the proliferation of counties revealed on Figs. 5, 6, and 7 is but a crude guide to population increase.

Two or more counties were grouped together for the purpose of establishing judicial districts. In these, a superior court met and dealt with cases of more consequence than those heard in the county courts.[35] On the other hand, counties were divided into smaller areas in order to facilitate the carrying out of some functions: thus there were, for example, road districts and patrol

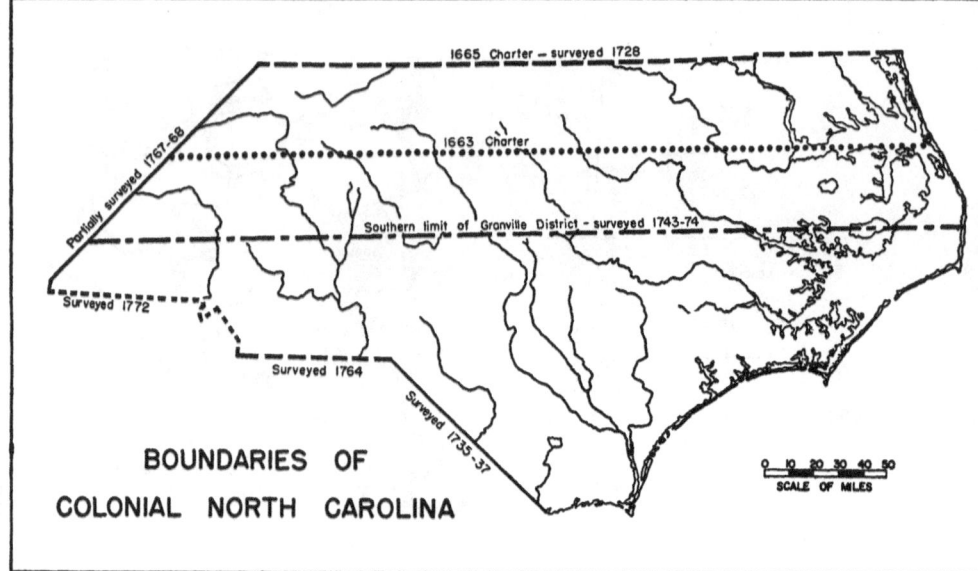

Fig. 8

districts, the former created for the supervision and execution of road building, the latter for the exercise of police functions. Such districts were small; the record of them is fragmentary and their significance was confined to local affairs. This is true too of other administrative divisions created in the territory of North Carolina.[36] Their bounds do not appear on any maps that have survived, and they could not now be reconstructed. That these internal boundary lines were not well known or clear to the settlers is not surprising when it is remembered that even the boundaries of the colony itself were for long undemarcated.

Throughout much of the colonial period the territorial extent of North Carolina was only loosely defined. Fig. 8 illustrates the gradual process by which its boundaries were established.[37] On the south, the boundary with South Carolina was a constant source of confusion and dispute, for there was a zone over which both North Carolina and South Carolina claimed jurisdiction. The issue was not finally settled until 1815, although by 1772 the

THE PROPRIETARY PERIOD AND AREAL ORGANIZATION　　　　31

two colonies had agreed upon a line (Fig. 8) that extended from the coast to about as far west as the foot of the mountains.

On the north, the Carolina Charters of 1663 and 1665 defined the boundary line between Virginia and North Carolina in different ways. The issue was further complicated by the unsatisfactory nature of the definition of the line in the second of these charters. After a series of controversies the two colonies worked out a compromise in 1715 and in 1728 marked out a line from the coast westwards to a point about thirty miles short of the Blue Ridge. Extensions and modifications of the course of the boundary were made from time to time during the succeeding two centuries, but the 1728 section of the line remained unaltered.[38]

The western limits of North Carolina did not receive as much attention as did the northern and southern limits during the colonial period. The second charter declared that the authority of the Carolina government extended as far west as the Pacific Ocean. More meaningful was the boundary established following the Royal Proclamation of 1763, which prohibited any colonial governor from granting land "beyond the heads or sources of any of the rivers which fall into the Atlantic Ocean from the west and northwest."[39] In an attempt to implement this decision a line was defined and partially demarcated a little to the east of the Blue Ridge by Governor Tryon a few years later. All land to the west of this line was to belong to the Cherokee. The prohibition did not deter some settlers from moving into the area, but with this delimitation of some sort of western limit the colony now had bounds not so very different from those of the present state territory.

CHAPTER III · THE LAND — IMAGE AND REALITY

At least as important as the qualities of the land included within the boundaries of eighteenth-century North Carolina was the colonial image of the qualities. These two closely related subjects are taken up in this chapter. Variations in environmental character are examined against the background of the contemporary view of these variations. Terrain is the aspect of the environment to which most attention is given, but the term "land" is used in its broadest sense and hence some reference is made to climate, to soil drainage conditions, and to the vegetation cover of the province. The detailed treatment of vegetation is relegated to Appendix I, partly in order to avoid burdening the text with an excessive amount of detail, and partly to allow greater scope for the development in Appendix I of an important but subsidiary theme, the effects of fire upon the vegetation of early North Carolina.

IMAGE OF THE LAND

The first accounts of North Carolina, whether written by travelers, visitors, residents, or officials in the colony, were generally based on limited first-hand knowledge. Few of the early writers hesitated to apply to the whole their impressions of a small section of the colony. Attempts at systematic description were rare, and the accounts were frequently exaggerated in tone. Well-founded or not, such writings created a contemporary image of the colony that influenced the subsequent course of settlement.

A few of the early accounts were unfavorable. One example will suffice to indicate the general tone of these deprecatory accounts. The Reverend John Urmstone, a Lancastrian, spent the period from about 1710 to 1721 as minister of a parish in the Albemarle area. His letters are full of complaints about the "wretched country," and he declared that he "would rather be Vicar to the Bear Garden than Bishop of North Carolina." Feeling "buried alive in this hell of a hole,"[1] he longed for the end of his tour of duty. When at last he got safely back to England, Urmstone wrote to the Secretary of the Society for the Propagation of the Gospel and lamented that during his period of residence in North Carolina he had ". . . struggled with great inconveniences of living in such an obscure corner of the world inhabited by the dregs and gleanings of all other English Colonies and a very unhealthy Country which have driven many Clergymen out of it not being able to stay so many months as I have years and brought others to their Graves. . . ."[2]

Urmstone's jaundiced view of North Carolina was perhaps partly a result of his own intemperate habits and disposition.[3] But there was some foundation for his reference to the settling in North Carolina of the "dregs and gleanings" of other English colonies. In the first decades of the eighteenth century, North Carolina was reputed to be a place to which debtors from other colonies might flee, because of a law that protected North Carolina settlers from foreign debts. Many of these debtors were regarded as being thieves and vagabonds.[4]

Urmstone represented the viewpoint of a minority. The dominant theme in the early accounts was a different one. The majority of writers emphasized instead the opportunities that awaited the settler in North Carolina, the abundance of desirable land that was available for settlement, and the temperateness of Nature in much of the colony. These writers gave North Carolina the reputation of being an especially attractive place in which to settle.[5]

Early visitors to the lands north of Albemarle Sound laid the basis of the reputation. One of the very first to view this area was John Pory, whose reports were printed in 1622 and again in 1650. Pory found a country full of pine trees and commented upon the abundant prospect of resources for the making of pitch, tar, potash, and masts for ships.[6] George Fox, the Quaker, visiting the same area about fifty years later, summed up his trip by noting that going from Virginia into North Carolina was like passing "from a very cold to a warm and spring-like country,"[7] an exaggeration that presaged what was to become a repeated theme—the delights of the climate of North Carolina. John Lawson, whose description of North Carolina was first published in 1709, ascribed the success of settlement in the Albemarle area to the mild winters and fertile soil: ". . . everything seemed to come by Nature, the Husbandman living almost void of Care, and free from those Fatigues which are absolutely requisite in Winter Countries, for providing Fodder and other Necessaries . . . the Fame of this new discovered Summer-Country spread through the neighboring Colonies, and in a few Years drew a considerable Number of Families thereto, who all found Land enough to settle themselves. . . ."[8] Von Graffenried, the leader of the settlement a little farther south, on the Neuse River, wrote in 1711 that settlers were flocking to North Carolina because cattle could be kept there in winter at no expense.[9] Those who actually cultivated the land rarely paused to record their impressions of it, but in the same year, one of the farmers of the Neuse River settlement wrote home that "we are in a very good and fat land."[10]

Even inhabitants of Virginia were beginning to look on North Carolina with envious eyes. One official noted in 1729 that the soil of North Carolina was better than that of Virginia and the timber larger.[11] Two years later, William Byrd II, a Virginian who had gained much first-hand experience of the northern part of North Carolina when he surveyed the boundary line, summed up his impressions as follows: "It must be owned North Carolina is a very happy Country where people may live with the least labour that they can in any part of the world, and if the lower parts are moist and consequently a little unwholesome every where above Chowan, as far as I have seen, people may live both in health and plenty. T'is the same I doubt not in all the uplands in that Province. . . ."[12] Byrd was so favorably impressed with the qualities of the land he saw along the boundary that he subsequently purchased a large amount of territory on the North Carolina side in the area adjoining the Dan River and called the region the "Land of Eden."

The habit of "describing" the whole colony on the basis of

highly subjective reactions to small parts of it gradually gave way to more systematic and better informed attempts at description. During the first half of the eighteenth century, the existence of regional differences within North Carolina began to receive attention. As the more observant and widely traveled writers came to recognize broad regional contrasts, so there began to develop a legend about the inland parts of North Carolina and, indeed, of all the Southern colonies.

The essence of this legend was that the interior Seaboard was basically different from the more maritime portion and that it afforded much superior resources for the would-be settler. The first North Carolinian to express the idea was one of the more systematic of the early writers, John Lawson, who combined the experience of an explorer, historian, topographer, and surveyor. Lawson's extensive travels in North Carolina were recorded in *A New Voyage to Carolina,* a popular volume published in several editions between 1709 and 1722, including one in German. Summarizing conditions in North Carolina, Lawson wrote:

It must be confessed that the most noble and sweetest Part of this Country is not inhabited by any but the Savages; and a great deal of the richest Part thereof, has no Inhabitants but the Beasts of the Wilderness. . . . Towards the Sea we have the Conveniency of Trade Transportation and other Helps the Water affords; but oftentimes those Advantages are attended with indifferent Land, a thick Air, and other Inconveniences; when backwards, near the Mountains, you meet with the richest Soil, a sweet, thin Air, dry Roads, pleasant small murmuring Streams, and several beneficial Productions and Species, which are unknown in the European World. One Part of this Country affords what the other is wholly a Stranger to.[13]

About twenty years later, another surveyor, Edward Moseley, gave cartographic expression to what was essentially the same idea. In his 1733 map, Moseley, perhaps to compensate for the lack of detail he was able to show on the section of his map representing the interior parts of North Carolina, placed there a long inscription describing in glowing terms the abundant wild life of the country 150 miles inland from the coast.[14]

Surveyors and map makers were not the only ones who recognized contrasts between the two areas. One of the most important early naturalists who visited the South was Mark Catesby.[15] After traveling extensively in Virginia and South Carolina during the first quarter of the eighteenth century, Catesby wrote a perceptive account of the contrasts:

> All the lower (which are the inhabited) parts of Carolina, are a flat sandy Country; the Land rising imperceptibly to the distance of about an hundred miles from the Sea, where loose stones begin to appear, and at length Rocks, which at the nearer approach to the Mountains, increase in quantity and magnitude, forming gradual Hills, which also increase in height, exhibiting extensive and most delightful prospects. Many spacious tracts of Meadow-Land are confined by these rugged Hills, burdened with grass six feet high. Other of these Vallies are replenished with Brooks and Rivulets of clear water, whose banks are covered with spacious tracts of Canes, which retaining their leaves the year round, are an excellent food for Horses and Cattle, and are of great benefit particularly to Indian Traders, whose Caravans travel these uninhabited Countries; to these shady thickets of Canes (in sultry weather) resort numerous herds of Buffelo's, where solacing in these limpid streams they enjoy a cool and secret retreat. Pine barren, Oak, and Hiccory-Land, as has been before observed to abound in the lower parts of the Country, engross also a considerable share of these upper parts . . . but as the geography of these extensive countries is hitherto imperfect, the western distances between the sea and mountains cannot be ascertained, though they are generally said to be above two hundred miles. The lower parts of the country, to about half way towards the mountains, by its low and level situation, differ considerably from those parts above them, the latter abounding with blessings, conducing much more to health and pleasure: but as the maritime parts are much more adapted for commerce, and luxury, these delightful countries are as yet left unpeopled, and possessed by wolves, bears, panthers, and other beasts.[16]

Catesby in fact was the first to appreciate and to record this fundamental difference between the maritime and inland portions of the southern Seaboard.

The contrast Catesby described was that between the two regions now called the Coastal Plain and the Piedmont. Some aspects of this contrast, particularly with respect to terrain, are about as marked today as they were then. A summary account of the salient features of the two regions will serve to suggest the broad basis of truth that lay behind the legend.

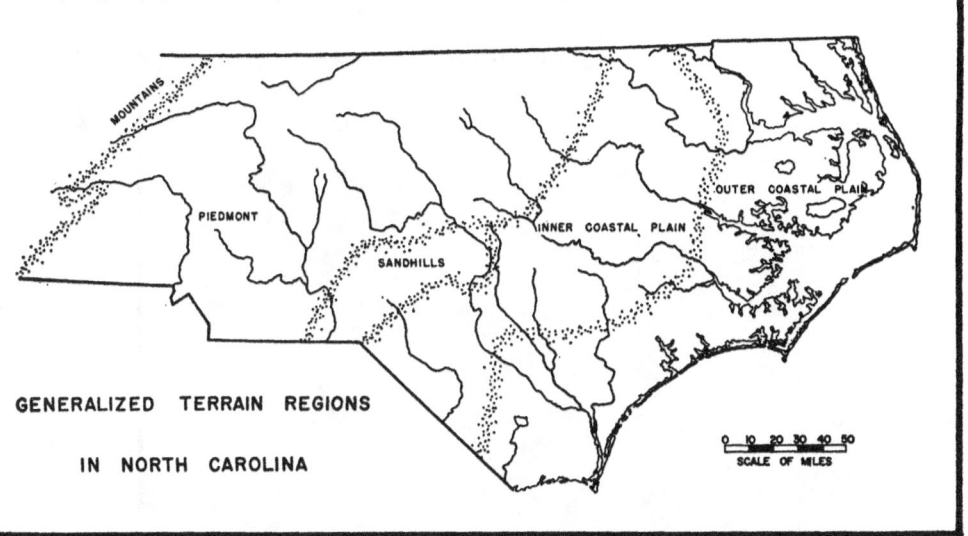

Fig. 9

THE LAND IN REALITY

The Coastal Plain (see Fig. 9)[17] as a whole is easily characterized. Imperceptibly rising from sea level in the east, most of the Coastal Plain is less than one hundred feet above sea level, although along the inner margins, adjacent to the Piedmont, elevations reach two hundred or three hundred feet in the north and even approach six hundred feet in the south. Flat or gently rolling surfaces predominate. Considerable portions of the region are imperfectly drained, and river valleys become less and less distinct towards the east as the rivers broaden into tidal estuaries. There are, however, important variations from east to west.

In the east, the coast is formed by a string of long narrow islands, composed of sand dunes and beaches, with scattered areas of tidal marsh on the mainland side.[18] Directly west of the fringing sand banks and shallow sounds of the coast is an amphibious landscape. Abundant water-logged areas blur the distinction between land and water surfaces. The series of necks of land projecting irregularly into the sounds are occupied by large areas of swamps and lakes,[19] and peat soils are widespread (see Fig.

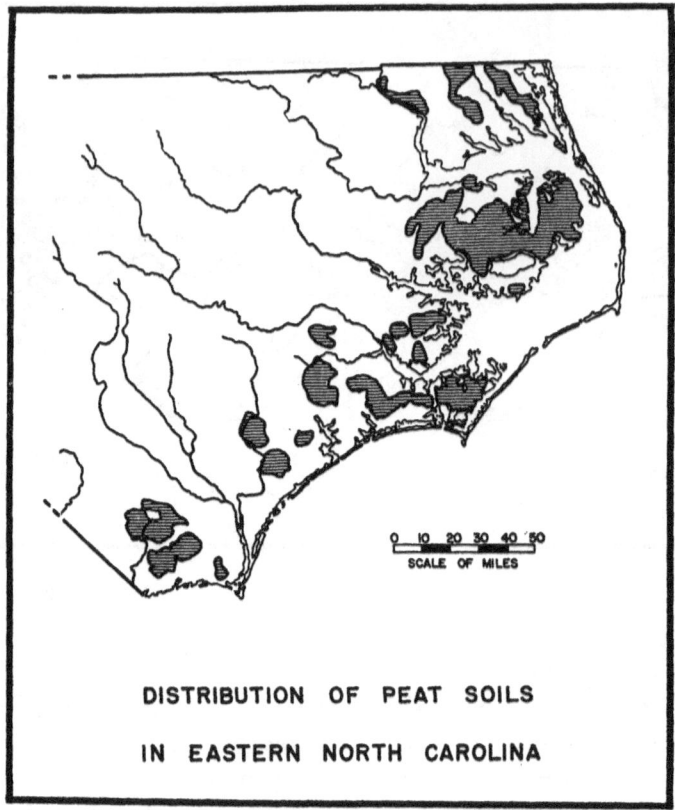

DISTRIBUTION OF PEAT SOILS IN EASTERN NORTH CAROLINA

Fig. 10

10).[20] Scarcely any of the land is more than fifty feet high, and much is less than twenty feet above sea level. The prevalence of flat, poorly-drained surfaces, combined with the absence of any strongly marked or conspicuous relief, imposes a semblance of uniformity on the landscape.

This eastern section of the Coastal Plain is sometimes called the Outer Coastal Plain (and also Tidewater or Flatwoods) to distinguish it from the Inner Coastal Plain that lies immediately to the west (Fig. 9). Although there is no sharp line of delimitation between them,[21] there are differences of some importance between the Inner and Outer Coastal Plain.

Compared with the Outer Coastal Plain, the Inner Coastal Plain lies at higher elevations and has more pronounced relief. Within the Inner Coastal Plain poorly drained areas are more scattered and occupy a smaller percentage of the total area. In a few places, the land is gently rolling or even hilly, and there is a gradual rise to the west at a rate of a little more than one foot per mile. The rivers in this section flow in well-defined valleys, bounded often either by a single bluff rising to the higher land above or by step-like forms, rising to the higher land in a series of two or more alternating low bluffs and flat benches; in places the cross-profiles of the valleys are markedly asymmetrical, with steep slopes adjacent to one side of the river, rising fifty to a hundred feet above the valley floor, with only swamps and low flats on the other side.[22]

In the north, the Inner Coastal Plain merges into the Piedmont. In the south, a distinctive zone of sand hills intervenes between them. The surface in this intervening region, known as the Sandhills (see Fig. 9), is rolling or hilly. Surface materials are sands or sandy loams, and internal drainage is excessive, so that there are no large areas of poor drainage. Here are found the highest elevations in the Coastal Plain (up to about six hundred feet), and in relief, slopes, and elevation the Sandhills are more like the Piedmont than the Coastal Plain, although lithologically they are a part of the latter. There are other areas of sand hills and sand ridges in the Coastal Plain, similar to the Sandhills in soil, drainage, and vegetation; but the Sandhills region constitutes the highest and largest single area of this type, occupying over a million acres.

The Coastal Plain as a whole occupied about three-fifths of the total area of colonial North Carolina. No sharp boundary distinguished it from the Piedmont to the west, either in North Carolina or in the rest of the southern Seaboard. Colonial observers recognized the gradualness of the transition between the western and eastern parts of the Seaboard, noting that the land became higher and hillier towards the west.[23]

DeBrahm alone among colonial writers mentioned the existence of some kind of boundary between the two.[24] In his account of South Carolina, DeBrahm refers to a *"quasi*-division

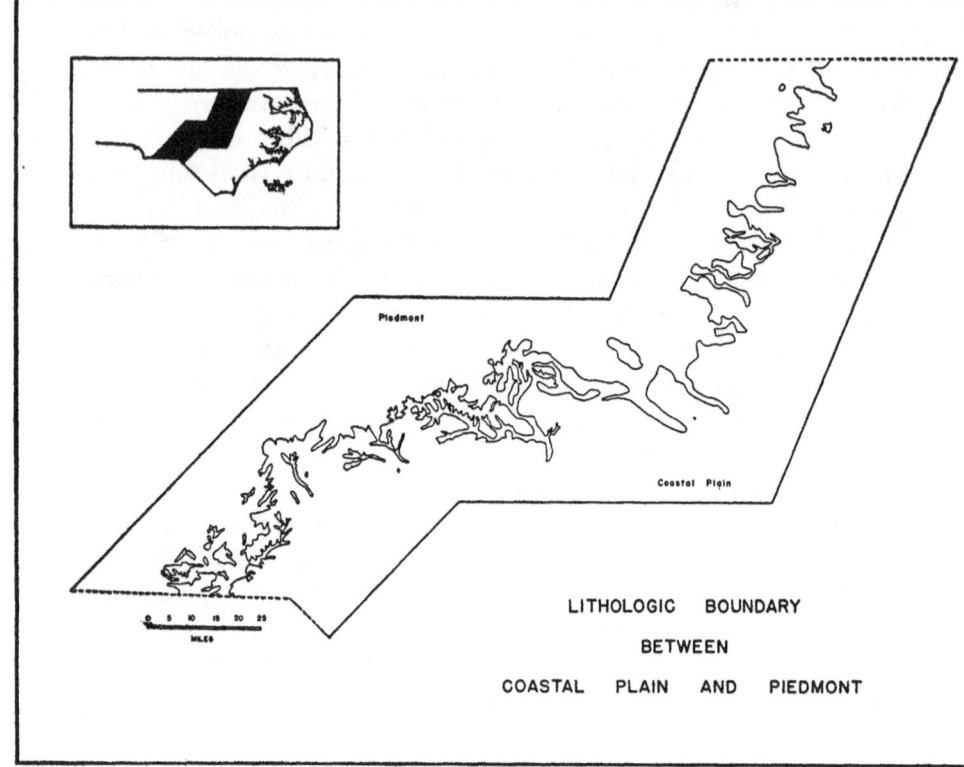

Fig. 11

line" between the coastal zone and the interior. He described the two zones in his accounts of South Carolina and Georgia; the line between them he regarded as being located generally 140 miles from the coast and as separating the lower parts, which were impregnated with sea air, marked by moss-hung trees, and suitable for rice-growing, from the higher land to the west.[25]

The "fall line" has been regarded by subsequent writers, and especially those of the twentieth century, as representing the boundary between the Coastal Plain and Piedmont. But this device has proved to be a confusing one. If one attempts to define the boundary in strictly geological terms, then the interdigitation of the Cretaceous and Tertiary deposits of the Coastal Plain, on the one hand, and the Cambrian and Triassic rocks of the Piedmont, on the other, gives the line boundary between them a very complex course; this is readily apparent from Fig. 11, which shows this lithologic boundary.[26] Nor is there any land-form feature that could serve as the basis of a delineation of the boundary in geomorphological terms. As in all such instances of regional contrasts, there is only a zone of transition between Coastal Plain and Piedmont, and any line drawn on a map to represent the boundary is only a *"quasi*-division line," as De-Brahm recognized.

Much of the Piedmont lies between five hundred and one thousand feet above sea level, and rises gradually, at the rate of three or four feet per mile, to the foot of the Blue Ridge on the west. It has a rolling upland surface. In some places relief is more marked, with rounded hills and southwest-northeast aligned ridges occurring above the general level of the surface. These higher features are chiefly evident in two localities, one near the Blue Ridge on the western fringe of the Piedmont, the other near

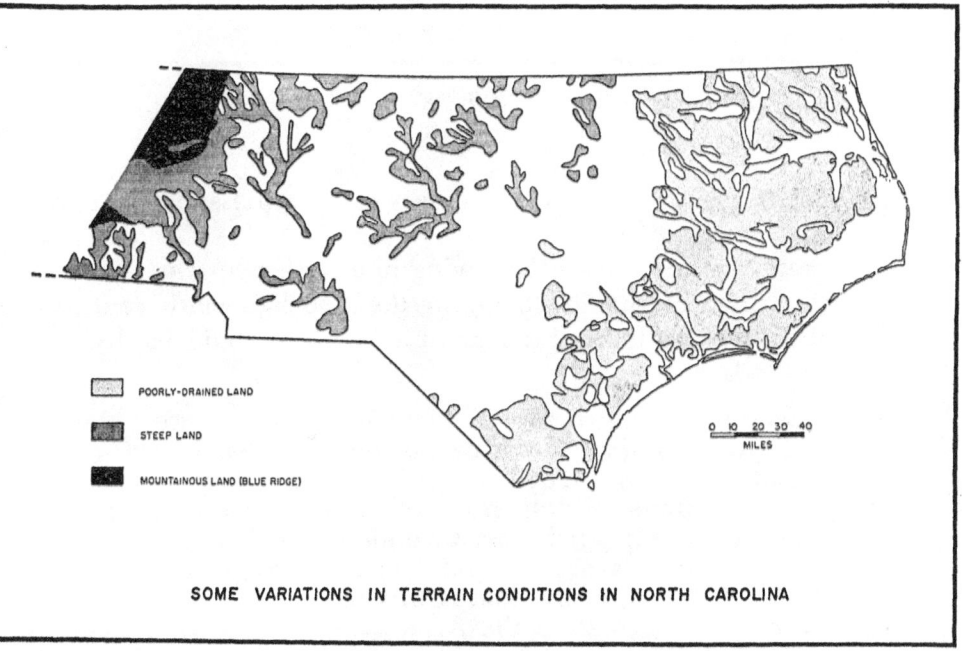

FIG. 12

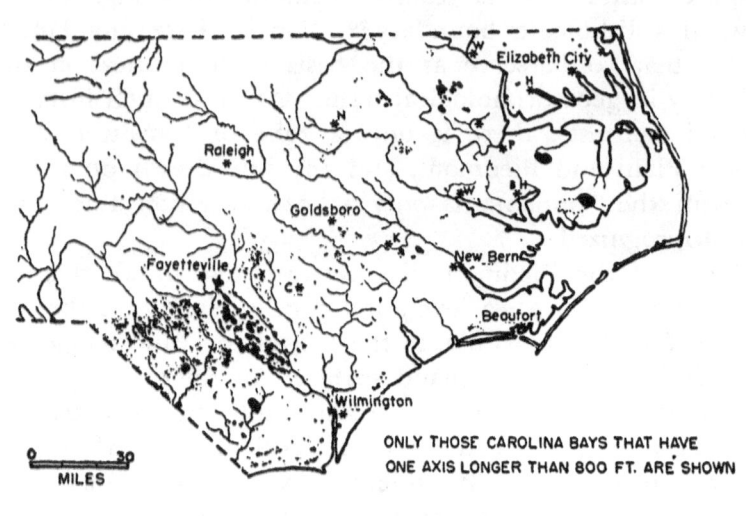

Fig. 13

its eastern edges (see the areas shown as "Steep Land" on Fig. 12).[27]

A surveyor and map maker living in a settlement close to the western fringe of the Piedmont in the mid-eighteenth century described the terrain of this area in a way that could hardly be bettered today:

> The ridges are so joined together that no matter where I stand it is possible to go to any other part of the land that I wish without crossing a stream, though the paths may resemble the moves of a piece in a game of draughts. And as the mountains are all about the same height it is easy to understand that one can get two different profiles of the land. The ridges give an almost straight horizontal line, and that is why the country looks practically level when seen from the Arrarat Mountains or from the Pilot. But the other and more correct profile can easily be pictured, especially when one takes a map and traces the hundreds

and thousands of valleys, some of them long valleys taking one, two or three, or even seven and eight hours to traverse.[28]

The complex pattern of stream valleys he described is considerably below the general level of the surface; the channels of a few major rivers are from two hundred to even five hundred feet below the interstream areas, and the valleys in general are markedly deeper than those of the Coastal Plain.

There is an important contrast between Piedmont and Coastal Plain in terms of the varying amount of wetland in the two regions. In the Piedmont, bottomlands vary from a few feet to about a mile in width, and these are, and were, the only commonly recurring type of wetland within the area. In the Coastal Plain, bottomland represents only one of several types of wetland, each one of which is fairly common; they vary in form from the few very large irregularly-shaped continuous blocks of swampland to the hundreds of small and remarkably uniform oval depressions known as "Carolina Bays."[29]

Maps of modern conditions provide fairly reliable guides to

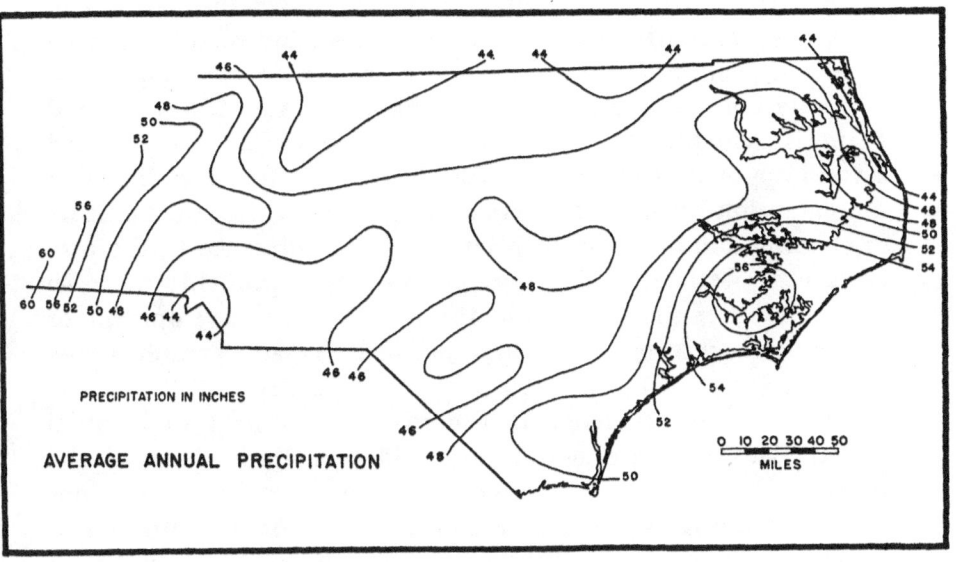

Fig. 14

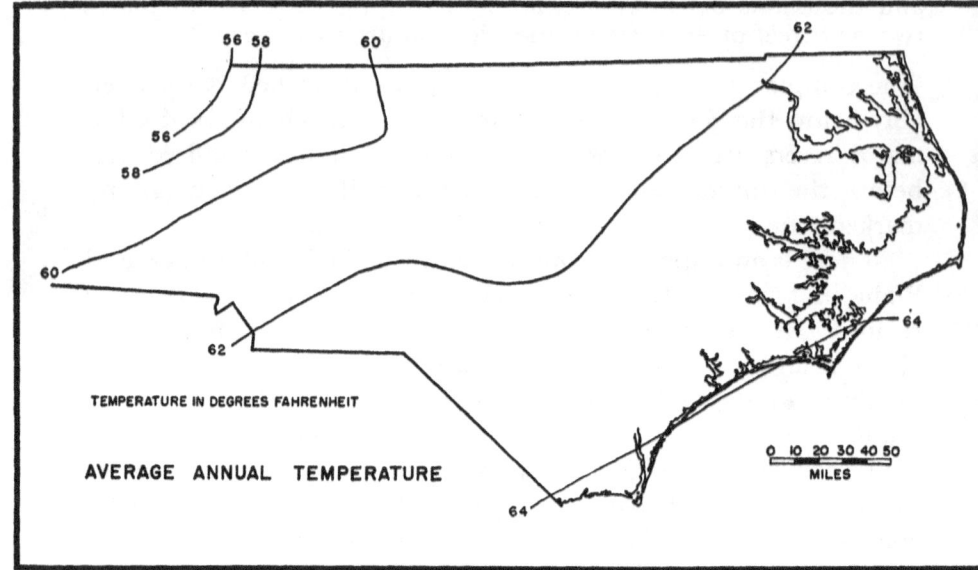

Fig. 15

the distribution of these wetlands; Fig. 12 shows the location of all kinds of poorly-drained lands, the distribution of Carolina Bays is shown on Fig. 13,[30] and the map of peat soils, Fig. 10, is also relevant. The strong predominance in the Outer Coastal Plain is evident. Although some of these wetlands did afford certain opportunities for the settler,[31] on the whole they impeded the extension of the settled area owing to the costs and difficulty of clearing and draining such land.[32] This difference in the proportion of wetland in the east and west was, probably more so than any other single contrast, the basis for the development of a legend concerning the greater productivity and greater settlement potential of the western part of the colony.[33]

There is no evidence that climatic conditions in colonial North Carolina were significantly different from those of the twentieth century. There is not now, and presumably was not then, any very great difference in the climate of the eastern and western portions of the land east of the Blue Ridge in North Carolina. Climatic conditions are fairly uniform throughout the

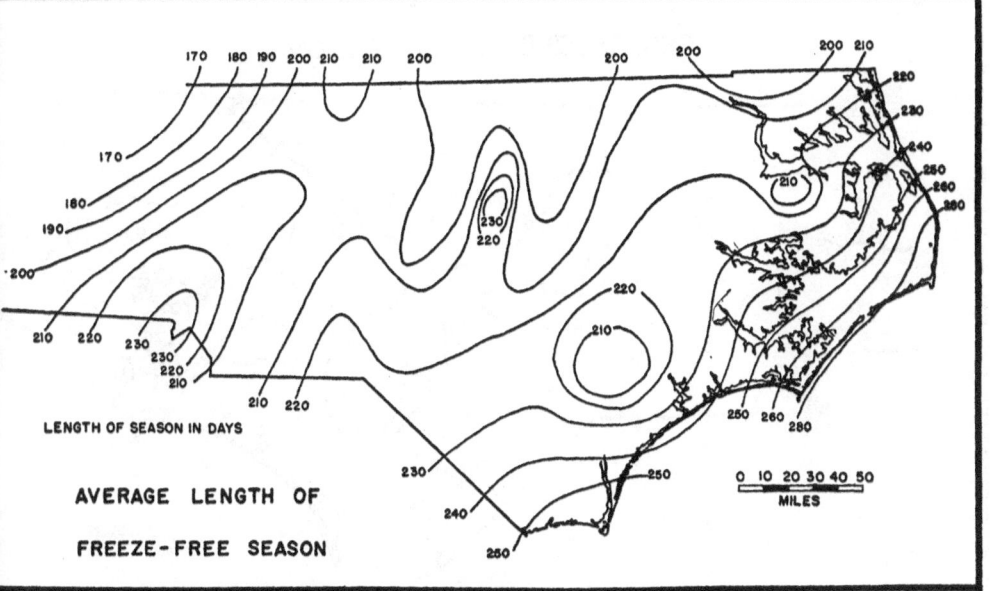

Fig. 16

area, as is apparent from Figs. 14, 15, and 16.[34] Although the average annual precipitation is considerable (Fig. 14) and most of North Carolina has between 45" and 55" of precipitation, dry spells are common in summer and fall, and a degree of drought occurs almost every year. The most marked climatic variation is in the length of the freeze-free season (Fig. 16), but the growing period is sufficiently long for the production of a great variety of field and vegetable crops. The areas closest to the Atlantic Ocean experience its moderating effects most markedly, with cooling sea breezes in summer and mild winter temperatures.

Although there were no important climatic variations in colonial North Carolina, the coastal parts were held to be less healthful, less temperate, and less pleasant than the interior parts.[35] Mosquitoes and hurricanes were probably the cause of this belief. Mosquitoes, sometimes mentioned in the early accounts,[36] were almost certainly a menace in the summer and fall months in the Outer Coastal Plain, where the abundance of low-lying land, poorly drained areas, and stagnant surface water must have pro-

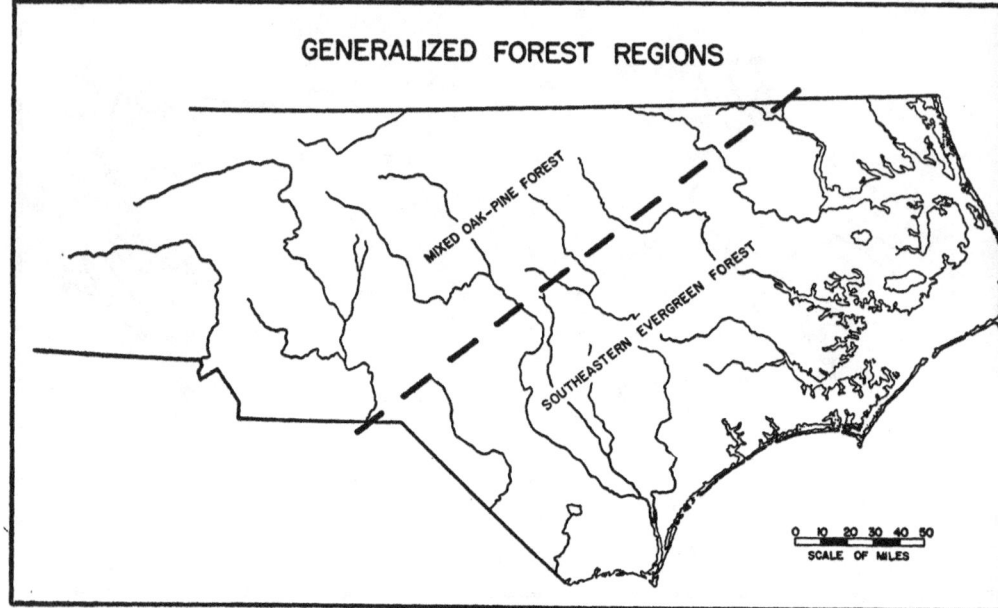

Fig. 17

vided excellent breeding grounds. In late summer and fall the hurricane danger was also present, and more serious in this area than farther inland; when hurricanes struck they caused much damage and attracted a great deal of attention.[37]

Much less is known about the vegetation cover of the colony than about its climate. While it is fairly safe to assume that the climatic conditions have not changed much in the last two or three hundred years, the degree of correspondence between the present and earlier vegetation cover is slight. Furthermore, the vegetation, unlike the climate, showed little semblance of uniformity.[38]

Forests were more widespread in the first half of the eighteenth century than they are now, and there was a broad contrast between the forest types of the eastern and western portions of the colony. Much of the Piedmont and a small part of the Coastal Plain was covered with oak-pine forest (see Fig. 17).[39] There were many local variations within this area, but in general

Virginia pine (*Pinus virginiana*) predominated in the western part of this belt, close to the Blue Ridge, while loblolly pine (*Pinus taeda*) predominated in the eastern part, and shortleaf pine (*Pinus echinata*) was most common in the central part; in all three sections oak and hickory trees were common. The forest in the remainder of North Carolina formed the northern limit of the southeastern evergreen forest (Fig. 17), and was dominated by loblolly, longleaf, and pond pines (*Pinus taeda, Pinus palustris,* and *Pinus rigida* var. *serotina,* respectively); in this section, too, local variations were common, and the bottomland hardwood forests formed a distinctive community along the rivers.

Parts of the colony were devoid of a forest cover. Some of the open areas, such as the freshwater marshes, tidal marshes, dunes, and beaches that were common in the Outer Coastal Plain, reflected distinctive soil and drainage conditions. There were also open areas made by man. Settlers commonly set fire to the vegetation during the colonial period,[40] as did Indians earlier, and one of the results of frequent fires was the creation and maintenance of expanses of open land in regions that would otherwise have been forest covered.

Savannahs and evergreen shrub bogs were common examples of such fire-induced open vegetation cover. Savannahs were upland grass-sedge bogs or flat, seasonally wet, treeless areas of grasses and sedges occurring in interstream locations, often only a few feet above surrounding areas. Evergreen shrub bogs also occurred on flat interstream sites, but were covered with a dense mass of shrubs and occasional scattered pond pines. Both were most common in the Outer Coastal Plain and probably once covered a considerable portion of it.

There were other kinds of fire-induced open land. Although they occurred in both regions, it seems that the proportion of such land in the Coastal Plain was more than in the Piedmont. For a variety of reasons,[41] fire was a more destructive agent in the Coastal Plain, with the result that fire subclimax types of vegetation were more common there.

While there was a larger proportion of nonforest vegetation in the Coastal Plain than in the Piedmont, this contrast did not necessarily make the former region relatively more attractive. In fact, the nonforested portions of the Coastal Plain, and particularly of the Outer Coastal Plain, were often also areas of excessive soil moisture for at least part of the year or were covered with a thick mass of shrubs and coarse grasses such as at best afforded only poor quality pasturage; and the coastal marshes and dunes were often of little use even as pasture grounds.

Existing conditions, and what can be surmised of former environmental variations, point towards the same conclusion: evidently, there was a basis in reality for the legend that developed early in the eighteenth century about the superior resources of the interior section of North Carolina as compared with the more maritime portion.

The sentiments of those who wrote about the wonders of the backcountry early in the eighteenth century were echoed by other writers as the colonial period drew to a close. British authors who had never even crossed the Atlantic, but based their accounts and "observations" upon the writings of those who had, took up the same theme. William and Edmund Burke, neither of whom had visited America, wrote of the pleasantness and "almost incredible" fruitfulness of the backcountry parts of Carolina and of the remarkable increase in the quality of the country from east to west.[42] Arthur Young, after studying several mid-eighteenth century accounts, came to essentially the same conclusion.[43] The author of a guide to the colonies, intended for the emigrants from Scotland who were setting out for the New World in the early 1770's, found words inadequate to convey a proper description of all the virtues of the interior parts of the Carolinas.[44]

The most elaborate of all accounts of the difference between the interior and maritime portions of North Carolina was drawn up by "An American," the anonymous author of *American Husbandry* (first published in London in 1775), who may or may not have seen the country he described. He summed up his account of the differences as follows: "In a word, all the necessaries, and many of the luxuries of life abound in the back parts of this province, which, with the temperate climate, renders it one of the finest countries in America; so fine, that every body must be astonished at finding any settlements made on the unhealthy sea coast, which is nearly the reverse."[45] He went on to recommend strongly that new settlers should fix themselves upon the hitherto neglected back parts of the country, for "every reason of effect conspires to shew the propriety of settling the back parts of this province in preference to the maritime ones. . . ."[46]

But these late recommendations were superfluous. By 1775, settlers had already discovered the attractions of the back parts for themselves and during the previous twenty or thirty years had been flocking into the area in large numbers. The first American West exerted an attractive force as impressive and consequential as that of subsequent ones beyond the Appalachians.

PART II
THE PEOPLE

CHAPTER IV · THE INFLUX OF SETTLERS AND DEMOGRAPHIC CHANGES

The population of North Carolina began increasing at a dramatic rate during the middle of the eighteenth century. In 1730, there were between 30,000 and 35,000 inhabitants in the colony; in 1750, there were between 65,000 and 75,000; and by 1770, the number was somewhere between 175,000 and 185,000.[1] The population thus doubled between 1730 and 1750, and then almost tripled between 1750 and 1770.

This rapid and substantial increase was primarily the result of immigration. In a sense, the increase was merely the continuation of a process that began with the founding of the colony. But the movement of people into North Carolina in the seventeenth and early eighteenth centuries proceeded by fits and starts.[2] Around the middle of the eighteenth century the flow had become a large, rapid, and accelerating stream. This influx, and the changes it caused in the make-up and distribution of the population in North Carolina, are the subject of this chapter.

MIGRATION AND MIGRANTS

The movement of settlers was so conspicuous in the 1750's that it aroused much comment. Early in 1751, Governor Johnston reported that people were flocking in daily. A few months later another official noted that "great numbers" of people were coming into the colony. Writing in the fall of 1752, Bishop Spangenberg claimed that four hundred families had already entered in that year. Two years later Governor Dobbs told the Board of Trade that settlers were coming in from the north in hundreds of wagons. A minister writing from Virginia, in 1756, reported that three hundred Virginians en route to North Carolina passed Bedford courthouse in one week, that between January and October of 1755 five thousand had crossed the James River bound for North Carolina, and that great numbers were following each day.[8] If the figures such observers cited were not always very accurate, at least they give some impression of the magnitude of the movement.

The Seven Years' War did not interrupt the flow, which continued unabated in the 1760's. In 1763, Benjamin Franklin estimated that ten thousand families, or forty thousand persons, had emigrated from Pennsylvania to North Carolina in the previous few years.[4] Other Southern colonies were also experiencing large increases, but Governor Tryon was not far wrong when, in 1766, he boasted that his colony was being settled faster than any on the continent. The rate of increase was greater only in Georgia, where much smaller increments sufficed to produce a greater rate of increase because of the smaller size of the total population involved.[5]

Many of the immigrants headed for the western part of the colony. A newspaper report from Williamsburg, Virginia, described the effect of the uneven impact of the incoming waves of settlers:

There is scarce any history, either antient or modern, which affords an account of such a rapid and sudden increase of inhabitants in a back frontier country, as that of North Carolina. To justify the truth of this observation, we need only to inform our readers, that twenty years ago there were not twenty taxable persons within the limits of the above mentioned County of Orange; in which there are now four thousand taxables. The increase of inhabitants, and flourishing state of the other adjoining back counties, are no less surprising and astonishing.[6]

The validity of these claims is borne out by figures of the yearly increase of population in certain counties. Fig. 18 shows the rate of increase between 1754 and 1770 in two counties, Onslow, along the coast, and Rowan, in the west.[7] While the eastern county did not quite succeed in doubling its population, the population in the western county almost quadrupled in size during the same period, and the difference between the two rates

THE INFLUX OF SETTLERS AND DEMOGRAPHIC CHANGES 55

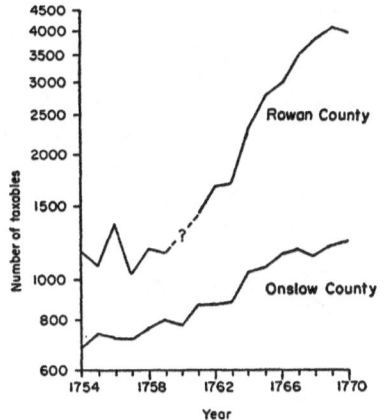

TWO NORTH CAROLINA COUNTIES—
POPULATION GROWTH, 1754-1770

FIG. 18

of increase became more and more marked from year to year as the volume of the immigration increased.

The higher rate of increase in the western part of the province could be attributed partly to the influx of large numbers into a hitherto fairly empty region. But more significant in accounting for the higher western rate was the fact that the fruitfulness of the west became legendary shortly before many migrants set out to seek land. That most immigrants went to the west was striking testimony to the effectiveness of the legend.

The migrants were a heterogeneous group. They represented a variety of religions, languages, nationalities, and social and economic classes. Distinctions made most commonly were based on place of origin: thus, Scotch-Irish, Scottish Highlanders, and Germans were generally distinguished. Each one of these three groups constituted an important element in the migration.

Of the three groups, the Scotch-Irish left least evidence of their part in the migration. Most of them probably came overland, chiefly from colonies to the north and particularly from Pennsylvania, where many of these eighteenth-century immigrants first disembarked.[8] One Philadelphia merchant even claimed that most of those who landed in the port went on to Virginia and North Carolina.[9] Others came directly from Ireland. Arthur Young, one of the most reliable of all eighteenth-century travelers, visited Ireland in the 1770's and mentioned the emigration of indentured servants to North Carolina.[10] Schemes organized to encourage this movement directly from Ireland accelerated the flow from time to time.[11] And a few Scotch-Irish probably entered by way of the port of Charleston and the overland route from South Carolina.

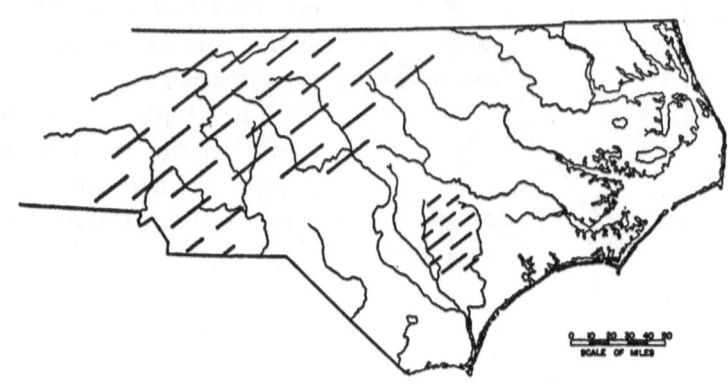

FIG. 19
Delineated area shows the approximate location of most of the Scotch-Irish settlers in North Carolina, 1750-1775.

The precise whereabouts of the Scotch-Irish who settled in the colony is uncertain. Their language, church affiliation, and surnames provide only very ambiguous means of identifying the localities to which they went. Fig. 19 shows the area within which the majority of the Scotch-Irish seem to have settled, but the evidence on which it is based is insubstantial.[12]

The migration of Scottish Highlanders to the colony is much more amply and specifically documented than that of the Scotch-Irish. It was part of a general emigration from Scotland to North America. This exodus began after the Treaty of Union in 1707, grew in volume as a "spirit of emigration" became common, and reached a peak shortly before the Revolution. By 1775, it was even celebrated in song and dance.[13] Some Scotsmen came to North Carolina before 1750, but the majority arrived during the third quarter of the eighteenth century,[14] when partisan authorities in the colony favored their migration, and merchants and shipowners fostered it.[15] As the "spirit of emigration" from Scotland reached its height in the 1760's and 1770's, more and more shiploads of Highlanders disembarked in North Carolina.[16]

One writer, who identified himself only as "Scotus Americanus," wrote an account of the colony for would-be emigrants from Scotland. So strongly did he emphasize the attractions of the colony that a few may have prepared to leave for the promised land immediately after reading it.[17] But promotional literature was probably superfluous. The letters sent by the new Carolinians to their friends and relatives still in Scotland served to illustrate the desirability of moving from the western Highlands and Islands of Scotland, where economic conditions were so unfavorable that even the less successful emigrants could hardly have failed to obtain a measure of security superior to that which they had been accustomed to in their former home.[18]

There is no way of calculating the numbers involved in the migration before 1763, but it has been estimated that about 25,000 Scotsmen came to North America between 1763 and 1775 and that over 5,000 of these went to North Carolina, the single most important receiving colony.[19] By 1775, there were perhaps as many as 10,000 Highlanders in the colony.[20] There were also some Scottish Lowlanders, few in number by comparison with the Highlanders but important because they included a small group of merchants who subsequently played a leading role in the economic development of the colony.

Most of the Highlanders settled within a fairly compact area, shown on Fig. 20.[21] The distribution shown on the map is probably fairly reliable, since virtually all of the references to Highlanders actually specifying the location of their settlements describe them as being in the same general area. It comprised the counties of Cumberland and Anson, with a particularly large concentration of Highlanders in Cumberland. The minority of Lowlanders, on the other hand, is difficult to locate. Unlike the more clan-conscious Highlanders, they seem to have dispersed and mingled with other settlers.

The third element in the peopling of the colony was the German-speaking group. The Germans were of different Prot-

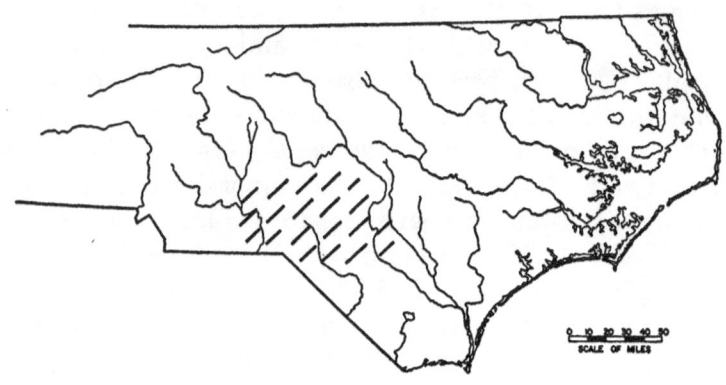

Fig. 20
Delineated area shows the approximate location of most of the Scottish Highlanders in North Carolina, 1750-1775.

estant denominations (of which Lutheran, Moravian, and Reformed were the most common), and came originally from different parts of Europe. The diversity among them in terms of place of origin was particularly marked: for example, of 42 whose birthplace is recorded in one extant list, 19 were born in German states, 1 in Switzerland, 4 in Denmark, 1 in Latvia, 3 in England, 17 in Pennsylvania, 1 in New England, 1 in Virginia, and 1 in Carolina.[22] The variety was accentuated because the Germans came into North Carolina only after more or less prolonged stays in colonies farther north.[23]

Despite their differences, the Germans were generally considered by others as a distinct group and regarded themselves as a separate and distinctive fraternity. One German minister, writing home from one of the more exclusively German settlements in western North Carolina, expressed this latter sentiment as follows:

Among the things to be especially emphasized for the younger people . . . was the admonishment not to contract any marriages with the English or the Irish. And even though this may seem very unreasonable to a European, it is in this region a very important matter. For in the first place, the Irish in this section are lazy, dissipated and poor, live in the most wretched huts and enjoy the same food as their animals (although in the cities this matter is reversed). In the second place, it is very seldom that German and English blood is happily united in wedlock. Dissensions and feeble children are often the result. The English wife will not permit her husband to be master in his household, and when he likewise insists upon his rights crime and murder ensue. In the third place, the English of this region do not adhere to any definite religion, do not have their children christened; nor do they send them to any school, but simply let them grow up like domestic animals. Finally, we owe it to our native country to do our part that German blood and the German language be preserved and more and more disseminated in America, for which the present indications in these regions are very favorable.[24]

The editor who published the letter late in the eighteenth century found it an especially interesting one and hoped that the "degenerating influence of race-mixture, especially by those of German blood" would be further investigated;[25] in a later volume, the same editor, Velthusen, reverted to the matter again and mentioned that he had been requested by a statesman to ask for more investigation of the deleterious influence of mixed marriages upon German blood.[26] If such sentiments were at all common they would go far to explain the German tendency to concentrate in exclusively German areas. (They also provide unusually early testimony to the rise of German nationalism, thirty years before Fichte delivered his famous address to the German people after the defeat of Jena.)

The Germans confined their settlements to western North Carolina to a greater extent than any other group of immigrants. Fig. 21[27] shows the approximate limits of the area within which they settled. The map also indicates the location of the Moravian tract, an especially important concentration of Germans. This piece of territory, officially known as "Wachovia," covered almost 100,000 acres. The Moravians purchased it from Lord Granville

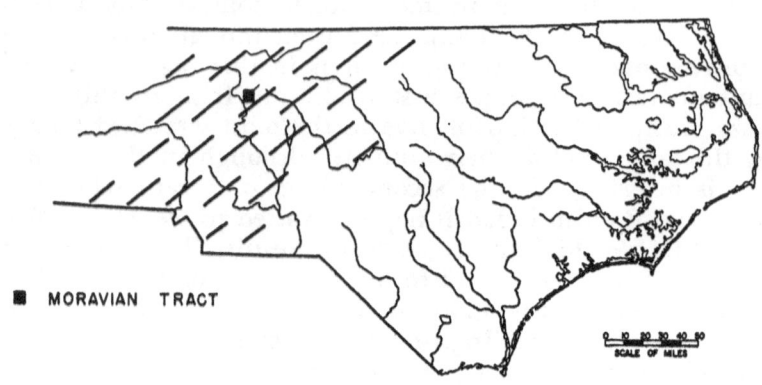

Fig. 21

Delineated area shows the approximate location of most of the German settlers in North Carolina, 1750-1775.

in 1752 and established themselves on the land the following year.

The history of the Moravians during the previous three centuries is an involved one. In short, they were the followers of the Protestant traditions and beliefs of the Unitas Fratrum, which was organized in Bohemia in the mid-fifteenth century by the followers of John Hus. After experiencing much opposition and persecution in various parts of Europe, they finally established a settlement in Georgia in the 1730's; this was soon abandoned and they then moved to Pennsylvania. The settlement of Moravians in North Carolina was an off-shoot of the Pennsylvania colony. The North Carolina branch was to be a self-supporting communal settlement, in which would be practiced the religion of the founders and from which the Gospel was to be spread among the Indians. It was a carefully supervised concentration of Germans, largely contained in one town and several villages.

The Moravian tract was not the only conspicuously German locality in western North Carolina. Evidence indicates that there were other more or less compact blocks of German-settled territory within the west. But the record of them is incomplete. The precise location of even those that are recorded is often impossible to establish, and in any event it is unlikely that any of the other German settlements were as highly organized as the Moravian colony.

Equally uncertain is the total number of Germans. The lack of a rational basis for calculating numbers of Germans in the colony before 1790 makes the existing estimates of doubtful value.[28] The 1790 Census does help to fill a little of the gap. Two analyses of this census produced calculations of the proportion of Germans in the white population of the state. Both calculations were obtained by inferring origins from surnames: one gives the German proportion as 2.8 per cent, the other as 4.7 per cent.[29] The white population was then almost 290,000, so that these proportions would put the number of Germans at about 8,000 and about 14,000, respectively. But since most of the Germans were still concentrated in the west the proportion there is more significant than the proportion in the state as a whole. Gehrke, also using the evidence of surnames in the 1790 Census, concluded that in two of the counties in western North Carolina that had strong German elements, they represented 22.5 per cent of the total white population.[30] Thus, in 1775, in the western counties of North Carolina, Germans probably constituted somewhere between 10 per cent and 30 per cent of the total white population.[31]

More important than the groups of Scotch-Irish, Scotsmen, and Germans who entered the colony was the great body of immigrants of English stock. Their influx into the colony was taken for granted, and there was nothing novel enough about either their settlements or their ways to warrant contemporary comment. They, the majority, set the patterns against which the divergences of the others become notable.

Many of the newcomers who were not otherwise labeled were of English origin, but their precise numbers are unknown. During the third quarter of the eighteenth century non-English immigrants taken as a whole may even have outnumbered the English. Certainly, the ratio of English to non-English was substantially altered by the immigration movement. At the end of the proprietary period most of the settlers were of English origin, with only small scattered groups of non-English settlers. By the time of the Revolution the proportion of the latter was far greater owing to the influx of numerous Scotch-Irish, Scotsmen, and Germans.

Many of the English settlers who came into North Carolina after 1750 seem to have come in from colonies to the north. But the record is fragmentary. Perhaps a few wanted to remain anonymous as they removed southward out of one colony and into another. Most of them achieved anonymity whether they sought it or not.

Occasionally one of the migrants wrote a letter about his trip, or kept a journal of it, or recollected it later in his life, and a few records of such writings do survive. Thus it is known that James Auld, leaving his wife and six children in Maryland, set out for North Carolina in February, 1765. He found a job there, as a clerk and storekeeper in the town of Halifax, returned to Maryland to collect his wife and children, and was back in North Carolina with them by September, 1765. Two years later Auld bought a farm, hired some help to run it, and then commuted each day between his farm and his job in the town.[32] Waightstill Avery was born in Connecticut and graduated from the College of New Jersey. Avery became a teacher and apprentice lawyer in Maryland, moved from Maryland to North Carolina in 1768 or 1769, and subsequently prospered as a lawyer.[33] William Few, born in 1743 the son of a Maryland farmer, recalled in his autobiography that his father had taken him along in his quest for a more fertile country and a milder climate. His father found in North Carolina the kind of country he was looking for and purchased lands on the Eno River in Orange County. He then went back with his son to Maryland, sold his lands there, packed his family and belongings into a wagon and a cart, and brought them all to North Carolina in the autumn of 1768.[34]

It so happens that these three instances all involved persons from Maryland, with means beyond those of the average settler.

As far as the incoming English settlers are concerned, the intermediate economic and social status of Auld, Few, and Avery may not have been unusual; but Maryland did not supply the disproportionately large share of newcomers that the three examples might suggest. English settlers moved into North Carolina from all the other colonies, and particularly from Pennsylvania, New Jersey, and Virginia, as well as Maryland.[35] In fact, Virginia seems to have been the most important single colony from which the English came.[36] Some also came from South Carolina and others directly from England.[37]

There could have been no single overriding motive that governed all of these thousands of English, Scotch-Irish, Scotsmen, and Germans, and led them all to seek a home in North Carolina. Migrations are not such simple things, nor are the motives of migrants generally unmixed. Some of those who came must have had their own individual and special reasons for doing so, others probably had a variety of motives, and perhaps a few arrived in the colony simply because they had taken a chance and followed the crowd.[38] Yet the very fact that so many different settlers did come into the colony within such a short space of time does indicate that it held some especially powerful and popular appeal.

There were probably two main components in this appeal. One, the legend about the western part of the colony, has already been noted (see Chapter III). The other was the cheapness and ease with which land could be acquired almost anywhere in North Carolina.[39] The low cost and ease of acquisition were a reflection of the lateness of settlement (much of the territory east of the Appalachians remaining fairly empty even as late as the 1740's) and of the absence of land speculation and aggregation on the large scale that was characteristic of the more northern colonies. Moreover, promoters of its settlement successfully advertised these contrasts.[40]

There are few data on the comparative prices of land in the various colonies, so that the force of this attraction is difficult to measure. But one travel account is informative. Smyth described the results of a venture he engaged in during the course of his travels shortly before the Revolution. Convinced that land was much cheaper in North Carolina than Virginia, he purchased

550 acres straddling the boundary between the two colonies. The 100 acres that were in Virginia cost him £200; the remaining 500 acres were in North Carolina and cost him but £250. Smyth then promptly sold all of the land to a Virginia planter for £50 more than he paid for it.[41]

For the immigrants not intending to earn their living primarily from farming, the attraction of the colony was somewhat different. Merchants, physicians, lawyers, and other professional persons, who came to sell their services and skills rather than to live off the land, formed a numerically small but economically significant minority of the incoming population. One of them was James Murray, a Scotsman who came to the colony as a merchant in 1735 and subsequently became a political figure of importance. Before he embarked for the colony, Murray wrote a letter in which he explained his reasons for emigrating. The letter represents a unique record of the motives of one immigrant and suggests some of the attractions, real or imagined, of the colony. Murray enumerated his reasons for going to North Carolina as follows:

1. It is a climate as healthy as England.
2. It is cheaper living there than anywhere in Scotland.
3. Land which may now be bought there for 1^s or 18^{ps} acre will in all probability double the value every year, the place growing more populous as the Land Lower down in that River has already done. This determines me to go daily so soon as August, that I may be there and purchase about one thousand acres before it is known that the Governor intends to remove thither.
4. I am sure of the Governor's interest to support me.
5. My own fortune is sufficient both to buy a handsome plantation and carry on as large a trade as I have occasion for; the profits of which I may expect will at least defray the charges of settling me the first two years and afterwards lay up £200 sterling pr. An.
6. The place by its situation is entirely out of the power of a foreign enemy, which is no small advantage in these uncertain times.
7. I have the advantage of two faithful correspondents, Gent^n of Substance and Experience, one in England and another in the West Indies, who are willing to join Interests with me so far as our little trade requires it.[42]

Murray's hopes were eventually realized. He prospered in the role of merchant-planter, his path to prosperity being smoothed by influential compatriot friends.[43]

The merchant-planter class that Murray represented was destined to play an important role in the economic development of the colony, but most of the immigrants were not of this class. The majority were plain folk. Included among them were indentured servants, others but recently released from their term of indenture who had decided to invest their free labor and freedom dues in North Carolina, and some who had never known servitude.

An analysis of some official lists concerning about twelve thousand persons, both English and Scottish, who left from England for North America between December, 1773, and April, 1776, has shown that more than half of them went as indentured servants, a third paid their own way, and that the rest were convicts or redemptioners.[44] The same analysis also revealed the numerical superiority of emigrants who described themselves as skilled workers, yeomen, or farmers over those calling themselves laborers.[45] More relevant to North Carolina is another study, which used some of the same lists employed in this analysis, together with some other lists of the same kind, and which drew upon only the information that related to emigrants bound for North Carolina. It showed that a fifth of the English were going as indentured servants, that artisans formed the largest single group among the English, and that the Scottish emigrants were mainly farmers and laborers from the Highlands.[46] Since both studies were based, necessarily, on the occupational labels immigrants attached to themselves, they may somewhat underrepresent the proportion of plain farmers and laborers.

If some of the English emigrants and many of those from the Scottish Highlands were driven from their homelands by economic hardships, they were not all penniless. Some came with at least modest reserves of cash,[47] and a few of the newcomers were merchants and men of property (such as Murray) seeking to expand their fortunes. Less is known about the Germans and Scotch-Irish who came overland from the north, but both of these two

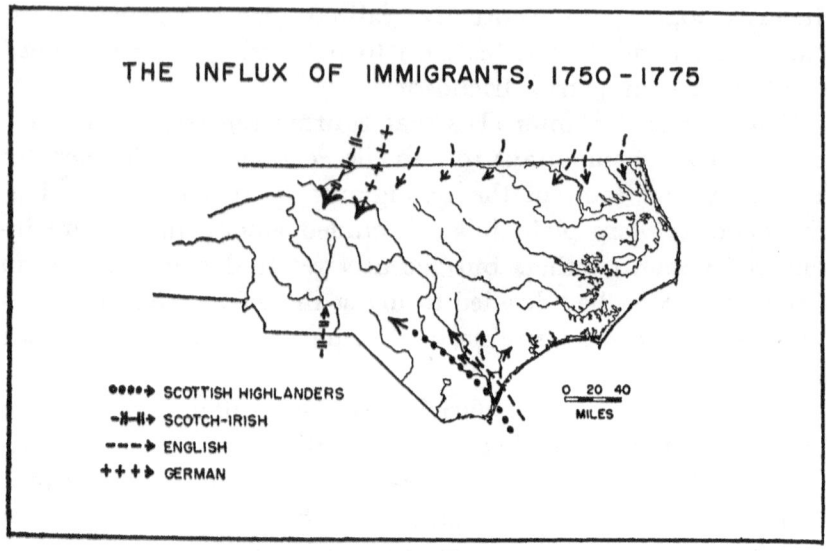

Fig. 22

Arrows indicate the generalized routes and directions of major streams of in-migration

groups seem to have been composed mainly of poor people, bringing few possessions with them.[48]

ENTRY AND DISTRIBUTION

The routes of entry of the immigrants are presented on Fig. 22.[49] The map is largely self-explanatory, but a brief commentary will help to summarize the relationships between place of entry and subsequent location of the several immigrant groups.

Most of the Germans and Scotch-Irish who entered the colony came overland from the north. They made use of the route grandly described on the 1755 edition of the Fry and Jefferson map of Virginia as "The Great Road from the Yadkin River thro' Virginia to Philadelphia distant 435 miles."[50] The Virginia section of this thoroughfare was being used in the 1740's, and possibly even earlier.[51] After following the Shenandoah Valley through most of north and central Virginia, the road led east through the Staunton River gap of the Blue Ridge, and then turned south; it crossed the Dan River in North Carolina and, in the early 1750's (and possibly earlier), reached the Yadkin

River in the vicinity of the Moravian tract. Although it seems to have lost its separate identity there, other roads extended from the Yadkin through the town of Salisbury and into South Carolina.

This was the route followed by the Moravians in their trek from Pennsylvania in 1753, and many other immigrants, particularly the Germans and Scotch-Irish from the north, came into North Carolina along it.[52] The "Great Road" thus provided a highway from the north into the legendary back lands of North Carolina. Part of its development was probably a result of the need for such a routeway, so that it was both a cause and effect of this movement.

Almost all the Scottish Highlanders, on the other hand, came across the Atlantic Ocean directly to North Carolina. After landing near the mouth of the Cape Fear River they moved inland into their favored area, a region that straddled the eastern and western parts of the colony (see Fig. 20). The Highlanders were clearly less interested in seeking out the westernmost lands than they were in joining their friends, relatives, and compatriots, the first of whom had come to south-central North Carolina at a time when that area was empty, or at least uncrowded, and thus had some of the same attractive attributes of lands farther west. Their desire to be among fellow countrymen, their initial entry at a place far from the westernmost regions and without the wagons that could have facilitated their movement there, and the initial existence of cheap land in the relatively sparsely populated area that the vanguard had elected to settle—all these factors probably played a role in determining the location of the main area of concentration of Highlanders. And subsequent expansion of this Scottish area in a westerly direction, onto the lands in the southern half of the colony between the Yadkin and Catawba rivers, was easy enough, since this was the very portion of the western territory farthest removed from the place of entry of most of the settlers coming into North Carolina from the north.

The English course of settlement differed from that of the Scottish Highlanders. The English came into the colony from all directions, by both land and sea, and they scattered into all parts of it. Only in the oldest settled parts of the colony, chiefly

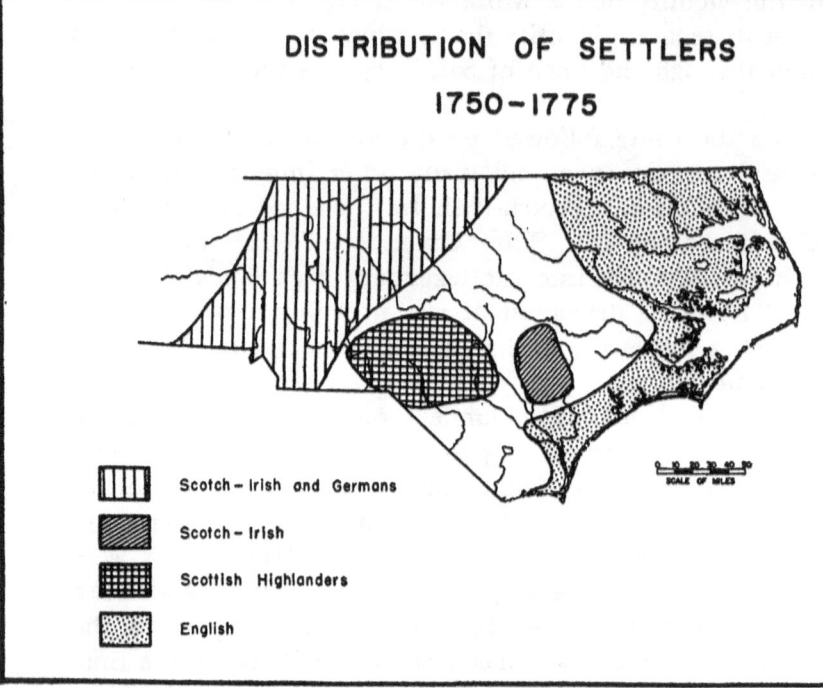

FIG. 23

Unshaded areas are those in which no particular category predominated. Boundaries are all approximate.

the northeast, was there anything approaching a markedly English area, since only here were they able to pre-empt much of the land before non-English settlers began moving into the colony in large numbers. There was probably a more or less constant infiltration of Virginians from across the boundary line into this same area.

The distribution of population changed rapidly during the third quarter of the eighteenth century as a result of the large-scale migration of settlers to the colony. Figs. 23, 24, 25, and 26 present a graphic summary of these changes. The first one, Fig. 23,[53] is necessarily nonquantitative and simply records the probable distribution of the major elements in the new population. Only those areas in which a particular group seemingly estab-

THE INFLUX OF SETTLERS AND DEMOGRAPHIC CHANGES

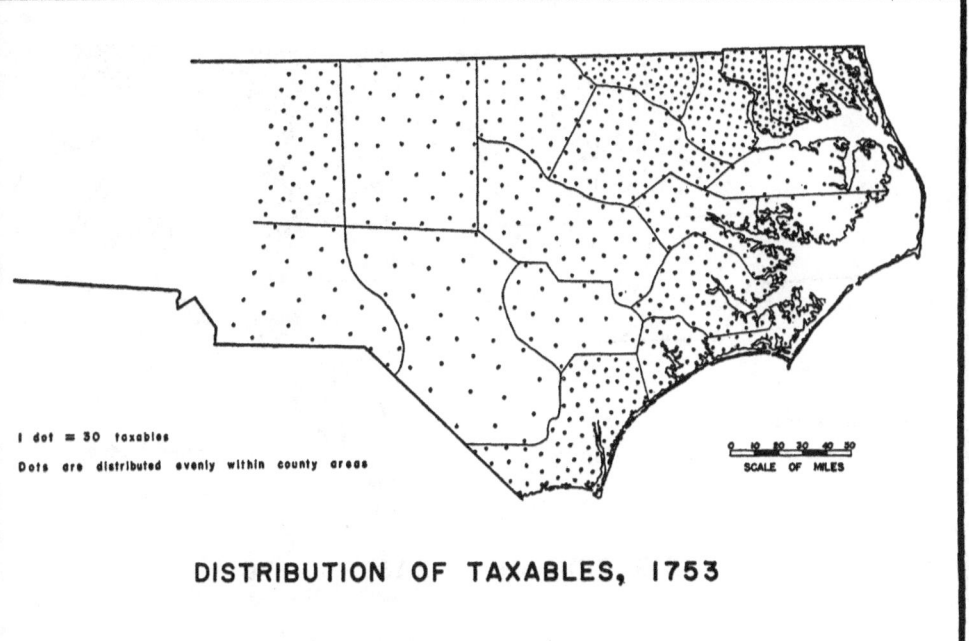

FIG. 24

lished a numerical superiority are distinguished, and large intervening areas where no single element predominated have been left blank. Comparison of this map with Fig. 4 reveals the radical transformation that the influx of migrants accomplished within a few decades.

Figs. 24, 25, and 26 show the changing distribution of the population in quantitative terms. The dots on the maps actually represent taxable persons, but to all intents and purposes they can also be taken as representing total population. The major deviation from this presumed correspondence, between taxables and population as a whole, is in western counties; more accurate data would probably reveal that densities of both taxables and total population were higher there than the maps suggest. (The nature and limitations of data on taxables are described in Appendix II, which also contains an account of the procedures employed in utilizing them.)

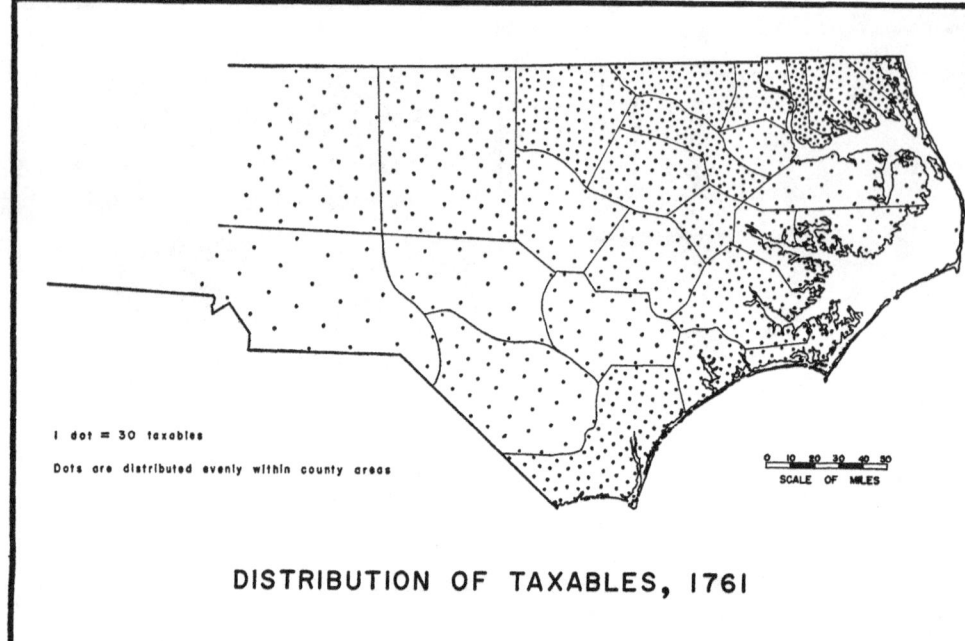

DISTRIBUTION OF TAXABLES, 1761

Fig. 25

In order to show graphically the changes that took place during the third quarter of the eighteenth century, three years were singled out, with eight-year intervals between them. Data on taxables are incomplete for the years before 1753, and from 1770 until 1775, so that it was decided to leave out of consideration these years at either end of the period. For the years 1753, 1761, and 1769 data were complete, with the single exception of Rowan County in 1753, for which county the 1754 total was used.

The unit areas within which the dots were placed were the counties. These are shown separately and named on Figs. 27, 28, and 29. The reconstruction of county boundaries was relatively simple, since most of this work has been done by others.[54] The only major drawback with regard to county boundaries was the constantly ill-defined, or undefined, western edge of the two westernmost counties. In order to resolve this problem, a line

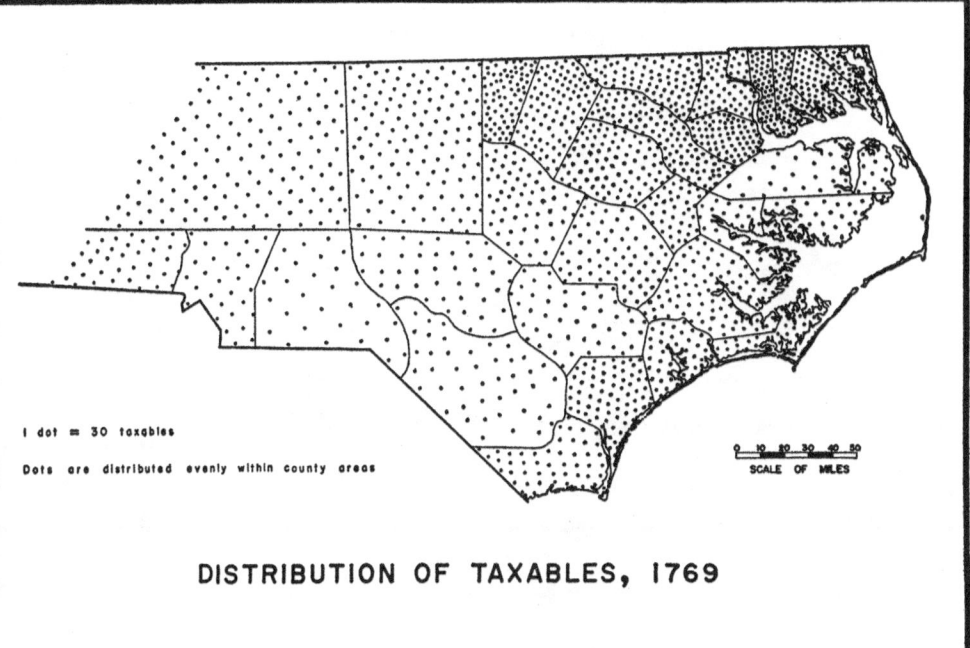

FIG. 26

was imagined, oriented approximately in a northeast-southwest direction, roughly parallel to the Proclamation Line of 1763, and located progressively further west from 1753 to 1769. This was considered to be the westernmost limit of the settled area and no taxables were shown to the west of the imagined line. Settlers almost certainly did not march westward in such smooth array, but the error inherent in the use of such a device is probably minor. The spreading of the dots evenly over the county areas in Figs. 24, 25, and 26 is also somewhat unrealistic.[55] The use of this procedure has the advantage, however, of revealing both the gross pattern of areal variations in the distribution of taxables and the changes in these patterns from year to year.

The three maps, despite their limitations, reveal several noteworthy features of population distribution. Most striking of all is the rapid settlement of the land west of the limit of the settled

FIG. 27

FIG. 28

FIG. 29

area in 1730 (see Fig. 4). Obvious too, is the fact that as the settled area was expanding, densities increased both in the east and in the west.

The highest densities, throughout the period covered by the maps, were in the northeast, mainly north of Albemarle Sound. If the dots had been located, rather than evenly distributed over the counties, the high densities would be even more striking in this area: a contemporary survey of a portion of this section reveals the extent to which settlements were concentrated along the rivers and inlets and were absent from the Dismal Swamp which straddled the boundary with Virginia.[56] The high densities probably reflect the fact that this was the oldest settled part of the colony, as well as its proximity to Virginia, whence many settlers were moving into North Carolina. The increasing densities north of Albemarle Sound also indicate that the area was filling up with settlers even though no observers seem to have mentioned this process. Observers often commented upon the increase in population in the west but they were probably somewhat misled by the more dramatic nature of the changes in the west, where farms were springing up in the wilderness, as compared with the east, where immigrants were moving into territory already partially settled.

To the south, between Albemarle Sound and Pamlico Sound, was a very different area. Here, the lack of increase in population is more in evidence. Throughout the period this region remained relatively sparsely settled and the persistence of the emptiness is evident on the maps. The large neck of land between the two sounds was occupied by the most extensive tract of flat, low-lying, poorly-drained land in the colony (see Fig. 12), which probably explains its lack of appeal. Even to the south, in the coastal counties as far south as the boundary with South Carolina, population densities were not high and increases were only slight. There too the prevalence of the same kind of land significantly diminished the attraction of the region for incoming settlers.

One broad variation appears on all of the maps. There is a general tendency for higher densities to occur in the northern half of the colony as compared with the southern half. It is not very pronounced but it is significant, particularly because any bias in the presumed validity of the correspondence between taxables and inhabitants is in an east-west direction and hence would not interfere with this north-south variation. The appearance of greater densities in the north reinforces the impression gained from contemporary descriptions that the settling of North Carolina in this period was accomplished predominantly by a southward flow of people into the colony and that the west was settled from the north, not by a simple westward thrust of pioneers.

NEGRO POPULATION

None of the maps presented thus far gives any indication of the distribution of the Negro component in the colony's population. Fortunately, the distribution of Negroes is more easily ascertained than that of any of the European groups. The simplest way of establishing where most of them were is through the use of data referring to Negro taxables, since they were almost always differentiated from whites on tax lists. There were so few Negro taxables who were not slaves that the terms "Negro taxables" and "slaves" can be regarded as being synonymous.

Table 1 is a compilation of data relating to size of slaveholdings. The data were taken from some of the more complete versions of tax lists that have survived and mainly from those in which each household was entered separately and a record made of its number of slaves.[57] Clearly, the locations and numbers of counties selected to represent each of the three major regions on the chart is not very satisfactory, and the fact that the data are for different years is also a drawback. But the collection of tax lists that is available is such a haphazard one that these shortcomings in the presentation of data are unavoidable. Despite the limitations of the method of presentation, and despite the inherent inaccuracy of the actual data, it is possible to draw certain conclusions from Table 1 concerning differences in slaveholdings from place to place within North Carolina.

Immediately apparent is the comparatively insignificant size of slaveholdings in the western portion of the colony, at least as exemplified by Orange County in 1755 and Anson County in 1763, where only a very small proportion (about 10 per cent) of the total number of households owned slaves, and those that did had very few.[58] In the southeast, really the lower Cape Fear River valley, slaves were much more widely held, and in larger numbers, so that the contrast between this region and the west was marked. In the northeastern region, slaveholding conditions were unlike those in either of the two other regions. While the proportion of households with slaves in the northeast was about the same as in the lower Cape Fear, the actual number of slaves per slave-owning household was generally much lower. In the virtual absence of households with twenty-one slaves or more the northeast more closely resembled the west than the southeast.

Although the chart does provide some measure of the occurrence of slaveholding in quantitative terms, it leaves much unsaid. To complete the picture, and at the same time to supplement the conclusions drawn from Table 1, two maps are included to show the distribution of Negro taxables in 1755 and 1767. The maps, Figs. 30 and 31, were based on tax returns which, although they did not record the number of slaves per household, did at least distinguish between the total number of Negro and white taxables in most of the counties.[59] The patterns revealed

TABLE 1. SLAVEHOLDING IN SELECTED

Region	County	Year	Total number of households	Households without slaves	
				No.	%
N.E.	Bertie[a]	1774	727	404	56
	Chowan[b]	1766	192	92	48
S.E.	New Hanover[c]	1755	264	118	44
	New Hanover[d]	1763	424	193	45
	New Hanover[e]	1767/69	550	268	49
W.	Orange[f]	1755	724	660	91
	Anson[g]	1763	?	?	90

SOURCES
a. Tax list in Legislative Papers, Tax Lists, 1771-74 (MSS).
b. Tax list in Chowan County, Lists of Taxables, 1766-98 (MSS).
c. Tax list in State Treasurer, Tax Lists, 1755 (MSS).
d. Tax list in N.C. Court Papers, 1763-77 (MSS).
e. The boundaries of New Hanover County were altered in 1764, when Brunswick County was

on Figs. 30 and 31 confirm the existence of the regional differences suggested by the chart on Table 1 and also suggest the presence of transitional areas between the three major regions singled out on the chart. The relatively high proportion of slaves in the total population of the southeast as compared with their occurrence in the west is striking.

The northeast is less easy to characterize, mainly on account of the critical location of some of the "no data" counties on Figs. 30 and 31. Slaveholding was not as prominent in the northeast as it was in the southeast, but it was more important in the northeast than it was in the west. The regional distinctiveness of the northeast that was conveyed by the form of presentation of the data on Table 1 is less evident on the maps. In terms of the occurrence of slaveholding, it seems from the maps that there was little basic difference between the area around Albemarle Sound and the adjacent areas to the south and west, but that there was a fairly small area immediately north of the sound in which slaveholding was more common than anywhere else in the colony outside of the southeast.[60] This area is a fairly small one, but since it embraced the two most densely settled counties in the colony (as is apparent from Figs. 24, 25, and 26), the total

THE INFLUX OF SETTLERS AND DEMOGRAPHIC CHANGES 77

AREAS OF NORTH CAROLINA, 1755-1774

Households with slaves		Slaveholding households							
		With 1-4 slaves		With 5-10 slaves		With 11-20 slaves		With 21 or more slaves	
No.	%	No.	%	No.	%	No.	%	No.	%
323	44	225	31.0	76	10.5	16	2.2	6	0.8
100	52	75	39.0	20	10.4	5	2.6	0	0.0
146	56	81	30.7	28	11.6	20	7.6	17	6.4
231	55	125	29.5	45	10.6	26	6.1	35	8.2
282	51	147	26.7	73	13.3	25	4.5	37	6.7
	9		8.3						
64		60		4	0.6	0	0.0	0	0.0
?	10	?	6.0	?	4.0	0	0.0	0	0.0

established. Data for New Hanover, 1767, and Brunswick, 1769, were added together in order to arrive at figures for an area approximately equivalent to that of New Hanover in 1755 and 1763. Tax list for New Hanover, 1767, in Comptroller's Papers, Box 40 (MSS); tax list for Brunswick, 1769, in Secretary of State, Tax Lists, 1720-1839 (MSS).
  f. Tax list in State Treasurer, Tax Lists, 1755 (MSS).
  g. Estimated from a mutilated tax list in Secretary of State, Tax Lists, 1720-1839 (MSS).

number of slaves in this area was larger than its extent would suggest.

While there was no major change in the distribution of Negro taxables between 1755 and 1767, there was a slight increase in the proportion of Negro taxables in each county. This change was a remarkably uniform one. Although the maps do not show how widespread the increase was, the change is revealed in the following table, which shows Negro taxables as a percentage of all taxables in the counties of North Carolina (and is derived from the same data on which the maps were based):

	Mean	Median	Highest in any county	Lowest in any county
1755 (19 counties)	33%	34%	73%	5%
1767 (22 counties)	46%	41%	87%	18%

In fact, only one county actually showed a decrease in the proportion of Negro taxables between 1755 and 1767; this was Hyde County, where the proportion decreased from 43 per cent to 41 per cent. Since this instance was both exceptional and negligible in amount, it can scarcely be regarded as being of any significance.

One other feature of the increase is suggested by the figures

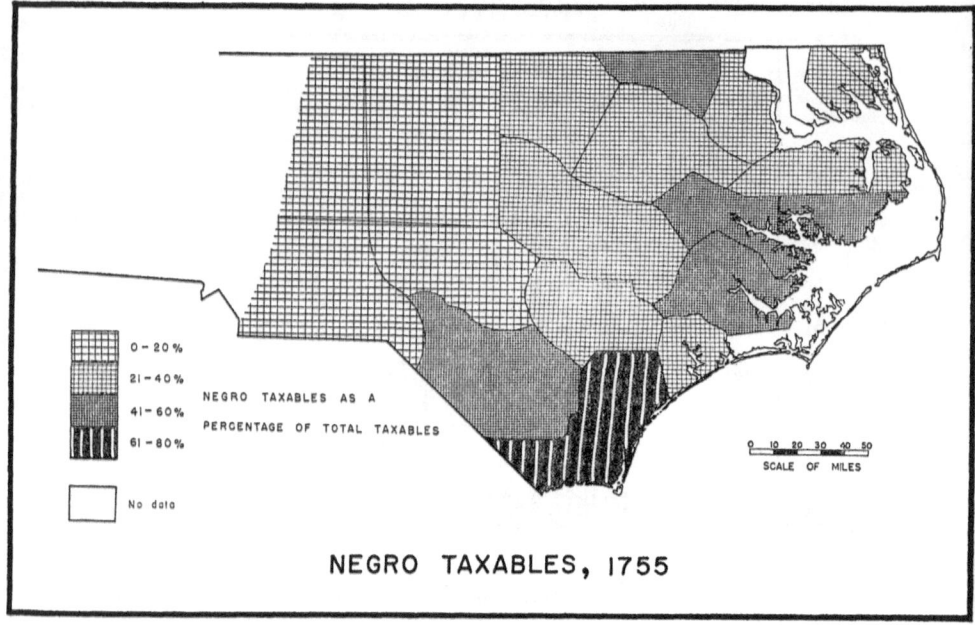

Fig. 30

on slaveholdings in New Hanover County for the years 1755, 1763, and 1767/69 (Table 1). The actual proportion of households that possessed slaves decreased slightly, so that most of the increase in the actual number of slaves during the period was probably a result of an increase in the numbers of slaves held by households that already possessed slaves. In other words, the practice of owning slaves was not becoming any more common, but there was a tendency for the actual slaveholding households to own more and more slaves.

The existence of this tendency in New Hanover County is suggested by the figures presented in the chart (Table 1). It is even more apparent if the proportionate sizes of each of the several slaveholding classes are presented in terms of slaveholding households rather than simply in terms of all households (see Table 2). Certainly the trends indicated in this chart are not entirely consistent. But that there was a trend towards an increase in the proportion of households with large slaveholdings is evi-

THE INFLUX OF SETTLERS AND DEMOGRAPHIC CHANGES

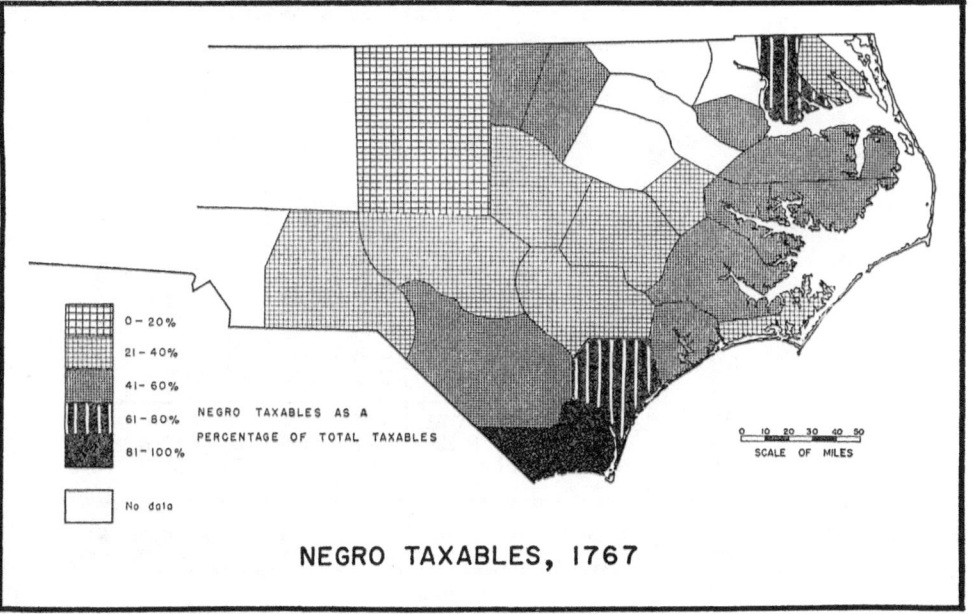

FIG. 31

dent if one compares the changing proportions of the largest (21 or more) and smallest (1-4) slaveholding households.

Thus, the nature of the change in New Hanover County and the broad similarity between the patterns depicted on Figs. 30 and 31 point towards the same conclusions. Briefly stated, it seems that three tendencies were proceeding concurrently during the third quarter of the eighteenth century: slaves were becoming more numerous in the colony, the actual proportion of the total population making use of slave labor was declining, and an increasing segment of the slaveholders was employing large rather than small numbers of slaves.

The three tendencies stemmed from a single cause. During the third quarter of the eighteenth century, the Negro population of North Carolina, in complete contrast with the white population, must have increased almost entirely as a result of natural increase, since very few Negroes were actually imported into the colony during the eighteenth century.[61] From 1755 to 1767 the

TABLE 2. SLAVEHOLDING IN NEW

Year	Total number of households with slaves	Households with 1-4 slaves			Households with 5-10 slaves		
		Number	As % of all households	As % of households with slaves	Number	As % of all households	As % of households with slaves
1755	146	81	30.7	55.4	28	11.6	19.2
1763	231	125	29.5	54.0	45	10.6	19.5
1767/69	281	147	26.7	52.0	73	13.3	25.9

SOURCES
Tax list for New Hanover, 1755, in State Treasurer, Tax Lists, 1755 (MSS); tax list for New Hanover, 1763, in N.C. Court Papers, 1763-77 (MSS); tax list for New Hanover, 1767, in Comptroller's Papers, Box 40 (MSS); tax list for Brunswick, 1769, in Secretary of State, Tax Lists, 1720-

Negro population increased by about 89 per cent.[62] This increase during the twelve-year period, resulting as it did almost entirely from natural increase, at a time when mortality rates were high, is extraordinarily large; it indicates a net annual rate of increase that must have been around 7 per cent.

The high net rate of increase and the absence of any considerable influx of slaves into the colony suffice to account for the three concurrent tendencies noted above. The white immigrants in the mid-eighteenth century rarely brought slaves with them. Those within the colony who held slaves increased the size of their holdings as their slaves multiplied; but since most of the incoming settlers did not bring slaves with them, the slaveholders represented a diminishing proportion of the population. Thus, while the actual distribution of slaveholding showed no important changes, slavery was actually becoming a more prominent feature in those areas in which it was already most conspicuous.

One qualification is necessary. While it is true that most immigrants into North Carolina did not bring slaves with them, a few probably did. The incoming settlers most likely to bring slaves with them would have been those coming from areas where

HANOVER COUNTY, 1755-1767/69

Households with 11-20 slaves			Households with 21 slaves or more			Households with 5 slaves or more		
Number	As % of all households	As % of households with slaves	Number	As % of all households	As % of households with slaves	Number	As % of all households	As % of households with slaves
20	7.6	13.7	17	6.4	11.6	65	25.6	44.5
26	6.1	11.3	35	8.2	15.1	106	24.9	45.9
25	4.5	8.9	37	6.7	13.1	135	24.5	47.9

1839 (MSS). The boundaries of New Hanover County were altered in 1764, when Brunswick County was established. Data for New Hanover, 1767, and Brunswick, 1769, were added together in order to arrive at figures for an area approximately equivalent to that of New Hanover in 1755 and 1763.

slaves were most abundant. These areas were Virginia and South Carolina, which had initially constituted the main areas whence slaves had been brought into North Carolina. In fact, the initial concentration of slaveholding in the lower Cape Fear, in the Albemarle area, and along the Virginia border, was a reflection of the proximity of these regions to, and their trade contacts with, the major sources of supply. But by comparison with the degree to which natural increase was serving to augment the number of slaves in these areas, this addition by (involuntary) immigration could not have been large. Furthermore, it was confined almost entirely to the east. Many of the immigrants to the west were coming from areas where slavery was relatively unimportant, often without the capital necessary to purchase slaves, and some (notably the Moravians and the Quakers) had more or less strong scruples about owning slaves.

PART III
THE CHANGING ECONOMIC GEOGRAPHY

CHAPTER V · UTILIZATION OF THE FORESTS

The settlers came to North Carolina with the immediate purpose of exploiting the land. As they used it, they inevitably transformed it. But the process of transformation did not impose any regular pattern on the land, and such patterns as were created were neither deeply etched nor widely recurrent elements in the rural scene. Exploitation was fairly unsystematic and small in scale. Irregular patches of roughly cleared land were worked by small numbers of men using primitive tools. Rectilinear surveying, wholesale vegetation clearance, contour farming, and other techniques that in later centuries contributed to the large-scale patterning of the land were not practiced.

If exploitation did not produce any dramatic or widespread patterns on the land, it did result in substantial differences from place to place within the colony. These differences, and the economic activities associated with them, are the subject of the three chapters that follow. In this first one of the three, the emphasis is upon the utilization of the forests for the commercial production of naval stores and wood products.

NAVAL STORES

Naval stores, or tar, pitch, and turpentine, were North Carolina's chief contribution to colonial commerce. One of the very first travelers recognized the great potential of the North Carolina forest for the making of naval stores (see p. 33, above). Even the traditional synonym for North Carolinians, "Tarheels," suggests the early importance of naval stores (though how and when this name first came into use has never been satisfactorily established). Throughout much of the eighteenth century the colony

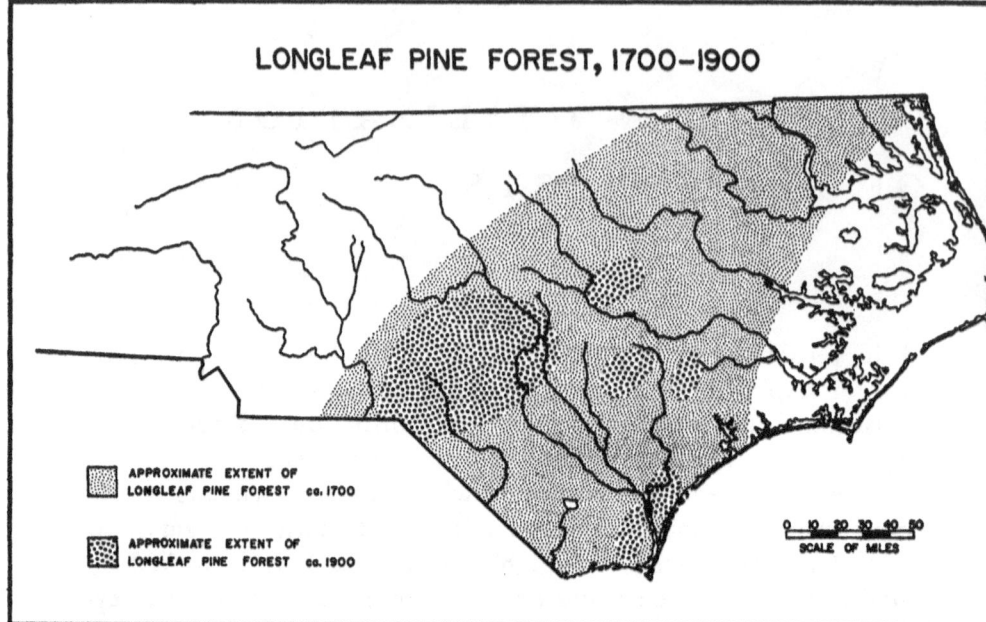

Fig. 32

was the leading American producer of tar, pitch, and turpentine. In 1768, a year for which comprehensive data are available, about 60 per cent[1] of all the naval stores exported from the North American colonies originated in North Carolina.[2]

Of critical importance in the naval stores industry was the colonial distribution of the longleaf pine (*Pinus palustris*). This tree, native to the sand hills and coastal plains of the southern Seaboard, yielded prolific amounts of resin and hence was the one most sought after by tar burners and turpentine collectors. But the distribution of longleaf pine forest during colonial times is not easily ascertained. Longleaf pine forest is a fire subclimax type of vegetation and its distribution has fluctuated in the past in response to changes in the incidence and frequency of burning. Furthermore, lumbering activities as well as the making of naval stores have drastically affected its distribution. The occurrence of the present longleaf forest consequently shows only a slight correspondence to its former extensive distribution.[3]

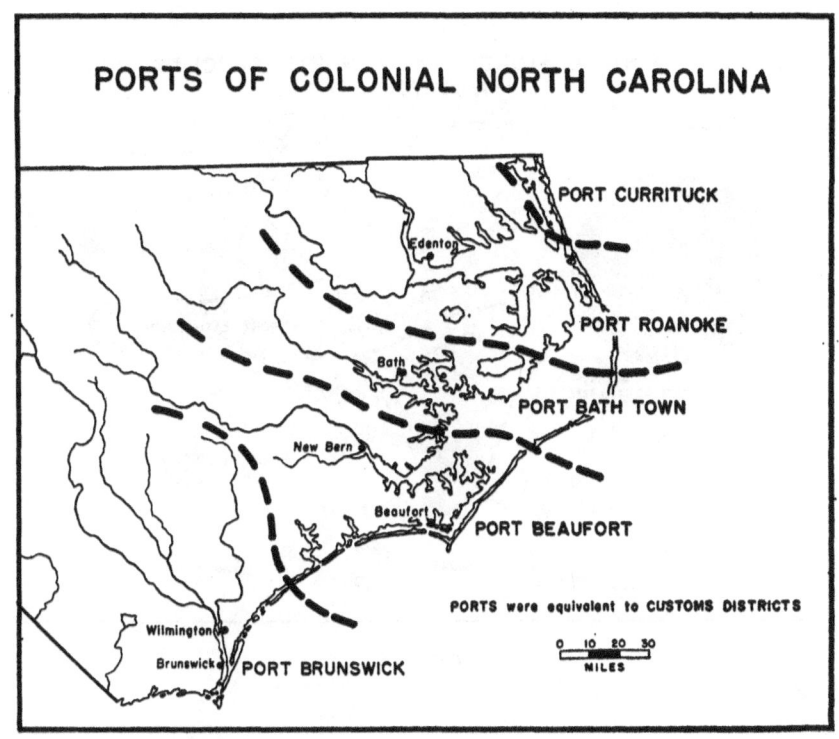

Fig. 33

The extent of longleaf pine about sixty years ago is shown on Fig. 32.[4] On the same map is shown the probable distribution at about 1700, or, more accurately, the area within which the longleaf pine may then have been the dominant tree. It probably occurred within the area in extensive, unmixed forests, often quite open in appearance,[5] and interrupted in places by the quite different tree associations of the river bottomlands. The map, little more than a tentative summary of an imprecisely-known change, does illustrate the most important feature of the earlier distribution, namely, the major concentration in the east.

Naval stores production was not uniformly distributed in the longleaf pine belt of eastern North Carolina. The most useful guide to the actual location of production is the record of exports, Customs 16/1, which is broken down by Ports or customs dis-

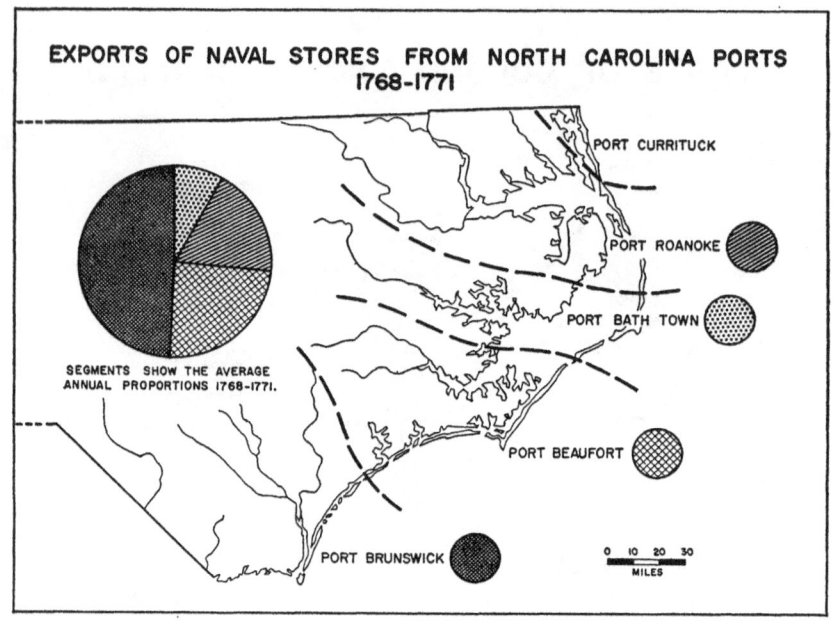

Fig. 34

tricts. The approximate locations of the Ports are shown on Fig. 33. (For an explanation of how the map was drawn, see Appendix II. In order to avoid confusing these Ports or customs districts with what is normally conveyed by the term port, the former has been capitalized throughout.) The bulk of the naval stores came from the two Ports serving the southern half of the colony, Ports Beaufort and Brunswick. In the years 1768 through 1772, almost 75 per cent of the total exports of pitch, tar, and turpentine were sent out of these two Ports (see Table 3 and Fig. 34).[6] Port Brunswick alone shipped out about one half of the total volume in each of the years 1768, 1769, 1770, and 1771. The sudden drop-off in 1772 apparently reflects the incompleteness of the export data for that year.[7]

The greater amount of naval stores produced in the southern part of the colony, and particularly in the Cape Fear Valley which was the area tributary to Port Brunswick, was a result of several factors. The larger role of the southern section could be attributed partly to the existence there of a greater extent of longleaf pine forest close to the coast (see Fig. 32). Of some significance, too, was the later date of settlement of the southern part. Since it was opened to settlement later, its potential as a source of naval stores stood unexploited while the reserves of the northern part were being diminished. But this time lapse was so short that it could not have been a major reason for the much greater production from the Cape Fear region in the third quarter of the eighteenth century. The making of naval stores only began on a large scale in 1705, when Parliament instituted bounty payments for colonial naval stores, and settlement of the Cape Fear region began some twenty years later.

A factor of more consequence was the facilities of the Cape Fear region for large-scale production. Two of the prime requisites for carrying out operations on a large scale were present in the area: relatively large holdings of land[8] within the belt of longleaf pine forests, and abundant slave labor that could be employed in extracting and making the naval stores.[9]

The availability of slave labor was especially advantageous. Unlike field crops, naval stores could be produced at almost any time of the year, which allowed slave labor to be used efficiently when few other tasks required their attention. There were other nonseasonal activities to which slaves were assigned, but none was as widespread or as lucrative as naval stores production.[10]

Although the possession of large landholdings was a help in the making of naval stores, some producers at least found a way of circumventing the lack of such a holding. They simply exploited the stands of trees on land not their own. Their actions sometimes attracted the attention of men with large estates, who resented such exploitation of vacant land. Henry McCulloh, for example, pointed out that "it has also been a practice of long standing in the Colony for people to Box pine trees for Turpentine and burn light wood for Pitch and Tarr without taking out Pattents for the Lands."[11] McCulloh went on to complain that this practice was making waste of the king's lands (i.e., unpatented land).

The possession of slaves, on the other hand, was almost a *sine qua non* for the large-scale production of naval stores. The

TABLE 3. EXPORTS OF NAVAL STORES

Port	1768		1769
	Number of barrels	% of N.C. total	Number of barrels
Roanoke	21,702	17	22,254
Bath Town	11,078	9	6,080
Beaufort	31,652	25	31,221
Brunswick	63,265	49	53,524
Total	127,697	100	113,079

SOURCE
Customs 16/1. "Naval stores" refers to pitch, tar, and turpentine. Tar was mostly "common tar," although the figures do include the small amount of "green tar" (made from living wood) that

making of tar, pitch, and turpentine was time-consuming and laborious, and without the labor of slaves the work could not be done efficiently enough to insure a healthy margin of profit. In Cumberland County,[12] for example, slavery was not important. A tax list for 1755 records a total of 205 households in the county, of which only 25 had slaves; of these 25 with slaves, 17 had 1 or 2 slaves, 5 had 3 or 4 slaves, and 3 had 5 to 8.[13] Yet despite the location of this county within the heart of the longleaf pine belt, the total volume of naval stores produced here was remarkably small, presumably because, without slaves, the production of naval stores did not represent an attractive prospect.[14]

Almost all of the naval stores produced in the colony were exported, either across the ocean to Great Britain, or coastwise to mainland or West Indian colonies. The methods employed to collect the barrels of tar, pitch, and turpentine preparatory to exporting them necessarily differed in the Cape Fear and Albemarle areas. This difference worked to the advantage of the former area.

The Cape Fear River and its tributaries represented an invaluable system of waterways flowing through the heart of the longleaf pine country and finally converging upon Wilmington and Brunswick, the two towns that constituted Port Brunswick. Thousands of barrels of tar, pitch, and turpentine were rafted or shipped down this arterial system, to be collected and entered by the merchants of the two towns. The barrels were then assembled

FROM NORTH CAROLINA PORTS, 1768-1772

1769	1770		1771		1772	
% of N.C. total	Number of barrels	% of N.C. total	Number of barrels	% of N.C. total	Number of barrels	% of N.C. total
20	19,533	19	21,682	17	15,538	24
5	6,736	7	13,104	10	11,316	18
28	23,276	23	29,118	23	27,082	42
47	52,425	51	63,223	50	10,379	16
100	101,970	100	127,127	100	64,315	100

was sometimes exported. Data on the exports of tar from Brunswick in 1772 are deficient (see Ch. V, n. 7). Port Currituck has not been included on this table because it played an insignificant role in the trade in naval stores.

into large lots and shipped out of the colony. Collection and dispatch was thus relatively inexpensive and expeditious.

The Albemarle Sound area, on the other hand, had no such advantageous water facilities. Instead of one unitary river system, there were numerous small streams flowing into the sound at various points. The few larger rivers that did flow into the sound passed through little of the longleaf pine area. Edenton, the largest town in Port Roanoke, had no "feeder" that could serve a function comparable to that which the Cape Fear River provided for Wilmington and Brunswick. And from Edenton to the open ocean was a circuitous and sometimes hazardous haul for all but the smallest vessels. Water facilities were thus somewhat unfavorable, and the barrels of naval stores had to be picked up from numerous little landings lining the small rivers entering Albemarle Sound.

Just how time-consuming and tedious the collecting process was in the Albemarle area is illustrated by the ship log of one vessel engaged in this task (see Fig. 35). In January, 1768, the brig "Joannah" left the West Indies for North Carolina in order to pick up a cargo for England. On February 25, Cape Hatteras was sighted. On March 1, the vessel reached Edenton Bay, after being piloted around Ocracoke Island and steering a slow course through the shallow waters of Albemarle Sound. The next day, the "Joannah" proceeded up the Cashie River and began picking up a cargo of naval stores (and some barrel staves) from landings

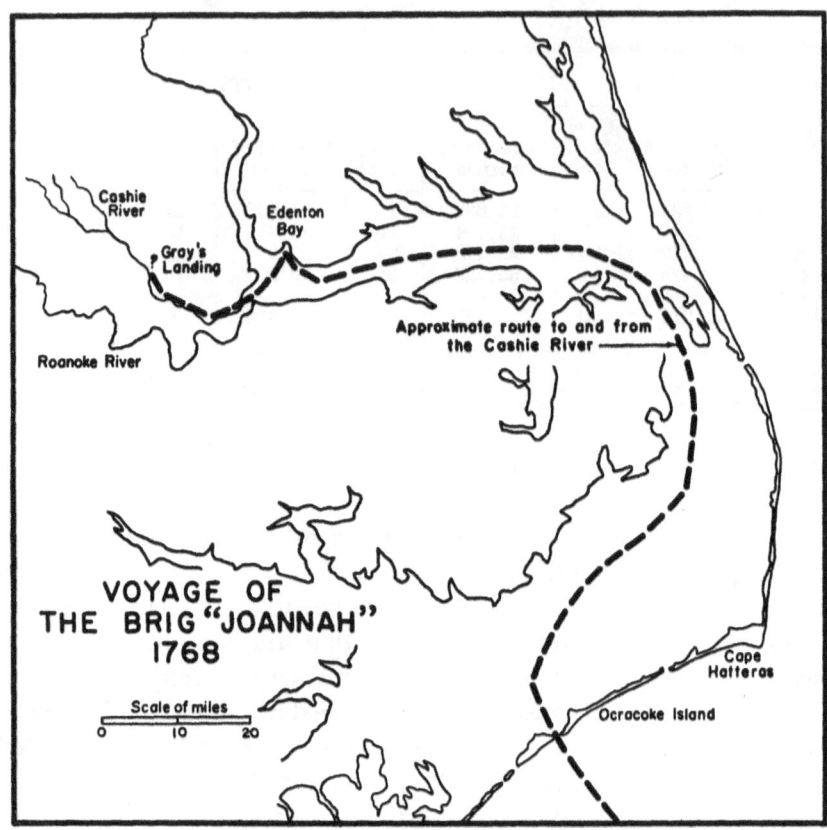

Fig. 35

along that river. It was April 30 before the brig was back in Edenton Bay with a full cargo. A week later, she set sail again, but not until May 17 was she clear of the Outer Banks and heading for London. The Atlantic passage took only forty-five days, or about one month less than the time spent in collecting the cargo. Even allowing for the likelihood that not all of the time spent in Albemarle Sound, Edenton Bay, and the Cashie River was spent strictly for commercial purposes, it is still clear that much time was lost because of the difficult job of loading a cargo from numerous landings, the hazards of shallow water, and the necessity for lightering in a couple of places.[15]

UTILIZATION OF THE FORESTS 93

WOOD PRODUCTS

Many other kinds of forest products besides naval stores were made in the colony on a commercial basis. Boards, planks, staves, heading, hoops, shook hogsheads, posts, oars, and masts, as well as other items, were all represented in the cargoes of vessels engaged in exporting the products of North Carolina. Even some of the vessels themselves were built in the colony. But the range of wood products was more impressive than was the total production. Only three items, shingles, staves, and sawn lumber were of major importance.

These three items were the only wood products regularly exported in significant amounts. In each of the years 1768 through 1772, the number of shingles exported from North Carolina amounted to between 5.6 million and 7.7 million, or about one-seventh or one-eighth of the total number exported from the North American colonies as a whole. The boards exported from North Carolina were somewhat less important in colonial commerce. Between three million and four million feet were annually shipped out of North Carolina, more than from any other Southern colony, but this amount was exceeded by Pennsylvania and by some of the New England colonies, representing only one-twelfth to one-fifteenth of the total exported from the colonies as a whole. North Carolina staves were a little more conspicuous in colonial commerce than were her boards. The colony's annual export of between about two million and three to five million staves constituted approximately one-tenth to one-twelfth of the total from the North American colonies.[16]

The exports of shingles, boards, and staves are presented on Tables 4, 5, 6, 7, 8, and 9, which show the amounts shipped out of each of the Ports of North Carolina, in both absolute and relative terms. Fig. 36, based on averages computed from Table 9, shows the relative importance of the several Ports in terms of exports of wood products. Since the destinations of the exports are not very relevant for present purposes they need only be summarized. Most of the shingles (over 80 per cent) were shipped to the West Indies, and the remainder entered the coastwise trade. An even greater proportion of the boards went to the West Indies,

TABLE 4
EXPORTS OF WOOD PRODUCTS FROM NORTH CAROLINA PORTS, 1768

Port	Sawn Lumber		Shingles		Staves	
	Amount in feet	% of N.C. total	Number of pieces	% of N.C. total	Number of pieces	% of N.C. total
Currituck	0	0	909,340	15	73,600	4
Roanoke	233,056	7	2,644,157	44	1,337,778	77
Bath Town	516,323	16	382,500	6	61,600	4
Beaufort	91,054	3	566,140	10	129,299	7
Brunswick	2,328,075	74	1,504,000	25	139,340	8
Total	3,168,508	100	6,006,137	100	1,741,617	100

SOURCE
Customs 16/1. "Sawn lumber" refers to all items listed in original data as planks and/or boards. "Staves" refers to all items listed in original data as pipe staves, barrel staves, hogshead staves, heading, and hoops.

and the balance either entered the coastwise trade or was sent to Great Britain. The export trade in staves was more complex; a little less than half of the total volume was generally shipped to the West Indies, the remainder going to Great Britain, southern Europe, or into coastwise trade, in proportionate amounts that varied from year to year.

The most conspicuous feature of the trade was the contrast between the northern and southern Ports (Fig. 36). Whereas most of the sawn lumber came out of Port Brunswick, most of the staves were shipped out of Port Roanoke. The latter Port also exported more shingles than any other Port, but to appreciate

TABLE 5
EXPORTS OF WOOD PRODUCTS FROM NORTH CAROLINA PORTS, 1769

Port	Sawn Lumber		Shingles		Staves	
	Amount in feet	% of N.C. total	Number of pieces	% of N.C. total	Number of pieces	% of N.C. total
Currituck	32,400	1	1,771,185	23	19,600	1
Roanoke	141,925	5	3,033,220	39	1,519,524	55
Bath Town	305,120	10	374,785	5	201,690	7
Beaufort	259,780	9	639,030	8	756,086	27
Brunswick	2,184,621	75	1,885,000	24	281,225	10
Total	2,923,846	100	7,703,220	99	2,778,125	100

(For source, see Table 4.)

TABLE 6
EXPORTS OF WOOD PRODUCTS FROM NORTH CAROLINA PORTS, 1770

Port	Sawn Lumber		Shingles		Staves	
	Amount in feet	% of N.C. total	Number of pieces	% of N.C. total	Number of pieces	% of N.C. total
Currituck	10,300	0.3	1,425,000	25	65,700	2
Roanoke	135,356	4	1,551,900	27	1,469,986	54
Bath Town	542,125	16	381,600	7	332,700	12
Beaufort	336,085	9.7	758,550	13	514,893	19
Brunswick	2,437,000	70	1,536,000	27	361,200	13
Total	3,460,866	100	5,653,050	99	2,744,479	100

(For source, see Table 4.)

the contrast with Port Brunswick in this trade it is necessary to add together the totals for Port Roanoke and Port Currituck and to regard them as one Port. (The areal connotations of the data are in no way distorted by this device, for the figures for Port Currituck merely represent the amounts exported from the shores of Currituck Sound, which was the northeasternmost of the many elongated extensions of Albemarle Sound; hence, it is more realistic to include the exports of Currituck Sound with those of Albemarle Sound as a whole than to treat the two Ports as separate entities.) In brief, the export trade in wood products from North Carolina presented a fairly simple pattern: most of the sawn lumber (about 70 per cent to 75 per cent) came from Port

TABLE 7
EXPORTS OF WOOD PRODUCTS FROM NORTH CAROLINA PORTS, 1771

Port	Sawn Lumber		Shingles		Staves	
	Amount in feet	% of N.C. total	Number of pieces	% of N.C. total	Number of pieces	% of N.C. total
Currituck	44,500	1	933,800	16	541,450	15
Roanoke	232,398	6	2,154,910	38	1,786,563	48
Bath Town	514,900	14	607,700	11	318,100	9
Beaufort	334,856	9	332,200	6	714,828	19
Brunswick	2,685,000	70	1,659,000	29	351,000	9
Total	3,811,654	100	5,687,610	100	3,711,941	100

For source, see Table 4.)

TABLE 8
EXPORTS OF WOOD PRODUCTS FROM NORTH CAROLINA PORTS, 1772

Port	Sawn Lumber		Shingles		Staves	
	Amount in feet	% of N.C. total	Number of pieces	% of N.C. total	Number of pieces	% of N.C. total
Currituck	0	0	669,820	11	316,266	10
Roanoke	172,236	4	2,565,850	41	1,544,762	50
Bath Town	653,500	16	683,700	11	206,600	7
Beaufort	428,641	10	530,800	9	606,269	19
Brunswick	2,864,000	70	1,766,000	28	445,800	14
Total	4,118,377	100	6,216,170	100	3,119,697	100

(For source, see Table 4.)

Brunswick, whereas most of the staves (about 55 per cent to 65 per cent) and shingles (about 50 per cent to 60 per cent) came from Ports Roanoke and Currituck. These differences in terms of Port of export are indicative of differences in terms of place of production; in order to analyze the latter variations, each of the three wood products must be considered separately.

Sawn lumber—The dominance of Port Brunswick in the export trade in sawn lumber was the result of the rise of an important sawmilling industry in the Cape Fear Valley. Almost as soon as

TABLE 9
NORTH CAROLINA EXPORTS OF WOOD PRODUCTS: RELATIVE IMPORTANCE OF PORTS, 1768-1772

Port	Sawn lumber—as % of all N.C. exports of sawn lumber					Shingles—as % of all N.C. exports of shingles					Staves—as % of all N.C. exports of staves				
	1768	1769	1770	1771	1772	1768	1769	1770	1771	1772	1768	1769	1770	1771	1772
Currituck	0	1	0	1	0	15	23	25	16	11	4	1	2	15	10
Roanoke	7	5	4	6	4	44	39	27	38	41	77	55	54	48	50
Bath Town	16	10	16	14	16	6	5	7	11	11	4	7	12	9	7
Beaufort	3	9	9	9	10	10	8	13	6	9	7	27	19	19	19
Brunswick	74	75	70	70	70	25	24	27	29	28	8	10	13	9	14
Total	100	100	99	100	100	100	99	99	100	100	100	100	100	100	100

SOURCE
Derived from Tables 4-8.

UTILIZATION OF THE FORESTS 97

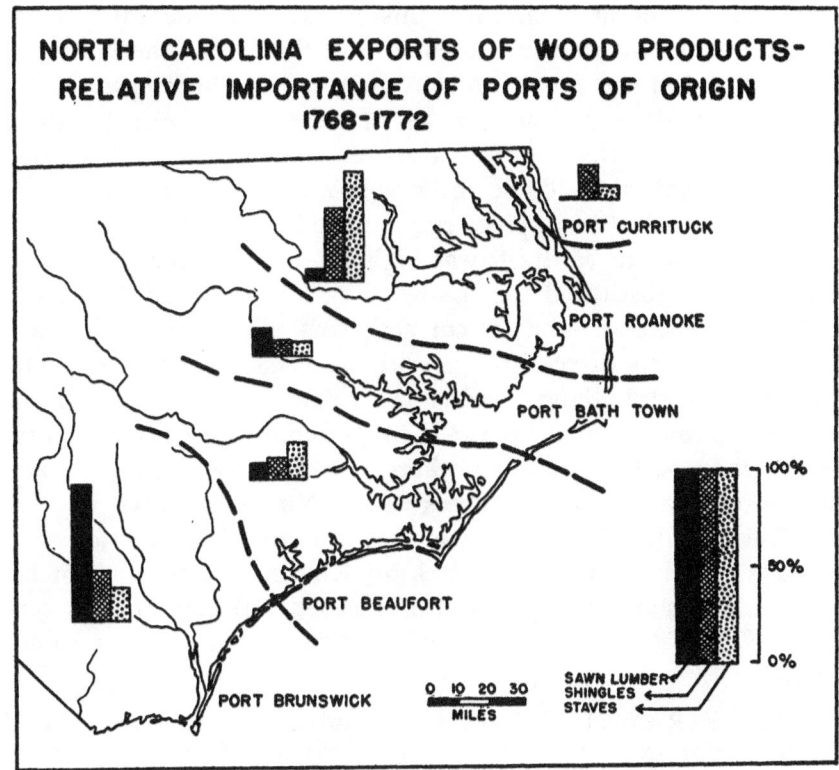

FIG. 36

the valley was opened to settlement, sawmills began to appear along the main river and its tributaries. In 1732, Governor Burrington reported that an abundance of sawmills was being erected, with the aim of developing a trade in sawn lumber.[17] In 1734, a visitor to the area around the confluence of the Northeast and Northwest branches of the Cape Fear observed five vessels in that vicinity loading with lumber for the West Indies.[18]

Thirty years later Governor Dobbs, in his report to the British government on conditions in the colony, stated that forty sawmills had been erected on branches of the Cape Fear River.[19] Dobbs's successor, Governor Tryon, was even more explicit. In a letter to the Board of Trade in 1766, Tryon, writing from Brunswick, noted that lumber was a "considerable staple in this port" and went on to amplify this point: "Of the lumber exported, plank and scantling are sawed in the mills, There are but few of these in the province, but what are on the creeks on the north east, and north west branches of Cape Fear River: On these creeks, there are fifty saw mills now in repair and more building, each with two saws; These mills will saw upon a medium two hundred thousand feet apiece per annum."[20] Tryon's estimate of the capacity of the sawmills was high (and in a letter the following year he substituted the figure of 150,000 feet for his earlier estimate of 200,000),[21] but he correctly singled out one of the most distinctive forms of resource use in the Cape Fear region. The records of Cumberland County and New Hanover County for the 1760's and 1770's contain many references to sawmills and their products.[22] By contrast, there is a marked paucity of such references relating to other areas within North Carolina.

The sawmills themselves were large units of production. An account of a mill belonging to John Rutherford, located on his "Hunthill" estate about thirty miles above Wilmington and very close to the Northeast Cape Fear, contains a number of pertinent details.

On this he [Rutherford] has a vast number of Negroes employed in various works. He makes a great deal of tar and turpentine, but his grand work is a saw-mill, the finest I ever met with. It cuts three thousand lumbers (which are our dales [i.e., sawn boards or planks]) a day, and can double the number, when necessity demands it. The woods round him are immense, and he has a vast piece of water, which by a creek communicates with the river, by which he sends down all the lumber, tar and pitch, as it rises every tide sufficiently high to bear any weight. This is done on what is called rafts, built upon a flat with dales, and the barrels depending from the sides. In this manner they will float you down fifty thousand deals at once, and 100 or 200 barrels, and they leave room in the centre for the people to stay on, who have nothing to do but prevent its running on shore, as it is floated down by the tides, and they must lay to, between tide and tide, it having no power to move but by the force of the stream. This appears to me the best contrived thing I have seen, nor do I think any better method could be fallen on; and this is adopted by all the people up the country.[23]

A coherent picture of sawmilling in the colony seems to emerge from the fragmentary record. By the third quarter of the eighteenth century, a few dozen large sawmills in the Cape Fear Valley furnished most of the sawn lumber exported from the colony. Each of the mills was situated on a body of water that served both as a source of power and as a means of transportation. The sawmills were, for their time, remarkably large units of commercial production, and the making of sawn lumber was apparently often combined with naval stores production. This was the case at "Hunthill" and the author of the description seems to imply that it was true also farther "up the country." Since both activities utilized similar resources (trees and water), and since they could both make profitable use of slave labor, it would therefore have been easy enough, and profitable, to combine the two kinds of production.[24]

Almost all the sawn lumber was pine wood, and the availability of this in large quantities in the Cape Fear Valley supported the prosperity of the sawmilling enterprises of the eighteenth century.[25] Although the forests were mined in a manner that guaranteed a life span for the sawmills which would be as short as it was profitable, there is no sign that output had begun to wane in the colonial period. On the contrary, the data on amounts exported between 1768 and 1772 indicate that production was actually increasing towards the end of the colonial period.

Several circumstances contributed to the growth and localization of the sawmilling industry in the Cape Fear Valley. The rivers and streams of the area were more significant than they were in the naval stores industry, providing water power as well as routeways. Large amounts of slave labor were less vital than in the naval stores industry, since power-driven saws did most of the work, and there was no need to have barrels made and packed in order to export the product. But if large numbers of slaves were not vital, sawmilling was nevertheless an industry for men of wealth. To set up and equip a large sawmill necessitated a considerable investment; and to provide trees to feed the mill, the owner needed either an extensive landholding, or else the means to purchase a steady supply of logs. Since the Cape Fear Valley, and particularly the lower part of it, was the region where men of substantial means were most numerous, it was there that the sawmilling industry was most important.

The estates of these men were generally known as "plantations."[26] "Hunthill" was one such plantation, and the account in which it is described contains references to others in the vicinity of Wilmington and the lower Cape Fear.[27] There is one particularly revealing report of another estate in this area. George Minot married a daughter of one of the Moore brothers who had earlier obtained large holdings in the lower Cape Fear (see p. 27, above). Through his wife, Minot inherited a six-hundred-acre property on Prince George's Creek, a tributary of the Northeast Cape Fear. In the mid-1740's, a few years after he had come into possession of the property, Minot tried to sell it. An account he wrote in an effort to advertise its more desirable qualities tells much about the character of this particular area. After noting that his land was situated in the "best Neighbourhood," Minot named the nearby residents, carefully appending to each of the names a military officer's rank, a "Mr." or an "Esq."; all of them, he wrote, are "Persons of Fashion & Education & Live in a Genteel manner & most of Em has had University Education, Who Keep 3 Packs of Dogs among Em for Deer hunting And verry often have matches of Horse Raceing in the Neighberhood, which they much delight in & are all Liveing within 3 miles of my House there."[28] The reader could hardly have been left with any doubts about the superior tone and wealth of the neighborhood, whatever his reaction to Minot's spelling.

Most of the lumber production probably came from sawmills belonging to substantial settlers and large landholders, but they were not the only ones with mills. There appears to have been a cluster of sawmills much farther up the Cape Fear, in the vicinity of Cross Creek. These were owned and operated by settlers of less affluent circumstances, including some of the Scottish Highlanders of Cumberland County, who seem often to have pooled their resources in order to establish a sawmill and then shared the profits accordingly. Frequently, too, a merchant had some hand in the operation, perhaps providing the initial impetus and some capital, or assisting in transporting and marketing the sawn lumber.[29]

There were areas outside the Cape Fear Valley in which sawn lumber was produced. The data on exports, for example, show that some was regularly shipped out of Port Bath Town. But the total amount was small, and there are no indications that commercial sawmilling was ever very important in colonial North Carolina outside the Cape Fear Valley. The output from sawmills elsewhere in the colony was either used (as in the west) for local needs, or, if exported, represented an amount overshadowed by the volume coming from the Cape Fear.[30]

Staves—The making of shingles and staves has to be distinguished from the making of sawn lumber. They were different in two important respects. First, whereas little manual labor was required in the production of boards, the making of shingles and staves necessitated the expenditure of much time and effort in the shaping of the finished product. Secondly, sawn lumber was made from pine wood, but shingles and staves were made from certain kinds of particularly durable, resistant woods.

The main stave-producing region was evidently located away from the area in which sawn lumber was made. A comparison of Ports of origin of exports of the two items for the years 1768 through 1772 (Table 9 and Fig. 36) reveals a notable dissimilarity. The ranking of the Ports, in terms of their relative importance as exporters of staves, is almost the complete reverse of that for sawn lumber. Most of the staves came from Port Roanoke. If its pre-eminence in this respect was not as marked as was that of Port Brunswick in the sawn lumber trade, it was nevertheless impressive. Between about 50 per cent and 75 per cent of the staves exported from the colony in each of the years 1768 through 1772 were cleared from Port Roanoke, and the proportion is even higher when the exports from Port Currituck (representing merely a portion of the same general area) are added to the Port Roanoke totals (see Table 9). Port Brunswick played but a minor role, furnishing only about 10 per cent of the total exports.

The reasons for the large export of staves from the Albemarle Sound Ports are not entirely clear. The staves themselves included pipe-staves, barrel-staves, and hogshead-staves. They were cut, shaped, and measured according to the purpose for which they were intended and, presumably, with the amount of care necessary to comply with the regulations governing the quality of such export items.[81] The wood from which they were made was generally referred to as "white oak" or "red oak." The "white oak" category probably referred to the same general group of oak trees that still bear this designation, and the most common representatives of this group in North Carolina would have been white oak (*Quercus alba*), post oak (*Quercus stellata*), overcup oak (*Quercus lyrata*), and live oak (*Quercus virginiana*). The term "red oak" is a little more puzzling. Presumably it was used with reference to wood from some of the group of trees now designated as "black oaks." The wood from certain members of the "black oak" group is still marketed as "red oak," as in the case of black oak (*Quercus velutina*), willow oak (*Quercus phellos*), and Southern red, or Spanish, oak (*Quercus falcata*). Water oak (*Quercus nigra*), which is also now classified as one of the black oaks, may have been regarded as a source of "red oak." These trees, or at least some of them, probably supplied most of the wood from which the staves were made.[82]

Bottomlands were of special significance in the making of staves. Several of these kinds of oak grew most abundantly on river and stream bottomlands and on the margins of swamplands; water oak, willow oak, and overcup oak, for example, were well represented in such locations. Fig. 37[83] shows the distribution of bottomland and swamp hardwoods in eastern North Carolina in the twentieth century. The floristic composition of these areas has, in detail, changed much since the colonial period, but it is safe to assume that they have always contained much oak woodland and hence were probably an important source of raw material for the makers of staves. The widespread occurrence of such land is a prominent feature of the map. There is also some indication of the relative prominence of bottomland in the area immediately to the north and west of Albemarle Sound, a factor which perhaps accounted for the large volume of staves shipped out of Port Roanoke.

The merchants and shippers who arranged for the picking up of quantities of naval stores from the landings along the shores of Albemarle Sound, and on the rivers leading into it, negotiated at the same time for the purchase and loading of staves. The latter were either taken on board ship at the same landings, or else

UTILIZATION OF THE FORESTS 103

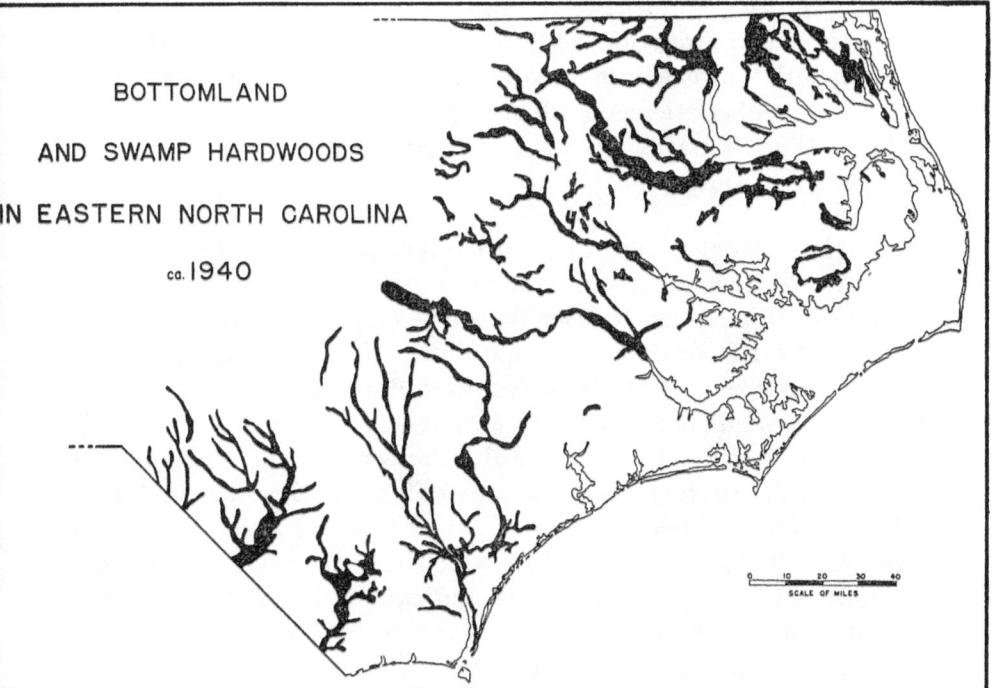

FIG. 37

they were piled together at a few convenient loading places. The brig "Joannah," for example, while loading a cargo of naval stores, was also taking in staves.[34] The letterbook and accounts of one merchant who was particularly involved with trade from Port Roanoke indicate that he concentrated on the purchase of naval stores and staves, together with some provisions.[35] And the cargo inventories of vessels clearing from Port Roanoke indicate that this three-fold emphasis was a very common one.[36]

Port Roanoke was not the only source of staves, but there is almost no information regarding their production elsewhere in the colony. The export data (Tables 4, 5, 6, 7, 8, and 9, and Fig. 36), showing that staves were exported in small amounts from all the other Ports, certainly suggest that the oaks of the bottomlands scattered in the eastern parts of the colony were here and there utilized in order to furnish staves for the export trade. Some of the sawmilling enterprises in the Cape Fear Valley were responsible for the production of part of the quantity exported. At "Hunthill," for example, the owner had trained some of his slaves in the arts of cooperage and carpentry and put them to work on the making of staves, hoops, and heading, which were then sold in the West Indies.[87]

Shingles—Shingles were the third important wood product. The export trade in them was more evenly distributed than was the trade in either sawn lumber or staves (Fig. 36). The Albemarle Sound Ports were the most important contributors to the shingle trade, but even when taken together Ports Roanoke and Currituck furnished only a little more than 50 per cent of total exports. Port Brunswick regularly supplied between 25 per cent and 30 per cent of the total, and the small Ports of Beaufort and Bath Town each supplied between 5 per cent and 15 per cent of the amount exported. The way in which the trade was apportioned among the several Ports is one indication that the commercial production of shingles was a comparatively widely distributed activity within eastern North Carolina.

Another indication is the distribution of the particular tree species sought out by the shingle makers. Shingles had to be made of wood that was light, soft, easily-worked, and resistant to frequent wetting and drying. White cedar and cypress trees (*Chamaecyparis thyoides* and *Taxodium distichum*) afforded such wood, and most shingles were made from them. Both white cedar and cypress are, and seem always to have been, remarkably spotty in their distribution.[88] They are associated with swampland, or at least with land which is under water for much of the year. Since both have been much sought after and are now much less common than formerly, their earlier distribution cannot be ascertained. But it is possible to recognize the general kind of area within which they were concentrated. They were probably well-represented in some of the bottomlands and in scattered patches here and there throughout all of the low-lying, flat lands and swamps of the Outer Coastal Plain (Fig. 37). Although not necessarily very abundant, white cedar and cypress trees were a fairly widely distributed resource.

The single most prominent producing region was in the area to the north of Albemarle Sound. This was partly because of the comparatively large amount of swampland in this area, including the Great Dismal Swamp.[39] There was another and at least equally important reason. This was the area first affected by what amounted to a southward migration of the shingle-making industry within the colonies. The demand for shingles in the West Indian islands was increasing at the same time as the ability of the Middle colonies to satisfy this demand was declining. The result was that the Southern colonies in general, and North Carolina in particular, began to play an increasingly important role in this branch of trade in the eighteenth century.[40]

In North Carolina, the large-scale production of shingles for export seems to date from about the 1750's. It was about then that several dozen families who had formerly been employed in the making of shingles in colonies farther north moved into the Albemarle area for the express purpose of finding similar employment in this new region. Furthermore, in the late 1750's at least one man entered into the business of producing shingles on a scale comparable to that of the large commercial sawmilling enterprises of the Cape Fear Valley. Thomas Macknight, having entered into a partnership with a Virginia merchant in 1757, began to organize shingle making on two large tracts of land that he held north of Albemarle Sound. He seems to have initiated a systematic attempt to make these lands profitable by opening roads through them, by cutting white cedar and cypress for shingles, and by clearing portions of them for agriculture. The labor was provided by Macknight's slaves and by immigrants to the area. Just how many of his ambitious projects were actually carried out is not clear, but his efforts must have contributed to the large volume of shingles exported from Port Roanoke.[41]

By comparison with the Albemarle Ports, Port Brunswick was of secondary importance in the export trade in shingles. But in each of the years from 1768 through 1772 more than 1.5 million shingles were cleared through Port Brunswick. Since this amount was between 25 per cent and 30 per cent of the total exported from North Carolina, the Cape Fear Valley was not insignificant in the production of shingles. Perhaps the volume exported from

Port Brunswick was also part and parcel of the southward migration of the industry. The large amounts of slave labor in this area would have facilitated the large-scale production of these handicraft items, although the appropriate trees were less abundant than they were in the Albemarle region. In any event, the lack of data on the exports of shingles during the years after 1772 makes it impossible to establish whether or not shingles were being produced here in increasing amounts.

The main features associated with the commercial production of forest products have been outlined. By way of summary, attention can be focussed upon the growth and distribution of the industry as a whole.

Throughout eastern North Carolina, the making of forest products of one kind or another became important during the eighteenth century. The general lack of commercial production before then was not a result of any predisposition against such production; nor was it because of a lack of raw materials, labor, or "know-how." The reason was rather the lack of easily-accessible and profitable markets. The commercial production of both shingles and naval stores was undertaken on a large scale almost as soon as market demands for these products made themselves strongly felt, as they did when the ability of other areas to compete in supplying shingles declined and when the bounty system was extended to naval stores.

The age or "stage" of settlement attained in any given area seems to have been of little or no consequence in determining when forests were utilized on a commercial basis. Settlers in the Cape Fear Valley began commercial production almost as soon as they arrived, while it was not until perhaps half a century or more had elapsed from the time of the first settlement in the Albemarle area that this region became noted for the export of forest products. Nor did settlers of different origins adopt significantly different attitudes towards commercial production; the Scottish Highlanders and the English settlers alike turned to the making of forest products as soon as markets became available and accessible.

Within eastern North Carolina there was some degree of specialization by area. Most of the naval stores and sawn lumber came from the Cape Fear Valley, whereas most of the shingles and staves were made in the region around Albemarle Sound. The reasons for these differences are complex, and no single factor suffices to explain the variations. The size of landholdings and slaveholdings, the nature of facilities for export, the amount of wealth and entrepreneurial energy possessed by a few leaders, the kind and amount of locally-available forest resources—these and other factors were important in one place or another within the colony.

By 1775 the forests of North Carolina were much altered and substantially diminished. They were not yet destroyed, for the large-scale manufacture of forest products had only just begun. Succeeding generations were able to find enough raw materials so that they could mine the forests and continue the tradition of commercial forestry that colonists had established. But the woodland they encountered was nowhere quite like that which the colonists had found, and in certain localities there was probably no resemblance at all.

CHAPTER VI · COMMERCIAL FARMING: CROPS, PLANTATIONS, AND LIVESTOCK

The subject of this chapter is the changing agricultural geography of colonial North Carolina. A topical breakdown is followed, each of the various major agricultural products being considered in turn. In the analysis of these topics, three themes are given most attention: the existence of regional variations within the colony, the influences of distinctive cultural groups, and the increasing commercialization of agriculture.

The last tendency will receive special emphasis because the quest for profits was a prominent factor in governing the rate and direction of agricultural change. Profit motives were present in the making of naval stores and wood products, the growing of food crops for sale off the farm, the experiments with commercial crops such as indigo and tobacco, and the cattle drives to distant markets, as well as in nonagricultural activities such as the building of roads and bridges to make market centers more accessible.[1] Farmers, in deciding what to grow, were paying more and more attention to market conditions and to the prospect for selling part of their farm output.

INDIAN CORN

As in the other colonies, Indian corn was ubiquitous. It was a popular crop because it was relatively easy to raise and could be put to many uses. Corn grew rapidly and well when planted in rough clearings among stumps and could be raised on a variety of soils and sites.[2] It was generally the grain most used for bread but could be eaten in several forms. Slaves were given rations

TABLE 10
INDIAN CORN EXPORTED FROM NORTH CAROLINA (IN BUSHELS)

Port	1753[a]	1764[b]	1768[c]	1772[c]	1771-76[d] annual average
Currituck			1,190	3,600	
Roanoke			92,853	114,456	ca. 97,000
Bath Town			9,037	18,490	
Beaufort		32,805	13,343	38,958	
Brunswick			966	1,238	
Total	61,528		117,389	176,742	

SOURCES
a. [Edmund and William Burke], *An Account of the European Settlements in America* (London, 1757), II, 253.
b. Refers to the period from Oct. 1, 1763–Oct. 1, 1764, and is from *North-Carolina Magazine; Or, Universal Intelligencer*, Oct. 12–Oct. 19, 1764.
c. Customs 16/1.
d. Derived from totals given in Ira W. Barber, "The Ocean-Borne Commerce of Port Roanoke, 1771-1776" (Master's thesis, University of North Carolina, 1931), Appendix I, p. 2.

in which corn was often the main item, and livestock was usually fed or at least fattened on corn.[3] Inevitably, corn was generally the first crop planted by newly-arrived farmers.[4]

Not all corn was consumed on the farm. Some farmers produced a surplus for market. Even before the seventeenth century, a few New Englanders were sending vessels to the Albemarle coast to pick up corn and other farm produce.[5] This trade continued through the early decades of the eighteenth century. A few years after settlers moved into the Cape Fear Valley this area too began to furnish a surplus.[6] As North Carolina's population began increasing rapidly, the amount exported showed a correspondingly large increment. In 1753, about 62,000 bushels were shipped out. Within fifteen years this amount had doubled, and within twenty years it had almost trebled (see Table 10).

A surplus of corn thus seems to have been one of the first consequences of settlement, and the volume of the surplus apparently increased at a rate roughly corresponding to the rate of increase of population.[7] But in order to establish how widespread was production for export, figures on the volume of exported corn must be converted to acreage equivalents. To convert volume to acreage, it is necessary to know the average yield of corn per acre.

Only three estimates of corn yields in colonial North Carolina are known to exist. The first is that reported by a visitor to southeastern North Carolina in the 1730's. He noted that corn grown on "overflow" lands there was said to yield eighty bushels per acre.[8] The second comes from an anonymous agricultural writer, who claimed that cleared land at first commonly yielded sixty to seventy bushels per acre, and sometimes as much as eighty to one hundred bushels.[9] The third estimate is in the records of the Moravians, who generally measured the product of their fields. They made one reference to a harvest of about twenty bushels per acre.[10] The disparity between the last estimate and the first two is large, but there are reasons to believe[11] that the Moravians' figure is the most reliable guide to average yield during the 1760's and 1770's.

If the figure of twenty bushels per acre is taken as a crude conversion factor,[12] then very little land could have been devoted to the commercial production of corn. The total exported in 1753 (Table 10) must have been produced on a mere three thousand acres. Although three times as much was exported in 1772, the nine thousand acres involved was still remarkably small.

The number of farmers producing corn for export may have been as insignificant as was the total acreage. Hypothetically, the 180,000 or so bushels of corn exported in 1772 could even have been produced by thirty farmers, growing no more than three hundred acres apiece. But the number was probably hundreds of times larger, and an estimate of nine thousand farmers with one acre apiece might well be a closer approximation to reality.

There are several reasons for preferring this latter figure. First, is the lack of evidence that any individual farmers produced large amounts of corn for export. Secondly, the few known contemporary references are to small acreages,[13] and if one can conclude anything from the heterogeneous collection of figures that survives, it would be that acreages rarely amounted to thirty and that totals of less than fifteen acres were more common than totals of over fifteen acres. There is a third reason. The major producing region was that which was served by Port Roanoke (Table 10), and there are records for a few years which described the Port's trade in great detail. Had the corn trade been dominated by a few producers, it is likely that individual corn shipments would have been relatively large. But the records show that the vessels sailing from Port Roanoke generally carried mixed cargoes. Corn was invariably only one of the items, and the amount of corn on each boat was typically small,[14] probably reflecting small purchases from individual farmers. These three reasons are grounds for believing that many farmers contributed to the trade in corn and that almost all of those who participated furnished only small amounts of surplus corn.

The leading position of Port Roanoke in the export trade seems to substantiate this view of corn production. Water transportation, the least expensive form of transportation, was vital for corn, because of its bulkiness, and because it was worth less per ton than any other commodity.[15] The distinctive disposition of land and water in the area served by Port Roanoke was particularly advantageous for the corn trade. A maximum number of producers were assured of convenient access to water transportation through their proximity to the innumerable landings that dotted the shores of Albemarle Sound and the banks of the many rivers flowing into it. And the relatively high, and increasing, density of population in this region must have guaranteed the proliferation of corn patches.[16]

WHEAT

Late in the seventeenth century, the author of a promotional account of Carolina informed his readers that some farmers there had experimented with wheat and had found that it grew "exceedingly well."[17] Promotional literature is not generally to be taken at its face value, but there are surer indications of successful wheat growing about twenty years later. The hundreds of bushels of wheat listed in the cargo inventories of vessels engaged in exporting the products of North Carolina bear witness to the fruitful efforts of wheat producers early in the eighteenth century.[18]

These shipments are also indicative of the special role of wheat. Seemingly, it was not grown primarily for bread (corn was used for that) but was raised mainly as a commercial crop. A ready market could be found for it, as the Reverend John Urmstone implied in 1714 when he noted that sloops from New England "sweep all our Provisions away—We have twice as many vessels this year as ever were wont to come, there are above 7 now waiting like as many vultures waiting for our wheat & more daily expected. . . ."[19]

As long as farmers had a commercial crop they could sell or barter it to obtain sugar, molasses, rum, and other items they regarded as necessities. Wheat afforded just such a crop. Naval stores, lumber products, and some corn were also exported, for much the same basic reason, but wheat was unique because it was a food crop apparently grown from the outset almost exclusively for export. In a letter written in 1711, Urmstone noted that many of the North Carolinians "live on a slender diet to buy rum sugar and molasses with other such like necessities which are sold at such a rate that the planter here is but a slave to raise a provision for other Colonies and dare not allow himself to partake of his own creatures except it be the corn of the Country in hominy Bread. . . ."[20]

There is very little information relating to wheat in the first half of the eighteenth century. Some farmers continued to grow it in the Albemarle area, or so it seems from an early account in which is mentioned the excitement generated by the annual wheat harvest.[21] Just before the middle of the century, one traveler reported that farmers were raising wheat in more westerly parts of the colony. The traveler, William Logan, only passed through the eastern section of the colony and took care to point out that his route never took him more than a few miles from the coast; but he did report hearsay to the effect that "at the Head of their Rivers they have very good Land, & raise a great quantity of Wheat, considering how thin their settlements are. . . ."[22] Since Logan's report is more or less contemporaneous with the large-scale movement of settlers into the western half of the colony, it carries with it the implication that wheat was grown here even in the first years of settlement.

During the third quarter of the eighteenth century, wheat became more important in the west. Several writers noted the increased output of wheat from the farms of North Carolina without associating the increase with any particular locality within the colony.[23] Others very definitely indicated that the increased emphasis on wheat growing was a feature of western, or backcountry, North Carolina. Thus the Moravians, for example, took note in 1775 of the fact that "our neighbors are steadily increasing the amount of wheat raised"—and the Moravians were located in the heart of the west (see Fig. 21).[24]

The Moravians had good reason to take note of the new emphasis upon wheat. They had concerned themselves with this crop ever since their arrival, and their own attitude towards the relative merits of corn and wheat was a rather special one. One Moravian summed it up in the notes he wrote next to the name of each of the cultivated plants listed in his catalogue of plants and animals: "Corn was and is the grain most generally used, and the people of this country live on it. Here not much is raised, though much is bought and sold." With reference to wheat he simply observed that "this is the proper grain for bread."[25]

Although precise acreages are not available it is clear from their records that the Moravians regarded wheat as the most important crop. It was the first crop they planted after their arrival in 1753, and in each of the succeeding years they grew far more wheat than corn.[26] They preferred wheat bread to corn bread and only ate the latter as a last resort,[27] but it was not this preference alone that accounted for the heavy emphasis they placed on wheat growing.

In addition to satisfying their bread preferences, wheat was also an eminently salable crop. Funds from its sale, as grain, flour, or bread, could be used to promote the well-being of the Moravian economy. As long as those around them concentrated on corn, and as long as wheat remained the highest priced grain, then its production represented an extremely profitable form of land use. Recognizing this, the Moravians sold grain, flour, and bread to customers who came to their community, or else they transported these items to markets elsewhere. When they needed more corn than they grew, they purchased some from their neighbors, which was more economical than increasing their corn acreage at the expense of wheat.

In 1755 they finished building a grist mill that served a dual purpose. The Moravians could grind their own grain more efficiently and could also do milling for others, who paid for this service with grain. The result was that the Moravians, three or

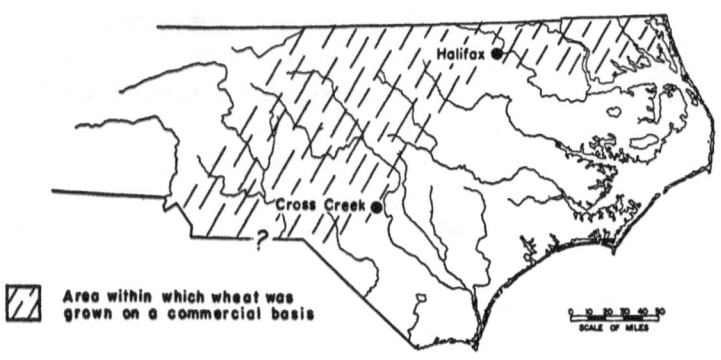

Fig. 38

four years after establishing their colony, were promoting a wheat trade within and from western North Carolina.[28]

The Moravian wheat trade seems to have developed smoothly until just before the end of the colonial period, when the amount of wheat grown by others in western North Carolina came to market in considerable quantities.[29] Some western farmers had been growing wheat as early as 1745.[30] As thousands more settled in the area the wheat crop steadily increased.[31] By the 1760's inventories of estates show distinctly larger amounts of wheat and there is evidence of flour exports from the area.[32] And ten years later advertisements for western lands were being phrased so as to appeal to commercial wheat growers.[33]

Fig. 38 is an attempt to show the location of the area within which most of the wheat was grown. It refers to the decade between 1765 and 1775, by which time wheat production had become most widespread, and is based on a heterogeneous collection

CROPS, PLANTATIONS, AND LIVESTOCK 115

of sources.[34] Since most of the details relating to wheat that were found in these sources were complementary rather than contradictory, the map is probably fairly reliable. Several aspects of the distribution require explanation and comment.

The amount produced within the wheat area was probably small. There are no data on total production, but there are some on the wheat trade.[35] In 1772, about 13,400 bushels of wheat officially cleared from the Ports of North Carolina.[36] The amount grown that year must have been much greater, since the figure does not include what was shipped as flour, does not allow for the overland exports of both wheat and flour to Virginia and South Carolina, and is in any case a figure for an unusual year.[37] While it is not possible to establish how seriously the figure under-represents production, North Carolina was certainly not one of the major wheat producing colonies.

More significant than the actual amount grown is the fact that wheat was becoming an increasingly popular crop. In 1768, only about 4,600 bushels were exported from the Ports of the colony, so that the equivalent figure of about 13,400 bushels in 1772 represents a three-fold increase.[38] Thus, the wheat area delimited in Fig. 38 was an area within which wheat was becoming an important crop rather than one in which it was already common.

The implications of the distribution shown on the map are clear enough. The location of the wheat area corresponds most closely with that portion of the colony into which had come, and were still coming, most of the immigrants from farther north. Within a few years of their arrival some of them began to produce wheat as a commercial crop. The Moravians were especially notable as wheat producers, turning to wheat raising and flour making so rapidly that they established a lead of a few years over their neighbors. But within one or two decades they had ceased to be exceptional in this respect, and many other western farmers were contributing to the growing trade in wheat and flour.

The northeastern portion of the wheat area on Fig. 38 was distinctive. This section, roughly embracing the land north of Albemarle Sound and east of the Roanoke River, was settled much earlier than the rest. Although it too received a large number of immigrants in the eighteenth century, it can scarcely be classed with the western part of the wheat area, since settlement of the northeast began in the seventeenth century, and some farmers were growing wheat here as early as the beginning of the eighteenth century. It was also exceptional because wheat growers enjoyed a special advantage in this area. This proximity to navigable waterways eliminated the necessity for converting the wheat into the less bulky form of flour before marketing the crop. They were close enough to water transportation, either along the lower Roanoke and Cashie rivers or Albemarle Sound, that the greater cost of transporting wheat (as opposed to flour) to loading points was not a consideration. This is reflected in export figures. Almost all of the wheat exported through the Ports of the colony was shipped out of Port Roanoke.[39]

In the west, marketing conditions were different. It was farther from the coast, there were no navigable waterways within the region, and transportation costs were inevitably higher. Most of the wheat was therefore made into flour before being exported. The export of the flour, as well as the movement of the wheat to milling centers, still necessitated wagon transportation overland for considerable distances. Flour from the northern portion of the backcountry wheat-growing area was carried into Virginia,[40] and from the southern part it was taken into South Carolina.[41]

Between the northern and southern sections of the wheat area there was a large intermediate region in which the flour and wheat trade centered on Cross Creek. This settlement served as a collecting center for both wheat and flour, and its growth owed much to the trade in these items. Some of the wheat received in Cross Creek was made into flour, and both wheat and flour were shipped from the town down the Cape Fear River.[42]

The function of Cross Creek was essentially similar to that of certain urban settlements in other colonies. The early growth of Alexandria, in Virginia, and of Bladensburg and Baltimore, in Maryland, was to a large extent a reflection of the wheat trade, for they served as centers to which wheat and flour of backcountry origin were brought for export.[43] This was true to a degree of Philadelphia too, though the growth of this metropolis was much less exclusively a function of the wheat trade. Even in South

CROPS, PLANTATIONS, AND LIVESTOCK 117

Carolina there was a small urban settlement, Camden, whose origin and early growth were associated with the wheat trade; backcountry wheat and flour were collected in Camden, milling was carried on there, and flour was forwarded to coastal markets.[44] The volume of the wheat trade carried on in these various places may have differed, but in all of them the trade assumed a similar pattern, was approximately contemporaneous, and an important component in their growth and function as commercial centers.[45]

The interrogation mark placed on the map (Fig. 38) at the southern edge of the wheat area indicates an unresolved question. The location of the wheat area in this vicinity clearly implies its continuance in South Carolina. This implication is apparently refuted by data on exports from South Carolina, since no wheat seems to have been exported from that colony, and at least some of the small amount of flour that was shipped out of South Carolina was of North Carolina origin.[46] Yet there is evidence that some wheat was grown in western South Carolina and that flour and possibly even wheat was sent from there to Charleston.[47] Presumably, then, the wheat area extended some distance into western South Carolina, and most of what was grown there was consumed in Charleston.

The inhabitants of the much smaller towns of Wilmington and Brunswick in southeastern North Carolina possibly pursued a similar policy. These town-dwellers, located in the midst of a non-wheat-growing area (see Fig. 38), may have consumed some of the wheat grown in the west.[48] In any event, they did not generate a demand for wheat strong enough to persuade farmers in the southeast to raise the crop, and there was no attempt at commercial wheat production in this area.

The absence of wheat raising in all the eastern portion of the colony south of Albemarle Sound is apparent on Fig. 38. Some of this area was undoubtedly too poorly drained for cultivation, particularly the section of it in the Outer Coastal Plain (see Fig. 9), which included large swampy patches. The drier parts of the area, however, were not basically very different from those north of Albemarle Sound, where wheat was raised. The absence of the crop probably reflected the ease with which items other than wheat could be produced on a commercial basis.[49]

Viewed in perspective, there seem to have been three stages in the extension of wheat growing. In the late seventeenth or early eighteenth century, some farmers began to raise it for sale off the farm. In succeeding decades the amount grown increased slightly. Then, around the middle of the century or a little earlier, wheat growing became appreciably more widespread as large numbers of farmers settled in the west, and some of them turned to wheat, again for commercial purposes. Finally, beginning sometime in the decade of the 1760's, wheat production received much more attention and was increasing rapidly as the colonial period came to an end.[50]

This last stage was in fact a reflection in miniature of what was going on in Virginia and Maryland at about the same time. There, wheat growing became remarkably widespread and supported an important export trade after 1760.[51] The small but expanding acreage sown to wheat in North Carolina (and part of South Carolina) represented the increasingly distinct southern end of an irregular, patchy, noncontinuous "belt" that extended through Virginia, Maryland, Pennsylvania, New Jersey, and New York, to at least as far north as the Hudson Valley.[52]

Whether or not farmers in North Carolina were consciously following the lead of farmers farther north is a moot point. Governor Martin thought they were. Writing from New Bern in 1773, he reported that "Indian Corn . . . is the Grain mostly cultivated in this Province, but I learn that the farmers here, after the example of the Virginians are going more and more upon wheat. . . ."[53] But to explain the rise of wheat production in North Carolina in terms of a deliberate imitation of events in Virginia is perhaps misleading. Farmers in North Carolina were attracted to wheat growing for many of the same reasons that made it seem appealing to Virginians. Wheat and flour were in demand in overseas markets, and after the middle of the century these markets strengthened.[54] Western settlers in North Carolina, looking around for a source of income, soon seized the opportunity presented by this demand. They did not need the guidance or stimulus of the Virginians. The Moravians had begun to raise wheat immediately after their arrival in North Carolina. In effect, the success of the Moravians, and the profitability of their policy, was a demonstration, to those of their western neighbors who were interested, of the virtues of wheat production.

The early Moravian emphasis upon wheat must be viewed in the context of their farm practices as a whole. At the end of the colonial period the Moravians were growing no important crops that were not also grown by others, but they used methods that were more productive than those of the generality of farmers. They farmed the land more intensively than most and exhibited attitudes we should now characterize as "conservationist."[55] Their agricultural activities, as well as their economy as a whole, were remarkably successful. Partly for this reason, and partly because they were such a compact and cohesive group of foreign immigrants, their settlements drew many visitors, including political leaders and merchants, as well as neighbors and travelers. These visitors invariably commented upon what they saw. As one traveler observed: "The moment I touched the boundary of the Moravians, I noticed a marked and most favorable change in the appearance of buildings and farms, and even the cattle seemed larger, and in better condition. Here in combined and well directed effort, all put shoulders to the wheel, which apparently moves on oily springs."[56] Earlier visitors expressed the same theme.[57] Although none of them was very specific about actual differences that could be observed, they were evidently impressed by the superior care and diligence of Moravian farming.

By way of a postscript, it is worth adding that wheat cultivation became a permanent element of North Carolina agriculture in postcolonial days. More farmers grew wheat, and the total acreage increased. It gradually ceased to be an important crop in the Albemarle region,[58] but with the exception of this area the location of the leading wheat producing section in the mid-twentieth century was remarkably similar to the wheat area that had developed by the last decade of the colonial period.[59] Neither the advance of cotton nor the increased acreage planted to tobacco very much altered the general distribution of the wheat crop. When traveling through the state in 1791, George Washington observed that the area between Charlotte and Salisbury was a "Wheat Country"; about 150 years later, this locality was still a prominent section within the wheat-raising region of the state.[60]

TABLE 11
TOBACCO EXPORTED FROM NORTH CAROLINA PORTS (IN POUNDS)

Year	All N.C. Ports	From Port Roanoke	From all N.C. Ports to Scotland only
1753	100,000[a]		
1766			324,000[d]
1767			399,000[d]
1768	? 358,000[b,e]		? 505,000[d,e]
1769	557,000[b]		460,000[d]
1770	1,056,000[b]		911,000[d]
1771	1,714,000[b]		993,000[d]
1772	1,605,000[b]	1,044,000[c]	
1773		1,525,000[c]	

SOURCES
 a. [Edmund and William Burke], *An Account of the European Settlements in America* (London, 1757), II, 253 (converted from hogsheads).
 b. Customs 16/1 (some data converted from hogsheads).
 c. James Iredell Notebooks, Vols. 1-5, Port of Roanoke Records, 1771-76 (MSS).
 d. *SC Gaz*, Dec. 17, 1772.
 e. One of these two figures for 1768 must obviously be wrong. In converting original data in sources a. and b. from hogsheads to pounds, it was assumed that 1 hogshead contained 1,000 lbs., a figure obtained by estimating the average number of lbs. per hogshead according to equivalents given in some of the Customs 16/1 data and in various merchant ledgers of the 1760's and 1770's.

TOBACCO

Among the nongrain crops, tobacco was the most important. Grown originally in the Albemarle area, the crop remained for some decades mainly confined to the northern part of the colony. From there it was exported, either through Port Roanoke, or through the Ports of Virginia, to which it was carried overland across the interprovincial boundary. Tobacco was a valuable source of income for those northern farmers who raised it, but the total amount they grew was very small compared with the vast quantities produced in Virginia and Maryland.[61]

Table 11 gives some impression of the amount exported. The table is incomplete, since it does not include the tobacco carried overland into Virginia. Furthermore, the figures are approximate (because of the conversions involved) and, at least for the year 1768, evidently inaccurate. The data at least show that tobacco production was increasing in the third quarter of the eighteenth century, although even at the end of the period the total amount exported was small,[62] and the total acreage devoted to the crop could not have been large. In 1772, the area planted to tobacco was perhaps between five thousand and seven thousand acres.[63]

As the amount of tobacco being raised was increasing, the distribution of the crop was changing. Contemporaries associated tobacco, rather vaguely, with the northern part of the colony. In fact, however, the crop was becoming increasingly common to the south of its original area, and the shift probably went unrecorded simply because the acreage devoted to the crop was everywhere small. Some impression of the changing distribution is conveyed by Fig. 39, which shows the locations, in 1754 and 1767, of the public warehouses set up for the inspection and storage of tobacco.[64] Since warehouses were only established in tobacco-growing areas,[65] the distribution of the former roughly corresponded to the distribution of the latter. Fig. 39 therefore shows that tobacco cultivation was being extended towards the southwest.

The change became more pronounced after 1767. In 1773, authorities noted with some concern that tobacco was being shipped from the port towns of Bath, New Bern, and Brunswick, despite the lack of tobacco inspectors in these places.[66] Ten years later, a traveler mentioned, parenthetically, that tobacco was the chief crop of the "middle parts" of North Carolina.[67] In 1791, George Washington reported that six thousand hogsheads of tobacco were annually exported from Fayetteville (in which was located the most southerly of all the warehouses shown in the 1767 map in Fig. 39). This amount was equivalent to approximately six million pounds, or about three and a half times the quantity that was exported from all of the North Carolina Ports twenty years earlier.[68]

As tobacco growing became more prominent towards the southwest it seems to have become slightly less common in the area north of Albemarle Sound and east of the Chowan River. Here there was a reduction in the number of warehouses between 1754 and 1767 (see Fig. 39). Some also disappeared from the region west of the Chowan River during the same period. The latter reduction was a reflection of a process of consolidation and enlargement of the 1754 warehouses,[69] but the reduced number east of the Chowan is less easily explained. Perhaps farmers were growing less tobacco, so that some of the warehouses became redundant and were abandoned. It is also conceivable that they fell into disuse because more and more of the crop was carried

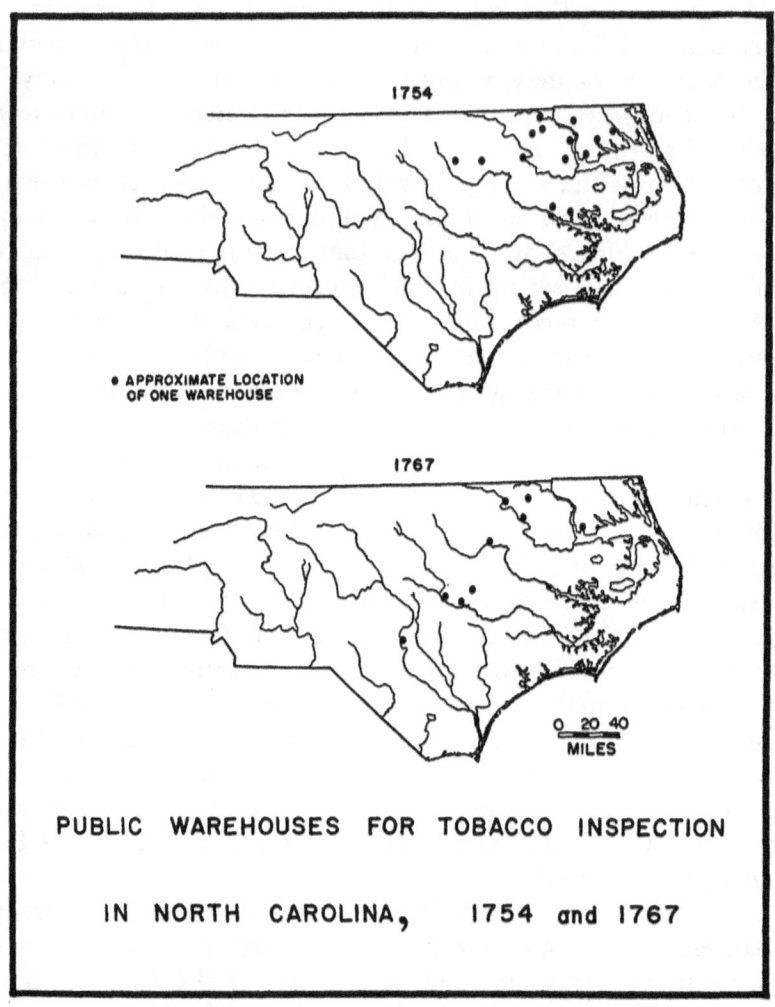

Fig. 39

overland to Virginia warehouses, or because greater use was made of the facilities at Edenton, the site of the one warehouse left in 1767 east of the Chowan River and north of Albemarle Sound.

The distribution of the tobacco crop and the extension of the area within which it was grown were a result of several interrelated factors. Tobacco was, and still is, a crop demanding a relatively large amount of labor. The consequences of this requirement are seen in the tobacco-growing regions of present-day North Carolina, in which some of the most densely populated rural areas in the United States are found. Earlier, in the middle of the nineteenth century, the demanding nature of the crop was common knowledge; one agricultural writer insisted that "it would startle even an old planter, to see an exact account of the labor devoured by an acre of tobacco. . . ."[70] In the colonial period, tobacco may have been less remarkable, since the cultivation of any and all crops called for laborious effort, but even then it was more demanding than most other crops.[71]

Since tobacco was a labor-demanding crop, there was a relationship between the distribution of slaves and the general location of the area within which the crop was grown. The nature of the relationship can be seen, albeit inconclusively, by comparing Fig. 39 with Figs. 30 and 31. The tobacco area was an area where slavery was moderately important. In tobacco-growing counties, perhaps 40 per cent to 60 per cent of the households owned slaves, and most of these households had few rather than many slaves (see data for Bertie and Chowan counties, on Table 1). Where slavery was much more important, as it was in the southeastern counties, the owners of large slaveholdings used their labor force to produce naval stores and lumber, export staples not subject to the notorious fluctuations in value that plagued tobacco farmers.[72] In the west, on the other hand, slavery was much less widespread; tobacco was not produced there and the chief export crop was wheat, whose cultivation consumed much less labor and was therefore a more feasible proposition for farmers with little or no slave labor.

Tobacco growing contributed to the agricultural distinctiveness of the area north of Albemarle Sound. Tobacco, wheat, and corn, were all produced in this region. But neither here nor elsewhere did any farmer grow both tobacco and wheat at the same time, although corn was grown in conjunction with either.[73] The production of all three north of Albemarle Sound was presumably a reflection of the intermingling within the region of some tobacco-and-corn farms and some wheat-and-corn farms. The tobacco-and-corn combination represented an especially practicable type of farm economy here, for about one-half of the households had at their disposal the labor of a few slaves. The writer of *American Husbandry* noted that "A man may be a farmer for corn and provisions, and yet employ a few hands on tobacco, according as his land or manure will allow him. This makes a small business very profitable, and at the same time easy to be attained. . . ."[74] He went on to report that this type of farming was common in Virginia and Maryland, but he might equally well have associated it with the Albemarle area of North Carolina.[75]

Finally, the role of Scottish merchants was also influential in tobacco production. In Virginia and Maryland, Scottish factors, representing the mercantile houses of Glasgow, promoted the growing of tobacco during the eighteenth century through the use of the direct purchase system. They facilitated the expansion of the area devoted to the crop there and engrossed most of the resulting trade.[76] Much the same process was at work in North Carolina. One firm of Scottish merchants, that of John Hamilton and Company, was located close to the town of Halifax, in the midst of the tobacco growing section. A contemporary described the business activities of this firm: ". . . this House was among the first to encourage and promote the Cultivation of Tobacco in No. Carolina: And the Planters of this Article requiring a considerable Stock to make any progress in it, the Merchants were obliged to give them large Credit to enable them to accomplish it; In consequence of which there are none in No. Carolina, and I believe very few in Virginia, who gave such extensive Credit to the Planters as they did."[77] The Hamiltons were an active company. Apparently they not only advanced more credit than any other, but they also bought more of the crop and sent more of it into Virginia for export than did any other firm.[78] The other Scottish trading establishments were probably smaller and played a less prominent role in furthering the production of tobacco,[79] but the net effect of the Scottish mercantile efforts was considerable. By extending credit services and marketing facilities to farmers they were boosting the trade of Glasgow at the same time as they were expanding tobacco cultivation in the colony to the south of the two more famous tobacco colonies.

RICE AND INDIGO

The three crops considered thus far, corn, wheat, and tobacco, were all fairly widespread, or at least were being grown in larger and larger quantities; and all are today significant elements in the agriculture of the state. Rice and indigo were not widely grown, neither was very important even at the end of the colonial period, and they are not grown at all in twentieth-century North Carolina. But rice and, to a lesser extent, indigo played a significant role in the economy of a small section of the colony.

The story of the introduction of rice and indigo is easily summarized. The production of both crops was a relatively late development in the economic life of the mainland colonies. Experiments with them were made towards the end of the seventeenth century.[80] Around the turn of the century, South Carolina began to establish itself as a rice-exporting province, and in the 1740's indigo production got underway. North Carolina lagged slightly behind its neighbor to the south. A little rice may have been grown earlier, but it did not attract any attention until about 1730, when one traveler observed rice swamps along the lower stretches of the Northeast Cape Fear River.[81] Growers began to produce indigo in North Carolina in the 1740's, but its cultivation remained largely on an experimental basis throughout the colonial period,[82] and only a handful of men apparently succeeded in growing amounts large enough to make it worth their while to export the finished product.[83]

The most important factor inhibiting any marked emphasis upon either rice or indigo in North Carolina was the fact that both required very large amounts of labor. The preparation of the ground, the planting of the crop, the cultivation, and the after-harvest tasks that had to be carried out before the product was ready for marketing were all so laborious and time consuming that both crops were notorious for the heavy strain they placed on available supplies of labor.[84] Certainly, the same producer could use his available labor force to maximum advantage by growing both crops on his holding, since the differences in their cultivation requirements were largely complementary. Rice was grown on sites that could be flooded, and indigo planted on

TABLE 12
RICE EXPORTED FROM NORTH AND SOUTH CAROLINA (IN BARRELS)

	1768	1769	1770	1771	1772	1775
Roanoke				1		
Bath Town						
Beaufort		2	8	8	24	
Brunswick	84	73	487	620	52	418
N.C. Total	84	75	495	629	76	
S.C. Total	132,000	122,000	136,000	130,000	108,000	

SOURCES
N. C. data, 1768-72, from Customs 16/1 (place names refer to Ports of N. C.). The 1775 figure is from Customs Records, Box 9, Port Brunswick (MSS); it refers to "casks," which were probably the same as barrels. S.C. totals from U.S. Bureau of the Census, *Historical Statistics*..., Series Z 264-65, p. 767. A barrel of rice weighed about 525 lbs. (see Ch. VI, n. 93).

adjacent dry lands; and the rice harvest required threshing and cleaning in the winter months, while the growing and making of indigo ended with the summer.[85] A large labor force could thus be switched from the one to the other, without any danger of a period of enforced and unprofitable employment. But there were very few persons in the colony who had such a large labor force at their disposal (see Chapter IV, above).

Climatic conditions were probably less significant as restrictive factors. North Carolina was located close to the northern limits of the area within which rice and indigo could be grown successfully.[86] But early colonists in Virginia had experimented with rice cultivation, and their efforts were rewarded with some success;[87] and farmers in Virginia and Maryland were able to produce indigo. If climatic conditions were not ideal in North Carolina, both crops could be grown.[88] Of the two, indigo production was the more precarious occupation, and those who grew it were barely able to compete with producers in colonies farther south. In the West Indian islands growers could depend upon three, four, and even more cuttings per year, but in South Carolina three cuttings was about the maximum, and in North Carolina it was possible to depend upon only one cutting.[89] That it was grown at all was possibly because of the tangible encouragement, in the form of a bounty, that was given by the British government. When the Revolution put an end to bounty payments, indigo growing was largely given up in North Carolina.[90]

TABLE 13
INDIGO EXPORTED FROM SOUTHERN COLONIES (IN POUNDS)

	1768	1769	1770	1771	1772	1775
Roanoke		40	180			
Bath Town						
Beaufort			326			
Brunswick	646	264	254	222	1,304	1,686
N.C. Total	646	304	760	222	1,304	
Va. & Md					2,423	
S.C. & Ga					777,000	

SOURCES
N. C. data, 1768-72, from Customs 16/1 (place names refer to the Ports of N. C.). Totals for Va. and Md., S.C. and Ga., from Customs 16/1, as compiled in Merrill Jensen (ed.), *English Historical Documents: American Colonial Documents to 1776* (London, 1955), p. 401. The 1775 figure is from Customs Records, Box 9, Port Brunswick (MSS).

Some impression of the total amount of rice and indigo production can be obtained from data on exports (see Tables 12 and 13). Again, the figures have to be interpreted cautiously, particularly as some of the rice and indigo was exported through Charleston,[91] and a portion of the rice harvest was consumed locally.[92] But total production was undoubtedly small, as can be seen by comparing North Carolina exports with those of other colonies (Tables 12 and 13).

The total acreage devoted to these crops was minute. It is unlikely that the area planted to rice in 1771 (when exports reached the highest point in the five-year period covered by the data from Customs 16/1) was as much as five hundred acres.[93] The indigo crop covered an even smaller extent. The 1772 data represent an area of only about eighty acres![94] But the amounts of rice and indigo grown did suffice to add a distinctive element to the economy of one region.

The production of rice and indigo was confined to a small area within the lower Cape Fear Valley.[95] The high degree of localization within this area is implicit in the data on exports (Tables 12 and 13): over 95 per cent of the rice and over 80 per cent of the indigo cleared from Port Brunswick. More precisely, the area of production was in New Hanover and Brunswick counties. It comprised the estuary of the river below Wilmington and

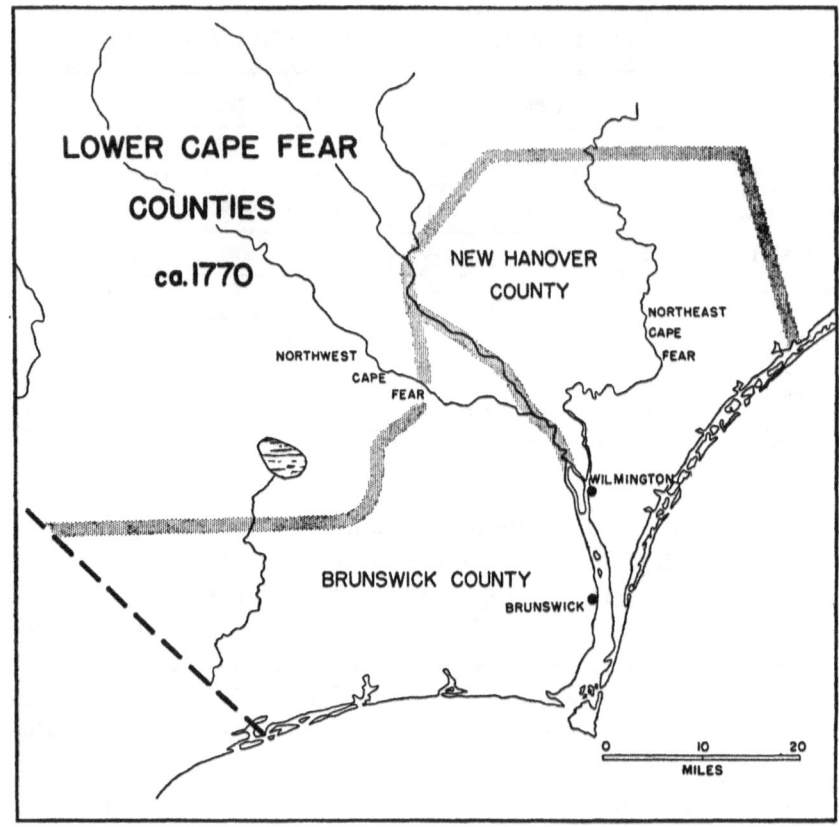

Fig. 40

the lower reaches of the Northwest and Northeast branches of the river a little way above Wilmington (see Fig. 40).[96]

The producers invariably owned slaves, often in large numbers. Thus, a visitor to the lower Cape Fear country in 1775 was impressed by the rice mills, indigo works, and lumber mills of Joseph Eagle(s). The mills and works had belonged to his recently deceased father, who had owned over seventy slaves on his death and whose estate was located on the Cape Fear River almost opposite Wilmington.[97] The seven leading indigo producers in 1749 were mentioned by name in a letter of Governor Johnston. Six of the seven were located on the Cape Fear River, and the sizes of the slaveholdings of five of these at about that time are known: William Moor(e) had over eighty slaves in 1755, John Swan had fifty-three slaves in 1755, John Ashe had twenty-five slaves in 1763, Thomas Jones had twenty-nine in 1767, and Maurice Moor(e) had seventy-two in 1769.[98] Some of the property of Henry Hyrne was advertised for sale in 1773, soon after his death, including eighteen Negroes and some fields suitable for rice cultivation. Almost certainly this was the same Henry Hyrne recorded as a resident of New Hanover County a few years earlier, when he was in possession of twenty-three slaves.[99] Other examples could be cited but the gist of the evidence is clear. Most of the rice and indigo was produced by a few men, living in the lower Cape Fear country, some of them owners of unusually large slaveholdings and most of them residents of the section of the colony where slavery was most prominent.[100]

The appearance of rice and indigo production in the lower Cape Fear accentuated a degree of regional individuality foreshadowed by the circumstances of settlement. The area was settled relatively late, beginning between about 1725 and 1730, by a prominent group of more than average wealth.[101] They took possession of large landholdings and employed slaves (which they had either brought with them or acquired soon after their arrival) in the large-scale production of naval stores and lumber, subsequently adding rice cultivation and indigo experiments to their commercial enterprises.

As early as 1737, the "rising" condition of the area was noted, and it was observed that the "Substantial Planters" there were becoming "very Rich."[102] When George Minot tried to sell a piece of land in this locality in the 1740's, he emphasized that his property was located in the "best Neighbourhood."[103] The net effect of the large-scale commercial and economic development of this region in the following few decades was to accentuate the accumulation of wealth. At the end of the colonial period, an observer wrote that in Brunswick County, particularly near the coast, there were "fewer of the lower class of country people than [in] any part of the whole province. . . ."[104]

The concentration of affluence was conspicuous, but there were remarkably few of the wealthy estates. Late in the 1760's, the two counties along the lower Cape Fear (Brunswick and New Hanover counties—see Fig. 40) contained only thirty-seven households owning twenty-one or more slaves; of these, only twenty households had more than thirty slaves, and only eight had more than fifty slaves.[105] There were probably a few more large estates a little farther up the Northeast and Northwest branches of the Cape Fear River but no very significant upstream extension of these distinctive units.[106] One of the remarkable features of the settlements in the lower Cape Fear was the way in which they remained constantly limited to their original area of distribution and did not proliferate farther up the valley. Contemporary maps clearly testify to this locational stability.[107]

Because there were so few of these large estates, information about them is scanty. References to them in travel accounts are invariably in general or impressionistic terms. References to them in advertisements sometimes furnish details, but it is the particularized information in newspaper advertisements that is most questionable; what was left unsaid by the advertiser, would, if reported, have placed the particulars in a more realistic perspective.[108] Neither travel accounts nor advertisements furnish detailed information on all-important elements such as land-use, size of fields and extent of cultivated land, the acreage planted to different crops, and the utilization of the woodland. But at least they do afford a few glimpses of other aspects of these holdings.

In the eyes of one traveler the "finest place in all Cape Fear" was the one called "Rocky Point,"[109] apparently a well-known and valuable property. When "Rocky Point" was put up for sale, some decades after the traveler saw it, the advertiser informed would-be purchasers that it comprised 1,920 acres.[110] Another tract, close to the town of Brunswick, was 1,280 acres in extent and called "Lilliput."[111] Both "Lilliput" and "Rocky Point" were probably smaller than other properties in the vicinity, and it is possible that what the advertisers were offering for sale were only portions of larger estates. There may have been ten or twenty estates of between two thousand and five thousand acres, and perhaps a few even larger ones.[112]

The same traveler who commented on "Rocky Point," added some information about other estates he visited along the lower

Cape Fear: "The plantations on this river are all very much alike as to the situation; but there are many more improvements on some than on others: this house [belonging to John Davis] is built after the Dutch fashion, and made to front both ways on the river, and on the land, he has a beautiful avenue cut through the woods for above two miles, which is a great addition to the house."[113] The visit was made in 1734. In the 1770's, while the amounts of improved land on these riverside settlements may have been as variable as in 1734, on the whole the acreages were small. Advertisers very rarely specified amounts of cleared land larger than one hundred acres. And if this much had been made available by the steady process of clearing on individual estates, it is still doubtful that all of it was under crops in any one particular year.

The owners gained more profit from the trees on their land than they did from patches of corn, rice, or indigo, and it was the marked emphasis on the making of naval stores and lumber products that differentiated the lower Cape Fear from adjacent areas of maritime South Carolina. The rice swamps of South Carolina represented the "Golden Mines" of that colony, and indigo was an important and valuable export item.[114] In the lower Cape Fear, on the other hand, the production of both of these crops was ancillary to the production of naval stores and lumber.[115] The difference did not go unobserved by contemporaries. A North Carolinian lamented the fact that "we grapple with lightwood knots" while South Carolinians had reached a "pitch of opulence" through "leaving the making of naval-stores to their more sharp-sighted neighbours, and pursuing the cultivation of rice, indigo and hemp; commodities which this province is equally capable of raising."[116] To this writer, it was astonishing that planters with slaves would waste their time "plodding over a tar kiln" even though these planters had fine rice-growing land at the very doors of their estates.[117] He would have been less astonished had he borne in mind that there was much more slave labor available in South Carolina than in his own province and that a large Negro work force was essential if the "Golden Mines" were to be worked.[118] Compared with the number in South Carolina, there were very few large-scale planters in the Cape Fear region, and the average size of their slaveholdings was much smaller.

The settlements in the lower Cape Fear, more so than those elsewhere in the colony, possessed features reminiscent of some of the many heterogeneous images evoked by the term "plantation." Whether they should or should not be called by this name is a problem in semantics, raised here in order to be dismissed briefly. Colonial usage does not help to solve the problem. Contemporaries called these large estates "plantations," but the term seems to have had no very specific connotations and was also used for small holdings, with or without slave labor, as well as for the colonies themselves. Nor is current usage very helpful, for the word is now used for a variety of phenomena. One fairly common current connotation of the word plantation is a sizable estate worked by slave labor. In this restricted sense the settlement units of the lower Cape Fear were plantations. Other current connotations are not applicable. The economy of these units was not based on cultivation (the utilization of the woodland was a major source of income), and their economy did not revolve around the export of any one single item (naval stores, lumber, wood products, rice, and indigo were all exported from the area, individual estates often supplying quantities of several of these items, and possibly some estates produced all).[119] Finally, insofar as the term implies a division of settlement units into two classes (plantations and nonplantations) it is unfortunately misleading, for there was no such dichotomy in reality. If all these reservations regarding usage of the word are borne in mind, then it is not misleading to refer to the large estates of the lower Cape Fear worked by slave labor as plantations.

The plantation system has recently been viewed as an institution brought to the mainland colonies by a process of diffusion. Thus, one historian has asserted that "we can trace, without a break, the transmission of the ways of setting up and running a plantation from Sicily and South Spain to the Atlantic islands," that the knowledge was then carried to Brazil and the West Indian islands, and that "it was from these islands that it made the jump to the American colonies."[120] This being so, one would expect to find evidence of this process at work in the settlement of the lower Cape Fear area.

The key to the emergence of the plantation system in the Cape Fear region was the prevalence of large landholdings in the initial settlement phase. Certainly prominent, possibly even dominant, among the men who obtained the large holdings were the South Carolinians who moved out of their own colony to settle in the valley of the lower Cape Fear.[121] Since the beginnings of the plantation system in South Carolina were promoted by persons of capital, at least some of whom came from the West Indies,[122] it is therefore possible to see a connection between the plantations of the West Indies and those of southeastern North Carolina. Also instructive are the documented circumstances attending the settlement of James Murray in the Cape Fear region.[123] In the process of establishing himself as a plantation owner there, Murray looked forward to the advantages that he planned to derive from drawing upon the wealth and experience of two connections, one in England, the other in the West Indies.[124] Furthermore, the cultivation of indigo on plantations represented the experimental transfer of a plantation crop into the Cape Fear via South Carolina and the West Indies.[125] These very different kinds of evidence seem to indicate that the emergence of the plantation system in the lower Cape Fear owed much to developments in South Carolina and in the West Indies.[126]

Today, very little remains of any of the elements that once set the lower Cape Fear region apart from adjacent areas in North Carolina. Naval stores, rice, and indigo are no longer produced here. The names of some of the original plantations survive, but the actual plantations have gone, and few of the famous plantation houses in the area contain any structural elements dating back to the colonial period. Even the neoplantation of the twentieth century is notable by its absence. The most enduring physical relics of the colonial plantation era have proved to be the tombs of some of the original owners of the large estates that once characterized this region, and, appropriately, the Moore family is well represented among the tombstones.[127]

LIVESTOCK

Animals were no less important than crops in the economy of colonial farms, and livestock raising was as universal as corn growing. The ubiquity of both was noted in a report on conditions in the colony: "Every proprietor of ever so small a piece of land, raises some Indian Corn and sweet potatoes, and breeds some hoggs and a calf or two; and a man must be very poor who walks a foot."[128] Domesticated animals were kept on almost every holding. Cattle, swine, oxen, horses, sheep, and fowl, in varying numbers and combinations, contributed to the subsistence of their owners, some of the animals providing raw materials for food, drink, and clothing, others furnishing a work force or a means of transportation. Livestock was not raised solely for consumption and use on the farm but also as a source of farm income. Live animals and animal products were traded in considerable amounts and represented an important segment of the commerce of the colony.

Some data are available on the amounts and kinds of livestock products exported from the five Ports, and the tabulation of the most useful of these data gives a crude impression of the relative importance of North Carolina as an exporting colony (see Table 14). The figures are of little value, however, as a guide to the absolute importance of commercial livestock raising within the colony, mainly because so much of what was produced was sent out overland into colonies to the north and south. While there are no data on the amount exported in this manner, it seems to have been substantial, at least if the number and variety of references to this overland trade in the contemporary record is any measure of its significance. Two different facets of this trade, livestock driving and the export of dairy products, will illustrate its importance.

Livestock driving was one of the more spectacular forms of trade engaged in by North Carolinians and was common during much of the eighteenth century. In 1728, a governor of the colony reported to the British government that beef and pork were exported live to Virginia and thought that he could "safely say thirty thousand Hoggs were drove out last year."[129] Five years later, another governor added more details: ". . . in a year when

TABLE 14
LIVESTOCK PRODUCTS EXPORTED FROM NORTH CAROLINA

Year	Beef and pork (in barrels)	Tallow and lard (in lbs.)	Butter and cheese (in lbs.)
1753	3,300[a]		
1764	(5,226)[b]	(19,960)[b]	
1768	3,584[c]	43,968[c]	1,400[c]
1769		90,865[c]	0[c]
1770		116,839[c,d]	725[c,e]
1771	5,917[c]	54,634[c]	2,020[c]
1772	4,831[c,f]	49,797[c]	9,517[c]

SOURCES
a. [Edmund and William Burke], *An Account of the European Settlements in America* (London, 1757), II, 253.
b. Figures refer to Port Beaufort only: *North-Carolina Magazine; Or, Universal Intelligencer*, Oct. 12-Oct. 19, 1764 (data are for year between Oct. 1, 1763, and Oct. 1, 1764).
c. Customs 16/1.
d. Total exported from all mainland colonies was 185,143 lbs.: U.S. Bureau of the Census, *Historical Statistics...*, Series Z 76, p. 761.
e. Total exported from all mainland colonies was 223,610 lbs.: *ibid*.
f. Total exported from all mainland colonies was 41,125 barrels: Merrill Jensen (ed.), *English Historical Documents: American Colonial Documents to 1776* (London, 1955), p. 395.

Mast abounds fivety thousand fatt hoggs are supposed to be driven into Virginia from this Province & allmost the whole number of fatted Oxen in Albemarle County with many Horses, Cows and Calves, much barreled Pork is also carried into Virginia...."[130]

Beginning apparently in the 1750's or 1760's livestock was driven to points much farther north, in Pennsylvania and New Jersey. One of the most important writers on colonial agriculture was a New Jersey farmer, Charles Read. Although most of his writings relate to conditions in his own colony, at one point in his diary Read notes that "the Cattle from Carolina generally arrive at any time from harvest till ye last of November."[131] The date of this note is uncertain, but most of the diary was written in the 1750's, and all of it between about 1746 and 1774. The lack of a precise time reference is not very important, for it is fairly clear from other sources that in the 1760's and 1770's cattle were regularly driven at least as far north as Philadelphia, while hogs continued to be taken into Virginia.[132] The number of livestock involved in this kind of trade is unknown, but the traffic was important. Pork, for example, was one of the most valuable surplus products raised in the colony.[133]

The exports of dairy products were much less valuable. Small amounts of butter and cheese were sent to Virginia at least as early as the 1730's.[134] In 1749, one letter writer reported that "Deary's [i.e., dairy houses] are growing much in esteem among us,"[135] but most of the butter and cheese made in the 1750's and early 1760's seems to have been for subsistence purposes or for a trade that was strictly local.[136] Dairy produce was less transportable than live animals. When, in the late 1760's, merchants and farmers did begin to send butter and cheese overland to points outside the colony, the produce was not hauled farther afield than Virginia and South Carolina,[137] and there are no indications that the trade was either regular or of much consequence. In terms of value, surplus dairy produce was a poor third after the exports of live animals and the trade in lard and tallow.

By the end of the colonial period it was widely held that ownership of large herds of livestock was commonplace. This contemporary opinion appeared frequently in writings on North Carolina (and "Carolina") and intrudes in a variety of sources with a repetitiveness that is almost convincing. Thus, the anonymous author of *American Husbandry*, in the chapter he devoted to North Carolina, reported, "It is not an uncommon thing to see one man the master of from 300 to 1,200, and even to 2,000 cows, bulls, oxen, and young cattle; hogs also in prodigious numbers. . . . Such herds of cattle and swine are to be found in no other colonies. . . ."[138] Another writer, who called himself "Scotus Americanus" and presented an account of conditions in the colony for the benefit of would-be emigrants from Scotland, pointed out that "to have 2 or 300 cows is very common; some have 1000 and upwards."[139] The theme was an oft-repeated one, and the wording in the various statements of it sometimes exhibits a remarkable sameness.[140] In reality, however, livestock holdings could scarcely have resembled the view of them that was presented in such statements. Inventories of colonial estates and lists of property held in the 1780's convey a different and probably more reliable picture, since both sources give the numbers of the various animals owned by North Carolinians.

The lists of property relate mainly to the early 1780's and have been analyzed by others. Among other things, it was found that the average number of cattle per cattleowner among the counties for which data were available varied between six and sixteen. Large herds were rare, and only about twenty-five cattleowners were in possession of herds of more than one hundred.[141]

Inventories of colonial estates cannot be analyzed as systematically as were the property lists.[142] But the numbers of cattle per estate in the third quarter of the eighteenth century seem to approximate the averages worked out for the early 1780's from the property lists. Furthermore, no holdings of over three hundred cattle were found in inventories, and even records of over one hundred were very rare. In short, contemporary statements about livestock holdings were exaggerated. Large holdings were rare rather than common.

Three instances of regional contrasts in livestock production were indicated by inventories of estates when they were used in conjunction with other sources. First, livestock holdings were apparently larger in the east than in the west, a difference which is especially significant in view of the tendency of many later writers to equate large-scale livestock production with the western part of the Southern colonies.[143] A comparison of inventories for eastern and western counties indicated not only that the average holding was larger in the former but also that the very largest holdings of livestock belonged to eastern farmers.[144] Secondly, commercial production of dairy commodities was confined to areas away from the coastal portion of the colony. The butter and cheese sent to coastal centers, for consumption or for export, seem to have been produced in the area west of Halifax and Cross Creek, since most of the surplus production passed through these two centers en route to the coastal ports of Virginia, North Carolina, and South Carolina.[145] The third regional variation was one for which the Scottish Highlanders were responsible. More so than any other segment of the population, they seemed to place an important emphasis on cattle raising and gave less attention than others to the breeding of hogs.[146] Each of these three instances of regional distinctiveness was a result of special factors.

The east-west difference was a result of several circumstances. In this era of extensive livestock raising, the ability of any one settler to raise large numbers of animals was limited only by the amount of open range to which he had access. The settlers in the west were not so closely crowded together that they had any concern about a lack of land for range. Their only problem was to prevent Virginians and South Carolinians from pushing into the territory of North Carolina with their stock to utilize and destroy range land that these intruders had no right to use.[147] There was plenty of range of one sort or another to meet the needs of the North Carolinians. But time was needed to build up large herds. The smaller size of the average holding of livestock in the western counties as well as the fact that the very largest holdings were to be found in the east rather than the west were probably a reflection of the relatively short space of time that had elapsed since settlers first began to move into the west in large numbers.

Conditions were more favorable in the east. The area had been settled for a longer period of time. Although population was growing steadily, there still remained a great deal of open range in the east. Much of the poorly drained land that failed to draw would-be cultivators to the region proved to be useful, if low quality, grazing land. As long as it remained unclaimed and unenclosed, this wetland served as open range for settlers living on its margins or fairly close to it.[148]

One area in which wet land was particularly common was a portion of the colony frequently commented upon by travelers. It comprised the territory between Albemarle Sound and the River Neuse, and was invariably visited or skirted by those travelers who took the main north-south coastal route through eastern North Carolina. Four who recorded their observations in this region, at various times between 1765 and 1784, present a fairly consistent picture of its general features: the area was a relatively sparsely settled one, with much of the land unclaimed or unpatented, and used as open range for large numbers of livestock.[149] This region was probably the single most important livestock-raising section of the colony. Most of the beef and pork exported by sea were cleared out of Port Bath Town and Port Beaufort, the two Ports that served this general area.[150]

Thus it seems that here, and presumably elsewhere in the

east, the substantial proportion of poorly drained land served to perpetuate the existence of relatively empty areas, but that much of this land could be, and was, used as open range.[151] Also in the east were the open forests of longleaf pine, or pine barrens, and these too were used for grazing purposes; in most seasons their carrying capacity was low, but grazing could be combined with other forms of forest utilization in these areas. Furthermore, because the east was settled earlier, those of the inhabitants who were raising livestock had had more opportunity to build up large herds.

The second example of regional distinctiveness, the restriction of the surplus butter- and cheese-producing area to the west, is less easy to understand. One early observer related it to the available kinds of grazing: "In the upper parts of the country the milk is well tasted, but where Cows feed in salt marshes, the milk and butter receives an ill flavour."[152] Since there was much grazing land in the east that was not salt marsh, this scarcely explains the almost complete absence of commercial production.[153] But contemporaries seem to have believed that all wet or swampy pasture land imparted a distasteful flavor to dairy products.[154] Perhaps it was this belief that resulted in the commercial production of butter and cheese becoming concentrated in parts of the colony away from the low-lying and, on the whole, more imperfectly drained coastal section. Or the difference may have stemmed from a predilection for this kind of production among one or more of the several cultural groups in the west, for it could have been the Germans, or the Scotch-Irish, or the Scottish Highlanders who supplied the dairy surplus.[155]

The third instance of regional distinctiveness noted above, the emphasis placed by the Scottish Highlanders of Cumberland County on cattle, is especially interesting. The Highlanders of North Carolina were pursuing the same activity that was being followed by their kinsmen who settled in Georgia.[156] Comparisons are difficult because the Highlanders of Georgia were turning to cattle in order to supply a special local market with beef, butter, and milk,[157] and there is no evidence of equivalent circumstances in North Carolina. In the Scottish Highlands, however, cattle had been the chief export, and before the enclosure movement the grazing of open range was a common practice there,[158] so that perhaps the Highlanders' predilection for cattle raising was responsible for their emphasis upon cattle in both North Carolina and Georgia.

Of a lesser order of importance than these regional contrasts were a few land-use features associated with livestock raising. Pens, generally referred to in colonial records as "cowpens," and more rarely as "sheep pens," "horsepens," and "hogpens," were often a feature of farms on which some livestock of one kind or another were raised. Such enclosures protected stock at night, probably from thieves as much as from wild animals, and those farmers who used them only allowed their stock to range at large during the day.[159] The term "cowpen" also seems to have been used for something else, being applied to more or less large tracts, chiefly in the east, which served as enclosures for cattle (and swine). These were not subsidiary features of farms, but were the essential element of more exclusively livestock oriented enterprises. The extremely limited usage of the term in this way suggests that these cowpens were very rare in colonial North Carolina.[160]

The closest thing to a description of a cowpen of the latter kind is the following statement, from a letter about economic conditions in North Carolina: "I have two places not far from your Lands, with Tennants on Shares with what we cal Cowe Penns, in which way Cattle and Hogs are easily raised under careful Industrious People."[161] This brief description is instructive because of the implication that cowpens were in fact a form of tenant farming. Other evidence indicates that the tenants were probably really overseers, managing and making productive a tract of land belonging to an (absent) owner. The overseer shared in the profits, being allowed to retain a portion of the increase in stock, as well as receiving some of whatever little crop harvest he produced.[162] Such arrangements, like cowpens, were probably rare.

Aspects of the changing agricultural geography of North Carolina have been examined, mainly in terms of the three themes stated at the beginning of the chapter. None of the three has

CROPS, PLANTATIONS, AND LIVESTOCK   141

been treated exhaustively. Thus, for example, in considering commercial agriculture no mention has been made of related activities carried on by farmers, such as horse breeding, local land speculation, or commercial fishing. These and other aspects have been omitted because they represent subjects of minor import, both in terms of the total area and numbers of persons involved.

Enough has been said, in this and the preceding chapter, to convey an impression of the changing geography of the primary economic activities carried on in the colony. A different type of economic activity will be taken up in the following chapter.

CHAPTER VII · URBAN SETTLEMENTS AND DECENTRALIZED TRADE

If the number, appearance, and population of towns in colonial North Carolina were taken as measures of importance, there would be little justification for devoting a separate chapter to them. By 1775 there were only about a dozen towns, all small and none very impressive in appearance. Most inhabitants lived on farms and at the end of the colonial period no more than 2 per cent of the total population, or less than five thousand persons,[1] resided in urban settlements. But none of these criteria is a true index of the significance of towns in the colony.

Urban settlements were an important and distinctive element in the geography of the colony. The ties between them and surrounding areas were instrumental in changing the character of these areas and in turn imparted certain distinctive qualities to each urban settlement. They played a key role in economic development and many of the changes taking place within the colony are only understandable in terms of the growth, function, and distribution of urban settlements. They were few and small, but the activities carried on by their inhabitants were of considerable significance.

Local historians have written histories of a few of the towns but their geography has never been analyzed. This task is attempted in the following pages. Most emphasis is placed upon the major urban centers. Some attention is also given to decentralized trade, a subject that helps to put urban growth in perspective. The treatment of towns with strictly local functions, confined to areas no more extensive than the county in which they were located, is cursory, because there is almost no contemporary information about most of them.

A couple of definitions are necessary at the outset. Contemporaries used the term "town" without any consistent connotations and the word is still used loosely today. "Towns," or "urban centers," will here refer to places performing functions and services for surrounding rural areas. Functions and services are used to embrace both secondary and tertiary forms of economic activity.[2] Towns, urban centers, urban places, and urban settlements are used synonymously.

URBAN SETTLEMENTS

In any society, the development of urban centers is dependent upon reliable and effective facilities for transportation. In seventeenth-century and early eighteenth-century North Carolina, since none of the settled area was more than a few miles from sounds, rivers, or coastal waters, these waterways were used for transporting goods from place to place.[3] Urban centers developed at locations alongside such waterways.

In the eighteenth century, roads became important. As large numbers of settlers moved into western portions of the colony, and as new settlers in the east took up holdings not fronting on waterways, the need for roads became widely felt. To meet this need the colonists developed a rudimentary road system, and a host of regulations provided for construction and maintenance. To be sure, many of the administrative provisions were never put into effect. But those that were, together with the work done by settlers who resorted to their own devices, furnished the colony with a serviceable network of paths and roads.

Travelers and other visitors who had occasion to use them, rarely failed to note how bad the roads were, often adding a vivid description of an accident in order to bring home their point.[4] But the badness of roads and mishaps along them have always been and still are themes invariably included in travel accounts. Constant reiteration bears testimony then as now to the time lag between highway needs and highway construction, as well as to popular fondness for stories of dramatic accidents. More important, there were roads and they were used.

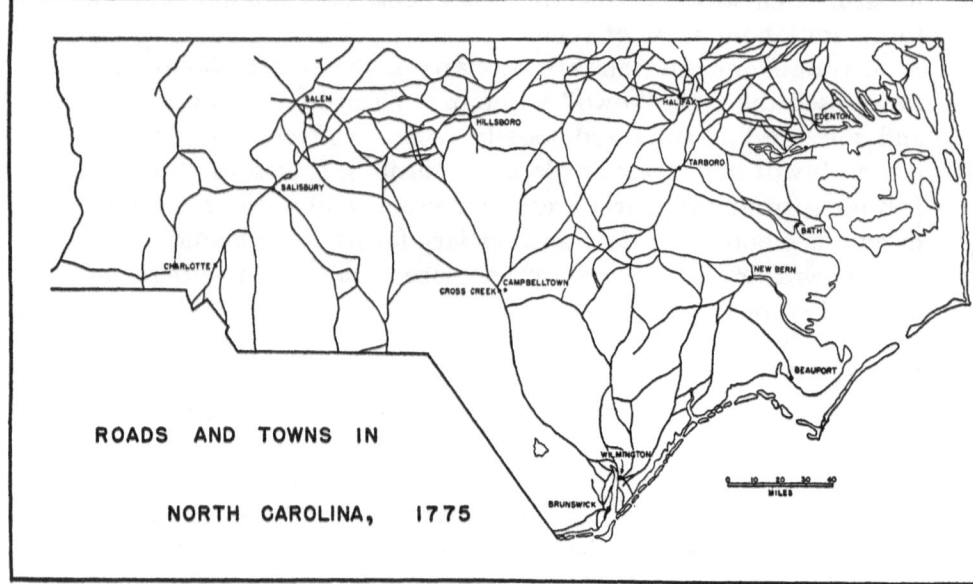

Fig. 41

The increasing importance of road transportation during the middle of the eighteenth century is clear from the record. The more detailed contemporary maps show numerous roads.[5] Documents drawn up in connection with land grants and sales contain frequent references to particular roads.[6] Advertisers of farms began about this time to include in their advertisements mention of roads near to or touching upon the land they were trying to sell.[7] Petitions and court minutes seem sometimes to be dominated by a preoccupation with more and better local roads.[8] Inventories of estates suggest that the ownership of wagons and carts was becoming increasingly widespread and common.[9] And in various sources there are indications of the emergence of a class of men specializing in wagon transportation.[10]

The network of roads that had come into being by 1775 is shown on Fig. 41.[11] The whole of the colony was by then linked by a system of roads, although there were significant variations in the density of the system. The network was clearly less dense in certain sections of the east. The relative paucity in places there was caused partly by the fact that the east included some of the more thinly settled parts of the colony and partly by the greater availability of navigable waterways in the areas along and close to the coast. The large number of roads in the west by 1775 is evidence of the speed and efficiency with which settlers turned to the task of furnishing themselves with lines of communication.

The existence of this system of roads is worth emphasizing, especially since it has received such scant attention in writings about the Southern colonies in general and North Carolina in particular.[12] The fact that roads existed and were used has been obscured by an undue emphasis upon various themes, such as the isolation of frontier settlers, the persistence of subsistence farming in areas other than those of plantation agriculture, the great importance of water transportation and the lack of it away from tidewater; or, if roads have been mentioned, it is their poor quality and condition that has most frequently been noted, in terms often as derogatory as those employed by the visitors from Europe who traveled along them.[13] But the use of overland transportation made possible the emergence of inland trading towns, as well as the expanded importance of the seaport towns.

Fig. 41 also shows the towns that had developed by the end of the colonial period.[14] The total number was still not large in 1775, although there were more than twice as many as there had been in 1730 (see Fig. 4, which shows the five towns in existence in 1730).

In all the urban settlements the single most important function was trade. The kind, amount, and direction of trade varied from place to place, but it was the one function common to all of the urban settlements and often the dominant factor in their growth (and decline). In terms of the kind of trade carried on in them, the urban settlements can be assigned to one of three types: there were the seaports of the east, the trading towns of the westernmost section of the settled area, and, in the middle country between the two, a third type of trading center that served as a link between the seaports and the westernmost towns. This highly schematic typology will serve as a framework for a discussion of the specific features and functions of the towns belonging to each of the three types.

Seaports—The seaports of North Carolina were the urban expressions of the colonial structure of the economy. Through them were funneled raw materials destined for export overseas and the items imported for sale and distribution within the colony. Little or no manufacturing was carried on in these towns. Such items as were produced came from the hands of a few specialized craftsmen, such as silversmiths and wigmakers, who worked only in a few of the largest urban places. Services other than trade were represented. Newspaper editors, tavern keepers, lawyers, physicians, teachers, as well as others, sold their services. The list could be extended but it would be more impressive than were the actual numbers of persons practicing such occupations in any one place. The most important service function, and the reason for the existence of the ports, was trade. The merchants who promoted this trade constituted the most important occupational class within the seaports.

The flow of products that the merchants directed moved across the sounds and oceans facing the ports and along the roads and rivers that led into them. The water served as a routeway to other colonies and to countries on the other side of the Atlantic. Some of the rivers were used as transportation routes to and from areas on the landward side of the ports. The roads supplemented and extended these ties back from the coast, and, since all of the larger ports lay along one main north-south coastal highway through the colony, the roads also served to connect the coastal towns with one another.

Included among the seaports were the oldest urban settlements in North Carolina. But by the end of the colonial period, the oldest were not the largest. There was a marked absence of any steady, cumulative process of urban growth. Trade was the predominant function in the seaports, and since the colony's trade was subject to relatively large and sudden changes the fortunes of the coastal centers fluctuated accordingly.

There were no ports ever comparable in size or importance to places such as Charleston or Boston. At no time in the colonial period did any one of North Carolina's ports contain more than a few hundred inhabitants; several probably had considerably less. As centers of consumption they were therefore much less influential than were the few metropolitan settlements of the Atlantic Seaboard. Nevertheless, the demands of the inhabitants of the ports were already beginning to induce changes in land use in the areas around them. There is at least one recorded instance of a form of intensive cultivation, not unlike truck farming, underway on the outskirts of Wilmington.[15] In this and other ways urbanization in the eighteenth century was initiating the changes that were to become much more pronounced in the nineteenth century.

The three largest seaports at the end of the colonial period were Edenton, New Bern, and Wilmington. The three other ports, Bath, Beaufort, and Brunswick, were small and declining in importance. All merit a few words.

Edenton was located at the northwestern end of Albemarle Sound, at the head of a bay just east of the mouth of the Chowan River. Founded early in the century, by the 1730's it had sixty houses and was then the largest town in the colony according to one of its inhabitants.[16] By the end of the period it was twice as large, with 135 dwellings in 1777.[17] While these figures give no indication of its importance as a trading port, its role in this respect is apparent from other sources. The presence of numerous merchants and British government officials whose job was to oversee trade and collect customs charges together with the constant references by visitors to the trade of the port, illustrate the relatively large role played by Edenton in the trade of the colony as a whole.[18]

The export specialties of Edenton's merchants were staves, shingles, tobacco, and corn. Many other items were cleared out of the port, but in these four it was pre-eminent among the North Carolina seaports.[19] The goods were shipped out by the small vessels engaged in the coastwise and West Indian trade,[20] and such ships were better equipped than the larger ones to navigate the shallow and circuitous route to and from the harbor of Edenton.[21]

As the county seat of Chowan, Edenton was also an administrative center. Indeed, the courthouse in Edenton in which the county court transacted its business of administration was one of the most imposing buildings in the Southern colonies; facing

Edenton Bay across the town green, it was (and still is) a distinguished eighteenth-century example of public building. A superior court probably met in the same building, for Edenton was also the center of one of the judicial districts into which the colony was divided. A different kind of legal activity was transacted in the land office, where the agent in charge of the disposal of land in the Granville District was located.[22] The colony's assembly sometimes met in Edenton, a meeting that was both a cause and an effect of the importance of the town. More mundane services were provided by the carpenters, laborers, blacksmiths, shoemakers, tanners, tailors, and other occupations represented among the inhabitants of the town.[23]

Land routes, as well as waterways, were of much service to the inhabitants of Edenton, and it was linked both to Virginia and more southerly parts of North Carolina by well-traveled roads. On the sound side of the town was the northern terminus of the ferry that carried the main north-south coastal highway across Albemarle Sound and led on to New Bern, Wilmington, and Charleston.[24] Several roads converged on the town from the north, including one known as the Virginia Road which was much used for communication between Edenton and a small section of Virginia across the intercolonial boundary line.[25] While the town probably had closer ties with Virginia than any other settlement in North Carolina, these connections were not enough to assure the town of continuing prominence. Neither land nor water routes sufficed to overcome the handicaps of a disadvantageous location.

It is not clear when these handicaps were first felt. Even before the end of the colonial period Edenton was apparently declining relative to the other two most important seaports, Wilmington and New Bern. In the 1760's and 1770's both of the other two were sometimes claimed to be the largest or most flourishing towns in the colony, whereas no one seems to have had such claims to make on behalf of Edenton. In all respects (save for its proximity to Virginia) the location of Edenton was disadvantageous. As a port, it was an unusually time-consuming distance away from the open ocean. Overland connections between Edenton and the rest of the colony were hampered on the south by the long ferry-crossing necessary to reach the other side of Albemarle Sound and on the west by the similar, though shorter, ferry across the mouth of the Chowan River. Both ferries caused delays and were out of operation in more extreme weather conditions.

Among the travelers who visited Edenton was Hugh Finlay, a surveyor of the post roads in North America. Observing the situation in 1774, he noted the troublesome delays occasioned by the ferries and found that travelers en route to Charleston from the north were generally taking the road through Halifax, thus by-passing Edenton. Finlay therefore proposed to re-route the post road from Williamsburg southwards through Halifax rather than Edenton, a change that was probably symptomatic of its declining relative importance.[26] And, as the more westerly portion of North Carolina was settled, there was less need for the post road to hug the coast quite so closely.[27]

By the end of the colonial period, New Bern had become a larger and more important port than Edenton. Founded in 1710 by Christoph von Graffenried, at the confluence of the Neuse and Trent Rivers, its early vicissitudes kept it from becoming much more than a village for most of the first half of the century. In 1741, only twenty-one families were living in New Bern.[28] But it soon began to grow rapidly. In 1765, it was reported to contain about a hundred houses and about five hundred inhabitants.[29] Two years later, Governor Tryon requested that a comptroller be appointed to serve there, "as the trade and town of Newbern are increasing very fast."[30] Governor Martin, in 1772, wrote that it was "growing very fast into significance."[31] The town contained about 150 dwellings in 1777, when, according to one traveler, it was the metropolis of North Carolina.[32] In the following year, it was visited by Ebenezer Hazard, during the course of a journey southward through the colonies on behalf of the postmaster general. Hazard stayed in New Bern and noted that it covered a larger area than any town he had seen since leaving Annapolis in Maryland.[33] Its growth continued in the following decade.[34]

The rapid growth of New Bern seems to have begun in the 1760's, when a group of successful merchants established themselves there.[35] Its central location, about halfway between the only two other important ports (Edenton and Wilmington), together with the roads that provided links to areas north, south, and west of the town, must have facilitated the business of the merchants; indeed, both factors may have influenced merchants in their decision to establish themselves in New Bern.[36] The selection of the town in 1765 as the site of the capital of the colony was followed by the construction of Tryon's Palace, to serve both as the governor's residence and as the meeting place of the government.[37] Trade flourished as a result.[38] A few years later, Governor Martin commented upon the way in which New Bern had grown at the expense of Beaufort, a small port to the southeast: ". . . the Trade that was formerly carried on through that Channel [i.e., Beaufort], is now derived almost entirely to this Town [i.e., New Bern], since it became the seat of Government, which has promoted its growth exceedingly, by inviting many considerable Merchants to settle in it."[39]

Facilities for water-borne trade were of some significance in the rising importance of New Bern. Although it was located closer to the open ocean than Edenton, New Bern was not significantly nearer to it than was Bath (which was declining in importance—see below) and was in fact farther away from the Atlantic than Beaufort. The voyage from the port to the ocean was a difficult one,[40] but the roads leading to the west from the town enabled the merchants to tap some of the trade from the interior. The Neuse River was of some use in this respect too, New Bern being a transhipment point on this river. Although large vessels could navigate no farther upstream than New Bern, very small craft could be used to float goods down the Neuse as far as the town, there to be loaded onto larger vessels for export.[41]

The two ports of Wilmington and Brunswick were located close to the mouth of the Cape Fear River, within fifteen miles of one another. Situated so close together and offering almost identical services, it was perhaps inevitable that one eclipsed the other. The story of their rivalry during the eighteenth century has been told elsewhere and need not be recounted here.[42] Although Brunswick was founded in the 1720's, about ten years before Wilmington, Governor Johnston's policy of favoring the newer settlement at the expense of the older was so effective that Wilmington soon outstripped Brunswick. By 1775, when Wilmington was one of the two largest urban settlements in the colony (and probably the largest), Brunswick was little more than a county seat and the location of a few port officials. One observer called it a "stragling village."[43] During the next few years Brunswick ceased to be a county seat, lost the right to borough representation, was given up by port officials, and, owing to the danger of its being raided by the English, was abandoned by its inhabitants.[44] When viewed by a traveler sometime during the winter of 1783/84, the former town of Brunswick was almost entirely demolished and deserted.[45]

Unlike Brunswick, New Bern, and Edenton, Wilmington flourished as a port from its earliest days and is still a port of considerable importance in the twentieth century. The basis of its commercial prosperity during the eighteenth century was the export trade of the Cape Fear Valley, the early growth of the seaport being a reflection of the settlement and development of this area. Large amounts of bulky naval stores and lumber produced in the area were sent down both branches of the Cape Fear River, as well as smaller quantities of farm products. Ocean-going vessels could not sail more than a few miles farther upstream than Wilmington, on either the Northeast or Northwest branch,[46] but it was relatively easy and inexpensive for producers to float down the exports on rafts or piragua,[47] for loading onto vessels downstream. Since Wilmington was located below the confluence of the two branches, but above Brunswick, its merchants were better able to intercept and handle this trade. Many of them seem to have used the island in the river opposite Wilmington as a collection point for the naval stores and lumber of the Cape Fear Valley before loading these goods onto larger vessels for export overseas.[48]

Not all of the trade of the valley, however, was handled at Wilmington, as Brunswick had one locational advantage. The exports were sent to the mainland colonies, to the West Indies and, more so than from any other of the ports of the colony, across the Atlantic to Great Britain. The importance of the transatlantic component reflected the large export trade in naval stores (see

Table 3 and Fig. 34), almost all of which were destined for the British market. The ships employed in the transatlantic trade were of necessity generally larger than those engaged in the coastwise trade, and the average tonnage of vessels entering and clearing the mouth of the Cape Fear was larger than the size using the other ports of the colony.[49] Some of these ships, when fully loaded, could not pass the stretch of the river between Wilmington and Brunswick; a little above Brunswick were the "Flats," where the shallow channel barred larger or heavily-laden vessels even at high tide.[50] Some shipmasters, desirous of calling at Wilmington, solved the problem by lightering. But others went no farther upstream than Brunswick and were content to take on a full load there. Brunswick seemed to have existed until the Revolution mainly to serve this function, and for that reason port officials, carrying out regulatory duties, were resident in the town.

Although the Cape Fear River was much utilized for trading purposes, road transportation was also of some consequence in the economic life of Wilmington and even of Brunswick. The main north-south coastal highway through the colony was extended as far south as the river almost as soon as settlers moved into the Cape Fear,[51] and contemporary maps show that before long there were several roads converging on Wilmington.[52] The court minutes of New Hanover County,[53] of which Wilmington was the county seat, reveal the inhabitants' constant concern to maintain and improve the road system within the county, and particularly those roads that linked up with others leading to more distant places. The colonial government itself took the initiative in arranging for the building of a road from the western part of the colony all the way to Wilmington and Brunswick; the road was designed to help divert to these two North Carolina ports some of the produce of the backcountry that had hitherto been exported via South Carolina.[54]

The concentration of large numbers of Scottish and Scotch-Irish merchants in Wilmington was a distinctive feature of the town and played an important role in its successful development as a seaport and trading center. There is abundant evidence of this concentration,[55] which was remarkable enough to attract the attention of those familiar with the town.[56] One example will show how the enterprise of such merchants contributed to the growth of trade in general and Wilmington in particular. Robert Hogg moved from Scotland to North Carolina in the 1750's, and within a few years he had helped establish the mercantile business of Hogg and Campbell, which rapidly became one of the notably successful firms in Wilmington. In 1774 his brother, James Hogg, emigrated to North Carolina, at the same time arranging for the transport of a shipload of Highlanders to Wilmington. After his arrival, James Hogg worked for a while as the representative of his brother's firm in Cross Creek, one of several stores that had been established as branches of Hogg and Campbell's Wilmington house. He shortly moved on to another branch of the firm, in Hillsboro, and in 1775 was forwarding goods in wagons from there to the headquarters office in Wilmington (and was also beginning to play a leading role in the Transylvania Company). The firm flourished. The annual profits of Hogg and Campbell amounted to about £1,200, and when the partnership was dissolved in 1778 the company had assets of £18,330.[57]

With such merchants operating out of Wilmington, its success as a commercial center was virtually guaranteed. Their contacts in Great Britain assured them of an advantageous market overseas. Their vigorous policy developed trade in the interior, funneled much of it into Wilmington, and expanded the hinterland of the port so that it included some of the backcountry as well as the Cape Fear Valley.

There is a little evidence of the size of Wilmington. In 1754, it included seventy families and was already larger than Brunswick, which then had only twenty families.[58] Sometime shortly before the Revolution, a traveler, while on his way through the town, estimated that it contained two hundred houses.[59] It was by then probably more populous than either New Bern or Edenton and almost certainly more important as a commercial center. In 1774, Wilmington was described as "the most flourishing town in the province"[60] and in the following year as the "principal Trading Town in this Province."[61] Smyth, however, wrote off Wilmington as "nothing better than a village."[62]

The other two seaports were Bath and Beaufort. Both were founded early in the eighteenth century, both were official ports of entry, and both were county seats. But both of them, after an initial phase during which they stood out as two of the most important port towns in the colony, dwindled into unimportance and were overshadowed by Edenton, New Bern, and Wilmington. While their decline was not so drastic as that of Brunswick, they barely survived as urban settlements and by the end of the eighteenth century had sunk into an obscurity from which they have not since emerged.[63]

Bath was the older of the two, and, indeed, the oldest town of all, having been incorporated in 1705. In 1708 it had about fifty or sixty inhabitants and was an important center of trade after the end of the war with the Tuscarora in 1715.[64] Brickell's description of Bath in 1737 gave no hint of its subsequent decline: "Bath Town, is the Second considerable Town in this Province, and is most delightfully seated on a Creek on the North-side of Pamticoe River, with the same beautiful Advantages of the former [i.e., Edenton]: It's Navigation is much better, being the most considerable and commodious for Trade in this Province, except Cape Fear."[65] But in 1745, New Bern already had as many houses as Bath,[66] and after the middle of the century the latter was never very important. Although it continued as an official port of entry for the remainder of the colonial period, the town was less appealing to merchants and shipmasters than Edenton to the north and New Bern to the south. In an area that remained sparsely settled, without any particular advantages in terms of either location or accessibility, it was by-passed when the main north-south coastal highway and post road was shifted farther west, to run through Halifax and New Bern.[67] Its failure to grow and its declining relative importance are implicit in the comments of the occasional traveler who still passed through the town.[68]

Beaufort's decline was no less marked. Bath and all of the other port towns were at least represented in the assembly. Beaufort was not; all towns with more than sixty inhabitants were entitled to representation, but although the people of Beaufort claimed they were eligible on this score they remained without one.[69] When first established, in the second decade of the eighteenth century, Beaufort was the only port close to the ocean, but this proximity alone was apparently not enough to induce many merchants to make it their seat of operations. Travelers very rarely included the port on their itinerary, since Beaufort was not on the main coastal highway that once passed through all the other seaports (see Fig. 41). Perhaps it failed to become an important port because of its disadvantageous overland ties. In any event, when New Bern began to flourish in the 1760's Beaufort's decline was one of the consequences.[70]

All six of the seaports were founded in the first half of the eighteenth century, and their differing fortunes in the colonial period were the result of a special process of urbanization. As the colony expanded, the increasing need and opportunity for merchandising services simply led to a proliferation of merchants in three of the pre-existing seaports, leaving the others without any very important commercial base. The large increase in population during the third quarter of the eighteenth century and the consequent increase in trade did not lead to the growth of any new, large urban centers along the coast. Instead, urban growth took the form of a reduction in the number of such centers, and the concentration of commercial facilities in a few large and expanding seaport towns.

Midland towns—West of the seaports was a second type of urban settlement, comprising Halifax, Tarboro, Cross Creek, and Campbelltown (see Fig. 41). Since all four were located in the area between the east coast and the most westerly portion of the settled area, they can be called "midland towns," a name which also serves to suggest something of their key function as links between east and west.

Each one of the midland towns originated in the third quarter of the eighteenth century. Their reason for existence was the handling of internal trade. In all four of them merchants utilized both overland and river transportation to move the goods involved in this trade. Tarboro was established too late to become of much importance before 1775, and little is known about its colonial phase. Campbelltown was really an offshoot of Cross Creek, located only about one and a half miles away from it. The two largest of the four were Halifax and Cross Creek.

Halifax was built on the south bank of the Roanoke River,

about sixty miles northwest of Edenton and only about fifteen miles from the boundary between Virginia and North Carolina. It was officially founded in 1757, at the request of a number of merchants anxious to promote trade and navigation on the Roanoke River.[71] This particular point alongside the river had a special advantage, since it was apparently the limit of navigability for small craft. One later visitor noted that shallops could navigate this far upstream,[72] and another writer declared that it was the limit for boats carrying between 150 and 200 barrels.[73] (It appears that some vessels could go even farther upstream, as far as the lower falls of the Roanoke about ten miles above Halifax and that the river was again navigable above the falls. But there is no evidence that any use was made of the river for transportation purposes above the town.)[74] The land chosen as the site belonged to James Leslie, who could conceivably have been one of the merchants who advocated the establishment of the town, and possibly a desire to promote the value of Leslie's land, through subdivision into town lots, had something to do with the choice of location.

In any event, the project was successful. Fifteen years after its establishment, the town was visited by the surveyor of post roads, whose brief description of Halifax in 1774 gives an inkling of its function: "This place contains about 50 houses, stores are kept here to supply the country round with European and West India Commoditys for which Pork, Tobacco, Indian corn, Wheat and Lumber are taken in return."[75] The town played a role as both a collecting and distributing trade center.

The ties of Halifax merchants to the east were probably with places in Virginia and with Edenton. The latter was the nearest seaport, easily reached by river or road, and in it were located the government agents who could officially clear goods destined for shipment outside the colony.[76] Westwards from Halifax, a number of roads afforded transportation and communication to and from the interior and were used by wagons carrying farm commodities into the town for subsequent export; a road linking it with Hillsboro apparently was especially important, even being used by something known as the "Halifax Express."[77] When the main coastal highway between Virginia and South Carolina through North Carolina was shifted west, it passed through Halifax instead of Edenton, symbolizing the rising importance of the former and in turn probably contributing to its growth.

The size of Halifax is uncertain. It was represented in the assembly in 1767,[78] so supposedly it had at least sixty resident families by then. A plan of the town, made in 1769,[79] shows that among the buildings were the county courthouse and jail, a tobacco store, hemp store, and even a playhouse. An incidental comment on the professions represented in the town in the same year, as well as on its social facilities, is provided by the diary of a visiting lawyer who, when he arrived in town, was greeted by three merchants and six attorneys and took part in a "splendid Ball" in the evening.[80] In 1774, it contained about fifty houses,[81] and ten years later was still "a small town but of an active trade."[82]

The size and importance of the town fluctuated during the course of each year. Periodic meetings of the county court[83] brought together leading members of the county, among them merchants who probably used this occasion to transact business. After 1768, Halifax was also the center of one of the five judicial districts of the colony; the twice-yearly meetings of the superior court were important occasions, and the town became a place "where all the inhabitants of the adjacent Country Come, to Deside their lawsuits and other Differences," and, probably, then also much business was carried on.[84]

Although Halifax and Cross Creek were essentially similar kinds of colonial trading centers, there is a great contrast between them today. Halifax did not subsequently become a larger urban center, and today has a population of only a few hundred. Enough relics remain to give ample scope to the restoration committee organized to preserve and reconstruct the once important town. Cross Creek, on the other hand, has become submerged in Fayetteville, an expanding urban center with about forty thousand inhabitants, serving important commercial, military, and educational functions; the development of Fayetteville has almost completely obliterated the physical remains of what was once Cross Creek. Fortunately, documentary evidence of its former role is unusually abundant.

Cross Creek developed around a small stream of that name,

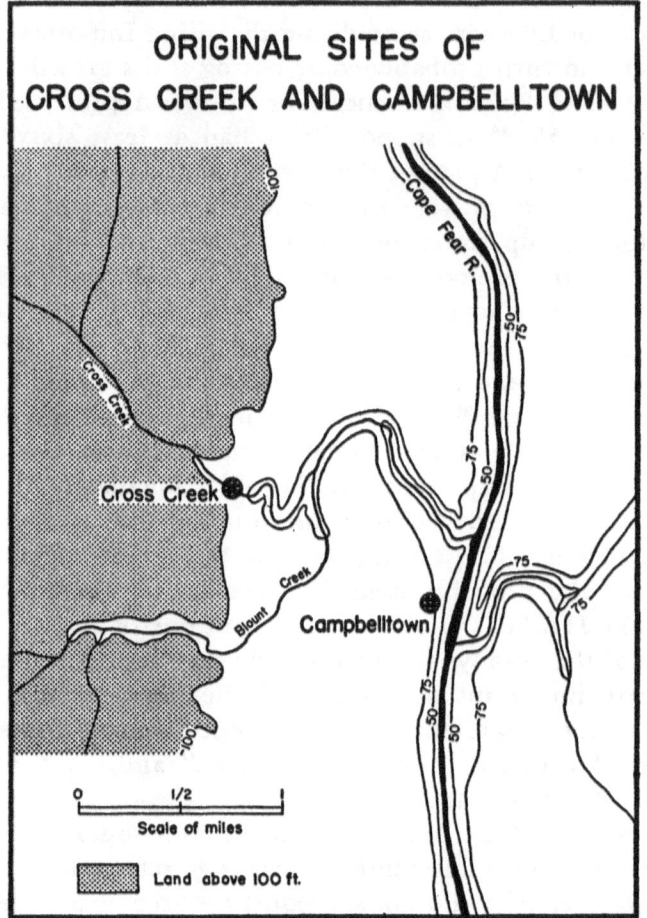

Fig. 42

about one and a half miles west of where the stream flowed into the Northwest Cape Fear River and on the western edge of a broad, flat bench above the Cape Fear (see Fig. 42).[85] Adjacent to the settlement on the north and west was the rougher terrain of the region known as the Sandhills. The settlement originally probably straddled the lower hill slopes and the flat benchland. The significance of the site, as well as the early growth and functions of the settlement, were described by William Bartram, who visited the town in 1776. His account of it is almost lyrical:

This creek [Cross Creek] gave name to a fine inland trading town, on some heights or swelling hills, from whence the creek descends precipitately, then gently meanders near a mile, through lower level lands, to its confluence with the river, affording most convenient mill-seats; these prospects induced active, enterprising men to avail themselves of such advantages pointed out to them by nature, they built mills, which drew people to the place, and these observing elegible situations for other profitable improvements, bought lots and erected tenements, where they exercised mechanic arts, as smiths, wheelwrights, carpenters, coopers, tanners, etc. And at length merchants were encouraged to adventure and settle; in short, within eight or ten years from a grist-mill, saw-mill, smith-shop and a tavern, arose a flourishing commercial town. . . .[86]

Bartram's account of the early growth was presumably based on hearsay, but it accords well with other evidence from the contemporary record.[87]

Since Cross Creek, unlike Halifax, was not established by administrative decree, its origins can not be dated so precisely. Although settlers were in the vicinity earlier, not until the late 1750's did the community begin to resemble a town.[88] By the 1760's, it was functioning as a prominent link for trade and communication between the eastern and western portions of the colony. At the end of the colonial period it probably contained a few hundred people, and a number of stores, grist mills, saw mills, and taverns.[89] At least some of the prominent merchants in the town were Scottish Highlanders, and there were others who were Lowland Scots and Scotch-Irish; despite the proximity of Cross Creek to the main area settled by Scottish Highlanders there is no evidence that they constituted the majority of the town's population, although it is perhaps safe to assume that Scottish and Scotch-Irish elements were more marked in this than in any other town.[90]

Roads from the interior converged on Cross Creek, and along these roads farmers sent their wagon loads of agricultural commodities to the town.[91] Produce was brought in from at least as far west and northwest of the town as Salem, Salisbury, Hillsboro, and Charlotte,[92] and in return goods purchased in the stores of Cross Creek were taken. Wheat was an especially important item in this trade with the interior.[93] One writer reported that forty or fifty wagons a day came into town.[94]

Strong ties existed between Wilmington and Cross Creek. Flour made in the town's mills, wheat, and other products of forest and field were sent from Cross Creek to Wilmington for export. Most of the Wilmington merchants had agents in Cross Creek, promoting the flow of goods between the seaport and the trading town, and drawing to Wilmington the trade that had formerly been attracted to South Carolina.[95] The goods themselves were sometimes hauled overland along the road that connected the two places, but perhaps the Cape Fear River was an even more important means of transportation.[96] The river could not be used by large vessels, but it was easy enough to float goods down it on rafts or small craft, though less easy to row them upstream from Wilmington.

A minor problem connected with the use of the river was the necessity of hauling back and forth over the mile-and-a-half stretch between Cross Creek and the Cape Fear landing, a flat stretch that became almost impassable in wet weather owing to the "constant intercourse of Waggons."[97] The point along the river to and from which goods were taken came to have a special significance. As Cross Creek began to grow and flourish, its leading inhabitants became embroiled with a group of men who tried to found a town around the river site. The efforts of the latter group (supported by a majority in the assembly) were partially successful. By about 1770 there was apparently a settlement growing up within a few hundred yards of the Cape Fear, a little more than a mile away from Cross Creek, known as Campbelltown (see Fig. 42).

The rivalry of the two settlements came to an end in 1778,[98] when they were united under the name of Campbelltown. The nominal union later became a physical one as the two expanded and joined together. The two settlements are now submerged in the town known as Fayetteville. All that remains as testimony to their once separate identities is the distinctive grid pattern of the systematically laid out town lots of the first Campbelltown, still discernible at the river (eastern) end of Fayetteville.[99]

Tarboro was the same type of urban center as Cross Creek

and Halifax, but smaller and less important. It was founded in 1760,[100] on the south side of the Tar River, but did not become very large during the next fifteen years. In 1773, Tarboro was denied a representative because it did not have as many as sixty resident families,[101] and about this time it was only half the size of Halifax.[102]

The land chosen for the town was the site of one of the many warehouses to which goods intended for export were brought for inspection.[103] The founders perceived that the site was advantageously located for trade and commerce,[104] and the town grew as a trading center. Surplus commodities from the interior were collected here for export, and imported goods were brought in for distribution. Tar, pork, and corn seem to have been the most important items brought into the town, but more and more tobacco was being handled by Tarboro merchants in the 1770's and 1780's.[105] Although much trade was carried on, and although Tarboro became the county seat of Edgecombe County, these functions did not very much enlarge the settlement. A visitor to the town shortly after the Revolution noted that "before the war there was every year brought in and sold there 7-8000 Pd. of English goods" but that Tarboro was "an inconsiderable place of itself."[106]

The use of both river and road transportation facilities emphasized the similarity between Tarboro and the other midland towns. Downstream from the town, the River Tar was used both for floating down goods and for rowing them up. The navigability of the river was not perfect, however, and was restricted to vessels of shallow draft. Even these were hampered by various obstructions, and apparently the river could not be used in all seasons. One writer described Tarboro as being at the head of navigation, but another noted that flat-bottomed craft carrying several hundred barrels could navigate the river for considerable distances above Tarboro.[107] For trade to and from points west of the town, roads rather than the river were used. Several roads led into the town from the west and also from north and south, as the settlement was located at a convenient crossing point along the river.[108]

Tarboro was in some ways less advantageously situated than

either Halifax or Cross Creek (see Fig. 41). It was somewhat farther from the western settlements, in an area that was not favorably located for tapping the trade that went out of the colony into Virginia and South Carolina and without any strong ties with an important seaport. It may have been for such reasons that Tarboro was the last of the midland towns to develop and remained the least important during the colonial period.

Western towns—The third type of urban settlement was the western town, a type including Hillsboro, Salem, Salisbury, and Charlotte.[109] These were all founded in the 1750's and 1760's. Their growth was a reflection of the influx of settlers into the backcountry and the development there of a rudimentary system of trade, transportation, and communications. The western towns provided the first generation of backcountry settlers with administrative, judicial, and commercial services. If the administrative and judicial functions were sometimes disrupted by political partiality and civil disorders, at least trade and commerce seem to have been uninterrupted.

Hillsboro and Salisbury can be taken together, since they were almost identical in important respects. Salem must be considered separately, for it was a rather special version of an inland town. Charlotte will be left to the last. It was probably the smallest and least important of the four and is certainly the least documented.

Hillsboro and Salisbury were both established about 1754 as the seats of the county governments of Orange County and Rowan County, respectively.[110] They were situated along a major routeway, known as the "Western Great Road" or "Western Path," which led southwestwards from Virginia through western North Carolina and which was once an important routeway for those trading with the Catawba and Cherokee.[111] The road subsequently became an important thoroughfare for settlers, and the founders of the two towns anticipated that a location along it would facilitate the commercial growth of the two new urban centers. Minor roads, perhaps really trackways, existed in the vicinity of both places before they were established, and the county courts of Orange and Rowan took care to see that roads to and from their county seats were further improved and extended. By 1767, both Hillsboro and Salisbury were also centers of judicial districts (the two westernmost of the meeting places of superior courts), and a few years later both were represented in the assembly.

The two towns grew rapidly. William Few, who removed to Hillsboro in 1764 as a young man, later recollected its condition then. It was, he reported,

... the metropolis of the county, where the courts were held and all the public business was done. It was a small village, which contained thirty or forty inhabitants, with two or three small stores and two or three ordinary taverns, but it was an improving village. Several Scotch merchants were soon after induced to establish stores that contained a good assortment of European merchandise, which changed the state of things for the better. A church, court-house and jail were built, but there was no parson or physician.

Two or three attorneys opened their offices and found employment. Superior and inferior courts of justice were established, and a fair field was opened for the lawyers.[112]

Governor Martin, in 1772, found settlements in the vicinity of Hillsboro "numerous beyond belief." He added that these settlements were as yet in a state of "infantine rudeness," a point which, in view of the growth and function of Hillsboro, emphasizes the simultaneity of rural settlement and the beginnings of urban development.[113] A lawyer who arrived in Salisbury in 1768, with the purpose of practicing there, found that it was in a "thick Settled" locality, "a small Town but in a Thriving way."[114]

The volume and destination of trade to and from Hillsboro and Salisbury can only be surmised from indirect evidence.[115] It seems that both towns fell within the trade orbit of merchants in Cross Creek and in Virginia and, furthermore, that some trade went from Salisbury to South Carolina and some from Hillsboro to Halifax. The local records of Rowan and Orange counties provide glimpses of the instruments of this trade. The Virginia Road and the Cross Creek, or Cape Fear Road, are frequently mentioned, as are the more local roads linking up with these major arteries, and the wagons used for carrying goods along them.

The agents of trade were merchants, and those in Hillsboro

were Scottish.¹¹⁶ In general, Scottish merchants played a singularly large role in the development of trade in the west and the related commercialization of agriculture. Through their efforts the trade of the backcountry was tapped. Congregating in Cross Creek, Wilmington, and various places in Virginia, with representatives in Hillsboro (and possibly Salisbury),¹¹⁷ with stores here and there in the west, and probably a few itinerant agents and factors seizing trade opportunities where they found them, Scottish merchants seem to have brought the surplus to the Cape Fear and to Virginia, sold imported goods in return, and, in effect, outflanked the mercantile efforts of the English merchants in the earlier settled Albemarle area.¹¹⁸

A third example of the western type of town is Salem. In an important sense, the Moravian settlement as a whole served as an urban center even before the founding of Salem in 1766. The Moravians were visited by farmers who came from considerable distances to purchase and sell goods and to buy services. Not all of those with whom the Moravians did business paid promptly, and in 1766 notices were posted calling on six hundred debtors, who owed the Moravians about £1,800, to pay off their debts.¹¹⁹ One Moravian was a physician, and as early as 1754 it was reported that he had a "large practice" and that "people have come more than a hundred miles to get medicine and advice from him"; he also traveled "far and wide to visit patients."¹²⁰ Even before there was a town in it, day laborers came to the Moravian tract to find employment there, as did a few itinerant craftsmen.

As the Moravians became better organized, they decided to realize their aim of building a central town, "not designed for farmers but for those with trades."¹²¹ After much careful deliberation a site was selected, a town laid off, buildings raised, and in 1767 Salem began to function as a compact, well-directed, urban center. The multifarious activities of its inhabitants provided goods and services for other western settlers. Among the institutions kept particularly busy were the tavern, store, pottery, grist mill, and saw mill, all of which were in or close by the town. Despite occasional setbacks, the newly founded town was a great success. The efforts of its tradesmen were so fruitful, and its commerce so prosperous, that by 1770 profits more than paid for the large expenses incurred in building the town. By 1775 it contained about 125 inhabitants.

Trade and transportation were all-important to the Moravian settlements in general and to Salem in particular. Moravian wagons regularly trundled to and from Wachovia, taking to more distant markets their own surplus, or goods purchased from others, and bringing back the few items even Moravian ingenuity could not produce, such as salt, iron, tea, and glass. Because they created considerable trade, the Moravians from time to time were visited by merchants who came to evaluate commercial possibilities. But neither solicitations nor unsolicited gifts distracted the Moravians in the constant search for the most advantageous trade destinations. More so than any other settlers, this group of Germans seems to have planned their trading activities with great care, diligently supervising them and organizing their economic activities with a view to exploiting the most profitable market possibilities.[122]

At first, and before Salem was founded, Charleston was the preferred destination. But early in the 1770's, Cross Creek became the trading place most used by the Moravians. There were several reasons for the changeover. In 1770, a road was opened directly from Salem to Cross Creek and this facilitated transportation between the two places. As Cross Creek grew, the stores there began to carry a wider assortment of goods and the Moravians found that it was no longer necessary to go to Charleston to obtain the special items they needed. The comparative advantages of trading directly with Charleston also fell off somewhat as hides and deerskins became relatively unimportant items among the products that the Moravians were taking to market. The best markets for the skins and hides were apparently in South Carolina. But within a decade after their arrival the Moravians were trading more and more in bulkier, less valuable, agricultural produce, which they found it more advantageous to carry only as far as Cross Creek. In 1772, they began sending a messenger once a month to Cross Creek to pick up copies of the Wilmington newspaper, to keep in touch with market conditions in these two places.

By 1775 the switch from Charleston to Cross Creek had been

accomplished. Finding that grain sold more profitably than flour at Cross Creek, the Moravians began the construction of a better and larger mill, thereby hoping to bring more customers to their mill and to put their trade on a sounder footing. In the same year and a few months before the Revolution began to disrupt trading patterns, the Moravians reported that their trade was largely with Cross Creek.[123]

Certain features of Salem were unique. Among the western towns it was distinctive because of the circumstances of its establishment as an integral part of a planned community, as well as on account of its exclusively German population. Salem was also unlike Hillsboro and Salisbury in that it was neither a county seat nor the center of a judicial district, and it was not represented in the assembly. But if administrative and judicial services were not among its functions, other kinds of service were, and in terms of its role as a center of trade and transportation Salem was merely one of a type.

The last and least important of the inland western settlements was Charlotte. It was established in 1768, in a location conceived to be advantageous for trade.[124] Seemingly, it became a trade center of more than local significance, although information concerning it in the contemporary records of North Carolina is fragmentary and inconclusive.[125] Because of its proximity to South Carolina much of its trade may have been directed there, and South Carolina records may contain pertinent details relating to Charlotte's early role. The founding of Queen's College in Charlotte by a law ratified in 1771 gives the settlement a small but special claim to some fame.[126] And whether or not Charlotte was very important in the eighteenth century it has subsequently become the largest urban settlement in the Carolinas.

Seaports, midland towns, and western towns were the three major types of urban center. Scattered here and there about the colony were some urban centers of strictly local importance. These can be treated much more briefly. Since their functions were confined to areas no more extensive than the counties in which they were located, detailed information concerning them can generally be found only in county records. But even when these records are more or less complete they contain very little about the local urban places. Exactly how many there were at any one time is not known, and the exact location of some is uncertain.

Some were really still-born towns. Land for them had been laid out in lots and optimistic legislation passed to regulate their growth. More often than not the hoped-for town failed to materialize. Portsmouth, for example, was laid out on one of the Outer Banks, adjacent to Ocracoke Inlet, in the hope that it might become a thriving seaport.[127] It never became more than a couple of houses around a tavern and eventually disappeared altogether.

The most common local urban centers were probably those that grew up around county courthouses. Whenever a new county was set up, provision was made for a courthouse, which was sometimes built at the approximate center of the county. Close by the courthouse a jail was erected, and generally an ordinary and at least a couple of residences. When court was in session the site was a scene of considerable activity. Some courthouse settlements subsequently became centers of year-round importance, as did Hertford, which had the additional advantages of a fairly accessible location on the banks of the Perquimans River, in an old and densely settled area.[128]

A few of the major colonial towns may have begun life as settlements of this type. But courthouses were sometimes moved from one location to another, especially in the early years of a county's existence. When this happened the original site was left stranded and generally never became a settlement of any note.

DECENTRALIZED TRADE

Some merchants in North Carolina bought and sold goods in places other than towns. A function normally associated with urban centers was in effect dispersed throughout the colony, since an important part of the colony's internal trade was carried on through the media of country stores and itinerant traders.

Country stores were the most important expression of this kind of merchandising. One such store was that of the Hamiltons', merchants from Glasgow who, in 1761, took over a store about six or eight miles from the town of Halifax. Its location appealed to them because it lay "at the meeting of two main Roads leading from the back parts of North Carolina to Halifax town."[129] Within fifteen years the Hamiltons had made their store into one of the largest and most prosperous in the colony, a pivotal point in their chain of establishments strung out from Suffolk, Virginia, to western parts of North Carolina. Siphoning some of the surplus off North Carolina farms into Virginia before dispatching it into coastwise or transatlantic commerce, the Hamiltons' store kept the same farmers supplied with imported goods via Virginia. Clustered around their main North Carolina store were several related buildings, including a tavern, warehouses, and an elegant dwelling house. Their complex of buildings may indeed be regarded as a miniature urban place, although it differed from other urban centers in that it was an enterprise exclusively concerned with trade, owned and operated by an individual company.

The Hamiltons were especially interested in tobacco. They promoted and financed its cultivation, and at the same time they arranged for its export in their own wagons and carts. The owner of a ferry in Halifax reported that he received more fees for ferrying from the Hamiltons than from any other merchant in the colony, and many of these fees were probably paid by tobacco-carrying wagons en route to Virginia.

There were other stores, although probably none was larger than that of the Hamiltons'. The Glasgow firm of Buchanans, Hastie, and Company had four stores in the colony, only one of which was apparently in a town, and at least one other store was located in Virginia.[130] Another Glasgow firm, that of John Alston, also had stores in North Carolina.[131] Additional country stores were scattered here and there in the colony.[132]

The record relating to all of them is fragmentary and scarcely warrants any but the most tentative generalizations. Stores were apparently somewhat more common in the northern half of the colony, perhaps because of the predominance in the store trade of Scottish merchants operating out of Virginia, or perhaps simply because of the slightly greater density of population in the north. Their location and business were related to overland transportation and the increasing use being made of roads. Stores seem to have become more numerous during the third quarter of the eighteenth century, which suggests that they were not entirely ephemeral phenomena, destined to disappear as soon as towns emerged, but were rather tributary merchandising sites, taking their place besides towns in the constantly expanding mercantile network that was blanketing the colony.

A less important form of decentralized merchandising was carried on by itinerant salesmen, who sold imported goods and in return took farm products. Since their activities were carried on by visits, and not through stores, they left almost no trace of their business operations. The Moravians were the only persons who have left even a mention of the visits of these traveling salesmen.[133] But Governor Dobbs, in a letter to the Board of Trade in 1763, noted with some concern the effect that their operations had on the trade of North Carolina. He told the board that he could not estimate the amount of British manufactured goods imported into the colony because most of it came in overland from Virginia and that ". . . from the number of Factors from that Colony dispersed through the Province it must greatly exceed the Import into any of our sea ports. The Quantity from South Carolina by Land is much smaller."[134] Settlers in the backcountry were also buying rum from Virginia, which led about a dozen North Carolina merchants to petition the governor for lower import duties on it so that they might better be able to compete with this indirect trade.[135]

The lack of information on the mechanics of trade in general, and on decentralized merchandising in particular, is unfortunate, for the relationship between trade and urban growth was a complex one. Contracts for trade were often neither made nor arranged in urban centers. Thus, factors and itinerant salesmen operated with no permanent business sites, urban or otherwise. The periodic get-togethers at meetings of county courts must also have been the occasion for the making of many business arrangements,[136] yet the couple of buildings around the courthouse scarcely represented an urban center for most of the year. Country stores disposed of more trade. Furthermore, the actual handling and carriage of goods may sometimes have had little to do with the urban centers within the colony, in so far as the goods were directed instead to ports, warehouses, and landings in Virginia.[187]

Hence, the making of the contracts on which trade was based and the actual movement of goods sometimes had no urban locus and contributed nothing to the growth of towns in North Carolina. Rural settlement in the colony expanded, the backcountry developed, commercial and economic life became more complex —but these changes were not necessarily accompanied by urban growth. Because of the degree of disassociation between urbanism and trade, the small number and size of the urban centers within the colony are misleading measures of its actual level of economic development.

This analysis of urban settlements and decentralized trade inevitably leaves unanswered questions. With regard to decentralized trade, for example, it would be important to know to what extent it was characterized by notable regional variations? Did it vary in incidence from one item of trade to another? Or were the major contrasts in terms of import versus export trade? Were conditions in North Carolina similar to or different from those in South Carolina and Virginia? When after the colonial period did decentralized merchandising begin to decline? And what forces led to its decline?

The single most important unanswered question with regard to urban settlements concerns the role of entrepreneurs. To what extent was differential urban growth a response to the actions of individual traders, promoters, or speculators? Perhaps too much weight has been attached here to the role of other, more tangible factors.

In any event, it is possible to make some summary generalizations concerning urban growth, with particular reference to relations between the coast and the interior. Implicit in the above account of three types of urban center is the fact that population increase in the third quarter of the eighteenth century had important consequences in terms of urban growth in the colony. Some of the pre-existing towns became more important, others declined. New towns emerged, even in the most recently settled areas and on the fringes of the occupied territory.

In turn, urban growth influenced rural activities. In their role as trade centers, urban settlements induced and facilitated changes in the areas they served. All were small, but their inhabitants performed important functions for farmers who had access to them.

Urban development was not uniform throughout the colony. Uneven growth was most evident along the coast, where three major port towns had eclipsed their rivals by the end of the colonial period. The three major ones, Edenton, New Bern, and Wilmington, were themselves by then showing evidence of differential growth rates, reflecting marked differences in the kind and extent of their trade hinterlands. Some of the backcountry trade was still moving to South Carolina and Virginia in 1775, but much was falling into the hands of merchants in Cross Creek and Wilmington, thereby promoting the rising importance of these two towns. The Moravians were trading through these Cape Fear Valley centers, and Scottish and Scotch-Irish merchants were successfully making of the valley a major thoroughfare of commerce to and from the west. The Moravians and Scottish merchants even seem to have joined forces in promoting this commerce.[138]

Edenton did not gain much of the backcountry trade, which was probably a major factor in its decline relative to Wilmington during the last few years of the period. New Bern was prospering for a somewhat different reason. Its intermediate location had something to do with its selection as the capital, and that it grew while Edenton did not was probably less a consequence of trade ties with the west than a reflection of the added importance attaching to any town of such political status.

For many years, various writers have linked the growth of towns along the Atlantic Seaboard to the fall line. It is therefore worth emphasizing that in fact there were no urban centers in the colony of North Carolina at any point along the fall line. The midland towns lay closest to this line, but they can scarcely be described as fall-line towns, since they were all located east of it, and neither their origin nor their subsequent development owed anything to it. Breaks in navigability may have had something to do with the growth of Halifax, Tarboro, and possibly Campbelltown, but the breaks involved were not those occasioned by falls.[139]

The colony of North Carolina was one of the least urbanized of all the colonies. In the mid-twentieth century the state of North Carolina is one of the least urbanized in the United States. But there is no warrant for interpreting this similarity as a holdover from the eighteenth to the twentieth century. Certainly, there is a modern parallel to decentralized merchandising, insofar as another kind of economic activity, manufacturing, is now notably rural and dispersed through the state. The parallelism is striking, but fortuitous. The two kinds of dispersion did not stem from a single cause, so that the low degree of urbanization then and now cannot be equated.

In another respect, urbanism in twentieth-century North Carolina shows remarkably little resemblance to conditions in the colony. The largest urban centers in the state are in the former colonial backcountry, while the easternmost part of the state is now the least urbanized section. A few of the colonial urban centers are still important. But most of them are not. Soon after the colonial period they subsided into a placid insignificance from which they are only now being rescued by the zealous efforts of restoration committees.

CHAPTER VIII · CONCLUSION

The previous chapters are an attempt to begin a study of the colonial Seaboard by analyzing the geography of a segment of it. In conclusion, a few generalizations and comments are offered. These concluding remarks concern the source materials used, the underlying factors responsible for geographical changes, regional differences within the colony and between the colony and its neighbors, and, finally, a retrospective view of eighteenth-century North Carolina.

SOURCE MATERIALS

The most serious drawback encountered when using colonial source materials for geographical purposes is the fragmentary and nonquantitative nature of much of the record. To remedy the deficiency as much as possible, the wealth of verbal descriptions found in official correspondence, in private diaries and letters, in travel accounts, and in various similar sources was exploited systematically. These materials were used in conjunction, so that the more unreliable descriptions could be sifted out. Travel accounts, for example, are sometimes deceptive. Too many travelers dwelt upon the bizarre and atypical, and hence their reports must be checked against one another, as well as against other sources.

The strong emphasis placed upon analysis of commodity production was partly dictated by the fact that the only systematically compiled data relevant to the changing economic geography of the colony are export figures. But in dealing with North Carolina or any other colony the commodity approach, admittedly old-fashioned, is entirely appropriate, because economic development was largely a matter of increasing primary production. Such considerations pointed to the advisability of placing emphasis upon production from forests and fields.

One means of partially closing the broad gap left by the general absence of statistics of the kind gathered in modern censuses is provided by inventories of estates. A systematic tabulation of all inventories for selected counties would be a profitable sampling procedure in future work on other colonies. Local records as a whole constitute a valuable corpus of material for the colonial period. The use made of them here was not exhaustive but perhaps it has demonstrated the role they must play in any future interpretation of the geography of the colonial Seaboard.

Important questions remain unanswered but some of them at least may be resolved by future work on South Carolina and Virginia materials. North Carolina records, for example, furnish little information on merchandising and decentralized trade within the colony. But in view of the ties between North Carolina and its neighbors to the north and south, records of Virginia and South Carolina merchants probably contain much that is pertinent to the study of North Carolina. Use of such material will lead to a better understanding of the complex relationships between decentralized trade and urban development in colonial North Carolina.

Despite gaps and unanswered questions, enough has been presented to show that the geography of the colonial Seaboard need not remain unstudied for lack of source materials. It is equally evident that the existing material is difficult to use. The nature of the contemporary record, often fragmentary, rarely quantitative, and ambiguous more often than not, does place many obstacles in the way of any study of colonial geography. But intractable sources are nothing new.

CAUSES OF CHANGES

The most basic factor causing changes in the colony's geography was the large-scale influx of migrants. This event had a deep impact over a wide range of activities. The rapid expansion of the settled area, the increasing densities in regions settled earlier, the multiplication of farms, and the expanded production from field and forest—changes such as these were all induced by the incoming stream of settlers. The resulting economic development was characterized by increases in the area devoted to primary economic activities, and the provision of an enlarged range of increasingly important tertiary activities. Secondary activities, mining and manufacturing, were notable chiefly for their absence.

Cultural differences among the settlers were of some significance in determining variations in the rate and direction of changes. The most obvious illustration is the Moravians, who systematically converted a small section of the wilderness into a productive, tightly organized, economic unit and demonstrated the rapidity with which commercial modes of agriculture could be established on the frontier of settlement. Frontier conditions and the availability of abundant land did not lead them to reject their familiar farming practices. On the contrary, the Moravians farmed as intensively and as methodically as if they were cultivating scarce acres in a densely settled peasant countryside of Europe.

Cultural differences may have been responsible for other variations. Because of the lack of quantitative information on farm holdings, the more subtle variations from place to place may have escaped unobserved. That there were some is at least suggested by the evidence found for one such variation, the emphasis placed by the Scottish Highlanders on cattle raising.

Other kinds of differences among the settlers were also reflected in the development of the colony. As significant as the role of the Moravians, though less striking because its effects were not so concentrated in one place, was the role of Scottish merchants. In seeking to expand the business profits of the firms they represented, they promoted the commercial production of crops such as wheat and tobacco by making sure that farmers had the means to produce a surplus and the markets in which to sell it.

Differences in terms of wealth, too, were a significant factor. They were most notable in the distinctive features bestowed on the lower Cape Fear country by the special group who settled it. Men of wealth and substance got a firm hold on large parcels of land in this region during the initial stage of occupation and subsequently applied large-scale capitalist methods to exploit the forests and soils. Their expansive estates gave a unique character to the Cape Fear region.

While there were no technological innovations to initiate widespread changes in economic activities, the increased use of available technology sufficed to stimulate economic growth and change. Thus, for example, increased use was made of roads. Large numbers of people came into the colony by road, and a rudimentary internal network of pathways was developed. Water transportation became relatively less important as more and more commodities moved in carts and wagons. The administrative framework utilized in making provisions for transportation facilities remained basically unchanged, so that material progress was not associated with either technical or administrative innovations in the field of transportation. Similarly, agriculture in the colony became increasingly oriented to market conditions, and crop patterns and distributions changed although farming was not marked by any significant technical advances. It is perhaps because these elements of drama were lacking that there has been a tendency in the past to overlook the importance of road transportation, and to regard agriculture in colonial North Carolina as being part of an unchanging and uniformly distributed subsistence economy.

Other factors responsible for change included those processes invariably found in all newly settled territories, such as the clearing of woodland and the extension of cultivated land. Even in those areas receiving fewest of the incoming settlers and remaining relatively empty, the widespread and frequent use of fire to create and maintain open grazing land helped to transform the wild landscape.

To sum up the geographical consequences of this variety of factors by resorting to a generalized scheme of frontier stages is impossible. The traditional view of the frontier as a series of westward migrating zones, each representing a different stage in development, scarcely bears any resemblance to the progress of settlement in colonial North Carolina. There was no such zonal and successional pattern of development. To take but three examples: the western part of the colony was settled mainly from the north rather than the east; urban settlements developed alongside the first rural settlements (in the Moravian tract the first western settlement was as much urban as it was rural); and cattle raising was most important in the east, not a preliminary to

CONCLUSION   177

pioneer farming either in the east or the west. The generalized scheme seems to apply neither to the colony as a whole nor to any one section of it.

REGIONS

The presence of regional differences within colonial North Carolina has long been recognized, as in the distinction commonly made between the eastern and western sections. Such criteria as the circumstances of settlement in the two areas, the incidence of slaveholding, the relative importance of forest utilization, the emphasis on particular crops, and the kind and number of urban places, can be used to differentiate the one section from the other. But two consequences of this generalized view of regional contrast are less acceptable: first, the underlying assumption of homogeneity in each one of the two sections; and secondly, the use of the "fall line" as a line of demarcation between them.

The first of these two consequences, the assumption of homogeneity, is apparently more valid for the west than the east. Contrasts within the west were, on the whole, of a minor order when compared with the broad distinction between it and the east. Possibly, however, the semblance of uniformity rests on nothing more than the lack of detailed information in the record, which is notably less informative with regard to the west.

Within the east there were certainly major variations from place to place. From north to south, this section embraced the most densely settled portion of the colony (north of Albemarle Sound), the emptiest area (between Albemarle and Pamlico Sounds), and the region within which the plantation unit of occupancy was most common (the lower Cape Fear). Although slavery was everywhere more important than in the west, the type of slaveholding household showed considerable variation in the east. There were differences in farming and forest utilization, contrasts which were expressed in the dissimilar export trade of Ports Roanoke and Brunswick. There were also variations from east to west within the eastern half of the colony, as, for example, with respect to tobacco growing and types of urban settlement. The east can scarcely be regarded as a homogeneous section.

The second consequence of the generalized view of regional contrast, the use of the fall line as a boundary of demarcation between east and west, has been a source of considerable confusion. That there was and is no one single line boundary between east and west should be obvious. There were as many boundaries as there were differentiating criteria, and all of them were more or less diffuse zones rather than lines.

In the last century the term fall line has come to be widely used with a variety of additional connotations, in the writings of both geographers and historians. Usage of the term in a general way to indicate the lithologic boundary between Coastal Plain and Piedmont is imprecise, because falls are actually farther upstream than the lithologic boundary. To assume, as is frequently done, that the line has other and related implications is more misleading. Topographic expression of the actual lithologic boundary is often lacking in North Carolina, and when present generally amounts to no more than a slight break in slope, barely perceptible on the ground. Nor are topographic contrasts in regions on either side of the line particularly significant: the Sandhills of the Coastal Plain are in many respects more like the Piedmont than the remainder of the Coastal Plain.

Certainly the lithologic boundary is often coincidental with an edaphic change. But so too are all such boundaries, and the soil contrasts on either side of this one are not notably more important than are those on either side of most other lithologic boundaries in the southern Seaboard. Furthermore, as far as colonial occupance was concerned, soil drainage conditions were more significant than soil composition. For eighteenth-century farmers, differences between the Inner and Outer Coastal Plain were more meaningful than those between the Inner Coastal Plain and the Piedmont.

Finally with respect to the fall line, and perhaps most important, is that much functional significance has been attached to the falls occurring on rivers not far from the point where they cross the lithologic boundary. As often as not such "falls" are really rapids, but the source of power in the falling water and the obstruction to navigability have been interpreted as prime factors in urban growth at fall-line sites. Admittedly, it is impossible to generalize on the basis of circumstances in colonial North Carolina. But the notable lack of any urban developments in

CONCLUSION   179

the colony at fall-line sites at least demonstrates that they were not universally important and suggests that perhaps they were also unimportant elsewhere along the Seaboard.

A few general contrasts between North Carolina and the adjacent colonies of Virginia and South Carolina are worth noting. The distinctiveness of North Carolina was evident in the concentration upon the production of naval stores and wood products, the comparatively low proportion of nonwhite inhabitants, the very small number of wealthy and extensive plantation units, and the nonreciprocal dependence of North Carolinians upon Virginia and South Carolina trade outlets. There were considerable differences in the process of settlement in the three colonies even though they all felt the impact of large numbers of migrants flocking in from farther north. There was nothing in North Carolina comparable to the deliberate and organized planting of townships of homogeneous cultural communities in South Carolina; nor was there a primate metropolis such as Charleston to serve as a focal point for the economic life of the colony. There was no large-scale westward movement of planters in North Carolina like that which took place in Virginia and which apparently diffused a certain amount of uniformity (in slaveholding and agriculture) from east to west across the Dominion. When the colonial geographies of Virginia and South Carolina have been subjected to study, a better understanding of the meaning and consequences of these differences should emerge.

RETROSPECT

Viewed in retrospect, the geography of the colony acquires added meaning. Although the subsequent settlement and development of the state of North Carolina has obliterated or transformed some elements of the earlier scene, other elements have persisted.

Among the colonial features that left an abiding imprint, the most widespread was the system of surveying according to metes and bounds. The haphazard arrangement of fields and farms that resulted is still characteristic of much of the state's rural landscape. The present urban scene also owes something to the colonial phase, since most of the earlier towns and villages have survived into the twentieth century, even if their size and importance have fluctuated.

As agricultural developments in the nineteenth century resulted in the introduction of new commercial crops, rice and indigo were abandoned, and the role of wheat became relatively less important. Tobacco, on the other hand, became much more valuable, and North Carolina eclipsed Virginia and Maryland in becoming the leading tobacco producing state in the country. The early staples, corn and swine, are still rural mainstays.

Some trends characteristic of the colonial period were subsequently reversed. The flow of migrants into North Carolina dwindled to a trickle in the nineteenth century, as the southern United States became the part of the country that held least attraction for incoming Europeans. The vision of the fertile western part of the colony that brought so many newcomers was subsequently transferred to the other side of the Appalachians, and the image of fabulous western acres soon became a traditional part of the mystique governing the settlement of the lands beyond the Mississippi.

For long, economic development remained a matter of increasing primary production and expanding trade. When manufacturing finally became important its emergence had two almost paradoxical consequences. First, much of the manufacturing in the state is nonurban in location, more so than in any other state. In the Piedmont, where most of it is carried on, there are no large urban centers (Charlotte, with about 270,000 persons in the standard metropolitan statistical area in 1960, is the largest), and few owe much of their growth to manufacturing. If the proportion of the employed population engaged in manufacturing is taken as a measure of industrial importance, North Carolina is about the fifteenth most industrial state in the country. But with less than 40 per cent of its population living in urban centers, it is also the seventh most rural state.

Secondly, the capital and employment opportunities that manufacturing brought in its wake were largely concentrated in what had been the western and least developed part of the colony. As a result, it is now the eastern part that is relatively underdeveloped, often isolated, and the section where rural poverty is

CONCLUSION 181

most common. Colonial conditions have been reversed. Perhaps it is not unduly straining the meaning of that term to call the easternmost part of the state the frontier section.

To place eighteenth-century North Carolina in a satisfactory perspective would require both an intensive study of the rest of the South during the same period and a similar study of developments in the state during the years that have elapsed since independence was achieved. Since the former represents the greater unknown, and since the material presented here has shown that colonial geography can be reconstructed, what is now needed most would seem to be an interpretation of conditions in other Southern colonies. This study meanwhile represents a preliminary step towards a better understanding of the geography of the thirteen colonies.

APPENDICES

APPENDIX I · FIRE AND OPEN LAND

Nowhere in North America has fire been a more persistent agent of alteration than in the Southeast. Its pervasive role in this region has been acknowledged but few attempts have been made to identify and locate the several kinds of open land created in historic time as a result of former burning practices.[1] While carrying out the research for this study of colonial North Carolina an attempt was made to find out whether a better understanding could be gained of the role man played in creating open land in a portion of the Southeast.

With this end in view, several different kinds of evidence were used.[2] Recent botanical literature dealing with the effects of fire on vegetation was studied, pertinent references encountered in the historical record were noted, and time was spent in field work in an effort to throw more light upon some of the questions that arose. The findings of such work are summarized in this appendix. The conclusions offered are not comprehensive, nor are most of them anything more than tentative.

The burning of vegetation was common in colonial North Carolina. Some fires were probably started accidentally and these could have been very destructive. Even though much of North Carolina has an average annual precipitation of between forty-five and fifty-five inches, the fire menace is a serious one. Conditions contributing to this danger include the dry spells that occur almost every year,[3] the generally high rates of evaporation, the very rapid downward percolation of rainwater falling on the large areas of sandy soils in the Coastal Plain, and the highly combustible nature of the peat soils of the Coastal Plain when the water table is relatively low. Thus, any fires initiated accidentally could have taken considerable toll of the vegetation cover.

Other fires were started deliberately. Settlers burned the cover regularly for a variety of purposes, among which were tick eradication, the improvement of pasturage, and clearing.[4] There may even have been an early law obliging colonists to burn the ground once a year;[5] not until 1777 was any legislation passed prohibiting deliberate burning, and even this proved ineffective.[6]

One of the most dramatic consequences of regular burning was the creation and maintenance of more or less open areas in localities that would otherwise have been forest covered. They were of several kinds. The most open kind were called "savannahs" or "savannah land."

Some writers who used the term savannah in eighteenth-century North Carolina[7] attempted to define it for the benefit of their readers. Their definitions, though often brief and sometimes little more than parenthetical asides, show a measure of agreement: a savannah was a flat, seasonally wet area, covered with grass, and distinguished from the surrounding area by a remarkable lack of trees.[8] One official claimed that there were "millions of acres" of savannah land in North Carolina in the early 1730's,[9] but his casual estimate seems to be an exaggeration. This kind of land was largely restricted to one section of the colony. A few travelers refer to savannahs in the Piedmont portion, but most of them used the word for features they observed in the Coastal Plain;[10] and local records show that while the term savannah was frequently employed for features in Coastal Plain localities, it was very rarely used in more interior areas.[11]

Nearly forty years ago, one savannah in North Carolina was subjected to careful analysis by two botanists, Wells and Shunk.[12] The one they studied was the Burgaw Savannah, or Big Savannah as it was also called. The site covered about 1,600 acres, lying between 50 and 60 feet above sea level, and was located near Burgaw, a county seat about 25 miles north of Wilmington. This savannah was a flat, treeless area, surrounded by pine woods, with peripheral, thin swamp forests along the few small streams flowing outwards from the area. The water table was generally at or close to the surface, but fell as much as several feet at

APPENDICES 187

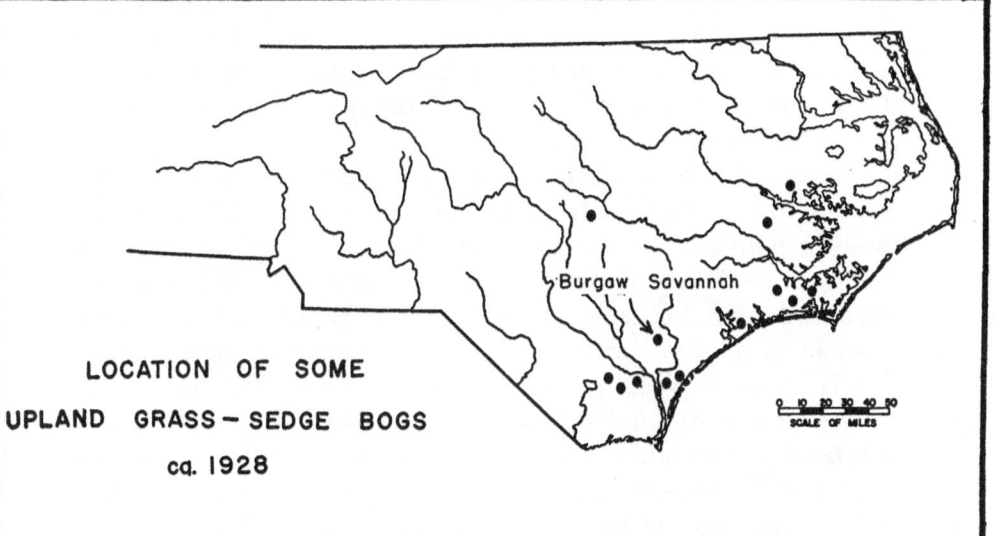

FIG. 43

times of drought. It was really an upland grass-sedge bog, for the surface carried a thick, close cover of grasses, sedges, and herbs.[13]

When the study of the Burgaw Savannah was undertaken, in the late 1920's, it was then the largest single site still bearing the name savannah. Fig. 43 shows its location, together with the location of other large savannahs still in existence at that time— on the map they are given their more precise name and called upland grass-sedge bogs.[14] The most notable feature of their distribution then was the concentration in the Coastal Plain, chiefly the outer section of it, a location that conforms in general terms with that indicated by references to savannahs in the colonial record.

Wells and Shunk found evidence indicating that the savannah owed its origin and persistence to regular burning. The perennial herbs and grasses survived the fires (their underground stems being protected by the sandy soils), while their competitors, the shade-making shrubs and pines, did not. This was substantially the same conclusion that John Bartram, a naturalist who visited the Coastal Plain of North Carolina in the 1760's, arrived at with reference to all savannahs: "ye bay swamps when fired in very dry weather burns furiously, which kills all, both trees and shrubs; which being often repeated turns it to Savana ground, producing much coarse grass. . . ."[15]

Savannah land was thus essentially a man-made phenomenon, created and maintained by deliberate burning.[16] The identity of those responsible for the burning is not recorded in any documents, but farmers living in North Carolina can recall who they were and why the burning was done.[17] While the high water table in savannahs during much of the year long deterred anyone from attempting to utilize them for growing crops, their grasses were a useful local resource. As long as savannahs were unfenced and uncultivated they were used, on a community basis, as sources of hay and as grazing land by those settled on near-by farms. The farmers set fire to the savannahs regularly in order to encourage the growth of the grass and to keep down tick infestation.

Possibly, savannah land attained its maximum extent before the end of the eighteenth century, while burning was widespread and the proportion of land in cultivation was still relatively low. There was still some savannah land left throughout the nineteenth century.[18] But by the mid-twentieth century it had largely disappeared (and authorities interested in preserving some of the distinctive flora and fauna associated with savannah land are currently finding it difficult to locate a specimen of this kind of land).[19] There seem to be two main factors causing its disappearance.

One is the declining incidence of deliberate burning, a decline which has been most marked during the past few decades. It in turn is a consequence of the ending of the free-range era (as stock law was finally extended over all of the eastern portion of the state)[20] and the introduction of stringent prohibitions against the use of fire (as conservation practices became common). With the greatly reduced incidence of burning, savannah land became rarer, much of it reverting naturally to a shrub or woodland cover.

The second factor is land reclamation. The fate of the Burgaw

Savannah exemplifies this factor. By the spring of 1960, the savannah had almost disappeared, much of it having been converted into cultivated land during the late 1950's. Large-scale farming operations and investment in extremely deep drainage ditches, together with heavy applications of fertilizer, had made economically feasible the cultivation of land formerly regarded as being uncultivatable and fit only for burning and grazing. Other savannah land was probably reclaimed in the same way.

A small portion of the Burgaw Savannah still remained uncultivated in 1960, and this remnant illustrated the effects of decreased fire incidence. Shrubs were beginning to assume dominance and it was ceasing to be primarily a grassland complex. This remnant may have been converted into fields since 1960. But even if it has not, if left unburned it will presumably revert to another kind of vegetation cover.

Savannah land was not the only type of open land created by the colonists. Evergreen shrub bogs were the most important of the other kinds of open cover and were probably even more in evidence during the colonial period than were the savannahs. Unlike the savannahs, evergreen shrub bogs occur on both mineral and peat soils. They now cover a much larger acreage than savannah land and are a somewhat less sharply defined type of vegetation cover, merging on their margins into a variety of other types. But both types of cover are fire maintained and occur mainly in the Outer Coastal Plain.[21]

Evergreen shrub bogs occur on flat interstream areas. An inch or two of standing water is often present at the surface, though the sites become quite dry during droughty periods. They are covered with a dense mass of shrubs and occasional scattered pond pines (*Pinus rigida* var. *serotina*). The evergreen shrub bogs vary greatly in size. It has been estimated that four-fifths of Holly Shelter Bay (the center of which is about 20 miles northwest of Wilmington), or about 35,000 to 40,000 acres, is one vast shrub bog;[22] at the other extreme are the Carolina Bays, many of which are occupied by this cover type, and the largest diameters of these are often less than one mile.

During the colonial period there was no one term reserved for such areas. Nor were the various appellations used to refer to shrub bogs always employed exclusively for this type of vegetation cover. "Pocosins," "bays," "open ground," "dismal swamps," "laurel swamps," and "laurel thickets" all seem to have been used to denote what were evergreen shrub bogs, as well as, on occasions, to refer to other types of cover.[23] Although the first two of these names, pocosin and bay, have come to be used more and more for shrub bogs in the nineteenth and twentieth centuries, there is still nothing approaching universal acceptance of this usage.

Botanists have shown that these shrub bogs are a result of regular and frequent burning and that variations in the characteristics of the vegetation within shrub bogs, or from one shrub bog to another, are largely caused by differences in fire frequency and intensity.[24] They have also suggested that when frequent fires occur on sandy areas, or on former peat areas where the peat has been burned off, the savannah complex tends slowly to displace the shrub bog community.[25] The successional relationships are imperfectly understood, but it is evident that the evergreen shrub bogs were once forested and that, if burning were to cease, the shrub cover would eventually be replaced by forest.[26]

The vegetation cover type labeled "pond pine–pocosin" on Fig. 44 corresponds roughly to the evergreen shrub bog type. On the original base map[27] from which Fig. 44 was compiled, pond pine–pocosin was defined as being "generally associated with the Carolina Bays in eastern North Carolina" and a note was added to the effect that it "chiefly consists of pond pine, cyrilla, wax myrtle, and other pocosin shrubs." The category included areas with stands of pond pine, so that the distribution shown is in fact more extensive than the actual area of shrub bog. But since there are no large blocks of shrub bog outside the area mapped as pond pine–pocosin, the distribution does give an impression of the general location of the shrub bogs about twenty years ago.

The predominance of the shrub bog cover in the more easterly section of the Coastal Plain is demonstrated by Fig. 44, despite undoubted imperfections in the presumed correspondence. The documentary evidence concerning the eighteenth-century distribution is not very conclusive, owing to the inconsistency in the usage of terms for shrub bogs. But the former occurrence was

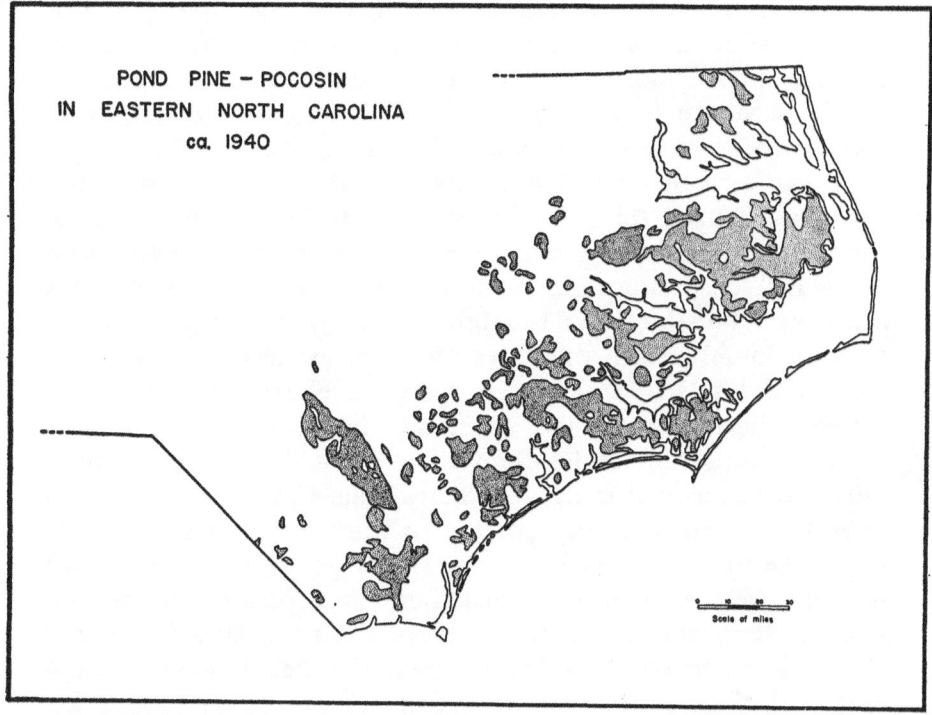

FIG. 44

probably not very different, judging at least from the colonial travel accounts and local records that are of some help.[28]

Evergreen shrub bogs and upland grass-sedge bogs were thus two types of open cover which, taken together, must have occupied a considerable portion of the total area of the Outer Coastal Plain. There were perhaps other kinds in the same region. "Meadows," for example, once existed in Onslow County. The term was used in colonial land grants for several sites in the county, and at least two localities, Starretts Meadows and Lloyds Meadows, still bore the name early in the twentieth century.[29] It is possible, however, that "meadows" was merely an alternative term for either shrub bog or savannah, rather than a name assigned to a quite distinctive type of open ground.

There is much less evidence relating to the colonial vegetation of the Piedmont than there is for the Coastal Plain. The historical record is much less useful, because the western region was settled later and for long was less frequently traversed and described. Furthermore, there are almost no botanical studies that can be used as a basis for reconstructing the details of the floral diversity of the Piedmont in the eighteenth century.

It can at least be said that there was some open land in the Piedmont during the colonial period. During the first half of the nineteenth century there was a tradition to the effect that there had been much open land in the west in the previous century.[30] This tradition is substantiated by scattered references in the colonial record, which testify to the existence of open land of several kinds in the western parts of North Carolina[31] and which indicate that the tree cover was thin in places.[32]

The proportion of fire-induced open land in the Piedmont must have remained much less than in the Coastal Plain, simply because burning was less common in the west during the eighteenth century. For at least a generation before colonists moved into the west in large numbers, there were present in the east many settlers who deliberately burned the vegetation for several purposes and set off other fires accidentally; their increasing numbers in the east, as well as the augmented scale of tar production there, were probably making accidental fires an increasingly common occurrence.[33] Furthermore, the existence of sand hills, sandy ridges, and extensive peat areas tended to make all fires more destructive in the Coastal Plain. Thus, both deliberate and accidental burning would have been more potent forces in the east than in the west during much of the colonial period.

There is a traditional view of the settler of Anglo-Saxon England as the "grey-haired enemy of the wood." The tradition is well founded, for the Angles, Saxons, and Jutes settled upon an island that was almost completely covered with forests. But the essentially similar traditional view that developed in the New World, to the effect that the first settlers in North America encountered a stubborn, forested world, stretching from Maine to Alabama, was much less securely founded and has been jettisoned in recent years.

In refuting this notion, great emphasis has been laid upon

the role of fire in the Indian economy and the effect of their fires upon the vegetation.[34] It is worth emphasizing therefore that in those areas, such as eastern North Carolina, where the white settlers displaced Indians the former quickly proved to be far more efficient than the latter in creating and maintaining open land. Rostlund's conclusion, stated with reference to the Old Southeast, that, "The maximum of cleared land was probably reached at some time before contact was made between the Indians and the Europeans, and thereafter, because the Indians were displaced from many regions and their frequent burning of the vegetation ceased, the area of cleared land diminished and the forested part increased"[35] would scarcely seem to apply in North Carolina. Indian openings were probably seized upon immediately by the European settlers and cultivated or regularly burned in order to improve the pasturage; and, at the same time, the settlers deliberately employed fire regularly and frequently to create and maintain new openings in the areas around their settlements. Thus, following immediately upon the Indians, came groups of settlers, more numerous than their precursors, originating fires more systematically over larger areas and doubtless being responsible also for a greater amount of accidental burning.

The whole subject of the effects of fire upon vegetation has only recently been given much attention and most conclusions are still tentative. As far as the colonial Seaboard is concerned, the bulk of the work remains to be done, especially the relating of information derived from the historical record to the studies and results of experiments carried out by botanists. Inevitably in such work, one is led into the detailed consideration, often species by species, of small areas. But the result is a better understanding of the vegetation cover that existed, or was created, in the colonial period.

APPENDIX II · DATA: TECHNIQUES AND SOURCES

North Carolina was one of the colonies in which no population census was carried out earlier than the first national census of 1790. This deficiency is bound to be a serious handicap in any analysis of the geography of the colony. Nevertheless, there are data on the numbers and distribution of people in North Carolina during the third quarter of the eighteenth century. These data are described in this appendix, their shortcomings are analyzed, and the procedures employed in tabulating and recording them are noted. Included at the end of the appendix is a briefer consideration of a better-known and more widely used source of colonial statistics, Customs 16/1.

POPULATION DATA

Most of the extant evidence that bears on the numbers and distribution of people in colonial North Carolina originated as a by-product of the system of taxation. Most colonists had to pay taxes for themselves and for their dependents. In an effort to make sure that the money due was actually paid, local officials drew up lists of everyone subject to taxation. These lists were compiled on a county basis.

"Taxables" were first defined in an act of 1715. The act stipulated that, ". . . all Males not being Slaves in this Government [of North Carolina] shall be Tythable at the Age of Sixteen Years And All Slaves Male or Female, either Imported or born in the Country shall be Tythable at the Age of Twelve Years."[1] Eight years later the act was amended slightly, in order to include all free Negroes, mulattoes, and persons of mixed blood over the age of twelve, both male and female.[2] Thus modified, the definition was the basis of the poll tax and remained unchanged until 1777.

Throughout all of the period under study taxables were therefore defined according to uniform criteria.

The annual duty of drawing up lists of taxables and collecting taxes fell to authorities in the individual counties. The tasks were not carried out very efficiently as a rule. Governor Dobbs, writing to the Board of Trade in 1755, noted with reference to the returns of taxables that "the returns are less than the Truth as all the Laws had been neglected and not put in execution. . . ."[3] They did not improve with the years, and Governor Martin, writing to Secretary Hillsborough in 1772, added a postscript to his letter: "The Lists of Taxables have been heretofore extremely erroneous by which your Lordship, the Governor and the Public have been imposed upon, of this I have lately obtained full proof."[4] He laid the blame for the errors upon the negligence and infidelity of the magistrates and county clerks. Although he assured the secretary that he would set about remedying the abuses there is no evidence that he attempted to do so.

Techniques—It is not possible to say precisely how accurate the returns of taxables were, but it is reasonable to assume that they understate the actual numbers of taxables and that the understatement is most pronounced in the western counties. The tax was frequently resented, particularly in the more recently settled areas of the west, and some of those who should have paid taxes probably successfully avoided being placed on the lists. It is also probable that the inefficiency of the system and the dishonesty of some collectors further reduced the numbers actually presented on the returns. And the whole system must have been more unsatisfactory in the west, where the administrative machinery ran less smoothly and the population was most mobile. Nor would the inevitable understatement of numbers have been counterbalanced by any boosting of the figures in the opposite direction; "padding" of the lists could rarely have been possible, for the appropriate amount collected from each recorded taxable was to be handed over with each list.

The relationship between the number of taxables and the total number of inhabitants is of critical importance. This problem has been tackled in the past by several students of colonial population. Greene and Harrington estimated that the taxables in the Southern colonies represented about a third of the total population.[5] They arrived at this ratio on the basis of the definition of taxables in Virginia and then applied it to all the Southern colonies even though the definition in Virginia was somewhat different from that which applied in North Carolina. (In Virginia, taxables comprised white males of eighteen and over, and Negro males and females of sixteen and over.) Friis followed the same method.[6] Sutherland estimated that it was necessary to subtract one-sixth of the total taxables in North Carolina, and then multiply by five, in order to arrive at the total population in the colony;[7] her reasons for this procedure are not apparent from the text.

In view of the impossibility of devising a precise conversion ratio, a rule-of-thumb method has to be used. Governor Dobbs believed that there were four times as many white inhabitants in North Carolina as there were white male taxables and consistently used a four-to-one ratio in calculating the number of white inhabitants.[8] Using this rule for whites as a guide, and allowing for the fact that Negro taxables must have represented about twice as high a proportion of the total Negro population (as compared with the proportion that white taxables represented of the total white population),[9] a ratio of one taxable to two inhabitants might not be too inaccurate for calculating the number of Negro inhabitants. If there were in the colony as many white inhabitants as there were Negro inhabitants, then the total population (white and Negro) could be obtained by multiplying the total number of taxables (white and Negro) by three (a simple average of the two ratios, 1:2 and 1:4). But throughout the colonial period there were more white inhabitants than Negroes, and even in 1790 there were still about three whites to every Negro in North Carolina. Hence, in working out a combined ratio, allowance has to be made for the preponderance of whites. If the total number of taxables, both white and Negro, is multiplied by 3.5, the product should approximately equal the total number of inhabitants.[10]

This ratio, of 3.5 inhabitants to every one taxable, has been used from time to time in this study to estimate the total population of North Carolina. It is no more than a very rough and ready rule-of-thumb guide, and the assumptions upon which it rests contain several possible sources of error:

1. Governor Dobbs's view that there were four white inhabitants to every one white taxable may be inaccurate.

2. The inference that there were two Negro inhabitants to every one Negro taxable may be wrong.

3. The backward extrapolation from the 1790 Census data to the effect that between 1750 and 1775 there were always three whites to every Negro may be erroneous for any or all of these years.

In any event, there is no more precise way than this of estimating the total population from the total number of taxables.

At least as important as changes in the total population of North Carolina are changes in the number and distribution of population from county to county within the colony. Even if the ratio of 1:3.5 represents accurately the proportion of taxables to population in North Carolina as a whole, this ratio can not be applied to the figures for individual counties. From county to county, the taxables constituted a varying proportion of the total population, and the ratio required for converting taxables to population would therefore vary from county to county. This is indicated for example, by the great differences in the numbers of Negroes in different areas (see Figs. 30 and 31). By definition, the total number of taxables always included a larger proportion of the Negro population than of the white population. Thus, in counties having the largest proportions of Negroes, the total number of taxables comes closer to representing the actual total county population than it does in other counties.

Furthermore, even if one were to arrive at a ratio valid for a given county in a particular year, the ratio would not necessarily be valid for any other year, even for that one county. This is because the proportion of taxables to population probably did not remain constant from year to year. If, for example, the Negro population increased at a rate differing from the rate at which the white population increased, then the ratio required for converting total taxables to total population would have to be altered accordingly. And when the study is extended to more than one county, over a period of years, the potential sources of error are vastly increased.

There are obviously many limitations upon the use of data on taxables as a substitute for population figures when analyzing variations from county to county within North Carolina. In mapping population patterns on a county basis, it is safer to map taxables rather than total inhabitants. The assumption is, of course, that variations in the distribution of the former bears some resemblance to the latter. The most significant likely deviations from this presumed correspondence are as follows:

1. The westernmost areas should probably show denser concentrations of dots, whether representing taxables or presumed population (for reasons noted above, p. 195).

2. In those counties where Negroes constituted the highest proportions of the total taxables, the number of taxables comes closer to the actual total population than it does where Negroes formed much smaller proportions of the total taxables. Since the Negroes were numerically much more significant in the east, it is safe to assume that if maps of all inhabitants were substituted for the maps of taxables, then the westernmost areas would gain more in densities than the easternmost ones.

Thus, on all the maps of taxables, dot densities in the west are misleadingly low.

Sources—All the source materials from which data on taxables were obtained are specified elsewhere, either in footnotes or in the Bibliography. Since, however, it is sometimes not apparent from the titles of such references that they do contain data, it will be appropriate to identify the relevant sources here and to mention some of the special features of each.

Most useful of all are the extant compilations of tax returns. Of such lists, the most comprehensive in its coverage is the list given in a broadside entitled "North-Carolina. A Table of the Number of Taxables in this Province from the Year 1748 inclusive . . . to the Year 1770." This list, printed in 1771, was drawn up by John Burgwin as a part of an official investigation into the finances of North Carolina that was undertaken in 1769 in connection with the Regulator Movement.[11] The number of taxables are given for each county, but Negro and white taxables are not differentiated. The returns for the years 1748 through 1752, and for 1770, are very incomplete; for the other years that the table covers, 1753 through 1769, totals are lacking for only occasional counties. Totals for the colony as a whole are not given, but were obtained by simply adding up the figures for the individual counties, year by year from 1753 through 1769.

There are also available official lists of tax returns for the year 1754 through 1756 and 1765 through 1767.[12] Here, too, the figures are presented by county, and there are occasional gaps or evidently incomplete returns, as well as obvious mistakes of addition. The chief advantage that the official lists have over the broadside table is their presentation of separate totals for Negro and white taxables in most of the counties. The numbers given for the total taxables, both Negro and white, in each of the counties should be the same as those given in the broadside table for the corresponding years, at least if both sources were entirely accurate. They are not, but the differences were found to be minor. The figures for the three years 1754 through 1756 are in fact approximately the same in both sources; for the three years 1765 through 1767 they show greater discrepancies, although the figure given in the one source for the total population of the colony is never more than 11 per cent greater or smaller than the corresponding figure given in the other source. This fair degree of similarity may well be indicative of the essential reliability of both sources.

Further information concerning taxables for particular counties in certain years was found in manuscript tax lists and local records. These tax lists are the original tax returns that were made in the counties. Although not many of these have survived, those that have are especially valuable.[13] On each list, next to the names of heads of households, the number of taxables in that household is recorded, the taxables often being differentiated, by age, sex, or color. The lists are useful for several purposes: gaps in the two sources described above sometimes could be filled in from them, or errors detected and sometimes remedied, and the more complete tax lists yielded systematic quantitative information on the size of Negro holdings that could have been obtained nowhere else.

Local records furnished another kind of information, less valuable than the tax lists, but useful for amplifying and occasionally correcting the tax returns presented in the broadside table and in the official lists. Entries were sometimes made in the records of the county court minutes when tax lists or tax revenues were handed over from one local authority to another. The entry invariably consisted in a simple statement of the total number of persons liable to pay taxes in the year and county to which the minutes refer.[14]

Information on numbers of taxables was procured from two other sources. One of them, the "Tax Book of Northern District 1757-1775," records the total number of taxables in fourteen counties (all in the Granville District) in successive years beginning about 1762 and ending about 1772.[15] The other source also gives simply the total number of taxables, and covers eleven of these counties for a slightly earlier period, from 1755 to no later than 1761.[16] These two sources are thus complementary to a certain extent; and both add to the more comprehensive coverage provided by Burgwin's broadside table.

Finally, there are kinds of information best lumped together and labelled "miscellaneous." The most useful are estimates made by officials and others, at various times, of the population of North Carolina, or of specified segments of the population (such as whites, slaves, militia, as well as taxables). Some of these represent guesses, but others are attempts at careful estimations made by persons familiar with conditions in North Carolina. The more reasonable ones are helpful when used in conjunction with all the other sources.[17]

Figures from all of the above source materials were recorded and finally collated. The result was a series of twenty-six charts, one for each year from 1750 through 1775. On each of these charts was listed, by county and for North Carolina as a whole, the total number of taxables, and, where possible, these totals were differentiated into Negro and white taxables. When, as often happened, more than one figure was available for any county in a particular year, and these figures were not the same, then the average was worked out and recorded.[18] The tables have not been included here, to save space, and because presentation of them in cartographic form is more appropriate (see Figs. 24, 25, and 26). The chief deficiency of the final compilations should be noted: none of the source materials provided figures for a considerable number of counties for several years at both ends of the period 1750-75. The incompleteness of the tables for the years before 1753, and after 1770, is such that it was decided not to attempt mapping data for these years.

DATA ON EXPORTS

Customs 16/1 are a useful collection of data. They provide a comprehensive picture of colonial commerce and serve as a substitute for production figures. But the data have to be used with circumspection.

They are certainly no more reliable than twentieth-century trade statistics, and there is every reason to suspect that they may well be considerably less accurate. Although there is no way of testing their validity, it is possible to spot at least the larger errors of omission, by simply comparing year to year totals (see, for example, the apparent omission described in Chapter V, note 7, above). In addition to the over-all possibility of unreliability inherent in any such compilation of data, three limitations of Customs 16/1 became particularly evident when they were used to analyze the trade and production of North Carolina.

First, some of the exports from the colony were carried overland to Virginia and South Carolina before being shipped to markets overseas. Since these exports are credited to Virginia and South Carolina, the amounts given in Customs 16/1 for North Carolina represent somewhat less than the total that was actually produced and sent out of the colony. Secondly, the official records inevitably fail to list any goods that were illegally shipped out of North Carolina ports. Since by the middle of the eighteenth century very little illegal trade seems to have been carried on along the coasts of North Carolina,[19] this particular limitation is probably of minor significance.

The third limitation is more important, and it stems from the format of the tables in Customs 16/1. The exports from North Carolina are broken down to show the amounts and kinds of goods shipped out of each of the "Ports" of the colony. The Ports were really customs districts, and there were five of them in North Carolina, known as Ports Currituck, Roanoke, Bath Town, Beaufort, and Brunswick. These customs districts were coastal outlets rather than subdivisions of the mainland. Although there is no record of their precise limits, they can be reconstructed, using as guides for this purpose the names of the districts, and the locations of the towns in which the customs officers were stationed;[20] it is also necessary to assume that the districts showed the application of some sort of rough and ready logic, designed to insure a minimum of overlap and a maximum of coverage, an assumption which is justified in view of the determination of the British government to establish an effective system for regulating colonial commerce.

Fig. 33 shows the probable location of the customs districts, or Ports. Some of the major coastal towns are shown, and the broken lines extending back from the coast, towards the interior, separate the major waterways that were tributary to the several Ports. Since these waterways were much used for transporting relatively bulky and low value items such as naval stores and lumber, the broken lines serve roughly to delimit the hinterlands of the Ports for these products. The map probably represents at least an approximate view of reality.

The bare enumeration of drawbacks associated with the use of tax returns and Customs 16/1 perhaps makes the obstacles appear more formidable than they actually are. Their deficiencies may seem awesome but they should not be compared, as sources of systematically compiled data, with the twentieth-century charts and tables of the U.S. Census Bureau. Their value resides in the unique opportunity they afford of obtaining some understanding of colonial conditions in quantitative terms.

ABBREVIATIONS
NOTES
BIBLIOGRAPHY
INDEX

ABBREVIATIONS

The following system of abbreviations has been employed for note references to sources:

AAAG—*Annals of the Association of American Geographers*
AH—*Agricultural History*
AHR—*American Historical Review*
BG—*Botanical Gazette*
BGSA—*Bulletin of the Geological Society of America*
BPRO—British Public Record Office (London)
BR—*Botanical Review*
BTBC—*Bulletin of the Torrey Botanical Club*
CRSG—*Colonial Records of the State of Georgia*
EG—*Economic Geography*
EM—*Ecological Monographs*
FHQ—*Florida Historical Quarterly*
GHSC—*Georgia Historical Society Collections*
GR—*Geographical Review*
JEMSS—*Journal of the Elisha Mitchell Scientific Society*
JHUSHPS—Johns Hopkins University Studies in Historical and Political Science
JSH—*Journal of Southern History*
JSHP—James Sprunt Historical Publications
JSSHPS—James Sprunt Studies in History and Political Science
JWAS—*Journal of the Washington Academy of Sciences*
LC—Library of Congress
MHSP—*Massachusetts Historical Society Proceedings*
MR—*Moravian Records*
NCCR—*Colonial Records of North Carolina*
NCDS—North Carolina Department of State (Raleigh, North Carolina)
NCGES—North Carolina Geological and Economic Survey
NCGS—North Carolina Geological Survey
NCHR—*North Carolina Historical Review*
NCSDAH—North Carolina State Department of Archives and History (Raleigh, North Carolina)
NCSR—*State Records of North Carolina*
NEHGR—*New-England Historical and Genealogical Register*
PMHB—*Pennsylvania Magazine of History and Biography*
SAQ—*South Atlantic Quarterly*
SCAG Gaz—*South Carolina and American General Gazette*

SC Gaz—South Carolina Gazette
SHAP—Southern History Association Publications
UNC—University of North Carolina (Chapel Hill, North Carolina)
USDA—United States Department of Agriculture
Va Gaz—Virginia Gazette
VMHB—Virginia Magazine of History and Biography
WMQ—William and Mary Quarterly

The locations of manuscripts have been specified in the Bibliography but not in note references. When page numbers have been given for manuscript items, the numbers refer to the pages of the volumes in which the manuscripts are bound. Where discrepancies arise because of the former practice of dating years from March 25, the two appropriate alternative years are indicated as follows: Feb. 1, 1735/36. Sources used in preparing particular maps are identified, either in the text or in a note, immediately after the first reference to the map. In quoting from colonial source materials, the original format (with regard to spelling, use of capitals, and punctuation) has generally been followed.

NOTES

CHAPTER I

1. Unless otherwise noted, all information referring to population numbers for colonies other than North Carolina, and for the colonies as a whole, were obtained from the two standard and most comprehensive compilations of colonial population figures. These are: Evarts B. Greene and Virginia D. Harrington, *American Population Before the Federal Census of 1790* (New York, 1932); and Series Z 1-19 in U. S. Bureau of the Census, *Historical Statistics of the United States, Colonial Times to 1957* (Washington, D.C., 1960). The former is particularly useful and is the only one of the two that includes data on urban settlements.

2. Fig. 1 is based on the maps for 1740 and 1760 that appear in Herman R. Friis, *A Series of Population Maps of the Colonies and the United States* ("American Geographical Society Mimeographed Publication," No. 3 [New York, 1940]). The distribution of the settled areas in North Carolina as presented in Friis's maps was slightly modified, using as a guide Figs. 24, 25, and 26. On the whole, however, Fig. 1 is probably less accurate than the dot maps of Friis on which it is based.

3. This farm was located 1½ miles from New York. It was described by Charles Read, one of the most informative observers of colonial farming, in Carl R. Woodward (ed.), *Ploughs and Politicks: Charles Read of New Jersey and His Notes on Agriculture, 1715-1774* (New Brunswick, N.J., 1941), p. 310. Tibout's full name is not given in Read's notes.

4. Official lists of the immigrants suggest that over thirty thousand of them came in in the six-year period, 1749-54, according to the calculations in Oscar Kuhns, *The German and Swiss Settlements of Colonial Pennsylvania: A Study of the So-Called Pennsylvania Dutch* (New York, 1901), p. 57.

5. For suggestive comments by contemporary observers on these features of land near Philadelphia, see the following: Gottlieb Mittelberger, *Journey to Pennsylvania*, ed. and trans., Oscar Handlin and John Clive (Cambridge, Mass., 1960), p. 90; Adolph B. Benson (ed. and trans.), *Peter Kalm's Travels in North America* (2 vols.; New York, 1937), I, 51; Harry J. Carman (ed.), *American Husbandry* ("Columbia University Studies in the History of American Agriculture," No. 6 [New York, 1939]), pp. 124-25.

6. William Douglass, *A Summary, Historical and Political . . .* (2 vols.; Boston, 1749-53), II, 333.

7. This figure of five hundred is taken from a study which presents a very comprehensive view of the trade of the port: Arthur L. Jensen, "The Maritime Commerce of Colonial Philadelphia," (Ph.D. dissertation, University of Wisconsin, 1954),

p. 9. There are no data on the actual amounts of the various products that were exported in the 1750's. But it is known that the exports of Philadelphia in the year ending April 5, 1766, included 367,522 bushels of wheat, 198,516 barrels of flour, 34,736 barrels of bread, 60,206 bushels of Indian corn, and 7,254 barrels of beef and pork: Franklin B. Dexter (ed.), *Extracts from the Itineraries of Ezra Stiles* ... (New Haven, Conn., 1916), p. 65.

8. Alfred Philip Muntz, "The Changing Geography of the New Jersey Woodlands, 1600-1900," (Ph.D. dissertation, University of Wisconsin, 1959), p. 155.

9. Andrew Burnaby, *Travels through the Middle Settlements in North-America. In the Years 1759 and 1760* ... (2nd ed.; London, 1775. Reprinted in "Great Seal Books," Ithaca, N.Y., 1960), p. 52.

10. "Itinerant Observations in America, reprinted from the London Magazine, 1745-6," *GHSC*, 4 (1878), 35.

11. William Eddis, *Letters from America* ... (London, 1792), p. 102.

12. It is, of course, unlikely that many of the migrants actually used the map. But the fact that there is a copy of one of the very rare early editions of this among the Moravian Archives in North Carolina (in a trunk!) suggests that possibly the Moravians at least did actually consult it.

13. This is the conclusion in Lawrence H. Gipson, *The British Empire Before the American Revolution*, Volume II, *The British Isles and the American Colonies: The Southern Plantations, 1748-1754* (New York, 1960), p. 82, and is based on the local records of one county. Gipson actually cites only one example of an estate with more than a hundred slaves, and he does not give precise acreages; but he does specify important supporting details on the size of slaveholdings from the records of Northumberland County, Virginia, for the years 1745 and 1746.

14. Chapman J. Milling (ed.), *Colonial South Carolina. Two Contemporary Descriptions by Governor James Glen and Doctor George Milligen-Johnston* ("South Caroliniana Sesquicentennial Series," No. 1 [Columbia, S.C., 1951]), p. 45.

15. *SC Gaz*, Feb. 21, 1774. Presumably, "20,000 l." means £20,000.

16. "Charleston, S. C., in 1774, as described by an English Traveler," *The Historical Magazine*, 9 (1865), 344.

17. *CRSG*, XXVI, 4.

18. George Wymberley-Jones (ed.), *History of the Province of Georgia ... by John Gerar William De Brahm* ... (Wormsloe, Ga., 1849), p. 37.

19. Hector St. John de Crèvecoeur, *Sketches of Eighteenth Century America* ..., eds., Henri L. Bourdin, Ralph H. Gabriel, and Stanley T. Williams (New Haven, Conn., 1925), p. 73.

20. The phrase has been taken out of its context and slightly altered in punctuation. The relevant passage in Smith's letter reads as follows: "When you send againe I intreat you rather send but thirty Carpenters, husbandmen, gardiners, fisher men, blacksmiths, masons, and diggers up of trees, roots, well provided; then a thousand of such as we have: for except wee be able both to lodge them, and feed them, the most will consume with want of necessaries before they can be made good for any thing." (John Smith, *The Generall Historie of Virginia, New-England, and the Summer Isles* ... [London, 1624], p. 72.)

Chapter II

1. Fig. 2 shows the location of these bounding parallels, though not as far west as the Pacific Ocean, which was in theory the western limit of the colony. A second charter in 1665 slightly extended the limits of Carolina, to 36°30′ and 29°N. The subsequent boundary lines of the colony of North Carolina are discussed at the end of this chapter and shown on Fig. 8.

2. In examining primary source materials, most attention was given to those relating to the royal period. For the proprietary period, much reliance was placed on the works of others. Hence, this chapter is based on secondary sources to a greater extent than the following ones.

3. Fig. 3 shows the locations of all major rivers, lakes, and sounds mentioned in the text.

4. See Greene and Harrington, *American Population* . . ., p. 156, in which are cited various estimates of the population about this time.

5. Figure from a report of Governor Burrington, Jan. 1, 1733, in *NCCR*, III, 433.

6. There is very little information on the actual numbers of Indians in the colony at this time, and what little there is is not very reliable. This estimate of a thousand is a liberal one, based on scraps of information in the following works: John Brickell, *The Natural History of North-Carolina* (Dublin, 1737; reprinted Raleigh, N.C., 1911), p. 282; Hugh Meredith, *An Account of the Cape Fear County, 1731*, ed., Earl G. Swem (Perth Amboy, N.J., 1922), p. 27; the prefatory notes of William L. Saunders in *NCCR*, III, xvii-xviii; Douglas L. Rights, *The American Indians in North Carolina* (Durham, N.C., 1947), *passim*; Stanley A. South, *Indians in North Carolina* (Raleigh, N.C., 1959), *passim*; and the estimates of individual groups, collated from various sources, in John R. Swanton, *The Indian Tribes of North America* (Smithsonian Institution, Bureau of American Ethnology, Bulletin 145; Washington, D.C., 1952), pp. 74-90.

7. *NCCR*, III, 433.

8. Information on this partnership, on Hugh Meredith, and on his subsequent trip to North Carolina was found in the following: Thomas A. Glenn, *Welsh Founders of Pennsylvania* (2 vols.; Oxford, 1911-13), I, 143, 193; Max Farrand (ed.), *The Autobiography of Benjamin Franklin: A Restoration of a "Fair Copy"* (Berkeley, Calif., 1949), pp. 64ff., 79; Leonard W. Labaree (ed.), *The Papers of Benjamin Franklin* (New Haven, Conn., 1959–), I, 175, 215-16, II, 234; Meredith, *An Account* . . ., *passim*. Unless otherwise noted, the details that follow concerning the Welsh in North Carolina are taken from these sources.

9. David Evans is mentioned in Meredith, *An Account* . . ., p. 21, and also in *NCCR*, III, 418, IV, 4, 46, 218, 274, 346, 598, 644, 804.

10. The three place names are mentioned in local records: Alexander M. Walker (ed.), *New Hanover County Court Minutes* (2 Parts; Bethesda, Md., 1958-59), Part I, pp. 4, 19, *et passim*. The Moseley map of North Carolina, 1733, shows a "Welch Settlement" in the same vicinity.

11. There are fragments of evidence suggesting that other Welsh people came to the colony both before and after the 1730's: see, for example, Tillie Bond Manuscripts, 1690-1828, Vol. I, p. 3. But nowhere does there appear to be any evidence indicating that their settlements were in any way distinctive. Although there always has been a slight consciousness in North Carolina of an early Welsh heritage, the Welsh are not associated with any distinctive features, traits, or contributions. Historians of North Carolina have generally included the Welsh in their lists of the diverse groups who came to the colony, but that is about all the attention they are accorded.

12. For the earlier group, see the following works: R. D. W. Connor, *Race Elements in the White Population of North Carolina* ("North Carolina State Normal and Industrial College Historical Publications," No. 1 [Raleigh, N.C., 1920]), p. 23; Hugh T. Lefler and Albert R. Newsome, *North Carolina: The History of a Southern State* (Chapel Hill, N.C., 1954), p. 49; and the prefatory notes of William L. Saunders in *NCCR*, I, x. The later group of French settlers is mentioned in Frances L. Harriss (ed.), *Lawson's History of North Carolina* (3rd ed.; Richmond, Va., 1960), pp. 84-85, 116-17.

13. The most important sources of information for this colonization project are: Kocherthaler, *Ausführlich und umständlicher Bericht von der berühmten Land-*

schaft Carolina . . . (Frankfurt am Mäyn, 1709); Vincent H. Todd and Julius Goebel (ed. and trans.), *Christoph von Graffenried's Account of the Founding of New Bern* (Raleigh, N.C., 1920); and, Hans G. Keller, *Christoph von Graffenried und die Gründung von Neu-Bern in Nord-Carolina* (Bern, 1953).

The Palatines involved in the project were part of a much larger group moving from Europe to North America early in the eighteenth century. Although the movement is generally referred to as the Palatine Migration, not all of the migrants came from the Rhine Palatinate: see the list in Moritz W. Höen and Anton W. Böhme, *Das verlangte nicht erlangte Canaan bey den Lust-Gräbern* . . . (Frankfurt and Leipzig, 1711), p. 99.

14. One historian has suggested that they finally settled in an area within the limits of the present-day counties of Craven, Jones, Duplin, and Onslow, i.e., no more than thirty or forty miles to the south and east of New Bern: Samuel A. Ashe, *History of North Carolina* (2 vols.; Greensboro, N.C., 1908-25), I, 273-74.

15. The report of the committee is in Leo F. Stock (ed.), *Proceedings and Debates of the British Parliaments respecting North America, 1542-1739* ("Carnegie Institution of Washington Publication," No. 338; 4 vols. [Washington, D. C., 1937]), IV, 851-57; for indications of earlier ventures of a similar nature, note especially pp. 851, 855, and Dr. Brickell's testimony on p. 856. Even the accounts of the historians of the Scotch-Irish in North America contain no details concerning Scotch-Irish in North Carolina during the proprietary period. A couple of examples of Scotch-Irish settlers in the colony earlier than 1735 are given in Lefler and Newsome, *North Carolina* . . ., pp. 76-77.

16. Fig. 4 is a summary view and interpretation of fragmentary information relating to settlers and settlements. It is based on many sources. All those cited elsewhere in this chapter which included references to settlers and settlements were relevant, and the following additional ones were used (though the information they contain was sometimes informative only in an oblique way): William K. Boyd (ed.), *William Byrd's Histories of the Dividing Line betwixt Virginia and North Carolina* (Raleigh, N.C., 1929), pp. 158, 160, *et passim; NCCR*, I, 380-81, III, 338; *NCSR*, XI, 29; the 1720 letter of Governor Boone of South Carolina cited in Marvin L. Skaggs, *North Carolina Boundary Disputes Involving Her Southern Line* ("JSSHPS," Vol. 25, No. 1 [Chapel Hill, N.C., 1941]), p. 5; "A New Voyage to Georgia. By a Young Gentleman. Giving an account of his travels to South Carolina, and part of North Carolina . . .," *GHSC*, II (1842), 56-57; Moseley map, 1733; Wimble map, 1738. The region shown for the Palatine settlers is the area in which they originally settled and does not indicate subsequent dispersion. The numerous doubts about the French colonists justify the question mark placed on the map. Unoccupied portions of the east were mainly swampland (which are discussed more fully in the next chapter). The maps for 1720 and 1740 in Friis, *A Series of Population Maps* . . ., seem to underestimate the extent of the settled area in North Carolina. Compare also two maps in the works of historians: Ashe, *History of North Carolina*, I, between pp. 376 and 377; Lefler and Newsome, *North Carolina* . . ., p. 254. These last two portray various aspects of settlement in the colony.

17. Apparently there was already a shortage of vacant land in sections of this region in the 1720's: *NCCR*, II, 289-90, 528.

18. The southern boundary of the Granville District is shown on Fig. 8. Not until the first decade of the nineteenth century were the claims of Granville's descendants finally extinguished, and parts of the course of the southern boundary of his district are still perpetuated in some of the county boundary lines within the state.

19. *NCCR*, III, 432.

20. One surveyor was shot when he went to view vacant lands in an area inhabited by fifty squatters' families: *NCCR*, V, 161. A land speculator, when he tried to sort out the legal tangles caused because squatters had moved onto the

lands held by himself, his father, and associates, found himself engaged in a "war" with the squatters; the group of visitors was violently treated, and one of them "very near had daylight let into his skull." The speculator nevertheless expressed his determination not to give in to such "a pack of ungrateful brutal Sons of Bitches": *NCCR*, VII, 32.

For two examples of official recognition at the end of the colonial period of the great extent to which settlers had resorted to squatting, see *NCCR*, X, 211; and, the broadside entitled "Advertisement. Whereas it appears that many persons have settled in the District of this Province, granted by his late Majesty to the Right Honourable John Earl Granville . . . Newbern, May 3, 1774. Jo. Martin."

21. For instructions concerning river lots, see *NCCR*, III, 102, V, 96, 1133. The other details about surveying are taken from an instruction brochure drawn up for a surveyor, John Clayton: the item is in Secretary of State Records, Box 1038 (MSS).

22. This account appears in a letter of Governor Dobbs to the Board of Trade, written August 24, 1755: *NCCR*, V, 361. Governor Burrington's earlier comments on the way in which Surveyor Moseley and his deputies carried out their duties are in a similar vein: *NCCR*, III, 434. Bishop Spangenberg, visiting North Carolina, found land matters there in "unbelievable confusion" in 1752: *MR*, I, 32.

23. A qualification should be made here. Some of the extant surveys of lands granted in eighteenth-century North Carolina seem to suggest that rectangular, or at least oblong, shapes were fairly common in western parts of North Carolina, more so than in the east. If a variation in shapes really did exist between east and west, it could have been a result of a more complete breakdown of the attempt to achieve rectangularity in the east, where there was a much greater proportion of wetlands of various kinds to contend with. Such was the abundance of streams in the western parts that rectangular lots there would not generally have been disadvantageous. The Moravians, when surveying the land within their large tract in the west, had initially intended to make the lots long and narrow, in order to secure water, meadowland, and woodland for each settler; but they soon turned to the use of square lots when they realized that these latter would still insure ample water, meadow, and wood in each lot: *MR*, II, 540-41.

It is conceivable that a prolonged study of all the extant colonial land grants and surveys could lead to more precise conclusions concerning shapes. But it is doubtful whether such a study would be worthwhile, particularly as the shapes and sizes of grants did not necessarily bear any relation to those of actual holdings, owing to the frequent modification of initial grants by later grants and purchases.

24. It is not clear whether family heads were allowed fifty or one hundred acres, and, furthermore, the amount seems to have varied from time to time. For relevant details on the headright system, see *NCCR*, I, 86-87, III, 101-2, IV, 60, V, 396-97, 1132-33. In 1754, Governor Dobbs asked the British government to allow him to make grants of up to 640 acres even to persons whose headrights would not have entitled them to such an amount: *NCCR*, V, 149, 156, 362, 396-97. Although the request apparently was not allowed, a few grants of 640 acres were made from time to time, presumably in disregard of the headright system.

25. This conclusion is based on a cursory sampling of some of the thousands of land grants and associated documents that are available: those that were examined are listed in the Bibliography. For examples of land grants made from 1749 to 1751, see *NCCR*, IV, 959-1255, *passim*, which shows that most grants at this time were for amounts between 100 and 400 acres. A study of the size of all the colonial grants of land in one particular locality has also shown that grants of over 640 acres were rare and that the average size was between 300 and 450 acres: Nannie M. Tilley, "Studies in the History of Colonial Granville County" (Master's thesis, Duke University, 1931), pp. 34-36.

26. The report is in *NCCR*, IV, 1086. The survey book is that of Henry

Eustace McCulloh, dated 1762-73 (MS). For a newspaper advertisement of McCulloh, inviting interested parties to purchase his land, see *Va Gaz*, P.D., Jan. 14, 1773. The tangled story of the land speculation ventures of the McCullohs, father and son, is briefly described in Charles G. Sellers, Jr., "Private Profits and British Colonial Policy: The Speculations of Henry McCulloh," *WMQ*, 3rd Ser., 8 (1951), 535-51. Also relevant is John Cannon, "Henry McCulloch and Henry McCulloh," *WMQ*, 3rd Ser., 15 (1958), 71-73.

27. Nina M. Tiffany (ed.), *Letters of James Murray, Loyalist* (Boston, 1901), p. 26.

28. James F. Shinn, "Edward Moseley: A North Carolina Patriot and Statesman," *SHAP*, 3 (1899), 33.

29. Information from Miss Beth Crabtree's manuscript notes on the Pollock Papers in NCSDAH.

30. These details are taken from Chapter V of E. Lawrence Lee, "The History of the Lower Cape Fear: The Colonial Period" (Ph.D. dissertation, University of North Carolina, 1955), pp. 151-81. On the attempts of "The Family" to engross Cape Fear lands, see also Sellers, "Private Profits and British Colonial Policy . . .," *WMQ*, 3rd Ser., 8 (1951), 536ff.

31. Some data on the sizes of landholdings in North Carolina are given in property lists drawn up in the early 1780's. The above conclusions are taken from a study of these lists: Francis G. Morris and Phyllis M. Morris, "Economic Conditions in North Carolina About 1780, Part I, Landholdings," *NCHR*, 16 (1939), Table 3, p. 120, and Table 6, p. 130.

32. Lee, "The History of the Lower Cape Fear: The Colonial Period," pp. 162-63.

33. The function of the counties was roughly the same as that of the precincts they replaced in the 1730's.

34. An invaluable aid in drawing Figs. 5, 6, and 7 was David L. Corbitt, *The Formation of North Carolina Counties, 1663-1943* (Raleigh, N.C., 1950), and particularly the maps (for 1700, 1740, 1760, and 1775) and chart at the end of this volume (between pp. 282 and 297). In fact, these maps and all maps in following chapters that show colonial county boundaries are largely based on Corbitt's work and the maps in it (drawn by L. Polk Denmark).

35. These groupings are listed in D. L. Corbitt, "Judicial Districts of North Carolina, 1746-1934," *NCHR*, 12 (1935), 45-61, an article also containing references to the legislative acts relating to the districts.

36. Examples of these other divisions were the parishes, created mainly for ecclesiastical purposes, and the cantons into which parishes were divided for regular processioning of land: acts of 1715, 1723, and 1741, dealing with these units are in *NCSR*, XXIII, 6-10, 103-7, 187-91. For an informative example of the ways in which the vestry of a parish functioned, see Records of the Proceedings of the Vestry of St. Paul's Church, Edenton, N.C., 1701-1841 (typewritten copy of MSS).

37. Fig. 8 is based on the following, all of which contain relevant details on the territorial limits of the colony: Boyd, *William Byrd's History* . . ., pp. xvi-xxiv; Skaggs, *North Carolina Boundary Disputes* . . ., *passim*; A. S. Salley, *The Boundary Line between North Carolina and South Carolina* ("Bulletin of the Historical Commission of South Carolina," No. 10 [Columbia, S.C., 1929]), *passim*; *NCCR*, VII, 470, 853-54; Charles O. Paullin, *Atlas of the Historical Geography of the United States* ("Carnegie Institution of Washington Publication," No. 401 [Washington, D.C., 1932]), pp. 82-83 and Plate 100A.

38. It should be noted that the line is not entirely an east-west one, since it runs in a roughly north-south direction for a short distance (of less than a mile) along a small creek, northeast of where the Meherrin River appears in Fig. 3. Thus, the portions of the dividing line east and west of this north-south section of it are not actually on the same parallel, although the displacement is a minor one. In some of the maps included in the present study the displacement of

the boundary is shown (in a slightly exaggerated form), while in others it is not; for various reasons, it was judged inadvisable to try to show the line in exactly the same way on all the maps. For an explanation of how this distinctive feature of the boundary line came into being, see Boyd, *William Byrd's Histories* . . ., pp. xx, 104, and 106.

39. The Proclamation is printed in Merrill Jensen (ed.), *English Historical Documents: American Colonial Documents to 1776* (London, 1955), pp. 639-43. There is a brief study of the line in Max Farrand, "The Indian Boundary Line," *AHR*, 10 (1904-5), 782-91; and the fixing of the line in North Carolina is described in *NCCR*, VII, 469-70.

Many of the maps of North Carolina presented in this and in subsequent chapters are "open-ended" on the west, a device resorted to because it seemed to be the most appropriate way of representing the western limit of the colony, even though a boundary was proclaimed in the 1760's.

CHAPTER III

1. The three quotations are from *NCCR*, II, 416, 374, 417.
2. *NCCR*, II, 431-32.
3. A biographer of Urmstone has emphasized his bitterness, indiscretions, and drunken habits: Samuel A. Ashe, Stephen B. Weeks, and Charles L. Van Noppen, *Biographical History of North Carolina* (8 vols.; Greensboro, N.C., 1905-1917), VI, 450-55. But one of Urmstone's contemporaries, Governor Eden, recommended him as being "really an honest pains taking Gentleman": *NCCR*, II, 293
4. *NCCR*, I, 371, 516, 527, 682-83, 691; "Journal of a French Traveller in the Colonies, 1765, I," *AHR*, 26 (1920-21), 738; letter of Seymour, 1705, cited in C. P. Nettels, *The Money Supply of the American Colonies before 1720* ("University of Wisconsin Studies in the Social Sciences and History," No. 20 [Madison, Wis., 1934]), p. 58.
5. This reputation was possibly reinforced by the writers of the stream of promotional literature that flowed from North Carolina. But such advertisements issued from all the colonies, the writers of them sparing no superlatives in extolling the virtues of whichever colony they happened to be writing about. The viewpoints expressed and the information given in promotional writings are clearly not as relevant here as are the opinions and details presented in the accounts of those who reported on the North Carolina scene more impartially and from first-hand experience. The illustrations that follow have been taken from the latter type of writing.
6. Cited in William S. Powell, "John Pory: His Life, Letters and Works" (Master's thesis, University of North Carolina, 1947), p. 92.
7. George Fox, *A Journal or Historical Account* . . . (Philadelphia, 1832), pp. 459-60.
8. Harriss, *Lawson's History* . . ., pp. 62-63. Another writer, in a later variation of the same theme, claimed that North Carolina was considered to be "the finest Winter country on the Continent & abounding with all the necessarys of Life & at the Cheapest Rate." The writer of these words, however, was George Minot, a Boston resident who had some interest in disposing of a plantation in North Carolina and was possibly more concerned with selling it than with accurate description. His letter, dated November 8, 1746, is in Samuel B. Doggett (ed.), "A Plantation on Prince George's Creek, Cape Fear, North Carolina," *NEHGR*, 52 (1898), 472. (I am indebted to Professor Louise Hall of Duke University for drawing my attention to this item.)
9. Todd and Goebel, *Christoph von Graffenried's Account* . . ., p. 289.

10. *Ibid.*, p. 306 (letter of Hans Ruegsegger—in the original German, *ibid.*, p. 204, he refers to "fetten" land).

11. *NCCR*, III, 49.

12. *NCCR*, III, 194.

13. Harriss, *Lawson's History* . . ., p. 84.

14. This map is reproduced in William P. Cumming, *The Southeast in Early Maps* (Princeton, N.J., 1958), Plates 51-54. In an editorial comment (p. 201) Cumming suggests that this inscription "may have had an appreciable influence in promoting the influx of settlers into the piedmont section of North Carolina during the next twenty or thirty years." It should be noted, however, that not all of the inscription actually refers to the inland country and that, as Cumming himself points out (p. 200), Moseley's map was very rare and was never published in convenient or inexpensive form. The inscription on the map is more significant as an instance of a legend that was beginning to become widespread and as one of the first crude cartographic expressions of it, rather than as a prominent factor in the diffusion of the legend.

15. Catesby's work, *The Natural History of Carolina, Florida, and the Bahama Islands* . . ., was published in two volumes, the first edition in 1731-43, with revised editions in 1754 and 1771; various complete or partial versions of this work were published in German, French, and Dutch during the eighteenth century. Catesby's extraordinarily detailed work has only recently begun to attract the attention it deserves: William H. Miller, "Mark Catesby, An Eighteenth Century Naturalist," *Tyler's Quarterly Historical and Genealogical Magazine*, 29 (1948), 167-80; George F. Frick, "Mark Catesby, Naturalist, 1683-1749" (Ph.D. dissertation, University of Illinois, 1957); George F. Frick and Raymond P. Stearns, *Mark Catesby: The Colonial Audubon* (Urbana, Ill., 1961).

16. Catesby, *The Natural History of Carolina, Florida, and the Bahama Islands* . . . (2 vols.; London, 1754), I, iv-v.

17. Fig. 9 shows the Coastal Plain and the Piedmont. The former is subdivided into three regions, the Outer Coastal Plain, the Inner Coastal Plain, and the Sandhills, each one of which will be described briefly in the following pages. Line boundaries have been avoided, for reasons that will be apparent from the discussion of the limits of the several areas; and bands of dots were used as a symbol because they convey a more realistic, or at least a less misleading, impression. The placing of the bounds was a largely subjective process, and was done almost entirely on the basis of terrain (including drainage) and geological conditions. The following two maps were used as guides to these conditions: U.S. Department of the Interior, Geological Survey, *State of North Carolina*, shaded relief map, scale 1:500,000, 1957; N.C. Dept. of Conservation and Development, Division of Mineral Resources, *Geologic Map of North Carolina*, scale 1:500,000, 1958.

18. The string of islands is known as the Outer Banks. Although these islands were a part of colonial North Carolina, they are given very little attention in this study, partly because their area is so small, and partly because there are already two accounts of them, *viz.*, Gary S. Dunbar, *Geographical History of the Carolina Banks*, ed., Fred Kniffen (Technical Report No. 8, Part A, of Project No. N7, onr 35608, Task Order No. NR388 002 of the Office of Naval Research [Baton Rouge, La., 1956]), and David Stick, *The Outer Banks of North Carolina, 1584-1958* (Chapel Hill, N.C., 1958). The two studies employ different approaches, but both contain information on the early geography of the Outer Banks.

19. The largest of the lakes is Lake Mattamuskeet (see Fig. 3), which, according to Indian legend, is of fire origin: William L. Hamnett and David C. Thornton, *Tar Heel Wildlife* (2nd ed.; Raleigh, N.C., 1953), p. 40. Attempts to drain it were made early in the twentieth century by the New Holland Company, but the project was abandoned and the lake is now a wildlife refuge. It is drained by

several canals; because it is not clear where the original course of the outlet was located, no drainage outlet has been shown for Lake Mattamuskeet on the maps that appear in this study.

It has been suggested that other North Carolina lakes in areas where peaty surface materials predominate are a result of peat destruction by fire during dry seasons: see N. B. Webster, "On the Physical and Geological Characteristics of the Great Dismal Swamp, and the Eastern Counties of Virginia," *American Naturalist*, 9 (1875), 260-61, but compare Nathaniel S. Shaler, "General account of the fresh-water morasses of the United States with a description of the Dismal Swamp District of Virginia and North Carolina," *U.S. Geological Survey, Tenth Annual Report, 1888-89* (1890), 319-20. More recently, it has been suggested that the formation of these lakes can be attributed to fire destruction of peat during an extended dry period in post-glacial times: B. W. Wells and Steve G. Boyce, "Carolina Bays: Additional Data on Their Origin, Age and History," *JEMSS*, 69 (1953), 133.

20. Fig. 10 is based on "North Carolina: Soil Association Map" by William D. Lee and E. F. Goldston, a map which appears inside the end cover of William D. Lee, *The Soils of North Carolina* (North Carolina State College, Agricultural Experiment Station Technical Bulletin No. 115 [December, 1955]). On the original map, the category shown on Fig. 10 as peat is described as follows: *"Muck-Peat. Wet upland bogs; black soft muck or brown fibrous peat . . . very difficult to drain and shrinks considerably when drained. . . ."*

21. Various attempts have been made in the past to locate and draw a boundary between the two areas. In his article on the "North Carolina Flatwoods," *EG*, 22 (1946), 203-19, Samuel T. Emory noted that it was difficult "to draw even a zone of transition" between the two and compromised by using county boundaries to delimit the boundary. Other recent writers have made the distinction on the basis of a combination of soil types and drainage conditions, e.g., Reece A. Jones, "The Inner Coastal Plain of North Carolina, An Agricultural Region" (Ph.D. dissertation, University of North Carolina, 1954), p. 4; and, Charles H. V. Ebert, "Soils and Land Use Correlation of the Outer Atlantic Coastal Plain of Virginia, The Carolinas, and North Georgia" (Ph.D. dissertation, University of North Carolina, 1957), pp. xiv, xvi.

Three early accounts of the Coastal Plain in Georgia are interesting in this respect. In an account of Georgia written in 1740, William Stephens seems to be referring to this contrast and notes that the "flat country" extends sixty or seventy miles inland: "A State of the Province of Georgia . . .," *GHSC*, 2 (1842), 75. De-Brahm, on the other hand, observed that the inner part of the province, where hills begin to form, was in general thirty-seven miles from the coast: *History of the Province of Georgia . . .*, pp. 19-20. William Bartram placed the inner limit of the "level plain" of Georgia about fifty miles from the coast: Francis Harper (ed.), *Travels of William Bartram* (New Haven, Conn., 1958), p. 19.

22. The Chowan, Roanoke, and Northwest Cape Fear rivers, for example, all flow in valleys that are markedly asymmetrical in places. None of the travelers in eighteenth-century North Carolina seems to have noticed the frequent occurrence of such valleys. Two nineteenth-century writers were apparently the first to describe the phenomenon: see, Griffith J. McRee, *Life and Correspondence of James Iredell* (2 vols.; New York, 1857-58), I, 31; and W. C. Kerr, *Report of the Geological Survey of North Carolina, Volume I, Physical Geography, Resumé, Economical Geography* (Raleigh, N.C., 1875), pp. 9-11. For an early reference to the asymmetry of the Northwest Cape Fear, see "A New Voyage to Georgia . . .," *GHSC*, 2 (1842), 55.

23. With reference to North Carolina, see: William K. Boyd (ed.), "Informations . . .," in *Some Eighteenth Century Tracts Concerning North Carolina* (Raleigh, N.C., 1927), p. 440 (more details concerning this pamphlet are given in

note 17, Chapter IV, below); and, Carman, *American Husbandry*, p. 236. With reference to South Carolina, see: Public Records of South Carolina (MSS), Vol. 32, pp. 281-82. Note also the quotation from Catesby, p. 36, above.

24. DeBrahm was as exceptional in this respect as he was in many other ways. For biographical information on DeBrahm, and for brief evaluations of some of his work as a geographer, map maker, and surveyor, see the following: A. J. Morrison, "John G. de Brahm," *SAQ*, 21 (1922), 252-58; Charles L. Mowrat, "That 'Odd Being,' De Brahm," *FHQ*, 20 (1942), 323-45; and Ralph H. Brown, "The DeBrahm Charts of the Atlantic Ocean 1772-1776," *GR*, 28 (1938), 124-32.

25. DeBrahm's account of Georgia is in Wymberley-Jones, *History of the Province of Georgia* . . ., and his account of South Carolina is in Plowden C. J. Weston (ed.), *Documents Connected with the History of South Carolina* (London, 1856), pp. 155-227. The reference to a *"quasi-*division line" is on p. 166 of the latter, although the two accounts should be read together. Note also that De-Brahm recognized a difference between the Inner and Outer Coastal Plain, at least in Georgia: see note 21, Chapter III, above.

26. The lithologic boundary shown on Fig. 11 was located from information on the *Geologic Map of North Carolina*.

27. Fig. 12 is based on J. F. Lutz and C. B. Williams, *Land Condition Map of North Carolina*, scale 1:500,000 (Dept. of Soils, N.C. State College, 1935). On the original, the Steep Land category is defined as "areas with a high percentage of the land too steep for cultivation"; it is quite probable that this area was originally defined in quantitative terms, although there is no longer any record of how the map was made. There is a crude recognition of both of these hillier regions within the Piedmont on the Mouzon map, 1775. The hills near the eastern border of the Piedmont occur within one of the Carolina Slate Belts, areas formed of metamorphic rocks, the more resistant of which are responsible for rougher terrain. A traveler who crossed this region in 1768 seems to have observed the distinctiveness of the terrain: Journal of a ride from Newbern to Salisbury, October 1768, with a map of the road (MSS). Governor Dobbs also commented upon the hilliness of the terrain in this area: *NCCR*, V, 355.

28. This description was apparently written by Reuter, the surveyor of the Moravian settlement, and is in *MR*, II, 557-58. The Arrarat and Pilot Mountains to which he refers are two of the most prominent outliers of the Blue Ridge.

29. Some of the Carolina Bays are still occupied by lakes, and many more were probably once lakes. Catesby seems to have been the first to note their existence and regularity of form: *Natural History of Carolina* . . ., I, iv. Schoepf, who traveled extensively in North America in 1783 and 1784, also noted the large number of little lakes that occurred here and there in North and South Carolina: Johann D. Schoepf, *Travels in the Confederation* . . ., trans. and ed., Alfred J. Morrison (2 vols.; Philadelphia, 1911), II, 135. (Schoepf's account of his travels is an exceptionally valuable source of information for geographical purposes; even though his travels were made a few years after the end of the colonial period, they contain much that is pertinent to a study of earlier conditions. For a sketch of his life and work, see the brief biography of Schoepf written by Friedrich Ratzel in Vol. 32 of the *Allgemeine deutsche Biographie* [Leipzig, 1891], pp. 350-52.)

30. Fig. 12 is based on the map by Lutz and Williams, cited in note 27, Chapter III, above. Again, there is no precise definition of the poorly drained category on the original map; seemingly, the category includes all land requiring some kind of artificial drainage before it can be used for crops. Owing to the scale of Fig. 12, it was not possible to show the linear strips of poorly drained land along river valleys.

Fig. 13 is a photostat copy of a portion of the map in W. F. Prouty, "Carolina Bays and Their Origin," *BGSA*, 63 (1952), Plate 1, following p. 170.

31. Thus, the cypress trees of some of the larger swamps were a highly prized source of timber, and some of the seasonally dry swamps afforded grazing.

32. Throughout the southern Seaboard the prevalence of poorly drained land in the Outer Coastal Plain has long inhibited agricultural settlement because the costs of reclaiming it have always been relatively high. The use of expensive modern equipment on a custom basis together with federal cost-sharing arrangements have facilitated the reclamation of much land in eastern North Carolina during the present century, and particularly since World War II. Recent developments in this area are examined in James R. Anderson and Henry W. Dill, *Land Clearing and Drainage in Eastern North Carolina* (USDA, Agricultural Research Service, Farm Economics Research Division [Washington, D.C., January, 1961]).

33. The distinction between the Coastal Plain and the Piedmont is frequently mentioned in histories and geographies of the South. But the contrast between the Inner and Outer Coastal Plain seems to deserve at least as much and, possibly, more emphasis. Indeed, a few writers around the turn of the eighteenth century did propose a three-fold regionalization of the southern Seaboard, dividing it into a lower, middle, and upper country: see John C. Fitzpatrick (ed.), *The Diaries of George Washington, 1748-1799* (4 vols.; Boston, 1925), IV, 193-94, and, John Drayton, *A View of South-Carolina* (Charleston, S.C., 1802), frontispiece map and p. 11.

34. Figs. 14, 15, and 16 are based on three maps that appear in Charles B. Carney, *Weather and Climate in North Carolina* (North Carolina State College, Agricultural Experiment Station Bulletin No. 396 [October, 1958]), pp. 8, 14, and 22, respectively.

35. "Journal of a French Traveller . . . ," *AHR*, 26 (1920-21), 735; Carman, *American Husbandry*, p. 263; Doggett, "A Plantation . . .," *NEHRG*, 52 (1898), 472; Richard J. Hooker (ed.), *The Carolina Backcountry on the Eve of Revolution: The Journal and Other Writings of Charles Woodmason, Anglican Itinerant* (Chapel Hill, N.C., 1953), pp. 195-96 (the reference is possibly to S.C. rather than N.C.); "Informations . . .," in Boyd, *Some Eighteenth Century Tracts . . .*, p. 438; Schoepf, *Travels in the Confederation . . .*, II, 114-16.

36. For a few examples, see the following: *NCCR*, I, 714; Doggett, "A Plantation . . . ," *NEHGR*, 52 (1898), 473; Evangeline W. Andrews and Charles M. Andrews (eds.), *Journal of a Lady of Quality . . .* (New Haven, Conn., 1923), pp. 179, 182.

37. There are many references to hurricanes. For examples, see the following: *London Magazine*, 30 (1761), 673; *Va Gaz*, P.D., Nov. 2, 1769, and Jan. 23, 1772.

38. Because of the presence of marked variations in the vegetation cover from place to place within the colony, any generalizations about the cover are subject to more than the usual number of qualifications. A more detailed account of the vegetation than that which follows is presented in Appendix I, which also contains some consideration of the effects of fire and fuller documentation than is given above on vegetation.

39. Fig. 17 and the details presented in this paragraph are somewhat conjectural. Further information on some points is given in Appendix I. The general works that were most useful in drawing the map are as follows: W. W. Ashe, "Notes on the Forest Resources of North Carolina," *JEMSS*, 10 (1893), 8-9; W. W. Ashe, *The Forests, Forest Lands, and Forest Products of Eastern North Carolina* ("NCGS," Bulletin No. 5 [Raleigh, N.C., 1894]), pp. 14-24; E. Lucy Braun, *Deciduous Forests of Eastern North America* (Philadelphia, 1950), pp. 259-304, and end plate; J. W. Cruikshank, *Forest Resources of the Northern Coastal Plain of North Carolina* (USDA, Appalachian Forest Experiment Station, Forest Survey Release No. 5, 1940), pp. 7-10; J. W. Cruikshank, *Forest Resources of the Southern Coastal Plain of North Carolina* (USDA, Appalachian Forest Experiment Station, Forest Survey Release No. 4, 1940), p. 7; Roland M. Harper, "A quantitative study of the more conspicuous vegetation of certain natural subdivisions of the coastal plain, as ob-

served in traveling from Georgia to New York in July," *BTBC*, 37 (1910), Fig. 1, p. 407; "Natural Vegetation," a map by H. L. Shantz and Raphael Zon, scale 1:8,000,000 (which appears as Fig. 2 in Section E of Part I of USDA, *Atlas of American Agriculture*, ed., O. E. Baker); N.C. Wildlife Resources Commission in cooperation with U.S. Fish and Wildlife Service, *Wildlife Cover Map of North Carolina*, scale 1:500,000 (drawn by Jean F. Outlaw, 1946-50).

40. See Appendix I for further details.

41. See Appendix I for an account of these.

42. [Edmund and William Burke], *An Account of the European Settlements in America* (2 vols.; London, 1757), II, 337. (Although this is the page number as printed, it should actually be p. 237 according to the proper pagination sequence.)

43. Arthur Young, *Political Essays concerning the present state of the British Empire* (London, 1772), pp. 250-51.

44. *A Present for an Emigrant; containing a brief Description of the Climate, Soil, and Produce of the British Colonies in North America* . . . (Edinburgh, 1774), pp. 28-30. (Through the assistance of the University of North Carolina Library, I was able to see a microfilm of the Yale University Library copy of this item.)

45. Carman, *American Husbandry*, p. 243.

46. *Ibid.*, p. 254.

Chapter IV

1. There are no precise figures available for any of these years. The number for 1730 was obtained by subtracting a few thousand from Governor Burrington's estimate of 36,000 for 1732: *NCCR*, III, 433. There are no complete lists of taxables available until 1753, when there were 22,605 taxables in the colony; the figure for 1750 was obtained by multiplying the number of taxables in 1753 by 3.5 to give the total population (the reasons for the use of this factor are explained at length in Appendix II) and again subtracting several thousand. There are no complete lists of taxables in 1770, but the total of taxables in 1769 was 52,151; to obtain the total number of inhabitants in 1770, the 1769 total of taxables was multiplied by 3.5 and a few thousand added. In view of the lack of precision in these numbers, a generous margin of safety was allowed for on either side of the probable totals. Information on the nature, use, source of origin, and reliability of data on taxables is given in Appendix II, below.

2. In his account, originally published in 1709, Lawson mentioned the "yearly abundance of Strangers" who were coming into North Carolina at this time, moving southwards in search of lands to settle: Harriss, *Lawson's History* . . ., p. 81. Governor Burrington, in a letter to the British government, dated September 4, 1731, reported that "a great number of people have come into this Country to Settle lately I hear of more that are coming from the Neighbouring Colonies . . .": *NCCR*, III, 210. If these descriptions are not exaggerations, they are indicative of brief precursory spells of immigration foreshadowing the prolonged and steady flow that soon got underway.

3. The sources of these five observations are as follows: *NCCR*, IV, 1073-74; letter of Rowan, September 19, 1751, in Arthur Dobbs Papers, 1731-1771 (MSS); *MR*, I, 41; *NCCR*, V, 149; "Letter of Rev. James Maury to Philip Ludwell, on the defence of the frontiers of Virginia, 1756," *VMHB*, 19 (1911), 293.

4. Franklin's estimate is recorded in Dexter, *Extracts from the Itineraries of Ezra Stiles* . . ., p. 64. For other references to population increase in the 1760's see: *MR*, I, 294; and *SC Gaz*, Oct. 10, 1768.

5. Tryon's remark appears in *NCCR*, VII, 248. Georgia still had a population of under 25,000 in 1770: U.S. Bureau of the Census, *Historical Statistics* . . ., Series Z 1-19, p. 756.

NOTES, pages 54-56

6. *Connecticut Courant,* Nov. 30, 1767 (LC).

7. There are no data available for the population as a whole, and the graph is based on numbers of taxables (for the relationship between taxables and population, see Appendix II, below). The choice of these two counties was determined by the completeness of data for them, and because the boundaries of both remained constant during the period plotted. Even for one of these counties, Rowan, the only total that is available for the year 1760 is incomplete and was therefore omitted from the graph (and an interrogation mark substituted).

The graph is on semi-logarithmic paper, so that the rate of increase is proportional to the steepness of the slope. In view of the shortcomings of the data on which the graph is based, it is doubtful whether any significance can be attached to minor fluctuations from year to year (such as the apparent peak in Rowan County in 1756 as compared with the years 1755 and 1757).

8. There is fragmentary evidence of this overland movement in the following sources: *NCCR,* V, 318, 356; *MR,* I, 41, II, 798; Chalmers G. Davidson, *The Life and Times of General William Lee Davidson* (Davidson, N.C., 1951), p. 3. One historian who has been particularly concerned with population changes in Pennsylvania, has suggested that the emigration of people from Pennsylvania to North Carolina began about 1740 and was well underway by 1750, and that the Scotch-Irish were the largest group among these emigrants: Wayland F. Dunaway, *The Scotch-Irish of Colonial Pennsylvania* (Chapel Hill, N.C., 1944), pp. 107-8. The author of one of the more reliable histories of North Carolina counties has noted that the bulk of the Scotch-Irish came into Orange County after 1750; relying apparently on the dates of establishment of Presbyterian churches, he specifies six Scotch-Irish settlements that were established between 1755 and 1765: Francis Nash, "The History of Orange County—Part I," *North Carolina Booklet,* 10 (1910-11), 63.

Although the exodus of large numbers of Scotch-Irish from Pennsylvania to North Carolina is a theme reiterated in all the standard histories of North Carolina, and in several histories of the Scotch-Irish in America, there is surprisingly little information in the historical record that actually testifies to the movement of Scotch-Irish settlers into North Carolina from the colonies to the north, either in groups or individually.

9. Dexter, *Extracts from the Itineraries of Ezra Stiles . . .,* pp. 64-65.

10. Arthur W. Hutton (ed.), *Arthur Young's Tour in Ireland (1776-1779)* (2 vols.; London, 1892), I, 402. Young is here referring to events of 1773 and earlier; he notes that one emigration of three hundred indentured servants to North Carolina had been "stopped by contrary winds, etc. There had been something of this constantly, but not of that amount." Young's account has some important details concerning emigration from Ireland to America before the Revolution—see, for example, *ibid.,* I, 115, 128, 144, 145, II, 56-58. The only two destinations within America that Young specifically mentions are North Carolina and, for seasonal moves, Newfoundland.

The arrival of five hundred Scotch-Irish in North Carolina in August, 1773, is mentioned in Abiel Holmes, *The Annals of America . . .* (2 vols.; 2nd ed.: Cambridge, 1829), II, 183, n.4.

11. See, for example, *NCCR,* IV, 686; and also the April, 1751, letter of Governor Dobbs to Rowan, quoted in Desmond Clarke, *Arthur Dobbs, Esquire, 1689-1765* (Chapel Hill, N.C., 1957), p. 96, with Clarke's comments on pp. 71-72, 95.

12. Fig. 19 is based on mention of Scotch-Irish settlers or settlements in the following sources: *NCCR,* IV, 686, V, 24, 25, 317, 356, VII, 102; *MR,* I, 46, 290, II, 791; letter from Dobbs to Rowan, April, 1751, quoted in Clarke, *Arthur Dobbs . . .,* p. 96; Land Grants, Vol. 6, 1701-1831 (MSS), p. 113; Rowan County, Court Minutes, Part I, 1753-55 (MSS), p. 8.

13. On his visit to the Island of Skye in 1733, Dr. Johnson was entertained by

the performance of a dance called "America." According to Boswell, the movements of the dance were designed to show "how emigration catches till all are set afloat": Frederick A. Pottle and Charles H. Bennett (eds.), *Boswell's Journal of A Tour to the Hebrides* . . . (New York, 1936), pp. 242-43. There was also apparently a popular song in the Highlands and Western Isles that was called "Dod a ah 'iarruidh an fhortain do North Carolina," or, "going to seek a fortune in North Carolina": this is cited in R. D. W. Connor, *North Carolina: Rebuilding an Ancient Commonwealth, 1584-1925* (4 vols.; Chicago, 1928-29), I, 152. A few of the emigrants to North Carolina brought Gaelic books with them, and some continued to speak the language and to listen to sermons given in Gaelic. Two verses of one of the earliest extant Gaelic poems composed in North Carolina are worth quoting, less for the poesy of the translation than for the imagery of the contents:

> In America now are we,
> in the shade of the forest for ever unfailing.
> When the winter departs and the warmth returns
> nuts and apples and the sugar will grow.
> . . . .
> We're turned into Indians surely enough.
> In the dark of the trees not one of us will be left alive,
> with wolves and beast howling in every lair.
> We've come into ruin since we left King George.

It was composed by John Macrae, who emigrated from Scotland to North Carolina in 1774, as a lullaby for his daughter: Charles W. Dunn, "A North Carolina Gaelic Bard," *NCHR*, 36 (1959), 474-75.

14. For convincing proof that most of them came after 1750, see Duane Meyer, *The Highland Scots of North Carolina, 1732-1776* (Chapel Hill, N.C., 1961), Fig. V, p. 91.

15. For instances of the partiality which was shown towards the Highlanders, see: *NCCR*, IV, 490, 532-33, VII, 543-44, 618, VIII, 144, 526, IX, 251. For the role of one merchant in particular, see the following: James Hogg Papers (MSS), Unit 2 (one folder, 1773-74), *passim*; *Weekly Magazine, or Edinburgh Amusement*, July 21, 1774.

16. The "spirit of emigration" is described in the following items, among others: *Weekly Magazine, or Edinburgh Amusement*, March 31, 1774; letter of Cathcart, dated March 8, 1774, in Folder 87 on Reel 3 of the Hayes Collection (microfilm in the Southern Historical Collection, UNC, Chapel Hill, N.C., from originals in the possession of Mr. John G. Wood, Edenton, N.C.). Incoming shiploads of Highlanders are mentioned in the following sources: Port Brunswick Shipping Register, 1765-75 (MSS); *SC Gaz*, Oct. 19-26, 1767, and Sept. 16-Oct. 2, 1769; *Va Gaz*, P.D., May 16, 1771, P.D., Sept. 23, 1773, R., 16 Dec., 1773, Pi., Dec. 30, 1775, D., Jan. 27, 1776; *NCCR*, VII, 543-44, IX, 259, 364, 1159, X, 324, 327-28, 346. Some of these references are seemingly made with respect to the same incoming group and are thus probably somewhat repetitious.

One letter, written from Pennsylvania on August 13, 1773, records the sending of agents by the "American Company of Farmers" in western Scotland to seek a large tract of land in North Carolina: T. W. J. Wylie (ed.), "Franklin County One Hundred Years Ago: A Settler's Experience Told In A Letter Written By Alexander Thomson In 1773," *PMHB*, 8 (1884), 322.

17. "Informations concerning the Province of North Carolina, addressed to emigrants from the Highlands and Western Isles of Scotland. By an impartial hand." This was printed in Glasgow in 1773 and has been reprinted in Boyd, *Some Eighteenth Century Tracts* . . ., pp. 427-51.

18. Not all the emigrants could write, of course, and not all of those who could, actually did write letters; but the effect of just one such letter would

probably have been important, particularly if news concerning the success of an emigrant was exaggerated a little before it was passed on to other interested parties. For James Hogg's views on the role of letters, see the item in the Hogg Papers cited in note 15, Chapter IV, above; also relevant is the testimony of the emigrants themselves, as given in A. R. Newsome (ed.), "Records of Emigrants from England and Scotland to North Carolina, 1774-1775," *NCHR*, 11 (1934), 130-43, *passim*.

19. These estimates are taken from Ian C. G. Graham, *Colonists from Scotland: Emigration to North America, 1707-1783* (Ithaca, N.Y., 1956), pp. 188-89. Graham based them on an examination of a variety of sources.

20. This is based on the "rough estimate" of twelve thousand for 1776 given in Meyer, *Highland Scots of North Carolina* . . ., p. 85.

21. Information on the location of Scottish Highlanders in North Carolina was found in the following sources, which were used as the basis of the distribution shown on Fig. 20: *NCCR*, VII, 540, 543-44, 618, VIII, 144, IX, 251; *Va Gaz*, D., Jan. 27, 1776; "Informations . . .," in Boyd, *Some Eighteenth Century Tracts* . . ., p. 440; English Records, American Loyalist Claims (MSS). Additional fragmentary evidence was found scattered through the following two works: Hugh E. Egerton (ed.), *The Royal Commission on the Losses and Services of American Loyalists 1783 to 1785* . . . (Oxford, 1915); and, *United Empire Loyalists. Enquiry into the Losses and Services in Consequence of Their Loyalty. Evidence in the Canadian Claims* (Province of Ontario, Bureau of Archives, Second Report, 1904; Toronto, 1905).

Sometime after Fig. 20 was drawn a series of maps based on the location of land grants and purchases secured by Highlanders was published: Meyer, *Highland Scots of North Carolina* . . ., pp. 97-100. Meyer's maps are more accurate than Fig. 20 in some ways, but there is evidence in the above sources of Scottish Highlanders living farther west than is indicated by Meyer's maps. In any event, the discrepancies between Meyer's maps and Fig. 20 are minor.

22. The birthplaces are those of a group of Moravians: *MR*, II, 818.

23. Referring to the Germans in a portion of northwestern colonial North Carolina, Gehrke has noted that they came *via* Pennsylvania from the Palatinate, Wurtemberg, Lorraine, the Upper Rhine, Hamburg, and Hanover, and that most of them spent a few years in Pennsylvania before trekking south: William H. Gehrke, "The German Element in Rowan and Cabarrus Counties, North Carolina" (Master's thesis, University of North Carolina, 1934), pp. 12-15.

24. This letter from Pastor Roschen appears in William K. Boyd (ed.) and Charles A. Krummel (trans.), "German Tracts Concerning the Lutheran Church in North Carolina during the Eighteenth Century. Part II. Velthusen's North Carolina Church Reports (I, II) with Ordination Address and Prayer," *NCHR*, 7 (1930), 244-45. It should be noted that it appears in translation and that it was written in 1789.

25. *Ibid.*, p. 249. The original German reads "von den Einflüssen der Vermischung auf das Verderbnis des deutschen Blutes" and appears in Johann C. Velthusen, *Nordcarolinische Kirchennachrichten* (Zweytes und letztes heft; Stade, 1792), 37n.

26. This view should be compared with the somewhat different attitude of another German pastor, Nüssman. Writing from North Carolina in 1787, Nüssman recommended that only unmarried settlers should come from Germany, for American wives were, he thought, far more suitable in this country: J. C. Velthusen, *et al.*, *Lehrbücher für die Jugend in Nord-carolina, entworfen von einer Gesellschaft Helmstädtischer Professoren* (Dritte Lieferung, Religionsgeschichte und Geographisches Handbuch: Leipzig, 1788), p. 22.

27. Fig. 21 is based on the numerous references that were found to German settlers in the west. Instances occur in the following sources: *NCCR*, V, 24-25,

356, VIII, 630-31, X, 231; Cora C. Curry, "Heidelberg Evangelical Lutheran Church Records (Old Dutch Meeting House), Rowan County (now Davie) North Carolina," *National Genealogical Society Quarterly*, 19 (March, 1931), 4-5. The Moravians settled in the Wachovia tract in western North Carolina, and there are references in their records to other (non-Moravian) Germans in this part of the west: *MR*, I, 78, II, 793, 797. Specific details in two German works are also relevant, although some of the settlements mentioned therein were not established until after 1775: Velthusen, *Nordcarolinische Kirchennachrichten*, pp. 16-17, 26; and, Velthusen, *Lehrbücher für die Jugend* . . ., pp. 15, 17, 19, 22, 25-26.

28. One historian claims that there were fifteen thousand Germans in the colony in 1760: Connor, *Race Elements* . . ., p. 18. Others suggest that there were that number in 1775, and yet another estimates that there were eight thousand in 1775: these last two figures are both in Lefler and Newsome, *North Carolina* . . ., p. 81, the first of the two being that of the authors, the second being that of "a leading authority." Contemporary estimates also showed considerable variation: see, for example, *NCCR*, V, 600-1, and compare *NCCR*, VIII, 630-31.

29. These are from the following two works: U.S. Bureau of the Census, *A Century of Population Growth: From the First to the Twelfth Census of the United States 1790-1900*, by W. S. Rossiter (Washington, D.C., 1909), Table 45, p. 116; and, American Council of Learned Societies, "Report of Committee on Linguistic and National Stocks in the Population of the United States," *American Historical Association, Annual Report, 1931, Volume I* (1932), p. 124. There can be little doubt that the method used in the latter was far sounder than that employed in the former, so that the estimate of 4.7% is probably closer to the truth.

30. Gehrke, "The German Element . . .," pp. 35-36.

31. This estimate rests on two assumptions: that the proportion of Germans in the population was constant between 1775 and 1790, and that the conclusions drawn from the evidence of surnames in the 1790 Census are reliable.

32. "The Journal of James Auld, 1765-1770," *SHAP*, 8 (1904), 255-61.

33. The biographical details are taken from Clement Eaton, "A Mirror of the Southern Colonial Lawyer: The Fee Books of Patrick Henry, Thomas Jefferson, and Waightstill Avery," *WMQ*, 3rd Ser., 8 (1951), 520-34, *passim*, and, Edward W. Phifer, "Saga of a Burke County Family, Part I, The Grandparents," *NCHR*, 39 (1962), 1-2.

34. "Autobiography of Col. William Few of Georgia. From the original MS. in the possession of William Few Christie," *Magazine of American History*, 7 (July-December, 1881), 343.

35. For evidence of a fairly widespread flow of settlers from colonies to the north, see the letter from Rowan to S. S., dated September 19, 1751, and the letter from John Campbell [to Arthur Dobbs?], written at about the same time, both of which are in the Arthur Dobbs Papers (MSS). The only fairly systematic type of record providing information on place of origin is furnished by Quaker certificates. While by no means all of the Quakers who came to North Carolina were of English descent, many of them were, and the lists showing the colony of origin of Quakers who joined two Quaker Monthly Meetings in North Carolina (at New Garden and Cane Creek) are of relevance here: of the 132 Quakers for whom a place of origin is given, 73 came from Pennsylvania, 50 from Virginia, 2 from Maryland, 2 from New Jersey, and 5 from elsewhere in North Carolina. These figures are compiled from data given in Stephen B. Weeks, *Southern Quakers and Slavery: A Study in Institutional History* ("JHUSHPS," Extra Volume 15 [Baltimore, 1896]), pp. 103, 105. Another group of Quakers moved from Nantucket Island to North Carolina; Weeks suggests they came in about 1771 (*ibid.*, p. 107), but Crèvecoeur gives their date of entry as 1766: J. Hector St. John de Crèvecouer, *Letters from an American Farmer* (Dutton Everyman Paperback; New York, 1957), pp. 127-28.

36. Settlers moving from Virginia into North Carolina after 1750 are mentioned in the following sources, though again, it is not certain that all of them were English: *NCCR*, IX, 349; "Letter of Rev. James Maury . . .," *VMHB*, 19 (1911), 293; the notes of a tour cited in George W. Paschal, *History of North Carolina Baptists* (2 vols.; Raleigh, N.C., 1930, 1955), I, 227; and there are many references to the settlement of Virginians in Granville County between 1746 and 1775 in Tilley, "Studies in the History of Colonial Granville County," pp. 30-42, *passim*. The extant record of English settlers coming from other colonies is less impressive. For some from Pennsylvania, see the Quaker lists cited in the previous footnote. Details on three from Maryland have already been given. For some coming from New Jersey, see *NCCR*, VI, 730: this item refers to a "few Poor families of Fishermen" who had come from Cape May to the southernmost coast of North Carolina and were New Light Anabaptists (Cape May at this time was a mainly Baptist community on the periphery of the main area of Quaker settlements in New Jersey). The New Light Baptists were elsewhere noted as being "very numerous" in this section of North Carolina: *NCCR*, VII, 164. There was also a "Jersey Settlement" in Rowan County.

37. Newsome found that about a hundred English emigrants were listed in the British customs house records for 1774-75, as compared with about five hundred Scottish leaving for North Carolina: Newsome, "Records of Emigrants . . .," *NCHR*, 11 (1934), 40. Also relevant here are some of the details in the biographical information compiled by Andrews and Andrews in *Journal of a Lady of Quality . . .*, pp. 8, 313-33, *passim*, and Mildred Campbell, "English Emigration on the Eve of the American Revolution," *AHR*, 61 (1955), 8.

38. F. W. Marshall, a Moravian who must have seen many of the migrants as they trekked by, close to the Moravian settlement, commented that "the migrations of men are like the movements of a flock of sheep, where one goes the flock follows, without knowing why": *MR*, I, 294. One of the finest accounts of the motivations that characterize emigrants involved in the peopling of colonies is that of Timothy Dwight, *Travels in New England and New York* (4 vols.; New Haven, Conn., 1821-22), II, 458-59.

In addition to the forces that "pull" men to a particular destination, there are, of course, the "push" forces that cause them to leave their homelands; but the latter are not treated in this analysis of immigration into North Carolina.

39. Since none of the incoming settlers stopped to record precisely what were the attractions of North Carolina for him, there is no very direct evidence to support this interpretation. There is, however, some fairly conclusive evidence that is relevant, in the following sources: *MR*, I, 40; Newsome, "Records of Emigrants . . .," *NCHR*, 11 (1934), 129-43, *passim*; the letter of Rowan to S. S., September 19, 1751, in Arthur Dobbs Papers (MSS); "Charleston, S.C., in 1774, as described by an English Traveler," *The Historical Magazine*, 9 (1865), 347; and the reason given by Meredith for his removal to North Carolina, described on p. 21, above.

40. For examples of this publicity, see the following: Harriss, *Lawson's History . . .*, pp. 177-78 (here Lawson, in a work that was published in several German-language editions, emphasizes the cheapness of land in North Carolina by comparison with prices in Virginia and Maryland); Stock, *Proceedings and Debates . . .*, IV, 852; "Informations . . .," in Boyd, *Some Eighteenth Century Tracts . . .*, pp. 427-51, *passim*; Höen and Böhme, *Das verlangte nicht erlangte Canaan . . .*, pp. 5-6 (even in this attempt to play down the overlaudatory tone of an earlier piece of promotional literature about Carolina, the authors came to the conclusion that land was much cheaper in Carolina than in Pennsylvania). Although the price of land in North Carolina rose during the eighteenth century, it remained comparatively cheap.

41. J. F. D. Smyth, *A Tour in the United States of America* (2 vols.; London,

1784), I, 152-53. There seems to have been a general tendency for land prices to decrease from New York at least as far south as North Carolina. This much is suggested by details and observations on land prices given in the following works: Percy W. Bidwell and John I. Falconer, *History of Agriculture in the Northern United States, 1620-1860* ("Carnegie Institution of Washington Publication," No. 358 [Washington, D.C., 1925]), pp. 70-71; William R. Shepherd, *History of Proprietary Government in Pennsylvania* ("Columbia University Studies in History, Economics and Public Law," Vol. 6 [New York, 1896]), pp. 34-35; Newton D. Mereness, *Maryland as a Proprietary Province* (New York, 1901), p. 77; William P. Palmer (ed.), *Calendar of Virginia State Papers ond other manuscripts, 1652-1781*, Vol. 1 (Richmond, Va., 1875), p. 218; Fairfax Harrison, *Virginia Land Grants: A Study of Conveyancing in Relation to Colonial Politics* (Richmond, Va., 1925), p. 140, n.2; R. D. W. Connor, *History of North Carolina*, Volume 1, *The Colonial and Revolutionary Periods, 1584-1783* (Chicago, 1919), p. 167.

42. Tiffany, *Letters of James Murray* . . ., pp. 18-19.

43. For further details on Murray see Sellers, "Private Profits and British Colonial Policy . . .," *WMQ*, 3rd Ser., 8 (1951), 537, 539.

44. Campbell, "English Migration . . .," *AHR*, 61 (1955), 4-5.

45. The occupational breakdown of the men, according to how they described themselves, was as follows: about 63 per cent craftsmen and tradespeople; about 16 per cent farmers, yeomen, or husbandmen; about 11 per cent laborers; about 5 per cent clerical workers or teachers; and about 3 per cent planters or gentlemen (*ibid.*, 6-7—the "missing" 2 per cent presumably were either unclassifiable or "lost" in rounding out the figures).

46. Newsome, "Records of Emigrants . . .," *NCHR*, 11 (1934), 40-41. Unfortunately, the findings of the two studies are not presented in comparable ways.

47. See Graham, *Colonists from Scotland* . . ., pp. 38-42, and the sources therein cited; and, the extract from a letter of March 16, 1774, sent from Wigton, in Galloway, and printed in *Weekly Magazine, or Edinburgh Amusement*, March 31, 1774.

48. Governor Tryon, in 1765, noted that settlers in the western counties, as compared with those in the eastern counties, were poor and had come from colonies to the north with "not more than a sufficiency to erect a Log House for their families and procure a few Tools to get a little Corn into the ground": William S. Powell (ed.), "Tryon's 'Book' on North Carolina," *NCHR*, 34 (1957), 411. See also *NCCR*, V, 318.

49. Fig. 22 is an interpretation of all the fragmentary evidence found relating to place and route of entry, particularly that which is specified in notes to the commentary that follows.

50. A valuable history, commentary, and bibliography pertaining to this map is given in Cumming, *The Southeast in Early Maps*, pp. 219-21. The map, when it was first drawn in 1751, showed only a section of the road, but subsequent editions, beginning in 1755, showed the entire stretch of the road that ran through Virginia.

51. Information on the origin of the road is given in the following works: Charles E. Kemper, "The Settlement of the Valley," *VMHB*, 30 (1922), 178; Charles E. Kemper, "Historical Notes from the Records of Augusta County, Virginia," *Historical Papers and Addresses of the Lancaster County Historical Society*, 25 (1921), 151; F. B. Kegley, *Kegley's Virginia Frontier: The Beginning of the Southwest: The Roanoke of Colonial Days, 1740-1783* (Roanoke, Va., 1938), pp. 143-44; William Couper, *History of the Shenandoah Valley* (3 vols.; New York, 1952), I, 345-56.

52. A summary account of the trip of the Moravians is given in *MR*, I, 77-79; a fuller version has been published in Newton D. Mereness (ed.), *Travels in the*

American Colonies (New York, 1916), pp. 323-56. For examples of others probably using the same route, see *NCCR*, V, 318, VII, 248.

53. The sources on which Fig. 23 is based are really all those cited in the above pages of this chapter that bear upon the distribution of the various elements in the population by the early 1770's. It should be emphasized, however, that it is no more than an impressionistic summary, since the exercise of a large amount of judgment is required in interpreting the fragmentary record of distributions.

54. Figs. 27, 28, and 29, for the years 1753, 1761, and 1769, were reconstructed from the maps for 1740, 1760, and 1775, which appear in Corbitt, *Formation of North Carolina Counties* . . ., as well as from some of the details and original definitions given in this work. Some of the county boundary lines are necessarily only approximately located.

55. This procedure is frowned upon by some cartographers. Perhaps there are occasions, however, when such dot maps are desirable. If a distribution that existed two hundred years ago is being mapped, and if the distribution has to be reconstructed on the basis of tenuous evidence and incomplete data, then the additional possibilities of error introduced by attempting to place the dots in what are assumed to be their appropriate locations are very great (and much greater than when preparing a located-dot map of a present-day distribution). On such occasions, the method of spreading dots evenly within the unit areas has its advantages. As an illustration of how this method can help, Fig. 25 (the 1761 map) should be compared with the maps showing population distribution in the colonies in 1760 that appear in three important works: Edward Channing, *A History of the United States*, Volume II, *A Century of Colonial History, 1660-1760* (New York, 1924), map at end of volume; Friis, *A Series of Population Maps* . . .; Jensen, *English Historical Documents: American Colonial Documents to 1776*, p. 454. The comparison shows that all three of these published maps somewhat misrepresent the distribution of North Carolina's population.

56. The contemporary survey is a manuscript map of the Albemarle Sound Region in the William L. Clements Library, Ann Arbor, Michigan (Clinton Collection, No. 293). Although undated it was almost certainly drawn up in the 1770's or early 1780's. The map is reproduced, in a slightly modified form which does not do justice to the original, in Ralph H. Brown, *Historical Geography of the United States* (New York, 1948), p. 61.

57. The process of extracting data from such lists, and then reordering them in order to calculate numbers of slaves per household, was a simple if time-consuming task. For a discussion of the origin and nature of data concerning taxables, see Appendix II, below.

58. The use of only two counties to represent the western portion of the colony is not a very satisfactory device. Unfortunately, there are no extant tax lists that show the number of slaves per household for any other western counties of colonial North Carolina. And the 1763 tax list for Anson County is torn in a few important places, so that instead of calculating totals it was necessary to resort to an impressionistic summary of conditions there; in view of the small number of slaves involved, the summary was not too difficult to make and is probably reasonably accurate.

59. The methods that were followed when using tax returns are explained in Appendix II, below. The particular returns that were used for Figs. 30 and 31 are specified in note 12, Appendix II, below. The data for Bertie County plotted on Fig. 30 refer to 1754; and on Fig. 31 the data for Bertie County refer to 1765, and those for Chowan and Perquimans are for 1766. There are no data at all for a few counties, and these had to be left blank on the maps.

60. This small area, shaded with the "herringbone" pattern in Fig. 31, comprised the two counties of Chowan and Perquimans. Inspection of the data on which the maps were based demonstrated that the greater intensity of this area was not

simply an artificial product of the class intervals used for the area shading on the map.

61. On the basis of a few scattered references to the numbers of Negroes that were imported into the colony, it would be reasonable to assume that even in the busiest years no more than one or two hundred were imported: *NCCR*, III, 430, 621, V, 314, IX, 179; *Commerce of Rhode Island, 1726-1774* ("Collections of the Massachusetts Historical Society," Seventh Series, Vol. 9 [Boston, 1914]), pp. 318, 414; *The North-Carolina Magazine: Or, Universal Intelligencer*, Oct. 12-Oct. 19, 1764; U.S. Bureau of the Census, *Historical Statistics* . . ., Series Z 290, p. 769. In the most important collection of documents relating to the slave trade, there is no section devoted to North Carolina because the editor was able to find almost no evidence of slave imports into the colony: Elizabeth Donnan (ed.), *Documents Illustrative of the History of the Slave Trade to America* ("Carnegie Institution of Washington Publication," No. 409; 4 vols. [Washington, D. C., 1930]), IV, 235-36.

62. Figures were obtained by comparing the total Negro population in 1755 with the total in 1767, using for this purpose only those counties in which Negroes and whites were differentiated; fortunately, they were differentiated in most of the counties in these two years. The figures were compiled from tax lists.

CHAPTER V

1. This figure was obtained by calculating the total number of barrels of naval stores exported from the mainland colonies and comparing this amount with the total exported from North Carolina. The figures were taken from the report made by the American Board of Customs: Exports and Imports, America, 1768-1773, a detailed document with invaluable data on colonial commerce. The original report is in BPRO, Customs 16/1, and I am indebted to Professor Merrill Jensen of the University of Wisconsin for the loan of his photostat copy of this material. In subsequent references, this source will simply be described as Customs 16/1. The limitations of Customs 16/1 as a source of statistical data are discussed at the end of Appendix II.

Background information concerning the development of the trade in naval stores in the eighteenth century is presented in Justin Williams, "English Mercantilism and Carolina Naval Stores, 1705-1776," *JSH*, 1 (1935), 169-85. Detailed descriptions of how these products were extracted from the forests have been given by several writers and will not be repeated here. The most useful accounts of production methods are in the following: Catesby, *Natural History of Carolina* . . ., I, xxiii-xxiv; Carman, *American Husbandry*, pp. 244-45; "Journal of a French Traveller . . .," *AHR*, 26 (1920-21), 733-34.

Other naval stores, such as resin, were of very minor importance in North Carolina, and are not considered here.

2. As long as the naval stores industry lasted it furnished an important source of income for North Carolina inhabitants. But it did not last very long. The large-scale production of naval stores began in the eighteenth century, reached a peak in the mid-nineteenth century, and declined rapidly thereafter. Today there is little left in North Carolina, either of the industry, or of the longleaf pine forests on which it was based.

3. The reduction in extent is not to be interpreted as a result primarily of fire upon the tree itself. Indeed, the longleaf pine seems to survive fire better than any other tree of the southeast. This quality has enabled it to survive on sites which, because of the high fiber content of the ground cover and the dryness of the very sandy soils, are, and have been, notoriously subject to fires. The openness of the stands in which it occurs can be attributed partly to the droughty

and infertile conditions of such sites and partly also, perhaps, to the inevitable destruction of some of the trees by fire at critical and susceptible periods in their growth cycle. While changes in the frequency or intensity of fires in historic time could have caused some decrease in the extent of longleaf pine forests, it seems more likely that this decline has been caused mainly by other factors. Widespread and long continued extraction of turpentine from longleaf stands, or severe cutting of the trees for lumber, or the destruction of longleaf seeds and seedlings by foraging hogs, or any combination of these factors probably played a more important role than fire in reducing the extent of longleaf pine forests.

The longleaf pine has been the subject of much investigation. The results of many earlier studies have been brought together and amplified in W. G. Wahlenberg, *Longleaf Pine* . . . (Charles Lathrop Pack Forestry Foundation, Washington, D.C., in cooperation with the Forest Service, USDA; 1946), which has a bibliography of over six hundred other items. A later study is also useful: David Bruce, "Thirty-two Years of Annual Burning in Longleaf Pine," *Journal of Forestry*, 45 (1947), 809-14.

4. In compiling Fig. 32, the following maps were used: "Map of North Carolina showing the distribution of the pine forests with special reference to the lumber industry," compiled 1881 (between pp. 514 and 515 in Vol. 9 of U.S. Dept. of Interior, Census Office, *Tenth Census of the United States* [1884]: *Report on the Forests of North America [Exclusive of Mexico]*, by Charles S. Sargent); Gifford Pinchot and W. W. Ashe, *Timber Trees and Forests of North Carolina* ("NCGS," Bulletin No. 6 [Winston-Salem, N.C., 1897]), Fig. 38, p. 132; G. F. Schwarz, *The Longleaf Pine in Virgin Forest* (New York, 1907), frontispiece map; W. W. Ashe, *Loblolly or North Carolina Pine* ("NCGES," Bulletin No. 24 [Raleigh, N.C., 1915]), Fig. 2.

5. "Pine barrens" were observed and commented upon by many travelers in North Carolina in the eighteenth century and later. What they generally meant by pine barrens were thin, distinctly open, stands of pine, growing on sandy hills or sandy upland sites throughout much of the Coastal Plain. While references in colonial materials to the particular species of which the pine barrens were composed are generally ambiguous, recent studies of the vegetation of sandy areas within the Coastal Plain have indicated that the dominant tree would almost certainly have been the longleaf pine. The scrub oaks and coarse grasses sometimes observed beneath the pine layer were probably mainly turkey oak (*Quercus catesbaei*) and wiregrass (*Aristida stricta*).

For references to the pine barrens in colonial North Carolina, see the following sources: *MR*, I, 39; *NCCR*, VI, 606; Catesby, *Natural History of Carolina* . . ., I, iv; Hugh B. Johnston (ed.) "The Journal of Ebenezer Hazard in North Carolina, 1777 and 1778," *NCHR*, 36 (1959), 362; Meredith, *An Account* . . ., pp. 17, 19, 20; Schoepf, *Travels in the Confederation* . . ., II, 127, 153-54; *NCCR*, V, 354; "Journal of an officer who travelled in America and the West Indies in 1764 and 1765," in Mereness, *Travels in the American Colonies*, pp. 400-1; "William Logan's Journal of a Journey to Georgia, 1745," *PMHB*, 36 (1912), 13, 15 (Logan briefly noted the similarity between the pine barrens in North Carolina and in New Jersey). Lederer, in a somewhat exaggerated vein, called what was undoubtedly a region of pine barrens, a "Deserta arenosa": William P. Cumming (ed.), *The Discoveries of John Lederer* (Charlottesville, Va., 1958), pp. 32, 85-86. For references to pine barrens in other Southern colonies, see: Smyth, *A Tour* . . ., I, 203 (South Carolina); Clarence L. Ver Steeg (ed.), *A True and Historical Narrative* . . ., ("Wormsloe Foundation Publications," No. 4 [Athens, Ga., 1960]), p. 137 (Georgia); John Bartram, *Diary of a Journey through the Carolinas, Georgia, and Florida from July 1, 1765, to April 10, 1766* . . . annotated by Francis Harper ("Transactions of the American Philosophical Society," New Ser., Vol. 33, Part 1, Dec., 1942 [Philadelphia, 1942]), pp. 22 (South Carolina), 32 (Georgia). For information on the pine barrens of New Jersey, see Muntz, "The Changing Geography of the New Jersey Woodlands, 1600-1900," pp. 127-31, 157-62; and the various relevant sources cited therein. In the New Jersey pine barrens the dominant pine is pitch pine (*Pinus rigida*); in the pine barrens of Virginia, according to Braun, *Deciduous Forests of Eastern North America*, p. 288, the dominant pine is loblolly (*Pinus taeda*). References in the colonial record to the longleaf pine by either its English or Latin name are rare; two of the few examples are in *NCCR*, VI, 606, and Harper, *Travels of William Bartram*, p. 20 (with reference to a description of the Coastal Plain in Georgia). The term yellow pine was used most frequently, but meant different species to different writers—see the comments on its usage in Schoepf, *Travels in the Confederation* . . ., II, 143-44. Thomas P. Keystone, on the basis of an early nineteenth-century travel account, also came to the conclusion that pine barrens were the longleaf pine stands: Ralph H. Brown, *Mirror for Americans* . . . ("American Geographical Society Special Publication," No. 27 [New York, 1943]), p. 235. For examples of the burning and grazing of the pine barrens in colonial times see *NCCR*, V, 354, and John Bartram, *Diary of a Journey* . . ., p. 32. For references to the production of naval stores from the pine barrens, see, for example, Catesby, *Natural History of Carolina* . . ., I, iv; *NCCR*, VI, 606; *MR*, I, 39. The most informative modern study of the vegetation of the pine barrens of North Carolina is B. W. Wells and I. V. Shunk, "The Vegetation and Habitat Factors of the Coarser Sands of the North Carolina Coastal Plain: An Ecological Study," *EM*, 1 (1931), 465-520.

6. Table 3 is a summary version of a series of tables compiled from Customs 16/1. On this series the exports were also broken down to show the overseas destination of all the exports; but this information is not relevant here, and it need only be mentioned that almost all of the naval stores either entered the coastwide trade, ultimately to be exported to Great Britain, or else were sent directly to the mother country.

Fig. 34 is based on averages computed from the data in Table 3. The data for 1772 were not taken into account (see note following), and no attempt was made to map the insignificant amount of trade from Port Currituck.

There are two estimates of the amount exported earlier in the century. One refers to about 1720, when 6,000 barrels were exported: *NCCR*, II, 296. The other refers to 1753, when 84,000 barrels were exported: [Edmund and William Burke], *An Account of the European Settlements in America*, II, 253.

7. It seems certain that the data for 1772 are incomplete, for there is no other way to account for the lack of a record of any exports of pitch and tar from Port Brunswick to Great Britain in 1772, even though in each of the four previous years such shipments had amounted to tens of thousands of barrels. It is as a result of this "lack" of shipments that the total volume of naval stores exported from North Carolina in 1772 amounted to only about three-fifths of what it had been in each of the four previous years, and the other three Ports in Table 3 suddenly seem to capture most of the trade in 1772. The figure for 1772 given in a table in Lefler and Newsome, *North Carolina* . . ., p. 92, seems more plausible, but no source for this figure is specified. In 1772, 130,000 barrels of naval stores were exported from North Carolina: Williams, "English Mercantilism and Carolina Naval Stores, 1705-1776," *JSH*, 1 (1935), 176, citing various manuscript trade papers.

8. See p. 27, above.

9. In all of the contemporary accounts in which mention is made of the type of person who actually made the naval stores, slaves are invariably specified; and it would seem, from the context of such references, that this was the normal practice. See, for examples, the following sources, all of which refer specifically to conditions in North Carolina: Brickell, *Natural History* . . ., p. 265; Powell, "Tryon's 'Book' on North Carolina," *NCHR*, 34 (1957), 411; "*Journal of a French Traveller* . . .," *AHR*, 26 (1920-21), 733; John Bartram, *Diary of a Journey* . . ., p. 16;

SCAG Gaz, July 29-August 5, 1768; Smyth, *A Tour* . . ., II, 95; Carman, *American Husbandry*, pp. 245-46; Schoepf, *Travels in the Confederation* . . ., II, 141, 143.

It is possible that the labor of indentured servants, where this was available, was also used in the making of naval stores: the first one of the above sources seems to suggest this.

10. The most significant of these other activities was the making and transporting of sawn lumber (discussed below), which probably served a fairly similar function. Lumbering, however, was a more localized phenomenon, dependent upon the availability of merchantable stands, while the making of tar and pitch only required a sufficiency of lightwood, or bits and pieces of living trees.

The resin from which turpentine was made flowed from cuts in the trees more freely in the summer months than it did in the winter months, and this seasonal variation was recognized by colonial turpentine makers. In this sense, turpentine making was not an entirely nonseasonal activity. Nevertheless, it could be, and was, made in the winter as well as summer; and in any case tar and pitch were the two most important naval stores, and the production of these bore no relation to seasonal conditions.

11. Letter to the Secretary of the Board of Trade, Jan. 1738, in *NCCR*, IV, 285. For statements of a similar nature see the following sources: *NCCR*, V, 149, IX, 294-95, 369; Schoepf, *Travels in the Confederation* . . ., II, 143.

12. The county was established in 1754 and the boundaries remained unchanged between 1754 and 1770; for their location, see Fig. 28.

13. These figures were compiled from the Cumberland County tax list in State Treasurer, Tax Lists, 1755 (MSS).

14. The absence of much naval stores production from Cumberland County was deduced from a fairly extensive examination of inventories of estates and merchants' account books relating to that area; the general lack of information indicative of production was judged to be significant. Only one source (the Robert Hogg Account Books, 1762-75, MSS), furnished evidence of even moderately large shipments of naval stores from Cumberland County; and it is significant that the persons mentioned in these accounts in connection with the largest sales of naval stores were the owners of the largest slaveholdings in Cumberland County—for example, Archibald McNeill, with seven slaves in 1767, and Farquhard Campbell, who had nine slaves in 1767 (figures from a 1767 list of Cumberland County taxables, in Comptroller's Papers, Box 40, MSS). Also significant is the fact that the settlers of Cumberland County who subsequently became Loyalists and filed claims after the Revolution for property and goods lost in North Carolina almost never claimed that they had lost naval stores, though they specified losses of just about every other item. (The statements of losses are in English Records, American Loyalist Claims, MSS.) There would seem to be no other way of accounting for the relative unimportance of naval stores in Cumberland County. The population of the county increased rapidly after its establishment in 1754, so that lack of settlements could not have been a factor. Cumberland County, and the area to the northwest of it, was the main area of the settlements of Scottish Highlanders (see Fig. 20), but to link the lack of naval stores production to the habits and predilections of this group would be misleading. It was not the fact that they were Scottish, but rather that most of them lacked slaves, that was of primary importance.

The low profit margins yielded by naval stores were caused by two reasons: those coming from North Carolina had early earned a reputation for being of particularly poor quality, owing to slipshod methods of production, packing, and shipping (see *NCCR*, IV, 5-6, VIII, 186-90); and freight rates on such bulky items were inevitably high.

Gray's view, that lumbering and the making of naval stores in eighteenth-century North Carolina was "mainly carried on by small farmers living in the vast pine forests," seems to be a misinterpretation: Lewis C. Gray, *History of Agriculture in the Southern United States to 1860* ("Carnegie Institution of Washington Publication," No. 430; 2 vols. [Washington, D.C., 1933]), I, 157. Compare the remarks and advice proffered by James Murray in a letter written at a time when he himself was engaged in producing naval stores in the lower Cape Fear Valley, much closer to Port Brunswick than Cumberland County: "If you intend to do any business here, a Cooper and a Craft that will carry about 100 barrels will be absolutely necessary. I have suffer'd much for want of them, and that want of Craft and negroes will be a great obstruction in securing the Quantity of Naval Stores at this time that otherwise I might do." (Letter to Henry McCulloh, dated May 11, 1741, published in Tiffany, *Letters of James Murray . . .*, p. 64.)

15. Details concerning this voyage were taken from Captain Jones, Ship Log, 1767-68, Edenton, N.C. (MSS). Fig. 35 was based on this log, and the Mouzon map of 1775. Further details on the difficulties of shipping out of Port Roanoke are given in *NCCR*, V, 316.

16. All these figures are based on compilations of data from Customs 16/1 and refer to the same five-year period.

17. *NCCR*, III, 369.

18. "A New Voyage to Georgia . . .," *GHSC*, 2 (1842), 55.

19. *NCCR*, VI, 1030.

20. *NCCR*, VII, 201-2.

21. *NCCR*, VII, 430.

22. Such references seem to be particularly frequent in the following local records: Walker, *New Hanover County Court Minutes*, Parts I and II; Cumberland County, Deeds and Grants (MSS), Vols. 3 (1766-1770), and 4 (1770-1772).

23. Andrews and Andrews, *Journal of a Lady of Quality . . .*, pp. 184-85. It has elsewhere been suggested that the "Hunthill" estate was one of four thousand acres: Boyd, *Some Eighteenth Century Tracts . . .*, p. 103. But the "vast number" of Negroes was really not so large—a 1767 tax list for New Hanover County shows that John Rutherford was in possession of forty-nine slaves at that time: the list is in Comptroller's Papers, Box 40 (MSS).

24. These generalizations are based on information in the sources cited in the previous five notes, on Tryon's letter of Feb. 22, 1767, in *NCCR*, VII, 440-41, and on the above-quoted account of "Hunthill." A comparison of account books with tax lists also proved helpful. The Robert Hogg Account Books, 1762-75 (MSS), provide the names of persons who sold large amounts of lumber, and a few of these could be identified in Brunswick County and New Hanover County tax lists, so that it was then possible to ascertain the number of slaves held by those few who were identified. The 1775 Mouzon map of the colony shows the location of a few sawmills, and identifies the owners of a couple of them; this evidence was of some slight use. But these sources, even when taken together, leave much unsaid, so that inevitably some of the generalizations rest on extrapolation from the existing evidence.

25. Some oak planks and boards were made in North Carolina, and between 1768 and 1772 about 50,000 feet were exported: Customs 16/1. Compared with the amount of pine boards and plank exported during the same period (about 15,000,000 feet), this is a trifling amount (and was omitted from Tables 4, 5, 6, 7, 8, and 9).

26. But the term "plantation" was not used with consistent connotations in colonial North Carolina; and because it has since acquired a variety of meanings, the use of it can be more confusing than enlightening. The term and its connotations are discussed in Chapter VI, below.

27. Andrews and Andrews, *Journal of a Lady of Quality . . .*, pp. 144-215,

passim. This whole account provides one of the most useful, albeit impressionistic, guides to this general area.

28. Doggett, "A Plantation . . .," *NEHGR*, 52 (1898), 471.

29. These generalizations are based on numerous references to sawmills in some of the local records of Cumberland County: Deeds and Grants, Vols. 3 and 4 (MSS). Some of these references are actually very informative, although the frequency of references to sawmills is a little misleading in that one and the same mill is often mentioned in several different places in the records. Also relevant are the Shaw Papers, 1735-1883 (MSS) and particularly the record of the agreement made between Colin Shaw and Angus McLarty on Jan. 18, 1766, as well as some of the other references to the activities of Colin Shaw in these papers.

30. The amount of sawn lumber exported from Port Bath Town, the second-ranking port after Port Brunswick in this trade, was only about a fifth of the volume shipped out of Port Brunswick (see Table 9). The only report of an important commercial sawmilling enterprise existing outside the Cape Fear Valley, actually refers to one the output of which must have been cleared through Port Beaufort rather than Port Bath Town. This mill was located fifteen miles by water from the town of Beaufort, and was on a two-thousand-acre tract from which were produced both naval stores and sawn lumber (according to the description of it in an advertisement in *North-Carolina Gazette* [New Bern], June 6, 1778). But see "Journal of a French Traveller . . .," *AHR*, 26 (1920-21), 735, for a reference to small mills that may have contributed to exports of sawn lumber from Port Bath Town.

31. Specifications for staves (and heading) are given in various regulatory acts: see, for example, the details in a 1755 act, in *NCSR*, XXIII, 354.

32. This is, as should be obvious, a tentative conclusion. Information on the various trees mentioned was obtained from some of the many guides to the trees of the southeast in general and North Carolina in particular. Two of the works found to be most helpful were: J. S. Holmes, *Common Forest Trees of North Carolina: A Pocket Manual* (8th ed.; Raleigh, N.C., 1958); and, W. C. Coker and H. R. Totten, *Trees of the Southeastern States* (3rd ed.; Chapel Hill, N.C., 1945).

33. Fig. 37 is based on the *Wildlife Cover Map of North Carolina*. On the original map, the vegetation cover type called "bottomland and swamp hardwoods" embraces several hardwood trees other than oaks.

34. See the source cited in note 15, Chapter V, above, and Fig. 35.

35. Nathaniel Williams, Letterbook and Accounts, 1758-1834, Cork, Ireland (MSS). The relevant items in this particular source refer to the period between 1758 and 1768.

36. These descriptions are in a ledger that contains a list of entrances and clearances relating to Port Roanoke, 1770-76 (MSS).

37. For a description of "Hunthill," see the account quoted on p. 98, above; the information on stave production there is given in Andrews and Andrews, *Journal of a Lady of Quality* . . ., p. 185.

38. Information on the past and present distribution of white cedar and cypress was found in the following: J. W. Cruikshank, *Forest Resources of the Northern Coastal Plain of North Carolina*, p. 10; B. W. Wells, *The Natural Gardens of North Carolina* (Chapel Hill, N.C., 1932), pp. 32-36; B. W. Wells, "Plant Communities of the Coastal Plain of North Carolina and Their Successional Relations," *Ecology*, 9 (1928), 233-34; Murray F. Buell and Robert L. Cain, "The Successional Role of Southern White Cedar, *Chamaecyparis Thyoides*, in Southeastern North Carolina," *Ecology*, 24 (1943), 85-93; B. W. Wells, "Ecological Problems of the Southeastern United States Coastal Plain," *BR*, 8 (1942), 539-43; Pinchot and Ashe, *Timber Trees and Forests of North Carolina*, pp. 173-78; Ashe, *The Forests, Forest Lands, and Forest Products of Eastern North Carolina*, pp. 15-31, *passim*.; Roland M. Harper, "Some Plants of Southeastern Virginia and Central North Carolina,"

Torreya, 3 (1903), 122-23; Roland M. Harper, "A November Day in the Upper Part of the Coastal Plain of North Carolina," *Torreya*, 6 (1906), 43; Thomas H. Kearney, "Report on a Botanical Survey of the Dismal Swamp Region," USDA, *Contributions from the U.S. National Herbarium*, Vol. 5, No. 6 (1901), 417, 423; and finally, an interesting map of the vegetation of North Carolina that appears in Eugene W. Hilgard, "Report on Cotton Production in the United States . . ." (this was published in 1884 as Volume 6 of the *Tenth Census of the U.S.*, and the map constitutes Plate 12 of this volume, preceding W. C. Kerr's "Report on the Cotton Production of the State of North Carolina . . .").

The white cedar now occurs here and there along the Atlantic Coastal Plain but is fairly rare in North Carolina. Although it was probably never very abundant or widely distributed, it was once more common that it now is. In the eighteenth and nineteenth centuries, burning and lumbering made great inroads on white cedar stands in North Carolina (as in New Jersey), with an efficiency that is not surprising in view of the tree's susceptibility to fire and its desirability for shingles. Paradoxically, in almost eliminating the white cedar stands, man was gathering the harvest of seeds whose growth he had earlier fostered. The white cedar apparently does not replace itself in the natural course of succession. Buell and Cain's study (cited above) of the reproductive habits of the tree has shown that it is dependent upon the existence of clearings in order to become established. Thus the stands so assiduously destroyed in the eighteenth and nineteenth centuries were themselves the product of activities in early centuries.

39. References to cypress trees, cypress swamps, and cypress ponds seem to be especially common in the records of Chowan County, as, for example, in Chowan County, Deeds, Book G, 1749-55 (MSS). In the Great Dismal Swamp, cypress trees were also once common: Kearney, "Report on a Botanical Survey . . .," USDA, *Contributions from the U.S. National Herbarium*, Vol. 5, No. 6 (1901), 418.

White cedar, too, was probably once more conspicuous in the Albemarle area than elsewhere. For mention of it here in the colonial record see the following: Harriss, *Lawson's History . . .*, p. 98; Powell, "Tryon's 'Book' on North Carolina," *NCHR*, 34 (1957), 408; Thomas Macknight's description of his estate of Campania, in English Records, American Loyalist Claims (MSS). For indications of the subsequent decline of white cedar, see: Kearney, "Report on a Botanical Survey . . .," USDA, *Contributions from the U.S. National Herbarium*, Vol. 5, No. 6 (1901), 417, 423; Ashe, *The Forests, Forest Lands, and Forest Products . . .*, pp. 30-31; Hamnett and Thornton, *Tar Heel Wildlife*, p. 9; A. E. Shearin, et al., *Soil Survey of Pasquotank County, North Carolina* (USDA in cooperation with the N.C. Agricultural Experiment Station, Oct., 1957), p. 48.

40. The interpretation in this paragraph is based on the following two sources: Benson, *Peter Kalm's Travels in North America*, I, 20, 298-301; and, the documents relating to Thomas Macknight's claim for compensation of losses in North Carolina, in English Records, American Loyalist Claims (MSS). Both sources leave much to be desired; because of this, and because of the lack of data on exports of shingles from the colonies before 1768, the interpretation is a tentative one.

Of special interest with regard to this southward movement is a mid-nineteenth-century account of how shingle makers, having virtually exhausted the resources of the Great Dismal Swamp, were then preparing to migrate southwards to a new field of operations, this time in the Florida Everglades: Frederick L. Olmsted, *A Journey in the Seaboard Slave States In the Years 1853-1854* (2 vols.; New York, 1904), I, 168, 170.

41. These details are taken from the second of the three sources noted in the previous note.

Chapter VI

1. All but the first and last of these activities will be described in this chapter. The first, the making of naval stores and lumber products, was discussed in the previous chapter, and for examples of evidence that indicate that these were generally made by farmers see the following sources: letter from Cullen Pollock to Joseph Anderson, dated May 11, 1747, in the Pollock Letter Book, 1708-61 (MSS); inventory of the estate of William Bartram, Senr., in J. Bryan Grimes [ed.], *North Carolina Wills and Inventories* (Raleigh, N.C., 1912), pp. 470-71 (this particular inventory is not dated but was drawn up *ca.* 1755). The last-named activity, the building of roads and bridges, is discussed briefly in the following chapter, in the context of transportation.

2. The most informative contemporary account of corn and its cultivation is that of Kalm: Esther L. Larsen (ed. and trans.), "Pehr Kalm's Description of Maize . . .," *AH*, 9 (1935), 98-117.

3. The use of corn for bread is indicated in the following: *NCCR*, I, 714, 765; "Journal of a French Traveller . . .," *AHR*, 26 (1920-21), 734, 737; Hooker, *The Carolina Backcountry on the Eve of Revolution* . . ., p. 196; and the tradition to this effect is repeated in the early nineteenth-century report published in A. R. Newsome (ed.), "Twelve North Carolina Counties, 1810-1811," *NCHR*, 6 (1929), 283. The allowance of corn rations to slaves is mentioned, or implied, in the following: *NCCR*, VII, 247; "William Logan's Journal . . .," *PMHB*, 36 (1912), 7. Use of corn as feed for livestock is mentioned in the following sources: Harriss, *Lawson's History* . . ., p. 76; Brickell, *Natural History* . . ., p. 16; Todd and Goebel, *Christoph von Graffenried's Account* . . ., p. 298; the letter from McCulloh to Iredell, Sept. 5, 1768, in McRee, *Life and Correspondence of James Iredell*, I, 23; and in several agreements with overseers among the papers in the Pollock Letter Book, 1708-61 (MSS).

4. Governor Dobbs and Governor Tryon, having made extensive tours of North Carolina (in 1755 and 1764, respectively), both reported that corn was the first crop planted by newly arrived farmers: *NCCR*, V, 363; Powell, "Tryon's 'Book' on North Carolina," *NCHR*, 34 (1957), 410.

5. Robert E. Moody (ed.), "Massachusetts Trade with Carolina, 1686-1709," *NCHR*, 20 (1943), 45.

6. The continued trade in corn from the Albemarle area is evidenced by various documents in Custom House Papers, Port of Roanoke, Vol. 1, 1682-1760 (MSS). The export of corn from the Cape Fear Valley is illustrated in "A New Voyage to Georgia . . .," *GHSC*, 2 (1842), 56.

7. But there were large variations from year to year in the amount of corn exported. In 1768, 117,389 bushels were exported; in 1769, 234,143 bushels; in 1770, 112,954 bushels; in 1771, 94,925 bushels; and in 1772, 176,742 bushels: Customs 16/1. These variations resulted mainly from regulations passed from time to time forbidding the export of corn when unusual climatic conditions had curtailed production: see *NCCR*, VII, 225-26, 428, VIII, 491, IX, 327-28. North Carolina's share of the total volume of corn exports from the mainland colonies also fluctuated from year to year. In 1770, it amounted to about one-fifth, whereas in 1772, it was only one-seventh (figures for the total exports from the colonies, compiled from Customs 16/1, are given in U.S. Bureau of the Census, *Historical Statistics* . . ., Series Z 76, p. 761—for 1770, and in Jensen [ed.], *English Historical Documents: American Colonial Documents to 1776*, p. 394—for 1772).

8. "A New Voyage to Georgia . . .," *GHSC*, 2 (1842), 56.

9. Carman, *American Husbandry*, p. 242.

10. *MR*, I, 250, 271 (both references are to the harvest of 1762).

11. The Moravians were meticulous record keepers and this is a good reason for preferring their figure. Furthermore, the visitor to southeastern North Carolina

was simply reporting hearsay about yields that referred to exceptionally fertile lands. And the anonymous author of *American Husbandry* (edited by Carman) sometimes inflated the virtues of the Southern colonies. Thus, he specified corn yields in New England, New York, and Pennsylvania (as on pp. 38, 73, 82, 141, 152); from these it would appear that yields of between twenty and forty bushels per acre were common in these areas. The figures he gave were mostly based on actual instances of corn farming, and the amounts are certainly credible. But when he came to describe yields in the Southern colonies the anonymous author was less careful, relying less on actual examples and more on generalizations. He invariably offered figures that would suggest the Southern colonies were much more productive. For corn yields in Georgia, he gave a figure of thirty-five to sixty bushels per acre, which was an estimate sent to him by a planter very well disposed to the virtues of farming in Georgia (p. 346; see also pp. 337-52). In Virginia and Maryland, the writer of *American Husbandry* claimed that yields of corn were seldom less than fifty bushels per acre and sometimes as high as eighty bushels (p. 188). But an observer of farming operations in Virginia in the 1770's estimated that the yields obtained there were between twelve and thirty bushels per acre: *The Journal of Nicholas Cresswell, 1774-1777* (New York, 1924), p. 197. The author of *American Husbandry* was, in fact, presenting an unduly favorable view of economic conditions in the Southern colonies. He was concerned to emphasize their importance to the Mother Country, and wanted to suggest that economic developments in the other colonies were detrimental to her interests. (These aims are most apparent in Chapters XXXIV-XXXVII; see, for example, pp. 504-5.) This bias led the author to present an inflated view of farming productivity in the Southern colonies.

12. It is safe both as an average and as a conversion factor. As an indication of average yields it is reasonable because, although under special circumstances (such as completely new land, or superior quality soils) greater yields may have been obtained, there were also probably many farmers who obtained smaller yields because they farmed with much less diligence than did the Moravians. As a conversion factor it is safe because even if the actual average were twice or half that assumed, the implication drawn from its use (see below) would not be invalidated.

13. Four sets of figures are relevant:
1. Nicholas Massy, who bought a tract of 310 acres on the Catawba River in 1767, mentioned in a letter to his brother that he had cleared and planted 8,700 corn hills. Since corn hills were generally spaced about 5 feet apart, an acre planted with corn must have contained on an average about 1,700 hills. Massy, therefore, had planted approximately 5 acres with corn. (Massy's letter, written to his brother in Maryland in 1767, is in Miscellaneous Papers, Series One, Vol. I, Sept. 20, 1755-Nov. 20, 1768, MSS; the size of his holdings is shown in his original deed of purchase, in Rowan County, Deeds, Vol. 6, MSS; the average of 1,700 hills per acre was obtained by working out the number of corn hills that could be disposed about a square-shaped acre of land, assuming that the hills were arranged in rows, the rows being 5 feet apart, and the hills along the rows being spaced 5 feet away from one another.)
2. The acreages planted to corn on a series of tracts offered for sale in a newspaper advertisement in 1773, seem to represent the other extreme. Again, the amounts were given in numbers of corn hills, but if the same method of conversion is employed it appears that the owner was referring to corn fields of 5 acres (on a tract of 500 acres), 30 acres (on a tract of 200 acres), 12 acres (on a tract of 700 acres), and 24 acres (on a tract of 500 acres). From some of the details furnished in the advertisement it is obvious that the advertiser was a person of considerable wealth, and that most of the tracts had been under cultivation for a longer time than had Massy's single farm. (The advertisement

is in *Va Gaz*, P.D., July 1, 1773—the tracts were all in Bute County, and tobacco and wheat were also grown on them.)
3. Very occasionally there is a mention in inventories of estates of the amount of corn grown by the deceased at the time of his death. Three such inventories were found, and they specify corn acreages of 8½ and 16, the latter twice. (The three inventories are in Orange County, Estates, 1758-85, MSS, and are on pp. 3-5, 223-26, and 254 of this volume. No particular significance attaches to the fact that these three inventories are all Orange County ones. There were many other references to corn, in Orange County inventories and in those of other counties, but none of them specifies the amount of corn being grown.)
4. There is a record of the fact that the Moravians, in 1762, had planted corn on 8 acres of their land, a remarkably small amount considering that this was the total for the whole community: *MR*, I, 250, 271.

Hence, it is reasonable to assume that small acreages predominated. There is one piece of evidence that runs counter to this view. In an advertisement of a farm near the River Roanoke, the advertiser claimed that this tract of 420 acres included over 100,000 corn hills: *Va Gaz*, P., June 9, 1766. This, presumably, was equivalent to about 60 acres of corn land. While it is conceivable that this was a more typical acreage than those cited above, it is more likely that it is either exceptional, or exaggerated, or both. No advertiser was likely to understate the amount he had planted, and it is worth noting that the largest acreages of corn, in item 2 above, were those taken from newspaper advertisements.

14. These features of the trade are apparent from a ledger containing lists of entrances and clearances, Port Roanoke, 1770-76 (MSS). For the earlier period, the following was relevant: Custom House Papers, Port of Roanoke, Vol. 1, 1682-1760 (MSS).
15. The comparatively low value of corn is abundantly illustrated by innumerable references to the prices of it and other colonial crops. Especially relevant is the "scale of value per ton" of various crops given in Carman, *American Husbandry*, p. 185.
16. An impression of population distribution and density in this area is given on Figs. 24, 25, and 26. See pp. 91-92, above, for a discussion of how these same water transportation facilities were more of a liability than an asset for the export of naval stores, an item produced on a completely different basis.
17. The account was by Thomas Ashe, and was written in 1682. It is reprinted in Alexander S. Salley (ed.), *Narratives of Early Carolina, 1650-1708* (New York, 1911), pp. 135-59—the reference to wheat experiments is on p. 146.
18. These cargo inventories can be found among the Custom House Papers, Port of Roanoke, Vol. 1, 1682-1760 (MSS). They record instances of wheat exports at least as early as 1703 (see pp. 11, 18).
19. Letter of 1714, in *NCCR*, II, 132.
20. *NCCR*, I, 764-65. The apparent lack of any evidence indicating that wheat was grown for consumption on the farm accords with the information indicating that corn was used for bread (see relevant sources cited in note 2, Chapter VI, above, and *MR*, I, 209).
21. Brickell, *Natural History* . . ., p. 40 (Brickell was an Edenton resident, and his account was first published in 1737). Apart from this, and the items cited above, the only other early references to wheat are in the following sources: *NCCR*, I, 127, 633 (which refer to 1714 and 1707, respectively, and are not very informative); and, Harriss, *Lawson's History* . . ., pp. 75, 83, 111, 173 (Lawson's remarks, first published in 1709, suggest that wheat yielded well, even on poor land, and that it was exported).
22. "William Logan's Journal . . .," *PMHB*, 36 (1912), 13.

23. See, for examples, the following: *NCCR,* IX, 621, 669; Mark A. De Wolfe Howe (ed.), "Journal of Josiah Quincy, Junior, 1773," *MHSP,* 49 (1915-16), 463.

24. The Moravian statement is taken from one of their reports: *MR,* II, 884. Also relevant are *NCCR,* VIII, 559; and, Carman, *American Husbandry,* p. 242. Even writers who had probably never been to North America and had obtained their information second-hand began to associate wheat production with western North Carolina: see [Edmund and William Burke], *An Account of the European Settlements in America,* II, 337 (correct pagination would have been 237); and, *A Present for an Emigrant . . .,* pp. 29-30. While some farmers in the east continued to grow wheat, it seems as though the practice there remained confined to the Albemarle area (for an indication of its persistence north of Albemarle Sound, see "Journal of a French Traveller . . .," *AHR,* 26 [1920-21], 738); no evidence of wheat growing in the southeastern part of the colony is known.

25. *MR,* II, 576 (the list was drawn up in 1764).

26. Although no comprehensive data are available for comparing acreages devoted to the two crops, there are a few production statistics that provide some measure of the relative importance of wheat and corn in the Moravian economy. The figures in the following table (from *MR,* I, 244, 271) show Moravian production of various crops, measured in bushels obtained after threshing:

YEAR OF HARVEST	WHEAT	CORN	RYE	BARLEY	OATS	BUCK-WHEAT	FLAX-SEED
1761	1009	114	163	328	300	40	72
1762	1198½	158	175½	220½	161½	48	29

It is apparent from these figures that wheat was by far the most important of the grain crops and that corn was merely one of several crops of much lesser significance. (The same feature is obvious from other figures in the *Moravian Records,* although these other data do not include the harvest of all the Moravian fields—see *MR,* I, 332, 358, 389, and 412.)

27. In the first couple of years, the Moravians ate bread made from corn, but by 1756 they were eating wheat bread regularly and gave up corn bread. At first they mixed some rye flour with the wheat, probably to stretch their supplies of the latter; but in 1764 one of the Moravians noted that "rye is more used in the distillery than for bread." (The quotation is from *MR,* II, 574. Information on bread preferences and bread making is in *MR,* I, 124, 142, 149, 155, 158, II, 576.)

The church diary of the Pennsylvania Moravians records the receipt of bread baked by their Brethren in North Carolina, which arrived in Pennsylvania in March, 1756, in two wagons (Fredric Klees, *The Pennsylvania Dutch* [New York, 1950], p. 221). The loaves were undoubtedly made from wheat flour, and the gift is eloquent testimony not only of their regard for such bread, but also of the pride the Moravians took in the early success of their community in North Carolina.

28. These two paragraphs are an interpretation of Moravian attitudes towards wheat raising, which is based on their records for the period between 1752 and 1780. Interpretation is necessary insofar as their motives for engaging in this or that kind of commerce are not always explicit. Information particularly relevant to the above paragraphs is given in entries on the following pages: *MR,* I, 159, 161, 173, 190, 206, 267, 368, 462, II, 698, 735, 736, 744, 762, 768, 891, 910.

29. It is not possible to establish how much wheat others were selling. The quantities were large enough to depress the price of wheat so that the Moravian trade was no longer as profitable as it had been: see *MR,* II, 884, 891, 893.

30. See Logan's report, cited on p. 112, above. And in 1753 the Moravians

were able to buy wheat for seed from a neighbor living six miles from their settlement: *MR*, I, 83.

31. But apparently there was no significantly large surplus for commercial purposes before 1760. The single exception is the unusually large amount of grain listed in the inventory of the estate of Matthew Patton in 1754, which included 25 bushels of wheat (as well as 100 bushels of corn, and 15 of rye, and a wagon which might have been used to carry his surplus to market); the inventory is in Anson County, Record of Wills and Inventories, Book 1, 1751-1795 (MSS).

32. See, for examples, the inventories of Aaron Vanhook, 1763 (which mentions 30 bushels of wheat in a mill, 20 bushels of wheat in a barn, and about 4,000 wheat sheaves "gathered in"); Duncan Bohannan, 1761 (50 bushels of wheat); and John McCallister (150 bushels of wheat—no date given, but probably belongs to 1769). The three inventories are all in Orange County, Estates, 1758-85 (MSS). The export of flour from the west was noted by Governor Tryon, in *NCCR*, VIII, 559 (refers to 1769).

33. A revealing advertisement in this respect is that for two tracts on the Dan River, in Guilford and Surry counties, which was inserted in *Va Gaz*, P.D., May 19, 1774. See also the advertisement for a tract of land in Wake County, in *Va Gaz*, P.D., Feb. 24, 1774.

34. While going through relevant source materials a note was made of those places (or counties) for which there was evidence associating them with wheat growing. It was a relatively easy matter to select from these references those that related to the period between 1765 and 1775 and then to draw a map showing the distribution of wheat at this time. The relevant sources are given in the list that follows, but in order to restrict its length it will be necessary to omit any discussion of the precise nature of the information found in each one of the sources and to resort to "blanket" references for large bodies of source material containing more than one mention of wheat: Secretary of State, Inventories and Sales of Estates, 1714-98 (MSS); Wake County, Clerk of Superior Court, Record Book No. 1, 1771-82 (MSS); Grimes, *North Carolina Wills and Inventories*; Anson County, Record of Wills and Inventories, Book 1, 1751-95 (MSS); letter from Alexr. Schaw, written to Lord Dartmouth in 1775, in Dartmouth Manuscripts, Transcripts of North Carolina Papers, 1720-83, p. 157; English Records, American Loyalist Claims (MSS—the materials relating to the claim of John Hamilton and Co. are especially useful); Cumberland County, Estates (eighty-three boxes of MSS—most of these do not refer to the colonial period, but by sampling them haphazardly about fifty estates were located that did refer to colonial Cumberland County, and a few of these contained relevant references to wheat); Chowan County, Inventories of Estates, Vols. 1-2, 1735-95 (MSS); Chowan County, Miscellaneous Court Papers, Vols. XII-XV (MSS); *NCCR*, V, 355-56, VIII, 559; "Journal of James Auld, 1765-1770," *SHAP*, 8 (1904), 261-62. In addition to these sources, a few of those that are cited elsewhere in this account of wheat growing also furnished relevant information. Two contemporary maps were useful because they showed the location of many mills: the maps were those of Collet, 1768, and of Mouzon, 1775.

35. There are three sources of data on trade in wheat, bread, and flour: Customs 16/1, which cover the period 1768-72; the James Iredell Notebooks, Vols. 1-5, Port of Roanoke Records, 1771-76 (MSS), which refer to only one of the Ports of North Carolina; and, Hogg and Campbell, Invoice Outward, 1767-82 (MSS), which contains a record of the flour purchases made by one large firm in Wilmington. These sources are not as valuable as the wealth of detailed information they contain would suggest. In attempting to use them to analyze trade in wheat, flour, and bread, it soon became obvious that they were of little value for this purpose. Each one of the three sources raised its set of intricate problems. It is not necessary to elaborate upon all of these intricacies here, but it is worth noting

three complicating factors that seriously restricted the use that could be made of any of the data in these sources. First, amounts are given in various weights and measures (bushels, barrels, tons, and so on), and are for three products (bread, flour, and wheat). No way could be found to convert these amounts to a common, significant index, such as acres. Secondly, the data throw very little light upon the volume of exports from the colony as a whole because much of the wheat and flour was carried into Virginia and South Carolina before being exported: *NCCR*, VIII, 559, IX, 328; Smyth, *A Tour* . . ., I, 161, II, 97-98. Although there are no data whatsoever on this overland trade, it was probably a much more significant part of the total export trade than in the case of corn, simply because wheat and flour were more valuable and hence better able to bear the costs of overland transportation. Thirdly, all of the sources pointed to the occurrence of large annual fluctuations in trade. In view of the few years covered by the data, and because the absolute amounts involved were small, these year to year variations created a problem. These three complicating factors very much restricted the use that could be made of the data in the sources.

36. Customs 16/1.

37. In 1772, a prolonged drought seriously injured crops, and particularly Indian corn. Learning of this, Governor Martin prohibited the export of wheat and flour in an attempt to relieve the distress expected to accompany the loss of the all-important corn harvest: *NCCR*, IX, 323-24, 327-28, 361. The fact that some wheat was exported may reflect the failure of his attempted interference with the export trade, or it may have been because this wheat was cleared from the Ports before the Governor's prohibition was announced. It is unfortunate that a figure has to be given for an unusual year, but the data are such that figures for most years are unusual for one reason or another. Those for 1772 at least have the significance of referring to the last year in which amounts for all the Ports are included.

38. Both figures were derived from Customs 16/1.

39. In 1772, for example, about 85 per cent of the 13,400 bushels of wheat shipped out of North Carolina Ports came out of Port Roanoke: Customs 16/1.

40. Smyth, *A Tour* . . ., I, 161, II, 97-98.

41. *NCCR*, VIII, 559.

42. The growth and function of Cross Creek is discussed in Chapter VII, below. Evidence of its role in the trade in wheat and flour was found in the following sources: letter from Alexr. Schaw to Lord Dartmouth, October, 1775, in Dartmouth Manuscripts; Harper, *Travels of William Bartram*, p. 302; *NCSR*, XV, 209; Robert Hogg Account Books, 1762-75 (MSS); Hogg and Campbell, Invoice Outward, 1767-82 (MSS); E. W. Caruthers, *A Sketch of the Life and Character of the Rev. David Caldwell* . . . (Greensborough, N.C., 1842), p. 113; and there are many references in Vols. I and II of the *Moravian Records* to trade between Cross Creek and the Moravian settlements, some of this trade being in wheat and flour.

43. For relevant contemporary comments on Alexandria and Bladensburg, see *Journal of Nicholas Cresswell, 1774-1777*, pp. 27, 47. The rise of Baltimore has frequently been associated with the wheat trade in Maryland; and some Virginians also took their wheat and flour there—see *Va Gaz*, P.D., March 22, 1770.

44. This interpretation of the function of early Camden rests more on surmise than on evidence, and perhaps the comparison should not be made until after all the relevant materials on South Carolina have been examined. But fragments of information from various sources suggest that the comparison might well be valid. See, for examples, the following: *SC Gaz*, Nov. 14, 1768; David Ramsay, *History of South-Carolina* (2 vols.; Charleston, S.C., 1809), II, 216; Thomas J. Kirkland and Robert M. Kennedy, *Historic Camden* (2 vols.; Columbia, S.C., 1905-26), I, 75-76, 87-88, 143; Leila Sellers, *Charleston Business on the Eve of Revolution* (Chapel Hill, N.C., 1934), p. 90.

45. This view of the wheat trade as a factor in the growth of urban settlements in various colonies obviously needs to be tested against the evidence relating to the early growth of the specified towns (and others), only a small fraction of which were examined.

46. Based on South Carolina exports, 1772, in Customs 16/1.

47. *South-Carolina Gazette and Country Journal*, July 15, 1766; *SC Gaz*, June 27, 1768, Nov. 14, 1768; Public Records of South Carolina (MSS), Vol. 32, p. 282; DeBrahm's account in Weston, *Documents Connected with the History of South Carolina*, p. 166.

48. The only known evidence on this point is both inconclusive and ambiguous: see *NCCR*, VI, 1030, and, the letter of Alexr. Schaw, cited in note 42, Chapter VI, above.

49. Such as naval stores and lumber products (see Chapter V, above) and, to a lesser extent, rice (see below).

50. The subject of soil "exhaustion" will not be entered into. At most, it was a minor factor as far as wheat growing was concerned. Only one contemporary writer actually associated soil "exhaustion" with wheat growing. He stated that, in the west, farmers were "exhausting" soil because of their habit of growing corn on the same piece of land without rotation and then turning to wheat when corn yields declined: Carman, *American Husbandry*, p. 242. With only this single piece of information to go on, it would be unwise to claim that views on soil "exhaustion" were a factor of major significance in the rising popularity of wheat.

51. This is the theme of Gaspare J. Saladino, "The Maryland and Virginia Wheat Trade from Its Beginnings to the American Revolution" (Master's thesis, University of Wisconsin, 1960)—see particularly p. 22. For contemporary comment summing up this change in Virginia and Maryland, see the following: *Va Gaz*, P.D., Oct. 29, 1767; *Va Gaz*, R., March 3, 1774 (in which a traveler seems to be including North Carolina with Virginia in respect to the rising importance of wheat).

52. "Belt" is not a very satisfactory term for this phenomenon. There was no continuous cultivated belt, and certainly no great band of contiguous fields devoted to wheat. At most there was probably a series of farms, the farms often being separated by nonagricultural areas, with a small portion of the cultivated part of the farms being used for raising wheat. But the term is much used to describe essentially similar agricultural features of the nineteenth and twentieth centuries, and this wheat "belt" was a colonial version of these later phenomena. One contemporary source throws an interesting sidelight on this colonial wheat "belt." The Committee of Husbandry of the American Philosophical Society published in 1771 a report about a "fly-weevil" that was causing much destruction of wheat. In their report, the committee observed that "It is said the injury of wheat from flies began in North-Carolina, about 40 years past. . . . That these mischievous flies have extended gradually from Carolina into Virginia, Maryland, and the Lower Counties, on Delaware; to the last of these places they did not arrive till seven years ago, and had not yet penetrated into Pennsylvania, or passed the Delaware." (*Transactions of the American Philosophical Society*, Vol. 1, Jan. 1, 1769-Jan. 1, 1771, 218.)

53. *NCCR*, IX, 621.

54. This conclusion on overseas markets is taken from Saladino, "The Maryland and Virginia Wheat Trade . . .," pp. 13, 91-144. The relationship between overseas markets and the production of wheat and flour in North Carolina is illustrated by a letter sent to Governor Martin from England in 1772 (*NCCR*, IX, 361), in which concern was expressed about the governor's attempt to prohibit the export of wheat and flour (see note 37, Chapter VI, above, for further details of this attempted prohibition).

55. It is difficult to pinpoint the particular respects in which their farming was

more productive, or more intensive, than farming elsewhere in the colony. Their agriculture is described in some detail in the voluminous records they left, but there are no such accounts of the farming of others that would provide a sure basis for comparison. Close examination of their records does, however, leave an impression of more careful and scrupulous farming than was practiced elsewhere, an impression essentially similar to that which was felt by contemporary visitors to the Moravian settlements (see below).

56. Winslow C. Watson (ed.), *Men and Times of the Revolution* . . . (New York, 1856), p. 255.

57. See, for examples, the following: Symth, *A Tour* . . ., I, 217; Schoepf, *Travels in the Confederation* . . ., II, 154; *NCCR*, VII, 285-86, IX, 329.

58. Wheat seems to have disappeared from here sometime in the last century, for even in 1861 an important agricultural writer observed that it was an especially important crop in Perquimans County, second only to corn: Edmund Ruffin, *Agricultural, Geological, and Descriptive Sketches of Lower North Carolina* (Raleigh, N.C., 1861), p. 85.

59. Compare Fig. 38 with the map showing the distribution of wheat in William Van Royen, *Atlas of the World's Resources*, Volume 1, *The Agricultural Resources of the World* (New York, 1954), Fig. 36, p. 32. The noncorrespondence of the scales and methods used in these two maps does not affect the validity of the comparison.

60. For Washington's comment, see Fitzpatrick, *Diaries of George Washington* . . ., IV, 186. The prominence of this area later is evident from the map in the atlas cited in the previous note.

61. For a variety of relevant supporting information, see the following: Boyd, *William Byrd's Histories* . . ., pp. 80, 103; *NCCR*, III, 622, IV, 170, V, 317; "William Logan's Journal . . .," *PMHB*, 36 (1912), 9; *MR*, I, 38; "Journal of a French Traveller . . .," *AHR*, 26 (1920-21), 736-37; Smyth, *A Tour* . . ., II, 97; Howe, "Journal of Josiah Quincy . . .," *MHSP*, 49 (1915-16), 463; Carman, *American Husbandry*, p. 237; Custom House Papers, Port of Roanoke, Vol. 1, 1682-1760 (MSS); Moody, "Massachusetts Trade with Carolina, 1686-1709," *NCHR*, 20 (1943), 45.

62. The smallness is immediately apparent when the figures are compared with those for Virginia and Maryland. Thus, in 1772, the amount exported from North Carolina Ports was only about 2 per cent of Virginia exports, and about 5 per cent of Maryland exports: Customs 16/1 data on tobacco in U.S. Bureau of Census, *Historical Statistics* . . ., Series Z 241-53. The exports from Virginia certainly included some tobacco actually grown in North Carolina; but even if it is assumed that as much tobacco was carried into Virginia from North Carolina as was exported directly from the latter, the comparative smallness of the North Carolina crop would still be evident.

63. The lower limit of 5,000 acres is a crude estimate, obtained by making the following assumptions:

1. that in 1772 as much tobacco was grown in North Carolina and then carried into Virginia for export, as was exported directly through the North Carolina Ports;
2. that in 1772 a hogshead of tobacco contained 1,000 lbs. of tobacco;
3. that 1 hogshead represented the average yield of 1½ acres of tobacco (an assumption made in Carman, *American Husbandry*, p. 168).

It was then a simple task to work out the acreage from the number of pounds of tobacco exported from the Ports in 1772. The upper limit of 7,500 acres was obtained by adjusting assumption 1. to allow for the fact that one traveler reported that twice as much tobacco was sent to Virginia as was exported via Edenton: "Journal of a French Traveller . . .," *AHR*, 26 (1920-21), 736-37.

64. Fig. 39 is based on two acts, of 1754 and 1767, which give full details of the tobacco inspection system, and specify the locations of the warehouses: *NCSR*, XXIII, 402-17, 728-41. (The 1767 act was first printed as a 1766 act in the *NCSR*, but this error was later corrected—see *NCSR*, XXV, 569.) It was not possible to locate all of these warehouses precisely on Fig. 39, because the sites of some of them were described in the acts with reference to long-vanished place names or personal names. All of the sites could be traced at least to the correct county, so that the inaccuracy incorporated in the map is not large.

65. There is one seemingly equivocal feature of the maps on Fig. 39. The value of the tobacco crop was such that it could stand the costs of transportation over considerable distances. A ton of it was worth twice as much as an equivalent weight of wheat, and four times as much as a ton of corn: Carman, *American Husbandry*, p. 185. Hence, it is possible that at least some of the crop was grown on farms well to the west of the warehouses and that it was simply brought to these before export. If this bringing in of tobacco from the west had been at all common, then of course warehouse locations would hardly serve as guides to the tobacco growing area. But there was no large-scale carriage of tobacco from the west, for virtually none was grown there. The counties containing tobacco warehouses were approximately those within which resided most of the tobacco-growing farmers. The existence of this rough correspondence was established by checking inventories of estates arranged on a county basis, in order to obtain an impression of the location of the counties in which resided most of the farmers whose inventories showed that they were growing tobacco. (The inventories examined are listed in the Bibliography and are for a number of counties in various sections of the colony.)

66. *NCCR*, IX, 539.

67. Schoepf, *Travels in the Confederation* . . ., II, 129-30. All earlier accounts associated tobacco with the northern part of the colony, and none described it as the chief crop; but Schoepf's statement was really an aside, and the context suggests that it would perhaps be misleading to attach too much significance to his use of the phrase "middle parts." Around this time, in the 1780's, tobacco cultivation was spreading southwards and had become of some importance in South Carolina and Georgia: see Jerome J. Nadelhaft, "South Carolina and the Slave Trade 1783-1787" (Master's thesis, University of Wisconsin, 1961), pp. 28-29.

68. Fitzpatrick, *Diaries of George Washington* . . ., IV, 167.

69. A series of legislative enactments made slight modifications to the warehousing system after 1754: *NCSR*, XXIII, 477-78, 488, 507-8, 512-14, 548. A host of minor matters were involved, but it is clear from some of the modifications, with regard to such issues as the numbers and salaries of inspectors at various places, that the disappearance of a few warehouses west of the Chowan River was simply a result of the enlargement of others in the same general area.

70. John Taylor, in an 1840 account, cited in Cornelius O. Cathey, *Agricultural Developments in North Carolina, 1783-1860* ("JSSHPS," Vol. 38 [Chapel Hill, N.C., 1956]), p. 119.

71. This is obvious from the account of its cultivation and preparation in Carman, *American Husbandry*, pp. 159-61.

72. The relationship between large slaveholdings and the production of naval stores and lumber in the southeast is discussed at length in Chapter V, above. For further details on the fluctuations in the value of tobacco, see Gray, *History of Agriculture* . . ., I, 272-76.

73. From all the inventories that were examined, it was evident that the farmers who were growing tobacco were not generally producing wheat and *vice versa*.

74. P. 177.

75. Provisions were also produced in the Albemarle area for export and included commodities such as peas, potatoes, honey, fish, and poultry, all of which appear

among the exports from Port Roanoke: see the two sources cited in note 14, Chapter VI, above, and Customs 16/1. Some of the provisions exported from here were used to supply vessels, such as the tobacco fleets sailing from Virginia: Harriss, *Lawson's History* . . ., p. 89.

If tobacco was really becoming less common in the area (see p. 121, above), then perhaps the decline was a result of soil "exhaustion," with declining yields following the nonrotation of the tobacco crop. There might thus have been a tendency for wheat-and-corn farms to replace tobacco-and-corn farms. All this is speculation, there being no evidence of such a tendency or for soil "exhaustion" in this area. But wheat was replacing tobacco to some extent in Virginia and Maryland: *Va Gaz*, P.D., Oct. 29, 1767. Gray has emphasized that small grains were being substituted for tobacco in tidewater Virginia and Maryland at about this time: *History of Agriculture* . . ., I, 166-68.

76. The following studies contain views of this process: Jacob M. Price, "The Rise of Glasgow in the Chesapeake Tobacco Trade, 1707-1775," *WMQ*, 3rd Ser., 11 (1954), 179-99; Robert P. Thomson, "The Merchant in Virginia, 1700-1775" (Ph.D. dissertation, University of Wisconsin, 1955), pp. 167-99; Calvin B. Coulter, Jr., "The Virginia Merchant" (Ph.D. dissertation, Princeton University, 1944), p. 2, *et passim*; Fairfax Harrison, *Landmarks of Old Prince William: A Study of Origins in Northern Virginia* (2 vols.; Richmond, Va., 1924), II, 371-96. Coulter's study is especially valuable and relevant.

77. From testimony of Rigdon Brice, among the supporting papers relating to the claims of John Hamilton and Company, in English Records, American Loyalist Claims (MSS).

78. See testimony of Robert Nelson, in source cited in previous note; but it should be noted that Nelson was referring to trade in general rather than to the tobacco trade in particular.

79. The Wilmington store of Hogg and Campbell was probably another such establishment, or so it seems from the detailed records of their transactions: Hogg and Campbell, Invoice Outward, 1767-82 (MSS). (Brief biographies of Hogg and Campbell are given in appendices appearing in Andrews and Andrews, *Journal of a Lady of Quality* . . ., pp. 323-25.) James Gammell and Company, of Greenock, sent Robert Gillies out to North Carolina to serve as their factor; he resided in Cross Creek, and even though there is no record of his activities there, it is very likely that he was doing on a small scale what the Hamiltons were doing so successfully on a large scale (information on Gammell and Gillies was found in English Records, American Loyalist Claims, MSS). The firm of John Cruden and Company, with stores at Cross Creek and Wilmington, was also involved in the tobacco trade and was apparently a branch of a Glasgow mercantile establishment (see advertisement in *Cape-Fear Mercury*, May 11, 1774, and English Records, American Loyalist Claims, MSS). But most of the Scottish traders interested in North Carolina tobacco probably operated out of Virginia (see *NCCR*, IV, 171), so that it is reasonable to suspect that the records of merchants there contain much further information relating to North Carolina trade.

80. The best compilation of background information is Gray, *History of Agriculture* . . ., I, 279-93.

81. Meredith, *An Account* . . ., p. 20. Note that Meredith mentions the use of tidal swamps, which suggests that this form of irrigation was used a few decades before the date suggested by Gray, *History of Agriculture* . . ., I, 279-80.

82. *NCCR*, V, 316, VI, 1029, IX, 270. See also: letter from Samuel Johnson to his son, October 5, 1755, in Hayes Collection (MSS), Folder 38 in Reel 2; Doggett, "A Plantation . . .," *NEHGR*, 52 (1898), 471.

83. *NCCR*, IX, 364; Tiffany, *Letters of James Murray* . . ., p. 78n.; letter of Governor Johnston to Thomas Hill, dated April 16, 1750—the original is in CO 5/296, p. 308 (LC copy of MSS in BPRO). I am much indebted to Mr. William

S. Powell, of the University of North Carolina Library, for drawing Governor Johnston's letter to my attention, for kindly sending me a copy of it, and for a great deal of help subsequently.

84. For information on these aspects of indigo growing, see the following: *Further Observations Intended for Improving the Culture and Curing of Indigo, etc. in South-Carolina* (London, 1747), pp. 14-25; C. W., [Account of the Culture and Manufacture of Indigo], *Gentleman's Magazine*, 25 (1755), 201-3, 256-59; *SC Gaz*, Aug. 25, 1757 (contains an extract from a poem, entitled "Indigo," with a wealth of detail about the growing of the crop). The demands of rice are well-known: among the more informative contemporary accounts is that of Carman, *American Husbandry*, pp. 275-77.

85. Carman, *American Husbandry*, pp. 279-80, 285; Milling, *Colonial South Carolina* . . ., p. 17 (remarks of Governor Glen). In both of these sources, the complementarity of rice and indigo production is emphasized.

86. The present northern limit for rice in the eastern United States is approximately 37°N, or about at the southern end of Chesapeake Bay: Van Royen, *Atlas of the World's Resources*, Volume 1, *The Agricultural Resources of the World*, p. 83.

87. Gray, *History of Agriculture* . . ., I, 277.

88. Both crops failed in 1773 because of a summer drought: *NCCR*, IX, 687.

89. Several references to the number of cuttings per year in South Carolina and the West Indies are cited in Gray, *History of Agriculture* . . ., I, 293; for North Carolina, see *NCCR*, VI, 1029, IX, 687.

90. Cathey, *Agricultural Developments in North Carolina, 1783-1860*, p. 19. But as late as 1791, Washington observed that some indigo was being grown: Fitzpatrick, *Diaries of George Washington* . . ., IV, 194.

91. *NCCR*, V, 356; Smyth, *A Tour* . . ., II, 97.

92. It is not possible to establish how large was the portion consumed locally. For an indication that some was kept aside for family use, see the inventory of the estate of John C. Bains, 1775, in Chowan County, Inventories of Estates, Vols. 1-2, 1735-95 (MSS). Gray cites evidence to the effect that a third of the rice produced in South Carolina in 1715 was consumed in that colony: *History of Agriculture* . . ., I, 287. It is quite possible that rice was a prominent element in the diet of those who lived in or near the rice-producing region of North Carolina, for it had certainly achieved such a status in the first half of the nineteenth century: Cathey, *Agricultural Developments in North Carolina, 1783-1860*, p. 141.

93. In 1771, 546 barrels of rice were exported from the Ports of North Carolina. If it is assumed that a similar quantity of North Carolina rice was actually exported through Charleston, and the amount consumed within the colony was equal to one-third of the total exported (through North Carolina Ports plus Charleston), then the total amount grown would have been of the order of 1,500 barrels. At this time a rice barrel weighed about 525 lbs.: see the various sources and conclusions given in U.S. Bureau of the Census, *Historical Statistics* . . ., pp. 750-51. A barrel of this weight probably represented the yield of approximately one-third of an acre: see various estimates of yields cited in Carman, *American Husbandry*, p. 278, and Gray, *History of Agriculture* . . ., I, 283-84. Hence, 1,500 barrels would have represented the harvest from 500 acres. Since some of the above assumptions are more likely to be over-estimations of rice production than under-estimations, this figure of 500 acres is best regarded as the upper limit. On the other hand, the most likely single source of error in the calculation may concern the quantity of North Carolina rice that was shipped to Charleston for export. Because facilities for handling rice at Charleston must have been so much better developed than at either Brunswick or Wilmington, it is possible that the South Carolina metropolis attracted much more of the North Carolina crop than has been allowed for in the calculation.

94. In 1772, 1,304 lbs. were exported from North Carolina Ports. Assuming

that an equal amount was exported via South Carolina, then total production in that year was about 2,600 lbs. Governor Glen of South Carolina estimated that good land yielded about 80 lbs. of indigo per acre, but that the land presently being cultivated (in South Carolina) would give only 30 lbs. per acre: Milling, *Colonial South Carolina* . . ., p. 17. If yields of 40 lbs. were obtained in North Carolina, then the total acreage there must have been about 80.

95. For indications of location in fairly imprecise terms, see the following: *NCCR*, IX, 270, 364; Smyth, *A Tour* . . ., II, 97. These sources specify the Cape Fear Valley, or the southern part of the colony. For more precise locational information and references, see below.

96. This map is based on numerous sources, primarily all of the references to rice and indigo production cited in the remainder of this account that could be placed in their locational context.

97. Details on Richard and Joseph Eagle(s) are taken from the following: Andrews and Andrews, *Journal of a Lady of Quality* . . ., pp. 148, 316; tax list for Brunswick County, 1769, in Secretary of State, Tax Lists, 1720-1839 (MSS); Grimes, *North Carolina Wills and Inventories*, pp. 486-90.

98. The letter from Governor Johnston was written in 1750 to Thomas Hill (see note 83, Chapter VI, above). The figures concerning the number of slaves owned by the individuals mentioned in the letter were obtained from the following tax lists: tax list for New Hanover County, 1755, in State Treasurer, Tax Lists, 1755 (MSS); tax list for New Hanover County, 1763, in N.C. Court Papers, 1763-77 (MSS); tax list for New Hanover County, 1767, in Comptroller's Papers, Box 40 (MSS); tax list for Brunswick County, 1769, in Secretary of State, Tax Lists, 1720-1839 (MSS).

99. These details relating to Hyrne are taken from an advertisement in the *Cape-Fear Mercury*, Sept. 22, 1773, and from a tax list for New Hanover County, 1767 (in Comptroller's Papers, Box 40, MSS).

100. For a view of the importance of slavery in this section, see data compiled for New Hanover and Brunswick counties in Table 2. There were, inevitably, a few exceptions to these generalizations. Fragmentary evidence of various kinds shows that from time to time a little rice and indigo was produced, on small estates, with the aid of only a few Negro slaves, in areas outside the Cape Fear region. The following sources record instances of such exceptions, or at least indications of possible exceptions: *NCCR*, V, 316, 356; letter of John Campbell, probably written to Dobbs around 1749, in Arthur Dobbs Papers, 1731-71 (MSS); inventory of the estate of John Bond, Jnr., 1750, in Secretary of State, Inventories of Estates, 1749-54 (pp. 7-9 in bound volume of MSS); inventories of estates of John White, 1746/47, John White, 1772, and John Wilson, 1761, all in Secretary of State, Inventories and Sales of Estates, 1714-98 (MSS); inventories of estates of Joseph Anderson, 1751, Cornelius Leary, about 1770, and John C. Bains, 1775, all in Chowan County, Inventories of Estates, Vols. 1-2, 1735-95 (MSS). These exceptions are less significant than their mere number would seem to indicate. A completely different kind of exception was a holding in Carteret County advertised for sale in 1777 and 1778: *North-Carolina Gazette* (New Bern), June 6, 1778. This estate was apparently one designed for the large-scale production of lumber, wood products, naval stores, and rice.

101. The course of settlement, and the economic development of this region have already been touched upon in a number of places in this and earlier chapters. What follows is a summary of the development of the area, with a few illustrative contemporary comments added.

102. Brickell, *Natural History* . . ., p. 4.

103. For further details of Minot's efforts, and for source, see p. 100, above.

104. Letter from Alexr. Schaw to Lord Dartmouth, Oct. 31, 1775, in Dartmouth Manuscripts, p. 157. The comments on the wealth of the region were borne out

by the few details found about the estates of individuals. Some examples of these estates have already been presented, and others were found but need not be presented here. Suffice it to say that the finding of these examples involved establishing the names and locations of both individuals and their estates, and the checking of such information against fragmentary evidence that seemed to provide further details on the nature of their settlements. The most useful sources for these purposes were the works and items cited in notes 97 and 98, Chapter VI, above, and particularly the editorial materials accompanying the text of Andrews and Andrews, *Journal of a Lady of Quality* . . ., and the tax lists. Other pertinent information was found in the following: the maps of Moseley (1733), Collet (1770), and Mouzon (1775); Alfred M. Waddell, *A History of New Hanover County and the Lower Cape Fear Region, Volume 1, 1723-1800* (N.p., n.d.); James Sprunt, *Chronicles of the Cape Fear River, 1600-1916* (2nd ed.; Raleigh, N.C., 1916). The last two of these items are local histories, often misleading in important respects; in particular, usage of the term "plantation" is so vague and flexible as to deprive of any meaning considerable portions of both accounts.

Doubtless, there were other, similarly large and wealthy estates scattered here and there in the colony. But in no other area were they so conspicuous and concentrated.

105. These figures are all either taken directly from Table 1, or derived from the 1767 New Hanover County tax list and the 1769 Brunswick County tax list noted on that table.

106. There are no detailed tax lists for the counties adjacent to New Hanover and Brunswick farther up the Cape Fear River, but Figs. 30 and 31 do suggest that slavery was much less important in this adjoining area, and there are no known records indicative of an extension of this concentration of wealth upstream. The property of James Pemberton, located in Bladen County, on the Northwest Branch of the Cape Fear, included 7 Negro slaves, a tar kiln, and 100 bushels of rice, and his holding was 250 acres in extent (English Records, American Loyalist Claims, MSS). Perhaps this was a transitional type of settlement, essentially the same as the settlements lower down the river, but on a smaller scale.

107. For the cartographic evidence, compare the Moseley map of 1733 with either the Collet map of 1770 or the Mouzon map of 1775.

108. This device, of leaving significant facts unsaid in newspaper advertisements, has always been a common one. Presumably, cautious readers of colonial papers made the necessary allowances for errors of omission.

109. "A New Voyage to Georgia . . .," *GHSC*, 2 (1842), 58.

110. *Cape-Fear Mercury*, Dec. 29, 1773.

111. *North-Carolina Gazette* (New Bern), Nov. 15, 1751. The name itself might have been ironical, implying that it was really a very large estate, or it might have been a recognition of the fact that it was but a small property among giant-sized ones. Or the name may have been bestowed for quite different reasons. The name was spelled "Lilleput" in the original. For further information on this estate, see Secretary of State, Inventories of Estates, 1749-1754 (MSS), pp. 52-58.

112. This is conjectural, although data compiled in Morris and Morris, "Economic Conditions in North Carolina About 1780, Part I, Landholding," *NCHR*, 16 (1939), 107-33, have been used as a crude guide. This work contains figures on landholdings in New Hanover County, 1782, and Brunswick County, 1784, which suggest that in these two counties there were then about thirty persons holding between two thousand and five thousand acres, and about 10 holding more acres (*ibid.*, Table 4); but the holdings of these individuals were not necessarily all in one piece, and some of their land was actually located in other counties. And the validity of extrapolating figures for the 1770's from data referring to the 1780's is questionable, simply because of the ever present possibility of land consolidation or fragmentation.

113. "A New Voyage to Georgia . . .," *GHSC*, 2 (1842), 56.
114. The "Golden Mines" are mentioned in Milling, *Colonial South Carolina* . . ., p. 119. Most of the indigo credited to South Carolina and Georgia (Table 13) probably came from the former colony.
115. The exports of naval stores and lumber products from the Cape Fear were obviously more important than were the exports of rice and indigo. For indications that the same landholder engaged in the production of both forest products and crops, see the following: *Cape-Fear Mercury*, Sept. 22, 1773 (advertisement of the estate of Henry Hyrne); Tiffany, *Letters of James Murray* . . ., p. 78n., *et passim*; Andrews and Andrews, *Journal of a Lady of Quality* . . ., p. 148.
116. *SCAG Gaz*, July 29-August 5, 1768.
117. *Ibid*. Also relevant are the following: Howe, "Journal of Josiah Quincy . . .," *MHSP*, 49 (1915-16), 462; Benson, *Peter Kalm's Travels in North America* . . ., I, 148; John Bartram, *Diary of a Journey* . . ., p. 22; and, "Journal of an Officer . . .," in Mereness, *Travels in the American Colonies*, p. 402.
118. It was estimated that thirty slaves were necessary for large-scale, specialized, rice production: see Milling, *Colonial South Carolina* . . ., p. 16, and Doggett, "A Plantation . . .," *NEHGR*, 52 (1898), 471.
119. It has recently been emphasized elsewhere that "product specialization probably never was so great on ante bellum plantations as popular accounts suggest": Merle Prunty, Jr., "The Renaissance of the Southern Plantation," *GR*, 45 (1955), 462.
120. Robert L. Reynolds, "The Mediterranean Frontiers, 1000-1400," in Walker D. Wyman and Clifton D. Kroeber (eds.), *The Frontier in Perspective* (Madison, Wis., 1957), p. 31. For a somewhat similar view, see Gottfried Pfeifer, "Historische Grundlagen der Kulturgeographischen Individualität des Südostens der Vereinigten Staaten," *Petermanns Geographischen Mitteilungen*, 98 (1954), 303 (in which is emphasized the West Indian component in the settlement of the Carolinas).
121. See p. 27, above, and note that the Moore family was from South Carolina. Editorial comments in Andrews and Andrews, *Journal of a Lady of Quality* . . . include very useful material relating to the South Carolina origins of many of the prominent early settlers in the Cape Fear area: see particularly pp. 8, 277, and 313ff.
122. Gray, *History of Agriculture* . . ., I, 322. See also Jno. P. Thomas, "The Barbadians in Early South Carolina," *South Carolina Historical and Genealogical Magazine*, 31 (1930), 75-92, *passim*; this article contains interesting details illustrating the ties between early South Carolina and Barbados, and the Moore mentioned (p. 89) as being one of the Barbadians who migrated to South Carolina was one of "The Family" of Moores who subsequently played such a large role in the lower Cape Fear. It is also worth noting that Barbadians played a very important part in the attempts that were made in the 1660's to settle the lower Cape Fear.
123. See item 7 in the quotation from one of his letters, p. 64, above.
124. The West Indian connection was Tullidelph (Tiffany, *Letters of James Murray* . . ., p. 19n.), apparently one of a family of wealthy, large, plantation owners in Antigua (see Andrews and Andrews, *Journal of a Lady of Quality* . . ., p. 100).
125. For its transfer from the West Indies to South Carolina, see Gray, *History of Agriculture* . . ., I, 290-92.
126. Source materials pertaining to South Carolina and the West Indian colonies will presumably throw further light on this transmission of the plantation system.
127. Details of these and a few other physical relics are given in Blackwell P. Robinson (ed.), *The North Carolina Guide* (Chapel Hill, N.C., 1955), pp. 265-69, and almost all of these were checked during the course of field work in the area. An impression of the unimportance of the neoplantation here can be gained from

Fig. 1 in Prunty, "The Renaissance of the Southern Plantation," *GR*, 45 (1955), 462. But one very carefully engraved nineteenth-century map does at least show the rice swamps that were then still in evidence along the estuary of the Cape Fear River: see U.S. Coast and Geodetic Survey, *Coast Chart No. 150, Masonboro Inlet to Shallotte Inlet including Cape Fear North Carolina*, scale 1:80,000, issued 1888 (topography surveyed between 1851 and 1878).

128. Letter of Alexr. Schaw, Oct. 31, 1775, in Dartmouth Manuscripts, p. 157.
129. *NCCR*, II, 762.
130. Speech of Governor Burrington, Nov. 8, 1733, in *NCCR*, III, 621-22. In a letter written about three years later, Burrington estimated that ten thousand oxen and fifty thousand hogs were driven into Virginia each year: *NCCR*, IV, 172.
131. Woodward, *Ploughs and Politicks* . . ., p. 331. Of some interest, though perhaps not very relevant here, is the fact that late in his life Read actually emigrated to North Carolina, and opened a store there; he died in 1774, about a year after his arrival in the colony: *ibid.*, 216-17.
132. The following diverse collection of source materials contains pertinent evidence for this: [Edmund and William Burke], *An Account of the European Settlements in America*, II, 239; *NCCR*, V, 322, 745-46, VI, 166, 1030; William W. Hening (ed.), *The Statutes at Large: Being a Collection of all the Laws of Virginia* . . . (13 vols.; Richmond, Va., Philadelphia, and New York, 1809-1823), VIII, 245; *Va Gaz*, R., Sept. 22, 1768; McRee, *Life and Correspondence of James Iredell*, I, 23; "Informations . . .," in Boyd, *Some Eighteenth Century Tracts* . . ., pp. 444-45; *Journal of Nicholas Cresswell 1774-1777*, p. 269; Smyth, *A Tour* . . ., I, 161, II, 97-98; Schoepf, *Travels in the Confederation* . . ., I, 213, II, 109-110; *MR*, I, 39, III, 1101, 1186, 1188, 1189, *et passim*.
133. See Boyd, *William Byrd's Histories* . . ., p. 55, and *NCCR*, IX, 269.
134. See, for example, *NCCR*, III, 622.
135. Letter from John Campbell, probably to Arthur Dobbs (undated, but almost certainly written in 1749), in Arthur Dobbs Papers, 1731-71 (MSS).
136. See *MR*, I, 151; *NCCR*, V, 356; and, "Journal of a French Traveller . . .," *AHR*, 26 (1920-21), 737.
137. For evidence of this overland trade, see the following: *SCAG Gaz*, Dec. 11, 1767 (advertisement of Atkins and Weston); inventory of John McGee, 1773, in Secretary of State, Inventories and Sales of Estates, 1714-1798 (MSS); Smyth, *A Tour* . . ., I, 161, II, 97-98; *MR*, II, 865.
138. Carman, *American Husbandry*, p. 241.
139. Boyd, *Some Eighteenth Century Tracts* . . ., p. 444.
140. See, in conjunction with the sources cited in the two previous notes, the following additional statements of the same theme: [Edmund and William Burke], *An Account of the European Settlements in America*, II, 238; Malachy Postlethwayt, *The Universal Dictionary of Trade and Commerce* . . . (2 vols., 4th ed.; London, 1774)—under the heading "Carolina"; *A Present for an Emigrant* . . ., p. 30; Schoepf, *Travels in the Confederation* . . ., II, 108. One early account of Carolina may well have been the source of most of the subsequent statements, and this early description was actually a piece of promotional literature: Thomas Ashe, "Carolina . . .," 1682, in Salley, *Narratives of Early Carolina, 1650-1708*, p. 149. Originally stated with reference to Carolina, the theme later appears in accounts of both North and South Carolina: for interesting examples with respect to the latter colony, see Milling, *Colonial South Carolina* . . ., pp. 76, 138. Later historians of agriculture have often accepted such statements as these at their face value: see, for examples, Cathey, *Agricultural Developments in North Carolina, 1783-1860*, p. 20, and, Gray, *History of Agriculture* . . ., I, 150.
141. Francis G. Morris and Phyllis M. Morris, "Economic Conditions in North Carolina About 1780, Part II, Ownership of Two Lots, Slaves, and Cattle," *NCHR*, 16 (1939), 316-22, *passim*.

142. A quantitative analysis of livestock holdings based on inventories would be feasible only if attention were concentrated upon the inventories of just one county, one for which there remains a relatively large number of comprehensive and roughly contemporaneous inventories. The use I made of inventories was necessarily broader in scope, and the findings impressionistic. For details of the inventories examined, see Bibliography. The interpretations that follow, above, are based on lists compiled from these inventories.

143. This Turnerian theme is an old and oft-repeated one: see, for example, Gray, *History of Agriculture* . . ., I, 149. Compare also Thompson's view that "in every one of the Colonies, stock raising on a large scale was primarily a frontier activity": James W. Thompson, *A History of Livestock Raising in the United States, 1607-1860* (USDA, "Agricultural History Series," No. 5 [November, 1942]), p. 65. Much confusion has stemmed from the attempt to view the history of colonial agriculture in the south as the story of the displacement of herders by farmers and the failure to analyze the livestock industry as such. In a recent attempt to resolve this confusion, Dunbar has substituted quite a different hypothesis (see note 161, Chapter VI, below).

144. Anson and Orange counties were used to represent the west; Chowan and Onslow to represent the east (see Bibliography for further details of the inventories examined). Instances of especially large holdings of livestock were those of the following persons: John Benbury of Chowan County, whose inventory (probably drawn up around 1767) lists 144 cattle, 254 hogs, 74 sheep, 10 oxen, and 6 horses; Edward Howard of Onslow County, whose inventory of 1746 specifies 123 cattle, 40 hogs, 8 horses, and 2 oxen; Caleb Wilson of Currituck County, whose inventory of 1754 lists 243 cattle, 454 swine, 142 sheep, and 22 horses (this inventory has been printed in Grimes, *North Carolina Wills and Inventories*, pp. 567-69, and possibly represents the largest of all livestock holdings at this time). The Morrises came to the same conclusion from their studies of property lists for the 1780's: Morris and Morris, "Economic Conditions in North Carolina About 1780, Part II, Ownership of Town Lots, Slaves, and Cattle," *NCHR*, 16 (1939), 316. And one traveler in the colony in the winter of 1783/84 observed that people inland kept fewer cattle than did the inhabitants farther east: Schoepf, *Travels in the Confederation* . . ., II, 121.

145. For suggestions of this localization, see the following: "Journal of a French Traveller . . .," *AHR*, 26 (1920-21), 737; Smyth, *A Tour* . . ., I, 84, 161, II, 97; Schoepf, *Travels in the Confederation* . . ., II, 121; letter from John Campbell, probably to Arthur Dobbs (undated, but almost certainly written in 1749), in Arthur Dobbs Papers, 1731-71 (MSS); Hogg and Campbell, Invoice Outward, 1767-82 (butter is specified in many of these invoices, and most of it seems to have been collected in Cross Creek before being sent to Wilmington); *MR*, I, 151, II, 820, 828, 865, 891; letter dated Nov. 23, 1761, from Peter Copland to Thomas Agnis, in Chowan County, Miscellaneous Court Papers (MSS), XI, 27. For an exception to the generalization, see Andrews and Andrews, *Journal of a Lady of Quality* . . ., p. 179.

146. The emphasis on cattle became apparent after listing the number of swine and the number of cattle recorded in the inventories examined. Owing to several complicating factors the making of these lists was of necessity a very crude process; but at least it was possible to carry out the listing on a county basis for six counties (Onslow, Chowan, Wake, Orange, Anson, and Cumberland). The list for Cumberland County differed from that of the other counties: whereas in the other five counties, a majority of the holders of livestock had more swine than cattle, in Cumberland County a noticeably higher proportion, possibly even a majority, of livestock holders had more cattle than swine. Since most of the Scottish Highlanders settled in Cumberland County, and probably comprised a majority of the population of the county, the above interpretation seems reasonable.

147. *NCSR*, XXIII, 60-61, 676-77. The first of these two references is to an act of 1715, designed, among other things, to stop Virginians from using land in North Carolina as range for their animals. The second reference is to an act of 1766 "to prevent the Inhabitants of South Carolina driving their Stocks of Cattle from thence to range and feed in this Province . . .," and it is clear from the preamble that South Carolinians had been trespassing on the range in several counties on the North Carolina side of the boundary.

148. This wet land was of many different kinds. The largest proportion of wet land in the colony was located in the Coastal Plain, especially the Outer Coastal Plain (see Figs. 9, 10, and 12). Further details about two particularly important kinds of wet land, the upland grass-sedge bogs and the pocosins, are presented in Appendix I and on Figs. 43 and 44. There are many references in the colonial record to the use of wet land of one kind or another for grazing purposes, and the following sources contain illustrative examples, mainly with respect to the savannahs, or upland grass-sedge bogs: *NCCR*, I, 715, V, 362; *North-Carolina Gazette* (New Bern), Jan. 16, 1778—advertisement of William Palmer; Meredith, *An Account* . . ., p. 17; Harriss, *Lawson's History* . . ., pp. 80, 118; Brickell, *Natural History* . . ., pp. 11-13; Todd and Goebel, *Christoph von Graffenried's Account* . . ., p. 298; "William Logan's Journal . . .," *PMHB*, 36 (1912), 6, 15; Schoepf, *Travels in the Confederation* . . ., II, 121. Also relevant is Ruffin, *Agricultural, Geological, and Descriptive Sketches* . . ., p. 91.

149. The four travel accounts are as follows: "Journal of a French Traveller . . .," *AHR*, 26 (1920-21), 736; Johnston, "Journal of Ebenezer Hazard . . .," *NCHR*, 36 (1959), 372; Watson, *Men and Times of the Revolution* . . ., p. 38; Schoepf, *Travels in the Confederation* . . ., II, 126-28, *passim*.

For a visual impression of the relative emptiness of this area, see Figs. 24, 25, and 26.

150. Based on tabulations of exports from Customs 16/1. Port Beaufort was especially important in this respect and was the single most prominent exporting Port in every one of the years for which data are available.

151. Not until 1922 did the era of free range come to an end in the eastern part of the state: *North Carolina General Statutes*, 68-39, 68-40, and 68-41. But the Outer Banks were not covered by this legislation, and even when it came to an end there, in 1958 (*North Carolina General Statutes*, 68-42, 68-43, 68-44, 68-45, and 68-46), a couple of minor exceptions were made. The Outer Banks of North Carolina are one of several areas, fringing the Atlantic coast of the United States, in which feral and semiferal livestock persisted until the late nineteenth century and even until the mid-twentieth century. Other areas are, or were, in New Jersey, Virginia, Maryland, and possibly elsewhere along the coast.

152. Catesby, *Natural History of Carolina* . . ., I, xxxi.

153. The absence was never quite complete during the colonial period. Very early in the eighteenth century, butter and cheese were being made on a commercial scale in the northeast (probably north of Albemarle Sound), as is evident from remarks in Harriss, *Lawson's History* . . ., p. 82. This seems to have been given up by the 1740's: "William Logan's Journal . . .," *PMHB*, 36 (1912), 7 (referring to the same area). Apparently it was also tried in the southeast: in 1775, one person near Wilmington was producing, among other things, cheese cakes and butter for sale in the town and was said to be "the only one who continues to have Milk": Andrews and Andrews, *Journal of a Lady of Quality* . . ., p. 179.

154. The only evidence for this is the statement of Schoepf, *Travels in the Confederation* . . ., II, 121.

155. There are fragments of inconclusive evidence associating both Scotch-Irish and Germans with the commercial production of butter and cheese; see, *NCCR*, V, 356, and advertisement in *SCAG Gaz*, Dec. 11, 1767. One can also conjecture

that the Scottish Highlanders, in view of their emphasis on cattle, may have had something to do with the surplus production.

156. Details illustrating the way in which the Scottish Highlanders in Georgia emphasized cattle raising are given in *CRSG*, V, 247, 381, 502, 556.

157. See references cited in previous note.

158. Further details on cattle raising in the Scottish Highlands are given in Meyer, *Highland Scots of North Carolina* . . ., pp. 36, 105, and the sources therein cited.

159. Details on this type of enclosure can be found in Brickell, *Natural History* . . ., p. 51, and *MR*, I, 156, *et passim*.

160. The following sources seem to contain references to this kind of cowpen (or sheep pen): Secretary of State Records, Box 726, Lists of Warrants Returned, 1751-80 (MSS)—see warrants of John Lay, of New Hanover County, 1760, and Francis Beatey, of Cumberland County, 1757; Cumberland County, Deeds and Grants, Vol. 4, 1770-72 (MSS)—see deed of land from Robert Stewart to Neill Ray, 1770; Land Grants, Vol. 16, 1755-60 (MSS)—see grant of land to John Costen, 1759; Onslow County Records, Deeds, 1747-54 (MSS)—see deed of land from Richard Chouston (?) to George Cooper, 1749; Walker, *New Hanover County Court Minutes*, Part I, pp. 24, 53—this last reference is to "sheep pens"; letter of William Faris to Arthur Dobbs, Feb. 18, 1750, in Arthur Dobbs Papers, 1731-71 (MSS). The above represent the sum total of references that were found in colonial records of North Carolina to cowpens. Less than ten instances are involved, though perhaps there are more in some of the local records that were not seen. The term also appears in a few pieces of legislation, though without reference to particular persons or places: *NCSR*, XXIII, 59, 167, 676.

161. Letter of Faris, cited in previous note.

162. This other evidence is in the form of information about contracts between overseers and landowners. The presumed relationship between overseers and cowpens is not entirely conjectural, for the few fragments of these contracts that survive do indicate that the chief function of the overseer may well have been the raising of stock. The following sources contain information about, or evidence indicative of, such contracts: Pollock Letter Book, 1708-61 (MSS), pp. 55ff.; agreement dated Sept. 23, 1764, in Hayes Collection, Vol. 8 in Reel 20; Wake County, Clerk of Superior Court, Record Book No. 1, 1771-82 (MSS), pp. 75-78; Cumberland County, Deeds and Grants, Vols. 1-2, 1741-63 (MSS), I, 299. The claim of John Cotton, in English Records, American Loyalist Claims (MSS) is also relevant. A generalized description of these contractual relationships is given in Brickell, *Natural History* . . ., pp. 268-69; although Brickell gives no specific examples of such contracts, his account is instructive.

A recent study of colonial cowpens (Gary S. Dunbar, "Colonial Carolina Cowpens," *AH*, 35 [1961], 125-30) was almost entirely about cowpens in South Carolina. Despite this limitation in coverage, the author's thesis was that "the cowpen complex was a South Carolina institution which was in time extended northward into North Carolina and westward into Georgia by South Carolinians" (*ibid.*, 125). The thesis is an intriguing one, but scarcely warranted by the record of circumstances in North Carolina. First, because the South Carolina cowpen complex, as described by Dunbar, was nowhere present in North Carolina; secondly, because even if a modified version of it were present in North Carolina, it hardly seems necessary to invoke this process of diffusion to account for its existence here; and thirdly, because the two sources the author cites to support the idea of diffusion into North Carolina are of questionable relevance. Nor is any evidence presented to support the diffusion into Georgia.

The problem of generalizing about several colonies on the basis of particular conditions in one colony is always a difficult one, particularly so in this case because little is known about livestock raising in Georgia, a subject certainly deserving of special study. Indeed, "cowpens" seem to have been more common and prominent in Georgia than in any other colony, at least to judge from the very frequent references to them in the early records of Georgia, from the existence there for some time of an official, large cowpen, and from the fact that grants of land were made to individuals for the specific purpose of setting up cowpens. But more important than the cowpens is the larger subject of livestock raising, and it is upon the larger issue that attention should be focussed in order better to understand the features associated with it.

Chapter VII

1. There is no way of calculating just how many people were living in towns. The few figures that are available for particular places are cited in the text of this chapter, and the number five thousand given above is nothing more than an impressionistic estimate.

2. For the purpose of defining urbanism, it is useful to distinguish between primary industries, on the one hand, and secondary and tertiary activities, on the other. The former require large surfaces, the latter have limited areal requirements: see Gunnar Alexandersson, *The Industrial Structure of American Cities* (Lincoln, Neb., 1956), pp. 11-13, for an elaboration of this point.

3. This is clear from the study of F. W. Clonts, "Travel and Transportation in Colonial North Carolina," *NCHR*, 3 (1926), 16-35; the title of this study is perhaps misleading, since Clonts was almost exclusively concerned with transportation in the Albemarle area, during the proprietary period.

4. Laments about road conditions and narrations of mishaps are liberally scattered through contemporary travel accounts and have so frequently been cited that there is little point in citing them again here. Occasionally, however, a traveler did express satisfaction with road conditions: see, for example, Johnston, "Journal of Ebenezer Hazard . . .," *NCHR*, 36 (1959), 376.

5. From time to time detailed plans were made of various sections of the southern boundary of North Carolina, and on these plans can be seen numerous named roads and paths; some of the plans consulted are listed in the Bibliography.

6. Land grants and deeds consulted are cited in the Bibliography.

7. See, for examples, the advertisement for 537 acres in Chowan County that appeared in *Va Gaz*, May 2, 1755, and another for 600 acres in Granville County appearing in *Va Gaz*, P.D., Jan. 26, 1769.

8. All the court minutes examined are listed in the Bibliography. The administrative powers of the local courts with regard to roads are described in Julian P. Boyd, "The County Court in Colonial North Carolina" (Master's thesis, Duke University, 1926), pp. 69-78.

9. The inventories of estates examined are listed in the Bibliography (see especially those for Orange County).

10. For instances of references to wagoners, see the following: Fanning-McCulloh Papers, 1758-1811 (MSS)—letter from Henry E. McCulloh to [Edmund Fanning], April 3, 1766; Shaw Papers, 1735-1883 (MSS)—Colin Shaw's disbursements in 1773 included a payment to a wagoner for his services.

11. Fig. 41 is based on the Mouzon map of 1775 and shows all of the roads represented on Mouzon's map. The outline of the colony as shown on Fig. 41 is based on the Mouzon map and hence is imprecise.

12. There are, however, several studies in which some emphasis is placed upon the significance of roads in the economic development of colonial Maryland.

13. For comments on the badness of roads see the following study: Charles C.

Crittenden, "Overland Travel and Transportation in North Carolina, 1763-1789," *NCHR*, 8 (1931), 239-42.

14. While the roads on Fig. 41 are shown just as they are on the original (the Mouzon map of 1775), some modifications of the Mouzon map were made with respect to towns. A few places shown on the Mouzon map are not represented on Fig. 41, and a couple of other settlements are added—the purpose of these changes simply being to insure that Fig. 41 showed all of the settlements classed as urban according to the definition used throughout this chapter.

15. Andrews and Andrews, *Journal of a Lady of Quality* . . ., pp. 178-79.

16. Brickell, *Natural History* . . ., p. 8.

17. Watson, *Men and Times of the Revolution* . . ., p. 37. Compare another traveler who was in the town in 1774 and claimed that it then contained 160 houses and about 1,000 people: *Journal kept by Hugh Finlay* . . . (Brooklyn, N.Y., 1867), p. 82.

18. Fragments about Edenton were found in the following: *NCCR*, VII, 491; Smyth, *A Tour* . . ., II, 92-93; "Journal of a French Traveller . . .," *AHR*, 26 (1920-21), 738. More valuable are the details about the town scattered throughout Chowan County, Miscellaneous Court Papers (MSS).

19. For a guide to the degree of specialization in corn, staves, and shingles, see the data on Port Roanoke presented on Tables 9 and 10, and Fig. 36. The specialization in tobacco was perhaps less marked, but does seem evident from data in Customs 16/1; also revealing on tobacco is Richard Brownrigg, Merchant's Ledger, 1757-59, Edenton, N.C. (MSS).

20. Customs 16/1 give information about the size of vessels and destination of trade: see the studies of Charles C. Crittenden, *The Commerce of North Carolina, 1763-1789* (New Haven, Conn., 1936), pp. 70-71, and, Byron E. Logan, "An Historic Geographic Study of North Carolina Ports" (Ph.D. dissertation, University of North Carolina, 1956), p. 54. Also relevant are the following: *Journal kept by Hugh Finlay* . . ., p. 82; *NCCR*, VI, 968.

21. "Journal of a French Traveller . . .," *AHR*, 26 (1920-21), 738; *Journal kept by Hugh Finlay* . . ., p. 82; Smyth, *A Tour* . . ., II, 92-93. See also the discription of the voyage of the brig "Joannah" in Chapter V, above.

22. See letter from Thomas Child, dated 25 Sept. 1759, in Chowan County, Court Minutes, Reference Docket, New Action Docket: 1755-61 (MSS).

23. Specific occupations are mentioned here and there in Chowan County, Miscellaneous Court Papers (MSS). Some of the occupations were probably carried on on a part-time basis.

24. This road can be picked out on Fig. 41.

25. There are many references to the Virginia Road in the local records of Chowan County: see, for example, Chowan County, Court Minutes, 1762-75 (MSS).

26. *Journal kept by Hugh Finlay* . . ., pp. 80-82, 87. See also Johnston, "Journal of Ebenezer Hazard . . .," *NCHR*, 36 (1959), 362. The route through Halifax, that is, the one farther west, was called the upper road, and the one through Edenton was known as the lower road. Even though the upper road came to be the more used road, the other was not abandoned.

27. There was a resurgence of port activity in Edenton during the Revolutionary War, when its inaccessibility gave it a special advantage: Schoepf, *Travels in the Confederation* . . ., II, 111-12.

28. There is an informative history of New Bern: Alonzo T. Dill, Jr., "Eighteenth Century New Bern: A History of the Town and Craven County, 1700-1800," *NCHR*, 22 (1945), 1-21, 152-75, 293-319, 460-89; 23 (1946), 47-78, 142-71, 325-59, 495-535. Much use was made of this study, and the figure of twenty-one for the number of families is taken from it: Dill, "Eighteenth Century New Bern . . .," *NCHR*, 22 (1945), 467.

29. "Journal of a French Traveller . . . .," *AHR*, 26 (1920-21), 735.

30. *NCCR*, VII, 499.
31. *NCCR*, IX, 281.
32. Watson, *Men and Times of the Revolution* . . ., p. 39.
33. Johnston, "Journal of Ebenezer Hazard . . .," *NCHR*, 36 (1959), 374.
34. When visited in 1783 it had a population of five hundred families: J. Fred Rippy (ed.), "A View of the Carolinas in 1783," *NCHR*, 6 (1929), 363. When Washington was in the town in 1791 it then included about two thousand persons: Fitzpatrick, *Diaries of George Washington* . . ., IV, 165.
35. A list of the number and names of New Bern merchants who advertised in North Carolina newspapers is presented in Wesley H. Wallace, "Advertising in Early North Carolina Newspapers, 1751-1778" (Master's thesis, University of North Carolina, 1954), p. 223.
36. On the significance of roads in the growth of New Bern, see Dill, "Eighteenth Century New Bern . . .," *NCHR*, 22 (1945), 475-77. Dill believes that roads were a cause rather than an effect of the growth of New Bern.
37. The central location of the town between the northern and southern portions of the colony was one of the reasons for its selection as capital: *NCCR*, VI, 1-2, 300-1, 879.
38. Dill, "Eighteenth Century New Bern . . .," *NCHR*, 23 (1946), 148-49.
39. *NCCR*, IX, 637.
40. See, for example, *NCCR*, IX, 281.
41. For fragmentary information on the navigability of the Neuse River, see the following sources: "Journal of a French Traveller . . .," *AHR*, 26 (1920-21), 735; Newsome, "Twelve North Carolina Counties . . .," *NCHR*, 6 (1929), 305; Todd and Goebel, *Christoph von Graffenried's Account* . . ., frontispiece map.
42. E. Lawrence Lee, "Old Brunswick, The Story of a Colonial Town," *NCHR*, 29 (1952), 233-34; E. Lawrence Lee, "The History of the Lower Cape Fear: The Colonial Period," pp. 196-203, *passim*.
43. Dartmouth Manuscripts, p. 161.
44. Lee, "Old Brunswick . . .," *NCHR*, 29 (1952), 243-44.
45. Schoepf, *Travels in the Confederation* . . ., II, 145. The site of Brunswick is currently being excavated by archaeologists.
46. *NCCR*, V, 158.
47. A piragua was a vessel consisting of two dugouts lashed together.
48. *NCSR*, XXIII, 748; see also the petition of justices of Brunswick County, in Legislative Papers, Box 5 (MSS).
49. See data in *NCCR*, VI, 968.
50. The "Flats" are mentioned in many accounts, but it is not clear just how shallow the river was at this point or what was the maximum size of vessels that could negotiate them.
51. See the information on the King's Road, in Bath County, N.C., Court Records, Onslow Precinct, 1731/32-1734 (MSS).
52. See, for example, the Collet map of 1768, and the Sauthier plan of Wilmington, 1769. Note also the road pattern on Fig. 41.
53. See Bibliography for these minutes.
54. *NCCR*, VII, 695-96. See also *NCSR*, XXIII, 753-54.
55. The following sources contain relevant evidence: English Records, American Loyalist Claims (MSS)—see, among others, the claims of Frederick Gregg, James Gammell and Co., William Mactier; *Proceedings of the Safety Committee for the Town of Wilmington, N.C., from 1774 to 1776* . . . (Raleigh, N.C., 1844), pp. 6-7, 9.
56. Andrews and Andrews, *Journal of a Lady of Quality* . . ., p. 155; *NCCR*, X, 48, 236.
57. Information on the Hoggs and on Campbell was taken from the following: Robert Hogg Account Books, 1762-75 (MSS); James Hogg Papers, 1772-1824, undated (MSS); Hogg and Campbell, Invoice Outward, 1767-82 (MSS); Andrews and

Andrews, *Journal of a Lady of Quality* . . ., pp. 323-25 (the reference is to biographical notes by the editors of the volume); Milnor Ljungstedt (comp.), "Items from southern records showing family and trade connections with northern colonies and the home countries," *American Genealogist*, 15 (Oct., 1938), 101; Archibald Henderson, "The Transylvania Company: A Study in Personnel. I. James Hogg," *Filson Club Historical Quarterly*, 21 (1947), 3-8, *passim;* Meyer, *Highland Scots of North Carolina* . . ., pp. 77, 129-30.

For an example of quite a different kind of tie between Hillsboro and Wilmington, see *Va Gaz*, P.D., Sept. 10, 1772, which contains a notice of a reward being offered for the return of one horse and one mare stolen from the race track at Hillsboro—the animals belonged to a Wilmington merchant.

58. *NCCR*, V, 158-59.
59. Smyth, *A Tour* . . ., II, 87.
60. *Journal kept by Hugh Finlay* . . ., p. 66.
61. *NCCR*, X, 48.
62. Smyth, *A Tour* . . ., II, 87. Yet Smyth referred to Brunswick, with no more than fifty or sixty houses, as a "little town": *ibid.*, II, 86, 88.
63. The growth of the nearby resort town and port of Morehead City has been an important influence in the survival of Beaufort. Bath is being restored by Colonial Bath, Inc.
64. Herbert R. Paschal, Jr., *A History of Colonial Bath* (Raleigh, N.C., 1955), pp. 9-12, 32-33.
65. Brickell, *Natural History* . . ., p. 8.
66. "William Logan's Journal . . .," *PMHB*, 36 (1912), 11.
67. *Journal kept by Hugh Finlay* . . ., pp. 80, 81, 87, 88; *NCCR*, VII, 148-49, 454-55.
68. Johnston, "Journal of Ebenezer Hazard . . .," *NCHR*, 36 (1959), 370; "Journal of a French Traveller . . .," *AHR*, 26 (1920-21), 736. See also the comments of Schoepf, *Travels in the Confederation* . . ., II, 126, who did not pass through the town.
69. *NCCR*, IX, 636, 639-41; compare *NCCR*, IX, 733-35, 1179.
70. See Governor Martin's comments, quoted on p. 150, above; and, "Journal of a French Traveller . . .," *AHR*, 26 (1920-21), 733.
71. *NCSR*, XXV, 354-55.
72. Schoepf, *Travels in the Confederation* . . ., II, 120.
73. Hugh Williamson, *The History of North Carolina* (2 vols.; Philadelphia, 1812), II, 218.
74. Schoepf, *Travels in the Confederation* . . ., II, 120. The falls upstream from Halifax are shown on the Collet map of 1770 and described in, Powell, "Tryon's 'Book' on North Carolina," *NCHR*, 34 (1957), 408.
75. *Journal kept by Hugh Finlay* . . ., p. 81.
76. The paucity of evidence referring to ties between Halifax and Edenton seems to suggest that they were neither very strong nor very important; for one of the few instances of specific evidence about them, see Chowan County, Miscellaneous Court Papers (MSS), XI, 27. Much of the export trade from Halifax was probably carried into Virginia rather than Edenton.
77. *NCCR*, IX, 356.
78. *NCCR*, VII, 473.
79. Sauthier plan of Halifax, 1769.
80. Diary of Col. W. A. Avery, 1769 (MSS).
81. See statement quoted on p. 156, above.
82. Schoepf, *Travels in the Confederation* . . ., II, 120.
83. Halifax had become a county seat in 1758, when Halifax County was created by a subdivision of Edgecombe County.
84. The quotation is from "Journal of a French Traveller . . .," *AHR*, 26 (1920-

21), 739. Since this business activity was not carried on through any formal commercial channels or institutions, there is no direct evidence relating to it. For a suggestive parallel, showing how the informal meetings of merchants in Williamsburg during "Public Times" greatly enhanced its economic importance, see James H. Soltow, *The Economic Role of Williamsburg* (Williamsburg, Va., 1956), pp. 5-18; but Halifax, of course, was much less important a center than Williamsburg.

The superior court district of which Halifax was the center embraced three counties. Wilmington, New Bern, and Edenton, were also the headquarters for superior courts; but the influx of persons that took place when these courts were in session was probably more noticeable in smaller towns such as Halifax.

85. Fig. 42 shows the approximate locations of the original sites of both Cross Creek and Campbelltown (the relationship between the two places is discussed below). Terrain was taken from several large-scale topographic quadrangles and is presented in a very generalized fashion; the one-hundred-foot contour, for example, is of no special significance and simply serves to indicate the approximate eastern edge of the rougher terrain of the Sandhills. Other sources for the map were the Sauthier plan of Cross Creek, 1770, and several of the references cited elsewhere in this chapter that deal with early conditions in the two settlements.

86. Harper, *Travels of William Bartram*, p. 302.

87. Much information on Cross Creek was obtained from the local records of Cumberland County (see Bibliography for further details), as well as from all the other sources specified in notes 88, 89, 90, Chapter VII, below.

88. Daniel Stanton, *A Journal of the Life, Travels, and Gospel Labours* . . . (Philadelphia, 1772), p. 126.

89. The figure of a few hundred is an attempt to reconcile conflicting contemporary estimates in Harper, *Travels of William Bartram*, p. 302, and, *NCSR*, XV, 209. The buildings specified above are mentioned in various records, and some are shown on Sauthier's plan of Cross Creek, 1770.

90. Fragments of information concerning the origins of the inhabitants were located in various sources (all specified in the above notes), and English Records, American Loyalist Claims (MSS) were especially useful for details about the inhabitants of Cross Creek. Some instances of Highlanders in the town are given in Meyer, *Highland Scots of North Carolina* . . ., p. 112. For an unusually informative example of the way in which one Scotch-Irish settler, living in the vicinity of Cross Creek, contributed to the trade of the town, see English Records, American Loyalist Claims (MSS)—claim of Connor Dowd.

91. For instances of references to this wagon trade from the interior, see the following sources: Harper, *Travels of William Bartram*, p. 302; Andrews and Andrews, *Journal of a Lady of Quality* . . ., p. 279; *NCSR*, XV, 209; "Informations . . .," in Boyd, *Some Eighteenth Century Tracts* . . ., p. 448. For a vivid account of the wagon trade through the town seventy-five years later, see Olmsted, *A Journey in the Seaboard Slave States* . . ., I, 397-98.

92. The trade to and from Salem is documented in *MR*, I and II, *passim*. The trade ties with Hillsboro, Salisbury, and Charlotte are less well documented, and, in fact, there is only oblique evidence for them: *NCCR*, IX, 356; *Va Gaz*, P.D., May 19, 1774—see advertisement for tracts of land in Guilford and Surry counties; "A Plan of part of the principal Roads . . .," 177— (see Bibliography for further details of this manuscript map, which reveals a very striking convergence of roads on Cross Creek).

93. See the sources cited in note 42, Chapter VI, above.

94. "Informations . . .," in Boyd, *Some Eighteenth Century Tracts* . . ., p. 448. The report is probably an exaggerated one.

95. There is abundant evidence on the ties between the two towns in the following items: Robert Hogg Account Books, 1762-75 (MSS); Hogg and Campbell,

Invoice Outward, 1767-82 (MSS); Byrne's Account Book, 1757-1854 (MSS); *Journal kept by Hugh Finlay* . . ., p. 69; *Proceedings of the Safety Committee* . . ., pp. 6-7; letter from a trader in Cross Creek, in *North-Carolina Gazette* (Wilmington), Feb. 12, 1766; notice regarding partnership between Sutherland and Cruden of Wilmington, and John Cruden and Co., of Cross Creek, in *Cape-Fear Mercury*, May 11, 1774; English Records, American Loyalist Claims (MSS)—claims relating to Neil McArthur, James Cruden, James Gammell, and William Mactier. The shift in trade, from South Carolina to Wilmington and Cross Creek, is discussed below, on pp. 165-66.

96. On the use of the river, see the following: Dartmouth Manuscripts, p. 157; Harper, *Travels of William Bartram*, p. 302; "Informations . . .," in Boyd, *Some Eighteenth Century Tracts* . . ., p. 448. In Hogg and Campbell, Invoice Outward, 1767-82 (MSS), there is a mention of a "Cross Creek Packet"; and one person at least earned his living by commanding a small trading vessel on the Cape Fear River—see claim of Duncan McRae, in English Records, American Loyalist Claims (MSS).

97. *NCSR*, XV, 209. Neil McArthur kept two wagons in business hauling between the river and Cross Creek: see claim of McArthur in English Records, American Loyalist Claims (MSS).

98. The gist of the story of their rivalry can be found in the following sources, which proved helpful because of the light they threw upon both Cross Creek and Campbelltown: *NCCR*, VI, 485-86, 682, 815-16, 820-21, 857, 865, 874, 883, 891, 937, 947, 953; *NCSR*, XXIII, 870-71, XXIV, 180-83, XXV, 209-11, 470-72; Legislative Papers, Boxes 5 and 6 (MSS); Cumberland County, Estates (MSS)—inventory of estate of John and William Russell; Governor's Office, Council Papers, 1761-79 (MSS)—Box 110.1 has several relevant items. The name "Campbelltown" was spelled in a variety of ways. The documents relating to the two towns have to be interpreted with care, particularly because in some of the official records the existence of Cross Creek was studiously ignored by those trying to promote the fortunes of Campbelltown.

99. See the area between Eastern Boulevard and Water Street on any detailed plan of Fayetteville.

It should be added that neither Cross Creek nor Campbelltown was a "fall-line" town and that the fall line was farther upstream. It was difficult for vessels to get even as far upstream as Campbelltown, and the river was apparently not utilized above the town: *MR*, I, 262; Diary of Col. W. A. Avery, 1769 (MSS); Williamson, *History of North Carolina*, II, 218; Isaac Winslow, Journal of a southern tour, 1824 (MSS).

100. *NCSR*, XXV, 451-53.
101. *NCCR*, IX, 746.
102. Smyth, *A Tour* . . ., I, 101.
103. This was Howel's Warehouse: *NCSR*, XXV, 379.
104. *NCSR*, XXV, 452.
105. Smyth, *A Tour* . . ., I, 101; Watson, *Men and Times of the Revolution* . . ., p. 58; Lida T. Rodman (ed.), *Journal of a Tour to North Carolina by William Attmore* ("JSHP," Vol. 17 [Chapel Hill, N.C., 1922]), pp. 28, 34-35; Fitzpatrick, *Diaries of George Washington* . . ., IV, 163-64.
106. Schoepf, *Travels in the Confederation* . . ., II, 124-25n.
107. There is almost no information in the contemporary record on the navigability of the Tar River. The above paragraph is based on details in two post-colonial sources: Rodman, *Journal of a Tour to North Carolina by William Attmore*, pp. 28, 34; and Newsome, "Twelve North Carolina Counties . . .," *NCHR*, 6 (1929), 74-86, *passim*.
108. The Collet map of 1768 shows a bridge over the river at this point. For roads, see Fig. 41.

109. Hillsboro was called Churton, Corbinton, and Childsburg before assuming its present name. Salem is now a small part of Winston-Salem. Much of colonial Salem has been preserved or restored, and a project to restore many structures in Hillsboro is currently underway.

110. Information on Hillsboro came from the following sources: *NCCR*, VII, 432, VIII, 80a, IX, 313; *NCSR*, XXIII, 691-92, XXIV, 22-24, XXV, 271-72, 402-4, 500-3; Sauthier plan of Hillsborough, 1768. Of some use was an early local history, Francis Nash, *Hillsboro, Colonial and Revolutionary* (Raleigh, N.C., 1903), particularly pp. 5-9.

For Salisbury, the following were used: Rowan County Records (see Bibliography); Sauthier plan of Salisbury, 1770; *NCCR*, V, 355, VII, 473; *NCSR*, XXIII, 621-22, 750-52, 810-13; *Va Gaz*, P.D., Oct. 27, 1774. As a guide, James S. Brawley, *The Rowan Story, 1753-1953* (Salisbury, N.C., 1953) proved to be of considerable use. The role of James Carter in the development of early Salisbury is discussed in a recent article: Robert W. Ramsey, "James Carter: Founder of Salisbury," *NCHR*, 39 (1962), 131-39.

111. This road, also known as the Indian Trading Path, appears on many eighteenth-century maps and plans.

112. "Autobiography of Col. William Few of Georgia . . .," *Magazine of American History*, 7 (July-December, 1881), 344. See also Smyth, *A Tour . . .*, I, 160-61.

113. *NCCR*, IX, 313.

114. The lawyer was Waightstill Avery and his account is in the MS, Journal of a ride from Newbern to Salisbury, Oct. 1768, with a map of the road. See also Smyth, *A Tour . . .*, I, 175.

115. The indirect evidence of most relevance was found in the following: Orange County, Estates, 1758-85 (MSS); Court Minutes of Rowan County (see Bibliography); Rowan County, Roads, 1757-1894 (MSS); English Records, American Loyalist Claims (MSS)—claim of James Munro; *NCCR*, V, 532, IX, 356; *Va Gaz*, P.D., Jan. 26, 1769—advertisement for the sale of a tract of land in Granville County; Smyth, *A Tour . . .*, I, 161, 175.

116. See quotation from Few, p. 163, above. Also relevant are English Records, American Loyalist Claims (MSS)—claim of James Munro, and, the information on James Hogg, p. 153, above.

117. The only specific reference to a Scottish merchant in Salisbury is in *MR*, I, 270.

118. Perhaps the system was neither as perfect nor as absolute as this conception of it implies, but the interpretation here does not assign to Scottish business acumen an incredible role. Records of Virginia merchants will undoubtedly furnish more information about some aspects of the trade discussed in this paragraph. For a summary of the role of Scottish merchants in Virginia at this time, see Coulter, "The Virginia Merchant," p. 2.

119. *MR*, I, 335.

120. *MR*, I, 105.

121. *MR*, I, 314.

122. There is abundant information on their trading activities in the *Moravian Records*. All of the information relating to these activities up to 1776, in Vols. I, II, and III, was extracted and tabulated. The analysis of these tables (not included here) forms the basis of the conclusions offered here about their trade. The only drawback, and the reason for some tentativeness, is that the editor and translator of the *Moravian Records* may have omitted some information about trade in preparing the records for publication.

123. See previous note for source. Especially relevant are *MR*, I, 339; II, 706, 828, 884, 891. As early as 1759, however, a trading wagon from Wachovia was being sent to the Cape Fear River once a month: *MR*, I, 212. And the Moravians, of course, still occasionally traded with other places.

124. *NCSR*, XXIII, 772-73 (the date of the act is 1768—see *NCSR*, XXV, 570-72).

125. On its smallness, even as late as 1791, see the following: Smyth, *A Tour . . .*, I, 177; Fitzpatrick, *Diaries of George Washington . . .*, IV, 185; *A Short Account of the Life and Religious Labours of Patience Brayton . . .* (New Bedford, 1801), p. 30. But in the early 1770's provision was made for the construction of a road from Charlotte to Bladen Courthouse (in the Cape Fear Valley): *NCCR*, IX, 657. A brief description of Charlotte in 1772 appears in Charles S. Davis (ed.), "The Journal of William Moultrie While a Commissioner on The North and South Carolina Boundary Survey, 1772," *JSH*, 8 (1942), 553.

126. *NCSR*, XXV, 519d, 519e, 519f.

127. *NCCR*, VI, 82, VII, 264; *NCSR*, XXV, 252-54.

128. Very little information about Hertford was found, though there is probably more in the records of Perquimans County. A few details are given in *NCSR*, XXIII, 752-53; XXV, 367-69.

For an example of the significance of courthouse sites in attracting other activities, see Paul M. McCain, *The County Court in North Carolina Before 1750* ("Historical Papers of the Trinity College Historical Society," Series 31 [Durham, N.C., 1954]), p. 107; also relevant is *MR*, II, 597.

129. Details concerning the Hamiltons are taken from English Records, American Loyalist Claims (MSS). They are also mentioned in Smyth, *A Tour . . .*, I, 90-91, and in an advertisement, in *Va Gaz*, P.D., June 9, 1774.

130. Advertisement in *Va Gaz*, D., Nov. 25, 1775.

131. Advertisement in *Va Gaz*, P.D., Sept. 24, 1772.

132. For information on other stores, see the following: Pettigrew Papers, Vol. 1, Mar. 9, 1772–Aug. 23, 1803 (MSS)—letter from James Lockhart, dated 17 May, 1774; Hogg and Campbell, Invoice Outward, 1767-1782 (MSS); *Va Gaz*, P.D., May 5, 1768—advertisement containing reference to George Robinson's store; Smyth, *A Tour . . .*, I, 98-100.

133. *MR*, III, 1038.

134. *NCCR*, VI, 969.

135. Legislative Papers (MSS), Box 2—petition dated Dec. 9, 1758. The Diary and Account Book of John Saunders, 1750-55 (MSS) is apparently the work of an itinerant merchant from Suffolk, Va., compiled on a trip through North Carolina. Connor Dowd and Colin Shaw were country merchants, among other things, operating through Cross Creek: for the former's activities, see English Records, American Loyalist Claims (MSS), for those of the latter, see the relevant items in Shaw Papers, 1735-1883 (MSS).

136. Much the same was true in Virginia, as was shown in an unusually valuable study of trade in that colony: Coulter, "The Virginia Merchant," p. 52.

137. Goods directed to warehouses and landings within North Carolina ultimately cleared through one of the seaports within the colony.

138. The ties between the Moravians and Scottish merchants are apparent from various fragments of information. See, in conjunction, the following sources: *MR*, I, 270, 307, II, 887, 912; Trade Letters from Robert Cochran of Cross Creek/Campbellton to Salem persons, 1775-83 (MSS); North Carolina Wills, 1663-1789, Vol. 9 (MSS)—will of Alexander Duncan, dated 1767; Andrews and Andrews, *Journal of a Lady of Quality . . .*, pp. 295, 299, 319 (biographical notes by the editors); Wallace, "Advertising in Early North Carolina Newspapers . . .," pp. 223-24 (information on various Wilmington merchants). The Cruden mentioned in *MR*, II, 887, was a Scotish merchant—see note 79, Chapter VI, above.

139. Traditionally, the association between the fall line and urban centers is based largely on the break in navigation presumed to occur where rivers cross the line as they flow from Piedmont to Coastal Plain. But each river had several breaks in navigation east of the falls, their location being dependent on the size and type of vessel using the river and on the practicability of upstream hauls as

compared with the facility of downstream movement. Furthermore, the limits inevitably shifted from season to season, as the river fluctuated in volume and depth. Hence, there was no single all-important absolute limit of navigability on any one of the rivers, but rather a series of limits.

Since the presumed correspondence between the fall line and urban growth has no relevance to actual conditions in colonial North Carolina, it is not worth elaborating upon it here, or even documenting the long history of the idea. It is enough to note that the whole subject of the fall line has been the source of confused thinking, much of which found its way into geography and history textbooks in the late nineteenth and early twentieth century. Misconceptions persist today, as is evident, for example, from a newly published and already widely used textbook (Rhoads Murphey, *An Introduction to Geography* [Chicago, 1961], pp. 31-32).

Appendix I

1. One exceptionally useful review article in which the significance of fire is emphasized is Kenneth H. Garren, "Effects of Fire on Vegetation of the Southeastern United States," *BR*, 9 (1943), 617-54. Although this is now somewhat out of date, it is still a very useful guide to botanical literature on the subject.

2. Garren, in the article cited in the previous note, made almost no use of the historical record. Rostlund, in another study which is relevant here, imposed upon himself a quite different limitation, using only the historical record and ignoring the findings of modern botanical studies: Erhard Rostlund, "The Myth of a Natural Prairie Belt in Alabama: an interpretation of historical records," *AAAG*, 47 (1957), 392-411. In the study upon which this appendix is based, both lines of evidence were used.

3. For two examples of particularly severe and prolonged droughts in the eighteenth century, see the following: *NCCR*, IX, 328; "William Logan's Journal . . .," *PMHB*, 36 (1912), 6.

4. For allusions to burning in eighteenth-century North Carolina, see the following sources: *NCCR*, V, 354, 363; Harriss, *Lawson's History* . . ., p. 219; *MR*, I, 49, 59; Smyth, *A Tour* . . ., I, 96; John Bartram, *Diary of a Journey* . . ., p. 15; Andrews and Andrews, *Journal of a Lady of Quality* . . ., p. 149; Boyd, *William Byrd's Histories* . . ., p. 228; *NCSR*, XXIII, 775.

5. For evidence pointing to the existence of this law, see the following two sources: Brickell, *Natural History* . . ., pp. 10, 84; Boyd, *William Byrd's Histories* . . ., p. 228. But there appears to be no mention of the law in the official records of the colony.

6. A bill to prevent deliberate burning had been introduced earlier but had not been passed: *NCCR*, VIII, 126, 138; IX, 389, 479, 663. The 1777 law is given in *NCSR*, XXIV, 134. An amendment to it was passed in 1782, making noncompliance a more severe offense: *NCSR*, XXIV, 460. But neither the law nor its amendment proved effective, and many other measures were introduced later.

7. Instances of the use of the term in the Southeast as a whole, from the sixteenth century on, are given in Rostlund, "The Myth of a Natural Prairie Belt . . .," *AAAG*, 47 (1957), 392-411, *passim*.

8. This description is based on the following sources: Harriss, *Lawson's History* . . ., pp. 12, 23, 63, 80-81; Brickell, *Natural History* . . ., pp. 11-12, 13; Meredith, *An Account* . . ., pp. 14, 17; "William Logan's Journal . . .," *PMHB*, 36 (1912), 15; *NCCR*, V, 354; John Bartram, *Diary of a Journey* . . ., pp. 15, 18; Smyth, *A Tour* . . ., I, 140-41; Johnston, "Journal of Ebenezer Hazard . . .," *NCHR*, 36 (1959), 376; Schoepf, *Travels in the Confederation* . . ., I, 153-54. For examples of descrip-

tions of similar features in Georgia and South Carolina, see: Steeg, *A True and Historical Narrative* . . ., p. 137; E. Merton Coulter (ed.), *The Journal of William Stephens, 1741-1743* ("Wormsloe Foundation Publications," No. 2 [Athens, Ga., 1958]), p. 246; Peter Force, *Tracts and Other Papers* . . . (4 vols.; Washington, D.C., 1836-46), Vol. 2, No. 12, p. 3; "A New Voyage to Georgia . . .," *GHSC*, 2 (1842), 50; Milling, *Colonial South Carolina* . . ., pp. 14, 118.

9. *NCCR*, III, 431. See also *NCCR*, III, 148.

10. Two writers, Lawson and Brickell, used the term for areas in both the Coastal Plain and the Piedmont. For mention of savannahs in the Piedmont in their accounts, see: Harriss, *Lawson's History* . . ., pp. 43, 48, 52; Brickell, *Natural History* . . ., p. 107. For the more customary usage of the term, to describe open areas in the Coastal Plain, see the accounts cited in note 8, Appendix I, above. One of the first travelers to apply the term to areas in North Carolina was John Lederer, whose journeys in 1669 and 1670 took him across the North Carolina Piedmont. Lederer tells of seeing savannahs in several places, including a particularly large one at the foot of the Blue Ridge: Cumming, *Discoveries of John Lederer*, pp. 34-35, *et passim*. But Lederer's account is often unreliable, as Cumming has noted: *ibid.*, pp. 85-86. For another misleading but nonetheless interesting mention of savannahs, this time apparently in the Coastal Plain, see the account cited in an early piece of promotional literature: Kocherthaler, *Ausführlich und umständlicher Bericht* . . ., p. 53.

11. This opinion is based on examination of deeds, court minutes, and other local records of selected counties, chiefly Rowan, Orange, and Anson in the Piedmont, and Chowan, Onslow, and Cumberland counties in the Coastal Plain (see Bibliography for details of these records). References to savannahs are far more common in Onslow County, the only county of those selected that is located entirely in the Outer Coastal Plain.

12. The results of this study are reported in B. W. Wells and I. V. Shunk, *A Southern Upland Grass-Sedge Bog: An Ecological Study* (North Carolina Agricultural Experiment Station, Technical Bulletin No. 32 [October, 1928]). Additional comments can be found in Wells, *The Natural Gardens of North Carolina*, pp. 79-108, and Wells, "Ecological Problems . . .," *BR*, 8 (1942), 544-46.

13. Insectivorous plants, including *Sarracenia flava* and *Dionaea muscipula*, added a note of drama to the extraordinary display of wild flowers on the Burgaw Savannah. The latter plant is known as Venus's-flytrap. It is almost entirely restricted in its distribution to a small portion of southeastern North Carolina, though it does also occur in a small section of South Carolina: see W. C. Coker, "The Distribution of Venus's Fly Trap *(Dionaea Muscipula)*," *JEMSS*, 43 (1928), 221-28, and, Austin H. Clark, "A New Locality for the Venus' Fly-Trap *(Dionaea Muscipula)*," *JEMSS*, 43 (1928), 221-28, and, Austin H. Clark, "A New Locality for the Vensus' Fly-Trap *(Dionaea Muscipula)*," *Science*, 88 (1938), 188. During the course of his travels in the 1770's, William Bartram observed extensive savannahs in southeastern North Carolina and noted the occurence of Venus's-flytrap in them: Harper, *Travels of William Bartram*, p. 299. And in his introduction to the account of his travels, William Bartram includes an account of the insectivorous plants that he found in "green meadows": *ibid.*, pp. liii-liv.

Harper notes that Governor Dobbs of North Carolina was, in 1759, the first to announce the discovery of Venus's-flytrap: *ibid.*, p. 494. In a letter Dobbs wrote the following year, the governor described the plant as follows: "But the great wonder of the vegetable kingdom is a very curious unknown species of sensitive; it is a dwarf plant; the leaves are like a narrow segment of a sphere, consisting of two parts, like the cap of a spring purse, the concave part outwards, each of which falls back with indented edges (like an iron spring fox trap); upon any thing touching the leaves, or falling between them, they instantly close like a spring trap, and confine any insect or any thing that falls between them; it bears a white flower; to this surprising plant I have given the name of Fly Trap Sensitive." (This letter of Dobbs to Peter Collinson is cited in Lewis W. Dillwyn, *Hortus Collinsonianus* . . . [Swansea, 1843], p. 18.)

The German traveler, Johann Schoepf, who mentioned the plant in his writings about twenty-five years after Dobbs announced the discovery, in all probability learned of its existence from John or William Bartram: Schoepf, *Travels in the Confederation* . . ., I, 90-92, II, 138. One of the German settlers in North Carolina then learned of its existence from reading Schoepf's account in the original German. Although this settler, Pastor Storch, had not seen the plant, he must in fact have been one of the few people in North Carolina who even knew that this remarkable plant, the habits of which later attracted the attention of Charles Darwin and many others, was to be found there. For Storch's observations, see Velthusen, *Nordcarolinische Kirchennachrichten*, p. 6; compare Lloyd, who suggests that the plant was well known in North Carolina by 1763—Francis E. Lloyd, *The Carnivorous Plants* (Waltham, Mass., 1942), p. 178.

14. Fig. 43 is adapted from Wells and Shunk, *A Southern Upland Grass-Sedge Bog* . . ., Fig. 4, p. 39.

15. John Bartram, *Diary of a Journey* . . ., p. 15 (the punctuation in the quotation was inserted by the editor of the modern published version).

16. It may well be that the patches of grassland that were once to be found in the generally wooded northeastern states, called "plains," had something in common with savannahs, at least in terms of their origin, maintenance, and subsequent reversion to forest. See the comments on "plains" made by Tax and Murphy in William L. Thomas (ed.), *Man's Role in Changing the Face of the Earth* (Chicago, 1956), pp. 413-14; also relevant is a description of one of these "plains" in Roland M. Harper, "The Hempstead Plains: A Natural Prairie on Long Island," *Bulletin of the American Geographical Society*, 43 (1911), 351-60.

17. I am much indebted to Mr. W. W. Spender, then farming in the vicinity of the Burgaw Savannah, for his generous assistance while I was visiting this area. His aid, in the field and in recalling local history, was invaluable.

18. A close study of the historical record of the nineteenth century would throw more light upon changes in the extent and distribution of savannahs during that century. For evidence of their existence then in the Coastal Plain, see the following: Ebenezer Emmons, *The Swamp Lands of North-Carolina* ("North-Carolina Geological Survey, Part II, Agriculture" [Raleigh, N.C., 1860]), pp. 89-91; Kerr, *Report of the Geological Survey* . . ., p. 19.

19. Two recent items circulated in an attempt to find sample sites for preservation were entitled "Wanted: an unspoiled savannah," and "Wanted—Homes for Fire Species," by the Natural Area Council (of the Nature Conservancy?), and by Richard H. Pough, respectively (neither item is dated).

20. Legislation passed by the North Carolina legislature in 1921, which became effective in 1922, officially brought to an end the era of free range: *North Carolina General Statutes*, 68-39, 68-40, and 68-41. All of the state (with the exception of the Outer Banks) thereby became stock-law territory. A marked decline in communal grazing and in the amount and frequency of deliberate burning was one of the consequences of this extension of the stock-law territory.

21. The evergreen shrub bogs have been studied extensively, partly because of their greater extent, and partly because of their association with the mysterious origin of the Carolina Bays. The most informative accounts can be found in the following works: Murray F. Buell, "Jerome Bog, A Peat-Filled 'Carolina Bay,'" *BTBC*, 73 (1946), 24-33; Alfred P. Dachnowski-Stokes and B. W. Wells, "The Vegetation, Stratigraphy, and Age of the 'Open Land' Peat Area in Carteret County, North Carolina," *JWAS*, 19 (1929), 1-11; B. W. Wells, *Vegetation of Holly Shelter Wildlife Management Area* ("North Carolina Department of Conservation and Development, Division of Game and Inland Fisheries," State Bulletin No. 2

[Raleigh, N.C., March, 1946]); Wells and Boyce, "Carolina Bays . . .," *JEMSS*, 69 (1953), 119-41.

22. Wells, *Vegetation of Holly Shelter* . . ., p. 4.

23. For examples of inconsistent usage of some of these terms in the eighteenth century, see the following sources: Harriss, *Lawson's History* . . ., pp. 4, 118; Brickell, *Natural History* . . ., p. 13; Smyth, *A Tour* . . ., I, 106; Schoepf, *Travels in the Confederation* . . ., II, 127, 135, 154; Johnston, "Journal of Ebenezer Hazard . . .," *NCHR*, 36 (1959), 369; Catesby, *Natural History of Carolina* . . ., I, iv; *NCCR*, V, 741, VI, 606.

The term pocosin was spelled in a variety of ways and is traditionally said to be of Indian (Algonquin) origin. It is scarcely used outside of North Carolina. The rarity of the term in the other southern states may well be related to the fact that although the shrub bogs occur on both mineral and peat soils, they are generally associated with the peat that covers a considerable portion of the Outer Coastal Plain in North Carolina; peat, however, occupies a much smaller proportion of the Coastal Plain elsewhere in the Southeast.

It is likely that the use of the term "bay" for shrub bogs derives from the frequent occurrence of several kinds of bay tree on the margins of these bogs: Wells and Boyce, "Carolina Bays . . .," *JEMSS*, 69 (1953), 119. Part of the Dismal Swamp, which straddles the eastern section of the border between North Carolina and Virginia, was an evergreen shrub bog according to the description made after a careful survey of the area about the turn of the century: Thomas H. Kearney, "Report on a Botanical Survey . . .," USDA, *Contributions from the U.S. National Herbarium*, Vol. 5, No. 6 (1901), 417, 426.

24. Wells, *Vegetation of Holly Shelter* . . ., pp. 29-30; Dachnowski-Stokes and Wells, "The Vegetation, Stratigraphy, and Age of the 'Open Land' . . .," *JWAS*, 19 (1929), 4, *et passim*; Buell, "Jerome Bog . . .," *BTBC*, 73 (1946), 30-32; William H. Brown, "The Plant Life of Ellis, Great, Little, and Long Lakes in North Carolina," USDA, *Contributions from the U.S. National Herbarium*, 13 (1909-12), 323; W. O. Shepherd, E. U. Dillard, and H. L. Lucas, *Grazing and Fire Influences in Pond Pine Forests* (North Carolina Agricultural Experiment Station, Technical Bulletin No. 97 [December, 1951]), *passim*.

25. Wells and Boyce, "Carolina Bays . . .," *JEMSS*, 69 (1953), 119; B. W. Wells, *Major Plant Communities of North Carolina* (North Carolina Agricultural Experiment Station, Technical Bulletin No. 25 [April, 1924]), pp. 8, 11; Karl F. Wenger, *Silvical Characteristics of Pond Pine* (USDA-Forest Service, Southeastern Forest Experiment Station, Station Paper No. 91 [April, 1958]), p. 12. Wells has even suggested that "this retrogressive change from shrub-bog to savannah is to be recognized as one of the major vegetational replacements of the historical period": Wells, "Ecological Problems . . .," *BR*, 8 (1942), 546.

26. On various aspects of the successional relationships involved, see: Wells, *Vegetation of Holly Shelter* . . ., p. 30; Buell, "Jerome Bog . . .," *BTBC*, 73 (1946), 32; Wells and Boyce, "Carolina Bays . . .," *JEMSS*, 69 (1953), 119, 139; Shepherd, Dillard, and Lucas, *Grazing and Fire Influences* . . ., *passim*. (This last work is of particular value for the quantitative analysis of the results of certain experiments.) Note also the contrasts observed in the cover of peat areas according to the degree of severity and the recency of burning in Shearin, *et al.*, *Soil Survey of Pasquotank County, North Carolina*, pp. 15-16, 48.

27. The map on which Fig. 44 is based is *Wildlife Cover Map of North Carolina*. The original map was compiled from field surveys and vertical air photographs (the latter probably taken in the 1930's and 1940's); the minimum area classified by field survey was one hundred acres, and the minimum area mapped was one thousand acres. Cleared areas were not represented on the original base map, and this in fact is a helpful omission, since much of the pond pine-pocosin that has recently been cleared, and probably much of it cleared in the past, was actually shrub

bog: Anderson and Dill, *Land Clearing and Drainage* . . ., p. 13, and photographs on p. 19.

A shrub bog area of approximately fifty thousand acres in Carteret County, about twelve miles northeast of Beaufort, has long been known as the "Open Ground," or "Open Land." One attempt to reclaim this area was abandoned in 1926; but much of it is now included in a large experimental farm.

28. For evidence from the accounts of travelers, see the sources cited in note 23, Appendix I, above. The local records used were mainly the court minutes and deeds of selected counties, chiefly Rowan, Orange, and Anson in the Piedmont, and Chowan, Onslow, and Cumberland counties in the Coastal Plain (see Bibliography for details of these records). Identification of the approximate location of all the pocosins mentioned in a series of land grants revealed that almost all of them were in coastal counties; the land grants used for this purpose were those in Land Grants, Vol. 16, 1755-60 (MSS).

29. Starretts Meadows and Lloyds Meadows appear on the 1923 Soil Survey map of Onslow County. Neither of these irregularly shaped areas covered more than one square mile. In the spring of 1960, Lloyds Meadows was still a mainly treeless area, more closely resembling a savannah than a shrub bog; although the area was at that time uncultivated, recent alterations made it impossible to ascertain what might have been the vegetation cover in earlier times. The 1949 vertical air photographs of the Lloyds Meadows area, however, do give some indication of the distinctively open nature of this site in an otherwise forested (or cultivated) area. The Soil Survey Report for Onslow County uses the category, "Portsmouth loam, prairie phase" for some of the soils of the poorly drained, practically treeless areas within the county: R. C. Jurney, *et al., Soil Survey of Onslow County, North Carolina* (Washington, D.C., 1923), p. 120, and accompanying map.

30. For one of the more exaggerated statements of this traditional view, see, William H. Foote, *Sketches of North Carolina, Historical and Biographical* . . . (New York, 1846), p. 189. This account has been cited frequently as evidence of the existence of much open land suitable for cattle raising, but it should be noted that in fact it has no more authority than that provided by a vivid imagination. There is a description in a similar vein in E. F. Rockwell, "An Ancient Map of the Central Part of Iredell County, N.C.," *Historical Magazine*, 12 (August, 1867), 87.

31. For references to these kinds, including meadows, Indian fields, old fields, highland ponds, savannahs, and licks, see the following sources: Harriss, *Lawson's History* . . ., pp. 43, 48, 85, *et passim*; Brickell, *Natural History* . . ., p. 107; Cumming, *Discoveries of John Lederer*, pp. 34-35, 85, *et passim*; Catesby, *Natural History of Carolina* . . ., I, iv; *MR*, I, 52; Boyd, *William Byrd's Histories* . . ., p. 212; William Byrd, *The Westover Manuscripts* . . . (Petersburg, Va., 1841), p. 112; Land Grants, Vol. 16, 1755-60 (MSS); Smyth, *A Tour* . . ., I, 141-43. (This last reference is to a "lick"—for an interesting account of a similar feature in Georgia see Harper, *Travels of William Bartram*, pp. 23, 343-44, and Fig. 7.) There are two modern studies of a special kind of open land that occurs in the Piedmont of North Carolina and other southern states, on granite rocks: Henry J. Oosting and Lewis E. Anderson, "Plant Succession on Granite Rock in Eastern North Carolina," *BG*, 100 (1939), 750-68; and, Rogers McVaugh, "The Vegetation of the Granitic Flatrocks of the Southeastern United States," *EM*, 13 (1943), 119-66.

32. *MR*, I, 45, 53, 59; Harriss, *Lawson's History* . . ., p. 48; Boyd, *William Byrd's Histories* . . ., p. 231; Byrd, *The Westover Manuscripts* . . ., pp. 110, 111, 112; Smyth, *A Tour* . . ., I, 164.

33. For mention of the long-standing habit of burning lightwood for pitch and tar, see: *NCCR*, IV, 285, V, 149, IX, 294-95.

34. For one of the earliest and one of the latest examples of this emphasis, see, Hu Maxwell, "The Use and Abuse of Forests by the Virginia Indians,"

William and Mary College Quarterly Historical Magazine, 19 (1910), 73-103, and, Rostlund, "The Myth of a Natural Prairie Belt . . .," *AAAG,* 47 (1957), 392-411.

35. Rostlund, "The Myth of a Natural Prairie Belt . . .," *AAAG,* 47 (1957), 409.

APPENDIX II

1. *NCSR,* XXIII, 72.
2. *NCSR,* XXIII, 106.
3. *NCCR,* V, 471.
4. *NCCR,* IX, 259.
5. See Greene and Harrington, *American Population* . . ., p. [xxiii], "Note on methods of calculation."
6. Friis, *A Series of Population Maps* . . ., p. 6.
7. Stella H. Sutherland, *Population Distribution in Colonial America* (New York, 1936), p. 211. It is only fair to note that it appears as though the author has since revised this method. Sutherland was one of the contributors to the chapter on colonial statistics in U.S. Bureau of the Census, *Historical Statistics . . .,* for which volume she compiled the table, Series Z 1-19, showing "Estimated Population of American Colonies: 1610-1780." It was she who presumably wrote the brief explanatory note for this table, in which it is pointed out that "no generalization can safely be made as to the ratio borne by the . . . southern taxables and tithables to the whole population of the Colonies. In every Province the figure was different." Appropriate ratios for particular colonies are then suggested, and the paragraph concludes with the remark that "the North Carolina white taxables were multiplied by 4 and the Negro taxables by 2": *ibid.,* p. 743.
8. *NCCR,* V, 600, VI, 614, 1040.
9. The higher proportion for Negroes is caused by the different policy followed in defining Negro taxables as compared to white taxables: see definition cited on p. 194, above.
10. In combining the two ratios, 1:2 and 1:4, a weighting had to be used that would take into account the fact that whites were three times as numerous as Negroes. The combined ratio was therefore obtained by averaging the two, but at the same time allowing the white ratio three times as much weight as the Negro ratio. The multiplier that has to be employed for calculating the total population from the total taxables is therefore $\frac{(4 \times 3) + (2 \times 1)}{4}$, or 3.5.
11. This table has been reproduced and printed in Boyd, *Some Eighteenth Century Tracts* . . ., opposite p. 416; it also appears in Greene and Harrington, *American Population* . . ., pp. 160-68, *passim.* The only known copy of the original is in the possession of the Massachusetts Historical Society. As the version of it in Boyd's book is difficult to decipher, I relied on Greene and Harrington's version of the original; following the practice adopted by Greene and Harrington, I corrected errors of addition in the broadside table, where these are obvious, and substituted zeroes for undecipherable digits.
12. *NCCR,* V, 320 (for 1754), 575-76 (1755), 603 (1756); VII, 145-46 (1765), 288-89 (1766), 539 (1767). These have also been published in Greene and Harrington, *American Population* . . ., pp. 162-67, *passim.* I used the latter version, which was easier to consult, only checking with the *NCCR* version for occasional minor points. The originals of the 1754-56 lists (which also had to be used to resolve minor difficulties), together with very fragmentary lists of the same kind for the years 1762-64, were obtained from Governor's Office: Lists of Taxables, Militia, and Magistrates; 1754-70, undated (MSS).
13. Almost all of the tax lists that have been preserved are available in NCSDAH.

(Two important exceptions are the tax lists of 1763 for Pitt and New Hanover counties, which are among the North Carolina Court Papers, 1763-77, in the manuscript collections of UNC Library.) They are dispersed among the following holdings of manuscripts there: Legislative Papers, Tax Lists, 1771-74; Secretary of State, Tax Lists, 1720-1839; State Treasurer, Tax Lists, 1755; Comptroller's Papers, Box 40, Tax Records, various counties, 1763-1835; Comptroller's Office, Box 41, Lists of Taxes, various counties, 1764-69; Pitt County, Miscellaneous Papers, 1762-1851, undated; Chowan County, Lists of Taxables, 1766-98. The format of these various tax lists is by no means uniform; and they vary also in many minor ways, not the least important of which is their state of preservation and degree of legibility.

14. The entries are not easily located, for they are generally embedded in single lines scattered here and there among the sometimes voluminous and often difficult to read manuscript minutes of the county courts. Not all of these were examined, but useful entries were found in the following (all are available in NCSDAH): Rowan County, Court Minutes, 1755-67; Rowan County, Minutes of Court of Pleas and Quarter Sessions, 1768-72, 1773-86; Onslow County, Precinct Court Minutes, 1734-37, County Court Minutes, 1741-49; Onslow County, Court Minutes, Vol. III, 1765-78; Cumberland County, Court Minutes, Book A (1755-59), Book B (1759-65); Chowan County, Miscellaneous Court Papers, Vols. 6-15. The same kind of data were found in the Records of the Proceedings of the Vestry of St. Paul's Church, Edenton, N.C., 1701-1841 (a typed copy in NCSDAH prepared from the original in the Church at Edenton). One volume of printed abstracts of county records also contained two relevant entries: May W. McBee (comp.), *Anson County, North Carolina: Abstracts of Early Records* ("May Wilson McBee Collection," Vol. 1 [privately reproduced, 1950]), p. 83.

15. This is a bound booklet in NCSDAH. The coverage of counties is as follows: Currituck 1763-71, Pasquotank 1763-71, Perquimans 1762-72, Chowan 1763-70, Tyrell 1761-71, Bertie 1763-71, Hertford 1763-71, Northampton 1763-71, Halifax 1762-71, Edgecombe 1762-70, Bute 1764-71, Granville 1760-72, Orange 1762-71, and Chatham (established 1770-71), 1771-72. Sutherland used this source, taking the figures for each county, but only for the last-named year in each case: Sutherland, *Population Distribution* . . ., pp. 208ff. This was appropriate for her own purpose, but Greene and Harrington concluded that this was all the information that the book contained: see footnote aw in Greene and Harrington, *American Population . . .*, p. 168.

16. Hayes Collection, Reel 2, Folder 37. The coverage of the counties is as follows: Granville 1755, 1758; Northampton 1755-57, 1761; Bertie 1755-59; Hertford 1759, 1761; Orange 1755-61; Currituck 1755-61; Perquimans 1755, 1757, 1761; Tyrell 1755-58, 1760-61; Pasquotank 1755, 1758; Edgecombe 1755; and Chowan 1755-56.

17. Most of these have been brought together in Greene and Harrington, *American Population* . . ., pp. 156-60.

18. Where, however, two or more figures were available for the same county in the same year and clearly showed one of the figures to be erroneous, then the obviously erroneous figure was discounted; if that still left more than two figures these were averaged, while if only one was left, then it was used as the presumed total. Most of the data that were clearly erroneous were so on account of incompleteness.

19. See Crittenden, *The Commerce of North Carolina* . . ., pp. 43-44.

20. *Ibid.*, pp. 35, 42, *et passim*, contains a useful summary of what little is definitely known about the locations of the Ports and the centers from which customs officials operated.

BIBLIOGRAPHY

I. PRIMARY SOURCES

A. MANUSCRIPTS

Unless otherwise indicated, all of the following manuscripts are available, in the original or on microfilm, in the North Carolina State Department of Archives and History, Raleigh, N.C.

American Board of Customs: Exports and Imports, America, 1768-73.
    British Public Record Office, Customs 16/1.
Anson County, N.C. Record of Wills and Inventories, Book 1, 1751-95.
Arthur Dobbs Papers, 1731-71.
    Photostat copies of MSS in Public Record Office of Northern Ireland.
Bath County, N.C. Court Records, Onslow Precinct, 1731/32-1734.
    University of North Carolina Library, Chapel Hill, N.C.
Byrne's Account Book, 1757-1854.
Captain Jones. Ship Log, 1767-68, Edenton, N.C.
    Duke University Library, Durham, N.C.
Chowan County, N.C. Court Minutes, 1730-34, 1740-48.
Chowan County, N.C. Court Minutes, 1762-75.
Chowan County, N.C. Court Minutes, Reference Docket, New Action Docket: 1755-61.
Chowan County, N.C. Inventories of Estates, Vols. 1-2, 1735-95. Book Q (1758-77).
Chowan County, N.C. Inventories of Estates, Vols. 1-2, 1735-95.
Chowan County, N.C. Lists of Taxables, 1766-98.
Chowan County, N.C. Miscellaneous Court Papers, Vols. 6-15, 19, 1751-75.
Comptroller's Office, Box 41. Lists of Taxes, various counties, 1764-69.

BIBLIOGRAPHY

Comptroller's Papers. Box 40. Tax Records, various counties, 1763-1835.
Cumberland County, N.C. Court Minutes, Books A-D, 1755-78.
Cumberland County, N.C. Deeds and Grants, Vols. 1-4, 1741-63, 1766-72.
Cumberland County, N.C. Estates.
Cumberland County, N.C. Lists of Taxables, 1777-83.
Cumberland County, N.C. Wills, 1757-1869.
Custom House Papers. Port of Roanoke, Vols. 1-2, 1682-1775.
Customs Records. Box 9. Port Brunswick, 1765-67, 1785-87.
Dartmouth Manuscripts. Transcripts of North Carolina Papers, 1720-83.
Diary and Account Book of John Saunders, 1750-55.
Diary of Col. W. A. Avery, 1769.
    In the collection of Draper Manuscripts in the Wisconsin State Historical Society, Madison, Wis.
Edgecombe County, N.C. Record Book of Marks and Brands, August, 1732-May, 1809.
English Records, American Loyalist Claims.
    Transcripts and photostats of MSS in the British Public Record Office.
Fanning-McCulloh Papers, 1758-1811.
    University of North Carolina Library, Chapel Hill, N.C.
Governor's Office. Council Papers, 1761-79.
Governor's Office. Lists of Taxables, Militia, and Magistrates. 1754-70; undated.
Hayes Collection.
    Microfilm in the Southern Historical Collection, University of North Carolina, Chapel Hill, N.C., from originals in the possession of Mr. John G. Wood, Edenton, N.C.
Henry Eustace McCulloh. Survey Book, 1762-73.
    University of North Carolina Library, Chapel Hill, N.C.
Hogg and Campbell. Invoice Outward, 1767-82.
Isaac Winslow. Journal of a southern tour, 1824.
    Duke University Library, Durham, N.C.
James Hogg Papers. 1772-1824; undated.
    University of North Carolina Library, Chapel Hill, N.C.
James Iredell Notebooks. Vols. 1-5, Port of Roanoke Records, 1771-76.
    University of North Carolina Library, Chapel Hill, N.C.
Journal of a ride from Newbern to Salisbury, October, 1768, with a map of the road.
    In the collection of Draper Manuscripts in the Wisconsin State Historical Society, Madison, Wis.
Land Grants. Vol. 6, 1701-1831; Vol. 16, 1755-60.
    Land Grant Office, North Carolina Department of State, Raleigh, N.C.

Ledger containing lists of entries and clearances, Port Roanoke, 1770-76.
 Chowan County Courthouse, Edenton, N.C.
Legislative Papers. 1689-1775.
Legislative Papers. Tax Lists, 1771-74.
Miscellaneous Papers. Series One, Vol. 1, Sept. 20, 1775-Nov. 20, 1788.
Nathaniel Williams. Letterbook and Accounts, 1758-1834; Cork, Ireland.
 Duke University Library, Durham, N.C.
New Hanover County, N.C. Lists of Taxables, Inventories of Estates, Miscellaneous Material, 1748-1858.
North Carolina Court Papers, 1763-77.
 University of North Carolina Library, Chapel Hill, N.C.
North Carolina Wills, 1663-1789. Vol. 9.
Onslow County, N.C. Accounts, Divisions, Inventories, Sales, etc. of Estates.
Onslow County, N.C. Court Minutes, Vols. II, III, 1749-78.
Onslow County, N.C. Deed Book, 1769-74.
Onslow County, N.C. Deeds, 1747-54.
Onslow County, N.C. Precinct Court Minutes, 1734-37; County Court Minutes, 1741-49.
Onslow County, N.C. Record of Land Grants, 1712-1800.
Onslow County, N.C. Tax Lists. 1774-90; undated.
Orange County, N.C. Estates, 1758-85.
Perquimans County, N.C. Court Minutes, 1738-74.
Pettigrew Papers. Vol. 1, Mar. 9, 1772-Aug. 23, 1803.
Pitt County, N.C. Miscellaneous Papers, 1762-1851; undated.
Pollock Letter Book, 1708-61.
Port Brunswick Shipping Register, 1765-75.
Port Roanoke, 1767-74. (Box 12 of Customs Records.)
Public Records of South Carolina (transcripts), Vol. 32, pp. 280-83.
 Photostat copy obtained from South Carolina Archives Department, Columbia, S.C.
Records of the Proceedings of the Vestry of St. Paul's Church, Edenton, N.C., 1701-1841. (Typewritten copy of the original.)
Richard Brownrigg. Merchant's Ledger, 1757-59, Edenton, N.C.
 Duke University Library, Durham, N.C.
Robert Hogg Account Books, 1762-75.
 University of North Carolina Library, Chapel Hill, N.C.
Rowan County, N.C. Court Minutes, Part I, 1753-55.
Rowan County, N.C. Court Minutes, 1755-67.
Rowan County, N.C. Deeds, Vols. 1-2 (1753-58), Vol. 6 (1764-68), Vol. 7 (1768-72).
Rowan County, N.C. Minutes of Court of Pleas and Quarter Sessions, 1768-72, 1773-86.

Rowan County, N.C. Roads, 1757-1894.
Rowan County, N.C. Tax Lists, 1758-1819.
Rowan County, N.C. Wills, 1743-1868, Vol. 8.
Secretary of State. Inventories and Sales of Estates, 1714-98.
Secretary of State. Inventories of Estates, 1749-54.
Secretary of State. Land Entries, Warrants, Surveys. Rowan County, 1751-1824.
Secretary of State. Petitions for Re-survey of Land Grants: Craven-Halifax, 1721-80 (Cumberland County folder).
Secretary of State. Tax Lists, 1720-1839.
Secretary of State Records. Box 726. Lists of Warrants Returned, 1751-80; undated.
Secretary of State Records. Box 1038. County Boundary Lines, 1747-1922.
Shaw Papers, 1735-1883.
State Treasurer. Tax Lists, 1755.
Tax Book of Northern District, 1757-75.
Thomas Oldham's Book, 1770-83.
    Chowan County Courthouse, Edenton, N.C.
Tillie Bond Manuscripts. 1690-1828; undated.
Trade Letters from Robert Cochran of Cross Creek/Campbellton to Salem persons, 1775-83.
    Moravian Archives, Winston-Salem, N.C.
Wake County, N.C. Clerk of Superior Court: Record Book No. 1, 1771-82. (Typewritten copy.)

B. NEWSPAPERS AND PERIODICALS

South Carolina Newspapers, 1732-82.
    Issued on microfilm by the Charleston Library Society, Charleston, S.C., 1956. 10 reels.
The Cape-Fear Mercury. Wilmington, 1769-75.
The North-Carolina Gazette. New Bern. 1751-59, 1768-78.
The North-Carolina Gazette. Wilmington. 1765-66.
The North-Carolina Magazine; or, Universal Intelligencer. New Bern. 1764-65.
The Virginia Gazette. Williamsburg. 1736-80.
    Issued on microfilm by The Institute of Early American History and Culture, Williamsburg, Va., 1950. 6 reels.
The Weekly Magazine, or Edinburgh Amusement. 1774.

C. OFFICIAL RECORDS AND DOCUMENTS

"Advertisement. Whereas it appears that many persons have settled in the District of this Province, granted by his late Majesty to the

Right Honourable John Earl Granville . . . Newbern, May 3, 1774. Jo. Martin."

A broadside in the University of North Carolina Library, Chapel Hill, N.C.

Chandler, Allen D. (ed.). *Colonial Records of the State of Georgia.* 26 vols.; Atlanta, Ga., 1904-16.

Clark, Walter (ed.). *The State Records of North Carolina.* 16 vols.; Winston and Goldsboro, N.C., 1895-1907.

Egerton, Hugh E. (ed.). *The Royal Commission on the Losses and Services of American Loyalists, 1783 to 1785.* . . . Oxford, 1915.

Grimes, J. Bryan [ed.]. *North Carolina Wills and Inventories.* Raleigh, N.C., 1912.

McBee, May Wilson [comp.]. *Anson County, North Carolina: Abstracts of Early Records.* ("May Wilson McBee Collection," Vol. 1.) Privately reproduced, 1950.

Newsome, A. R. (ed.). "Records of Emigrants from England and Scotland to North Carolina, 1774-1775," *North Carolina Historical Review,* 11 (1934), 39-53, 129-43.

Proceedings of the Safety Committee for the Town of Wilmington, N.C., from 1774 to 1776: printed from the original record. Raleigh, N.C., 1844.

Saunders, William L. (ed.). *The Colonial Records of North Carolina.* 10 vols.; Raleigh, N.C., 1886-90.

Stock, Leo F. (ed.). *Proceedings and Debates of the British Parliaments respecting North America, 1542-1739.* ("Carnegie Institution of Washington Publication," No. 338.) 4 vols.; Washington, D.C., 1937.

United Empire Loyalists. Enquiry into the Losses and Services in Consequence of Their Loyalty. Evidence in the Canadian Claims. (Province of Ontario, Bureau of Archives, Second Report, 1904). Toronto, 1905.

Walker, Alexander M. (ed.). *New Hanover County Court Minutes.* 2 Parts; Bethesda, Md., 1958-59.

Weeks, Stephen B. (comp.). *The State Records of North Carolina: Index.* 4 vols.; Goldsboro, Charlotte, and Raleigh, N.C., 1909-14.

D. TRAVEL ACCOUNTS, NARRATIVES, TOPOGRAPHIES, JOURNALS, HISTORIES, AND GEOGRAPHIES

Andrews, Evangeline W., and Charles M. Andrews (eds.), *Journal of a Lady of Quality.* . . . New Haven, Conn., 1923.

"A New Voyage to Georgia. By a Young Gentleman. Giving an account of his travels to South Carolina, and part of North Carolina . . . ," *Georgia Historical Society Collections,* 2 (1842), 37-66.

(A reprint of the second edition [1737] of a pamphlet first published in 1735.)

A Present for an Emigrant; containing a brief Description of the Climate, Soil, and Produce of the British Colonies in North America. ... Edinburgh, 1774.

Bartram, John. *Diary of a Journey through the Carolinas, Georgia, and Florida from July 1, 1765, to April 10, 1766* ... annotated by Francis Harper. ("Transactions of the American Philosophical Society," New Ser., Vol. 33, Part 1, Dec., 1942.) Philadelphia, 1942.

Benson, Adolph B. (ed. and trans.). *Peter Kalm's Travels in North America.* 2 vols.; New York, 1937.

Boyd, William K. (ed.). *William Byrd's Histories of the Dividing Line betwixt Virginia and North Carolina.* Raleigh, N.C., 1929.

Brickell, John. *The Natural History of North-Carolina.* Dublin, 1737; reprinted Raleigh, N.C., 1911.

[Burke, Edmund and William]. *An Account of the European Settlements in America.* 2 vols.; London, 1757.

Burnaby, Andrew. *Travels through the Middle Settlements in North-America. In the Years 1759 and 1760. With Observations upon the State of the Colonies.* 2nd ed.; London, 1775; reprinted in "Great Seal Books," Ithaca, N.Y., 1960.

Byrd, William. *The Westover Manuscripts: containing The History of the Dividing Line betwixt Virginia and North Carolina; A Journey to the Land of Eden, A.D. 1733; and A Progress to the Mines.* ... Petersburg, Va.; printed by Edmund and Julian C. Ruffin, 1841.

Catesby, Mark. *The Natural History of Carolina, Florida, and the Bahama Islands.* ... 2 vols.; London, 1754.

"Charleston, S.C., in 1774, as described by an English Traveler," *The Historical Magazine*, 9 (1865), 341-47.

Coulter, E. Merton (ed.). *The Journal of William Stephens, 1741-1743.* ("Wormsloe Foundation Publications," No. 4.) Athens, Ga., 1958.

Cumming, William P. (ed.). *The Discoveries of John Lederer.* Charlottesville, Va., 1958.

De Crèvecouer, J. Hector St. John. *Letters from an American Farmer.* Dutton Everyman Paperback; New York, 1957.

———. *Sketches of Eighteenth Century America: More "Letters from an American Farmer."* Edited by Henri L. Bourdin, Ralph H. Gabriel, and Stanley T. Williams. New Haven, Conn., 1925.

Dexter, Franklin B. (ed.). *Extracts from the Itineraries of Ezra Stiles, D.D., LL.D., 1755-1794, with a selection from his correspondence.* New Haven, Conn., 1916.

Douglass, William. *A Summary, Historical and Political, Of the first Planting, progressive Improvements, and present State of the British Settlements in North-America.* 2 vols.; Boston, 1749-53.

Drayton, John. *A View of South-Carolina.* Charleston, S.C., 1802.

Eddis, William. *Letters from America, Historical and Descriptive; Comprising Occurrences from 1769, to 1777, Inclusive.* London, 1792.

Finlay, Hugh. *Journal kept by Hugh Finlay, Surveyor of the Post Roads on the Continent of North America, during his Survey of the Post Offices between Falmouth and Casco Bay in the Province of Massachusetts, and Savannah in Georgia; begun the 13th Septr. 1773 and ended 26th June 1774.* Brooklyn, N.Y., 1867.

Fitzpatrick, John C. (ed.). *The Diaries of George Washington, 1748-1799.* 4 vols.; Boston, 1925.

Harper, Francis (ed.). *Travels of William Bartram.* ("Naturalist's Edition.") New Haven, Conn., 1958.

Harriss, Frances L. (ed.). *Lawson's History of North Carolina.* 3rd ed.; Richmond, Va., 1960.

Höen, Moritz W., and Anton W. Böhme. *Das verlangte nicht erlangte Canaan bey den Lust-Gräbern.* . . . Frankfurt and Leipzig, 1711.

Hooker, Richard J. (ed.). *The Carolina Backcountry on the Eve of Revolution: The Journal and Other Writings of Charles Woodmason, Anglican Itinerant.* Chapel Hill, N.C., 1953.

Howe, Mark A. De Wolfe (ed.). "Journal of Josiah Quincy, Junior, 1773," *Massachusetts Historical Society Proceedings,* 49 (1915-16), 424-81.

Hutton, Arthur W. (ed.). *Arthur Young's Tour in Ireland (1776-1779).* 2 vols.; London, 1892.

"Itinerant Observations in America, reprinted from The London Magazine, 1745-6," *Georgia Historical Society Collections,* 4 (1878), 1-64.

Johnston, Hugh B. (ed.). "The Journal of Ebenezer Hazard in North Carolina, 1777 and 1778," *North Carolina Historical Review,* 36 (1959), 358-81.

"Journal of a French Traveller in the Colonies, 1765, I," *American Historical Review,* 26 (1920-21), 726-47.

Kocherthaler. *Ausführlich und umständlicher Bericht von der berühmten Landschaft Carolina.* . . . Frankfurt am Mäyn, 1709.

Meredith, Hugh. *An Account of the Cape Fear Country, 1731.* Edited by Earl G. Swem. Perth Amboy, N.J., 1922.

Mereness, Newton D. (ed.). *Travels in the American Colonies.* New York, 1916.

Milling, Chapman J. (ed.). *Colonial South Carolina: Two Contemporary Descriptions by Governor James Glen and Doctor George Milligen-Johnston.* ("South Caroliniana Sesquicentennial Series," No. 1.) Columbia, S.C., 1951.

Mittelberger, Gottlieb. *Journey to Pennsylvania.* Edited and translated by Oscar Handlin and John Clive. Cambridge, Mass., 1960.

Newsome, A. R. (ed.). "Twelve North Carolina Counties, 1810-1811,"

North Carolina Historical Review, 5 (1928), 413-46; 6 (1929), 67-99, 171-89, 281-301.
Pottle, Frederick A., and Charles H. Bennett (eds.). *Boswell's Journal of A Tour to the Hebrides.* . . . New York, 1936.
Powell, William S. (ed.). "Tryon's 'Book' on North Carolina," *North Carolina Historical Review*, 34 (1957), 406-15.
Rippy, J. Fred (ed.). "A View of the Carolinas in 1783," *North Carolina Historical Review*, 6 (1929), 362-70.
Rodman, Lida T. (ed.). *Journal of a Tour to North Carolina by William Attmore.* ("James Sprunt Historical Publications," Vol. 17.) Chapel Hill, N.C., 1922.
Salley, Alexander S. (ed.). *Narratives of Early Carolina, 1650-1708.* New York, 1911.
Schoepf, Johann D. *Travels in the Confederation, 1783-1784, from the German of Johann David Schoepf.* Translated and edited by Alfred J. Morrison. 2 vols.; Philadelphia, 1911.
Smyth, J. F. D. *A Tour in the United States of America.* 2 vols.; London, 1784.
Steeg, Clarence L. Ver (ed.). *A True and Historical Narrative of the Colony of Georgia by Pat. Tailfer and Others with Comments by the Earl of Egmont.* ("Wormsloe Foundation Publications," No. 4.) Athens, Ga., 1960.
[Stephens, William.] "A State of the Province of Georgia, Attested upon Oath in the Court of Savannah, November 10, 1740," *Georgia Historical Society Collections*, 2 (1842), 67-85.
"The Journal of James Auld, 1765-1770," *Southern History Association Publications*, 8 (1904), 253-68.
The Journal of Nicholas Cresswell, 1774-1777. New York, 1924.
Todd, Vincent H. (ed.), and Julius Goebel (trans.). *Christoph von Graffenried's Account of the Founding of New Bern.* Raleigh, N.C., 1920.
"William Logan's Journal of a Journey to Georgia, 1745," *Pennsylvania Magazine of History and Biography*, 36 (1912), 1-16, 162-86.
Williamson, Hugh. *The History of North Carolina.* 2 vols.; Philadelphia, 1812.
Wymberley-Jones, George (ed.). *History of the Province of Georgia: with maps of original surveys. By John Gerar William De Brahm.* . . . Privately printed; Wormsloe, Ga., 1849.

E. AUTOBIOGRAPHIES, BIOGRAPHIES, CORRESPONDENCE, AND PERSONAL PAPERS

"Autobiography of Col. William Few of Georgia. From the original MS. in the possession of William Few Christie," *Magazine of American History*, 7 (July-December, 1881), 343-58.

Brayton, Patience. *A Short Account of the Life and Religious Labours of Patience Brayton.* . . . New Bedford, 1801.
Caruthers, E. W. *A Sketch of the Life and Character of the Rev. David Caldwell.* . . . Greensborough, N.C., 1842.
Davidson, Chalmers G. *The Life and Times of General William Lee Davidson.* Davidson, N.C., 1951.
Farrand, Max (ed.). *The Autobiography of Benjamin Franklin: A Restoration of a "Fair Copy."* Berkeley, Calif., 1949.
Fox, George. *A Journal or Historical Account of the Life, Travels, Sufferings, Christian Experiences and Labour of Love, in the Work of the Ministry.* . . . Philadelphia, 1832.
Labaree, Leonard W. (ed.). *The Papers of Benjamin Franklin.* New Haven, Conn., 1959—.
"Letter of Rev. James Maury to Philip Ludwell, on the defense of the frontiers of Virginia, 1756," *Virginia Magazine of History and Biography,* 19 (1911), 292-304.
McRee, Griffith J. *Life and Correspondence of James Iredell.* 2 vols.; New York, 1857-58.
Stanton, Daniel. *A Journal of the Life, Travels, and Gospel Labours.* . . . Philadelphia, 1772.
Tiffany, Nina M. (ed.). *Letters of James Murray, Loyalist.* Boston, 1901.
Watson, Winslow C. (ed.). *Men and Times of the Revolution; or, Memoirs of Elkanah Watson . . . 1777 to 1842.* New York, 1856.
Wylie, T. W. J. (ed.). "Franklin County One Hundred Years Ago: A Settler's Experience Told In A Letter Written By Alexander Thomson In 1773," *Pennsylvania Magazine of History and Biography,* 8 (1884), 313-27.

F. MISCELLANEOUS

Boyd, William K. (ed.). *Some Eighteenth Century Tracts Concerning North Carolina.* Raleigh, N.C., 1927.
Boyd, William K. (ed.), and Charles A. Krummel (trans.). "German Tracts Concerning the Lutheran Church in North Carolina during the Eighteenth Century. Part II. Velthusen's North Carolina Church Reports (I, II) with Ordination Address and Prayer," *North Carolina Historical Review,* 7 (1930), 225-82.
Carman, Harry J. (ed.). *American Husbandry.* ("Columbia University Studies in the History of American Agriculture," No. 6.) New York, 1939.
Commerce of Rhode Island, 1726-1774. ("Collections of the Massachusetts Historical Society," Seventh Series, Vol. 9.) Boston, 1914.
Curry, Cora C. "Heidelberg Evangelical Lutheran Church Records (Old Dutch Meeting House), Rowan County (Now Davie) North

Carolina," *National Genealogical Society Quarterly*, 19 (March, 1931), 4-10.
C. W. [Account of the Culture and Manufacture of Indigo], *Gentleman's Magazine*, 25 (1755), 201-3, 256-59.
Doggett, Samuel B. (ed.). "A Plantation on Prince George's Creek, Cape Fear, North Carolina," *New-England Historical and Genealogical Register*, 52 (1898), 469-73.
Force, Peter. *Tracts and Other Papers*. . . . 4 vols.; Washington, D.C., 1826-46.
Fries, Adelaide L., and Douglas L. Rights (eds.). *Records of the Moravians in North Carolina*. 8 vols.; Raleigh, N.C., 1922-54.
Further Observations Intended for Improving the Culture and Curing of Indigo, etc. in South-Carolina. London, 1747.
Jensen, Merrill (ed.). *English Historical Documents: American Colonial Documents to 1776*. London, 1955.
Larsen, Esther L. (ed. and trans.). "Pehr Kalm's Description of Maize . . .," *Agricultural History*, 9 (1935), 98-117.
Ljungstedt, Milnor (comp.). "Items from southern records showing family and trade connections with northern colonies and the home countries," *American Genealogist*, 15 (Oct., 1938), 95-104.
Postlethwayt, Malachy. *The Universal Dictionary of Trade and Commerce*. . . . 2 vols., 4th ed.; London, 1774.
Velthusen, Johann C. *Nordcarolinische Kirchennachrichten*. Zweytes und letztes heft; Stade, 1792.
Velthusen, J. C., et al. *Lehrbücher für die Jugend in Nordcarolina, entworfen von einer Gesellschaft Helmstädtischer Professoren*. Dritte Lieferung, Religionsgeschichte und Geographisches Handbuch; Leipzig, 1788.
Weston, Plowden C. J. (ed.). *Documents Connected with the History of South Carolina*. London, 1856.
Woodward, Carl R. [ed.]. *Ploughs and Politicks: Charles Read of New Jersey and His Notes on Agriculture, 1715-1774*. New Brunswick, N.J., 1941.
Young, Arthur. *Political Essays concerning the present state of the British Empire*. London, 1772.

II. SECONDARY SOURCES

A. PUBLISHED WORKS

American Council of Learned Societies. "Report of Committee on Linguistic and National Stocks in the Population of the United States," *American Historical Association, Annual Report, 1931, Volume I* (1932), 105-441.

Anderson, James R., and Henry W. Dill. *Land Clearing and Drainage in Eastern North Carolina.* U.S. Department of Agriculture, Agricultural Research Service, Farm Economics Division, Washington, D.C., January, 1961.

Ashe, Samuel A. *History of North Carolina.* 2 vols.; Greensboro, N.C., 1908-25.

———, Stephen B. Weeks, and Charles L. Van Noppen. *Biographical History of North Carolina.* 8 vols.; Greensboro, N.C., 1905-17.

Ashe, W. W. *Loblolly or North Carolina Pine.* ("North Carolina Geological and Economic Survey," Bulletin No. 24.) Raleigh, N.C., 1915.

———. "Notes on the Forest Resources of North Carolina," *Journal of the Elisha Mitchell Scientific Society,* 10 (1893), 5-25.

———. *The Forests, Forest Lands, and Forest Products of Eastern North Carolina.* ("North Carolina Geological Survey," Bulletin No. 5). Raleigh, N.C., 1894.

Bidwell, Percy W., and John I. Falconer. *History of Agriculture in the Northern United States, 1620-1860.* ("Carnegie Institution of Washington Publication," No. 358.) Washington, D.C., 1925.

Braun, E. Lucy. *Deciduous Forests of Eastern North America.* Philadelphia, 1950.

Brawley, James S. *The Rowan Story, 1753-1953.* Salisbury, N.C., 1953.

Brown, Ralph H. *Historical Geography of the United States.* New York, 1948.

———. *Mirror for Americans: Likeness of the Eastern Seaboard, 1810.* ("American Geographical Society Special Publication," No. 27.) New York, 1943.

———. "The DeBrahm Charts of the Atlantic Ocean, 1772-1776," *Geographical Review,* 28 (1938), 124-32.

Brown, William H. "The Plant Life of Ellis, Great, Little, and Long Lakes in North Carolina," U.S. Department of Agriculture, *Contributions from the U.S. National Herbarium,* Vol. 13 (1909-12), 323-41.

Bruce, David. "Thirty-two Years of Annual Burning in Longleaf Pine," *Journal of Forestry,* 45 (1947), 809-14.

Brun, Christian. *Guide to the Manuscript Maps in the William L. Clements Library.* Ann Arbor, Mich., 1959.

Buell, Murray F. "Jerome Bog: A Peat-Filled 'Carolina Bay,'" *Bulletin of the Torrey Botanical Club,* 73 (1946), 24-33.

——— and Robert L. Cain. "The Successional Role of Southern White Cedar, *Chamaecyparis Thyoides,* in Southeastern North Carolina," *Ecology,* 24 (1943), 85-93.

Campbell, Mildred. "English Emigration on the Eve of the American Revolution," *American Historical Review,* 61 (1955), 1-20.

Cannon, John. "Henry McCulloch and Henry McCulloh," *William and Mary Quarterly*, 3rd Ser., 15 (1958), 71-73.

Cappon, Lester J., and Stella F. Duff. *Virginia Gazette Index, 1736-1780*. 2 vols.; Williamsburg, Va., 1950.

Carney, Charles B. *Weather and Climate in North Carolina*. North Carolina State College, Agricultural Experiment Station Bulletin No. 396, October, 1958.

Cathey, Cornelius O. *Agricultural Developments in North Carolina, 1783-1860*. ("James Sprunt Studies in History and Political Science," Vol. 38.) Chapel Hill, N.C., 1956.

Clark, Austin H. "A New Locality for the Venus' Fly-Trap (*Dionaea Muscipula*)," *Science*, 88 (1938), 188.

Clark, Thomas D. (ed.). *Travels in the Old South*. 3 vols.; Norman, Okla., 1956-59.

Clarke, Desmond. *Arthur Dobbs, Esquire, 1689-1765*. Chapel Hill, N.C., 1957.

Clarke, William B., et al. *The Coastal Plain of North Carolina*. ("North Carolina Geological and Economic Survey," Vol. 3.) Raleigh, N.C., 1912.

Clonts, F. W. "Travel and Transportation in Colonial North Carolina," *North Carolina Historical Review*, 3 (1926), 16-35.

Coker, W. C. "The Distribution of Venus's Fly Trap (*Dionaea Muscipula*)," *Journal of the Elisha Mitchell Scientific Society*, 43 (1928), 221-28.

―― and Henry R. Totten. *Trees of the Southeastern States*. 3rd ed.; Chapel Hill, N.C., 1945.

Cole, Arthur H. *Wholesale Commodity Prices in the United States, 1700-1861, Statistical Supplement*. Cambridge, Mass., 1938.

Connor, R. D. W. *Cornelius Harnett: An Essay in North Carolina History*. Raleigh, N.C., 1909.

――. *History of North Carolina*, Volume 1, *The Colonial and Revolutionary Periods, 1584-1783*. Chicago, 1919.

――. *North Carolina: Rebuilding an Ancient Commonwealth, 1584-1925*. 4 vols.; Chicago, 1928-1929.

――. *Race Elements in the White Population of North Carolina*. ("North Carolina State Normal and Industrial College Historical Publications," No. 1.) Raleigh, N.C., 1920.

Corbitt, David. L. *The Formation of North Carolina Counties, 1663-1943*. Raleigh, N.C., 1950.

――. "Judicial Districts of North Carolina, 1746-1934," *North Carolina Historical Review*, 12 (1935), 45-61.

―― (comp.). *Calendars of Manuscript Collections, Volume 1*. Raleigh, N.C., 1926.

Couper, William. *History of the Shenandoah Valley*. 3 vols.; New York, 1952.

Crittenden, Charles C. "Inland Navigation in North Carolina, 1763-1789," *North Carolina Historical Review*, 8 (1931), 145-54.
——. "Means of Communication in North Carolina, 1763-1789," *North Carolina Historical Review*, 8 (1931), 373-83.
——. *North Carolina Newspapers Before 1790* ("James Sprunt Historical Studies," Vol. 20, No. 1.) Chapel Hill, N.C., 1928.
——. "Overland Travel and Transportation in North Carolina, 1763-1789," *North Carolina Historical Review*, 8 (1931), 239-57.
——. "Ships and Shipping in North Carolina, 1763-1789," *North Carolina Historical Review*, 8 (1931), 1-13.
——. *The Commerce of North Carolina, 1763-1789*. New Haven, Conn., 1936.
——. "The Seacoast in North Carolina History, 1763-1789," *North Carolina Historical Review*, 7 (1930), 433-42.
—— and Dan Lacy (eds.). *The Historical Records of North Carolina*, Vols. 1-3, *The County Records*. Raleigh, N.C., 1938.
Cruikshank, J. W. *Forest Resources of the Northern Coastal Plain of North Carolina*. U.S. Department of Agriculture, Appalachian Forest Experiment Station, Forest Survey Release No. 5, 1940.
——. *Forest Resources of the Southern Coastal Plain of North Carolina*. U.S. Department of Agriculture, Appalachian Forest Experiment Station, Forest Survey Release No. 4, 1940.
Cumming, William P. *The Southeast in Early Maps*. Princeton, N.J., 1958.
Dachnowski-Stokes, Alfred P., and B. W. Wells. "The Vegetation, Stratigraphy, and Age of the 'Open Land' Peat Area in Carteret County, North Carolina," *Journal of the Washington Academy of Sciences*, 19 (1929), 1-11.
Dill, Alonzo T., Jr. "Eighteenth Century New Bern: A History of the Town and Craven County, 1700-1800," *North Carolina Historical Review*, 22 (1945), 1-21, 152-75, 293-319, 460-89; 23 (1946), 47-78, 142-71, 325-59, 495-535.
Dillwyn, Lewis W. *Hortus Collinsonianus*. . . . Swansea, 1843.
Dunaway, Wayland F. *The Scotch-Irish of Colonial Pennsylvania*. Chapel Hill, N.C., 1944.
Dunbar, Gary S. "Colonial Carolina Cowpens," *Agricultural History*, 35 (1961), 125-30.
——. *Geographical History of the Carolina Banks*. Edited by Fred Kniffen. (Technical Report No. 8, Part A, of Project No. N7, onr 35608, Task Order No. NR 388 002 of the Office of Naval Research.) Baton Rouge, La., 1956.
Dunn, Charles W. "A North Carolina Gaelic Bard," *North Carolina Historical Review*, 36 (1959), 473-75.
Eaton, Clement. "A Mirror of the Southern Colonial Lawyer: The

Fee Books of Patrick Henry, Thomas Jefferson, and Waightstill Avery," *William and Mary Quarterly*, 3rd Ser., 8 (1951), 520-34.
Edwards, Everett E. *References on American Colonial Agriculture*. U.S. Department of Agriculture, Bibliographical Contributions No. 33, September, 1938.
Elkins, Stanley M. *Slavery: A Problem in American Institutional and Intellectual Life*. Chicago, 1959.
Emmons, Ebenezer. *The Swamp Lands of North-Carolina*. ("North-Carolina Geological Survey, Part II, Agriculture.") Raleigh, N.C., 1860.
Emory, Samuel T. "North Carolina Flatwoods," *Economic Geography*, 22 (1946), 203-19.
Farrand, Max. "The Indian Boundary Line," *American Historical Review*, 10 (1904-5), 782-91.
Foote, William H. *Sketches of North Carolina, Historical and Biographical.* . . . New York, 1846.
Ford, Worthington C. "Early Maps of Carolina," *Geographical Review*, 16 (1926), 264-73.
Fowler, Malcolm. *They Passed This Way: A Personal Narrative of Harnett County History*. N.p., 1955.
Frick, George F., and Raymond P. Stearns. *Mark Catesby: The Colonial Audubon*. Urbana, Ill., 1961.
Friis, Herman R. *A Series of Population Maps of the Colonies and the United States*. ("American Geographical Society Mimeographed Publication," No. 3.) New York, 1940.
Garren, Kenneth H. "Effects of Fire on the Vegetation of the Southeastern United States," *Botanical Review*, 9 (1943), 617-54.
Gipson, Lawrence H. *The British Empire Before the American Revolution*, Volume II, *The British Isles and the American Colonies: The Southern Plantation, 1748-1754*. New York, 1960.
Glenn, Thomas A. *Welsh Founders of Pennsylvania*. 2 vols.; Oxford, 1911.
Graham, Ian C. G. *Colonists from Scotland: Emigration to North America, 1707-1783*. Ithaca, N.Y., 1956.
Gray, Lewis C. *History of Agriculture in the Southern United States to 1860*. ("Carnegie Institution of Washington Publication," No. 430.) 2 vols.; Washington, D.C., 1933.
Greene, Evarts B., and Virginia D. Harrington. *American Publication Before the Federal Census of 1790*. New York, 1932.
Guide to the Manuscript Collections in the Archives of the North Carolina Historical Commission. (North Carolina Records Survey Project, Division of Community Service Programs, Work Projects Administration.) Raleigh, N.C., 1942.
Guide to the Manuscripts in the Archives of the Moravian Church in America, Southern Province. (North Carolina Historical Records

Survey, Division of Community Service Programs, Work Projects Administration.) Raleigh, N.C., 1942.

Guide to the Manuscripts in the Southern Historical Collection of the University of North Carolina. ("James Sprunt Studies in Historical and Political Science," Vol. 24.) Chapel Hill, N.C., 1941.

Hamnett, William L., and David C. Thornton. *Tar Heel Wildlife.* 2nd ed.; Raleigh, N.C., 1953.

Harper, Roland M. "A November Day in the Upper Part of the Coastal Plain of North Carolina," *Torreya,* 6 (1906), 41-45.

———. "A quantitative study of the more conspicuous vegetation of certain natural subdivisions of the coastal plain, as observed in traveling from Georgia to New York in July," *Bulletin of the Torrey Botanical Club,* 37 (1910), 405-28.

———. "Some Plants of Southeastern Virginia and Central North Carolina," *Torreya,* 3 (1903), 120-24.

———. "The Hempstead Plains: A Natural Prairie on Long Island," *Bulletin of the American Geographical Society,* 43 (1911), 351-60.

Harrison, Fairfax. *Landmarks of Old Prince William: A Study of Origins in Northern Virginia.* 2 vols.; Richmond, Va., 1924.

———. *Virginia Land Grants: A Study of Conveyancing in Relation to Colonial Politics.* Richmond, Va., 1925.

Henderson, Archibald. "The Transylvania Company: A Study in Personnel. I. James Hogg," *Filson Club Historical Quarterly,* 21 (1947), 1-21.

Holmes, J. S. *Common Forest Trees of North Carolina: A Pocket Manual.* 8th ed.; Raleigh, N.C., 1958.

Johnston, Frances B., and Thomas T. Waterman. *The Early Architecture of North Carolina.* Chapel Hill, N.C., 1947.

Jurney, R. C., et al. *Soil Survey of Onslow County, North Carolina.* Washington, D.C., 1923.

Karpinski, Louis C. *Early Maps of Carolina and Adjoining Regions from the Collection of Henry P. Kendall.* Second edition prepared on the basis of the 1930 Catalogue compiled by Priscilla Smith. [Charleston, S.C., 1937.]

Kearney, Thomas H. "Report on a Botanical Survey of the Dismal Swamp Region," U.S. Department of Agriculture, *Contributions from the U.S. National Herbarium,* Vol. 5, No. 6 (1901), 321-550.

Kegley, F. B. *Kegley's Virginia Frontier: The Beginning of the Southwest: The Roanoke of Colonial Days, 1740-1783.* Roanoke, Va., 1938.

Keller, Hans Gustav. *Christoph von Graffenried und die Gründung von Neu-Bern in Nord-Carolina.* Bern, 1953.

Kemper, Charles E. "Historical Notes from the Records of Augusta County, Virginia," *Historical Papers and Addresses of the Lancaster County Historical Society,* 25 (1921), 89-92, 147-55.

Kemper, Charles E. "The Settlement of the Valley," *Virginia Magazine of History and Biography*, 30 (1922), 169-82.
Kerr, W. C. *Report of the Geological Survey of North Carolina*, Volume I, *Physical Geography, Resumé, Economical Geography*. Raleigh, N.C., 1875.
Kirkland, Thomas J., and Robert M. Kennedy. *Historic Camden*. 2 vols.; Columbia, S.C., 1905-26.
Klees, Fredric. *The Pennsylvania Dutch*. New York, 1950.
Kuhns, Oscar. *The German and Swiss Settlements of Colonial Pennsylvania: A Study of the So-Called Pennsylvania Dutch*. New York, 1901.
Laney, Francis B., and Katharine H. Wood. *Bibliography of North Carolina Geology, Mineralogy, and Geography, with a list of maps*. ("North Carolina Geological and Economic Survey," Bulletin No. 18.) Raleigh, N.C., 1909.
Lee, E. Lawrence. "Old Brunswick, The Story of a Colonial Town," *North Carolina Historical Review*, 29 (1952), 230-45.
Lee, William D. *The Soils of North Carolina*. North Carolina State College, Agricultural Experiment Station Technical Bulletin No. 115, December, 1955.
Lefler, Hugh T. *A Guide to the Study and Reading of North Carolina History*. Chapel Hill, N.C., 1955.
—— and Albert R. Newsome. *North Carolina: The History of a Southern State*. Chapel Hill, N.C., 1954.
—— and Paul Wager (eds.). *Orange County, 1752-1952*. Chapel Hill, N.C., 1953.
Lloyd, Francis E. *The Carnivorous Plants*. Waltham, Mass., 1942.
Maxwell, Hu. "The Use and Abuse of Forests by the Virginia Indians," *William and Mary College Quarterly Historical Magazine*, 19 (1910), 73-103.
McCain, Paul M. *The County Court in North Carolina Before 1750*. ("Historical Papers of the Trinity College Historical Society," Series 31.) Durham, N.C., 1954.
McVaugh, Rogers. "The Vegetation of the Granitic Flat-rocks of the Southeastern United States," *Ecological Monographs*, 13 (1943), 119-66.
Mereness, Newton D. *Maryland as a Proprietary Province*. New York, 1901.
Meyer, Duane. *The Highland Scots of North Carolina, 1732-1776*. Chapel Hill, N.C., 1961.
Meynen, Emil. *Bibliography on German Settlements in Colonial North America*. Leipzig, 1937.
Miller, William H. "Mark Catesby, An Eighteenth Century Naturalist," *Tyler's Quarterly Historical and Genealogical Magazine*, 29 (1948), 167-80.

Moody, Robert E. (ed.). "Massachusetts Trade with Carolina, 1686-1709," *North Carolina Historical Review,* 20 (1943), 43-53.
Morris, Francis G., and Phyllis M. Morris. "Economic Conditions in North Carolina About 1780, Part I, Landholdings," *North Carolina Historical Review,* 16 (1939), 107-33.
———. "Economic Conditions in North Carolina About 1780, Part II, Ownership of Town Lots, Slaves, and Cattle," *North Carolina Historical Review,* 16 (1939), 296-327.
Morrison, A. J. "John G. de Brahm," *South Atlantic Quarterly,* 21, (1922), 252-58.
Mowrat, Charles L. "That 'Odd Being,' De Brahm," *Florida Historical Quarterly,* 20 (1942), 323-45.
Nash, Francis. *Hillsboro, Colonial and Revolutionary.* Raleigh, N.C., 1903.
———. "The History of Orange County—Part I," *North Carolina Booklet,* 10 (1910-11), 55-113.
Oosting, Henry J. "An Ecological Analysis of the Plant Communities of Piedmont North Carolina," *American Midland Naturalist,* 28 (1942), 1-126.
——— and Lewis E. Anderson. "Plant Succession on Granite Rock in Eastern North Carolina," *Botanical Gazette,* 100 (1939), 750-68.
Pascal, George W. *History of North Carolina Baptists.* 2 vols.; Raleigh, N.C., 1930, 1955.
Paschal, Herbert R., Jr. *A History of Colonial Bath.* Raleigh, N.C., 1955.
Paullin, Charles O. *Atlas of the Historical Geography of the United States.* ("Carnegie Institution of Washington Publication," No. 401.) Washington, D.C., 1932.
Pfeifer, Gottfried. "Historische Grundlagen der Kulturgeographischen Individualität des Südostens der Vereinigten Staaten," *Petermanns Geographischen Mitteilungen,* 98 (1954), 301-12.
Phifer, Edward W. "Saga of a Burke County Family, Part I, The Grandparents," *North Carolina Historical Review,* 39 (1962), 1-17.
Pinchot, Gifford, and W. W. Ashe. *Timber Trees and Forests of North Carolina.* ("North Carolina Geological Survey," Bulletin No. 6.) Winston-Salem, N.C., 1897.
Powell, William S. *North Carolina County Histories: A Bibliography.* ("University of North Carolina Library Studies," No. 1.) Chapel Hill, N.C., 1958.
Price, Jacob M. "The Rise of Glasgow in the Chesapeake Tobacco Trade, 1707-1775," *William and Mary Quarterly,* 3rd Ser., 11 (1954), 179-99.
Prouty, W. F. "Carolina Bays and Their Origin," *Bulletin of the Geological Society of America,* 63 (1952), 167-224.

Prunty, Merle, Jr. "The Renaissance of the Southern Plantation," *Geographical Review*, 45 (1955), 459-91.
Ramsay, David. *The History of South-Carolina*. 2 vols.; Charleston, S.C., 1809.
Ramsey, Robert W. "James Carter: Founder of Salisbury," *North Carolina Historical Review*, 39 (1962), 131-39.
Rights, Douglas L. *The American Indians in North Carolina*. Durham, N.C., 1947.
Roberts, Patricia R., and H. J. Oosting. "Responses of Venus Fly Trap (*Dionaea Muscipula*) to Factors Involved in its Endemism," *Ecological Monographs*, 28 (1958), 193-217.
Robinson, Blackwell P. *A History of Moore County, 1747-1847*. Southern Pines, N.C., 1956.
—— (ed.). *The North Carolina Guide*. Chapel Hill, N.C., 1955.
Rockwell, E. F. "An Ancient Map of the Central Part of Iredell County, N.C.," *Historical Magazine*, 12 (August, 1867), 84-90.
Rostlund, Erhard. "The Myth of a Natural Prairie Belt in Alabama: an interpretation of historical records," *Annals of the Association of American Geographers*, 47 (1957), 392-411.
Ruffin, Edmund. *Agricultural, Geological, and Descriptive Sketches of Lower North Carolina*. Raleigh, N.C., 1861.
Salley, A. S. *The Boundary Line between North Carolina and South Carolina* ("Bulletin of the Historical Commission of South Carolina," No. 10.) Columbia, S.C., 1929.
Schwarz, G. F. *The Longleaf Pine in Virgin Forest*. New York, 1907.
Sellers, Charles G., Jr. "Private Profits and British Colonial Policy: The Speculations of Henry McCulloh," *William and Mary Quarterly*, 3rd Ser., 8 (1951), 535-51.
Sellers, Leila. *Charleston Business on the Eve of the Revolution*. Chapel Hill, N.C., 1934.
Shaler, Nathaniel S. "General account of the fresh-water morasses of the United States with a description of the Dismal Swamp District of Virginia and North Carolina," *U.S. Geological Survey, Tenth Annual Report, 1888-1889* (1890), 255-339.
Shearin, A. E., et al. *Soil Survey of Pasquotank County, North Carolina*. U.S. Department of Agriculture in cooperation with the North Carolina Agricultural Experiment Station, October, 1957.
Shepherd, William R. *History of Proprietary Government in Pennsylvania*. ("Columbia University Studies in History, Economics and Public Law," Vol. 6.) New York, 1896.
Shepherd, W. O., E. U. Dillard, and H. L. Lucas. *Grazing and Fire Influences in Pond Pine Forests*. North Carolina Agricultural Experiment Station, Technical Bulletin No. 97, December, 1951.
Shinn, James F. "Edward Moseley: A North Carolina Patriot and

Statesman," *Southern History Association Publications*, 3 (1899), 15-34.
Skaggs, Marvin L. *North Carolina Boundary Disputes Involving Her Southern Line.* ("James Sprunt Studies in History and Political Science," Vol. 25, No. 1.) Chapel Hill, N.C., 1941.
Soltow, James H. *The Economic Role of Williamsburg.* Williamsburg, Va., 1956.
South, Stanley A. *Indians in North Carolina.* Raleigh, N.C., 1959.
Sprunt, James. *Chronicles of the Cape Fear River, 1600-1916.* 2nd ed.; Raleigh, N.C., 1916.
Stick, David. *The Outer Banks of North Carolina, 1584-1958.* Chapel Hill, N.C., 1958.
Stuckey, Jasper L., and Stephen G. Conrad. *Explanatory Text for Geologic Map of North Carolina.* ("North Carolina Department of Conservation and Development Bulletin," No. 71.) Raleigh, N.C., 1958.
Sutherland, Stella H. *Population Distribution in Colonial America.* New York, 1936.
Swanton, John R. *The Indian Tribes of North America.* (Smithsonian Institution, Bureau of American Ethnology, Bulletin 145.) Washington, D.C., 1952.
Swem, E. G. *Virginia Historical Index.* 2 vols.; Roanoke, Va., 1934-36.
Thomas, Jno. P. "The Barbadians in Early South Carolina," *South Carolina Historical and Genealogical Magazine*, 31 (1930), 75-92.
Thompson, James W. *A History of Livestock Raising in the United States, 1607-1860.* (U.S. Department of Agriculture, "Agricultural History Series," No. 5.) Washington, D.C., 1942.
Thornton, Mary L. (comp.). *A Bibliography of North Carolina, 1589-1956.* Chapel Hill, N.C., 1958.
———. *Official Publications of the Colony and State of North Carolina, 1749-1939: A Bibliography.* Chapel Hill, N.C., 1954.
Tilley, Nannie M., and Noma Lee Goodwin (comps.). *Guide to the Manuscript Collections in the Duke University Library.* ("Historical Papers of the Trinity College Historical Society," Series 27-28.) Durham, N.C., 1947.
U.S. Bureau of the Census. *A Century of Population Growth: From the First to the Twelfth Census of the United States, 1790-1900.* By W. S. Rossiter. Washington, D.C., 1909.
———. *Historical Statistics of the United States, Colonial Times to 1957.* Washington, D.C., 1960.
U.S. Department of the Interior, Census Office. *Report on the Forests of North America (Exclusive of Mexico).* By Charles S. Sargent. Published as Vol. 9 of the *Tenth Census of the United States.* Washington, D.C., 1884.

Waddell, Alfred M. *A History of New Hanover County and the Lower Cape Fear Region, Volume 1, 1723-1800.* N.p., n.d.

Wahlenberg, W. G. *Longleaf Pine: Its Use, Ecology, Regeneration, Protection, Growth, and Management.* Charles Lathrop Pack Forestry Foundation, Washington, D.C., in cooperation with the Forest Service, U.S. Department of Agriculture, 1946.

Webster, N. B. "On the Physical and Geological Characteristics of the Great Dismal Swamp, and the Eastern Counties of Virginia," *American Naturalist,* 9 (1875), 260-62.

Weeks, Stephen B. *Southern Quakers and Slavery: A Study in Institutional History.* ("Johns Hopkins University Studies in Historical and Political Science," Extra Volume 15.) Baltimore, 1896.

Wells, B. W. "Ecological Problems of the Southeastern United States Coastal Plain," *Botanical Review,* 8 (1942), 533-61.

———. *Major Plant Communities of North Carolina.* North Carolina Agricultural Experiment Station, Technical Bulletin No. 25, April, 1924.

———. "Plant Communities of the Coastal Plain of North Carolina and Their Successional Relations," *Ecology,* 9 (1928), 230-42.

———. *The Natural Gardens of North Carolina.* Chapel Hill, N.C., 1932.

———. *Vegetation of Holly Shelter Wildlife Management Area.* ("North Carolina Department of Conservation and Development, Division of Game and Inland Fisheries," State Bulletin No. 2.) Raleigh, N.C., March, 1946.

——— and Steve G. Boyce. "Carolina Bays: Additional Data on Their Origin, Age and History," *Journal of the Elisha Mitchell Scientific Society,* 69 (1953), 119-41.

——— and I. V. Shunk. *A Southern Upland Grass-Sedge Bog: An Ecological Study.* North Carolina Agricultural Experiment Station, Technical Bulletin No. 32, October, 1928.

———. "The Vegetation and Habitat Factors of the Coarser Sands of the North Carolina Coastal Plain: An Ecological Study," *Ecological Monographs,* 1 (1931), 465-520.

Wendel, G. W., T. G. Storey, and G. M. Byram. *Forest Fuels on Organic and Associated Soils in the Coastal Plain of North Carolina.* U.S. Department of Agriculture—Forest Service, Southeastern Forest Experiment Station, Station Paper No. 144, July, 1962.

Wenger, Karl F. *Silvical Characteristics of Pond Pine.* U.S. Department of Agriculture—Forest Service, Southeastern Forest Experiment Station, Station Paper No. 91, April, 1958.

Williams, Justin. "English Mercantilism and Carolina Naval Stores, 1705-1776," *Journal of Southern History,* 1 (1935), 169-85.

Wroth, Lawrence C. *An American Bookshelf, 1755.* Philadelphia, 1934.

Wyman, Walker D., and Clifton D. Kroeber (eds.). *The Frontier in Perspective*. Madison, Wis., 1957.

B. THESES AND DISSERTATIONS

Barber, Ira W. "The Ocean-Borne Commerce of Port Roanoke, 1771-1776." Master's thesis, University of North Carolina, 1931.
Boyd, Julian P. "The County Court in Colonial North Carolina." Master's thesis, Duke University, 1926.
Cotton, William D. "North Carolina as seen through the eyes of travellers, 1524-1729." Master's thesis, University of North Carolina, 1949.
Coulter, Calvin B., Jr. "The Virginia Merchant." Ph.D. dissertation, Princeton University, 1944.
Ebert, Charles H. V. "Soils and Land Use Correlation of the Outer Atlantic Coastal Plain of Virginia, the Carolinas, and North Georgia." Ph.D. dissertation, University of North Carolina, 1957.
Frick, George F. "Mark Catesby, Naturalist, 1683-1749." Ph.D. dissertation, University of Illinois, 1957.
Gehrke, William H. "The German Element in Rowan and Cabarrus Counties, North Carolina." Master's thesis, University of North Carolina, 1934.
Hall, Arthur R. "Soil Erosion and Agriculture in the Southern Piedmont: A History." Ph.D. dissertation, Duke University, 1948.
Henline, Ruth. "Travel Literature of Colonists in America, 1754-1783: An Annotated Bibliography." Ph.D. dissertation, Northwestern University, 1947.
Jensen, Arthur L. "The Maritime Commerce of Colonial Philadelphia." Ph.D. dissertation, University of Wisconsin, 1954.
Jones, Reece A. "The Inner Coastal Plain of North Carolina: An Agricultural Region." Ph.D. dissertation, University of North Carolina, 1954.
Lee, E. Lawrence. "The History of the Lower Cape Fear: The Colonial Period." Ph.D. dissertation, University of North Carolina, 1955.
Logan, Bryon E. "An Historic Geographic Study of North Carolina Ports." Ph.D. dissertation, University of North Carolina, 1956.
Muntz, Alfred Philip. "The Changing Geography of the New Jersey Woodlands, 1600-1900." Ph.D. dissertation, University of Wisconsin, 1959.
Nadelhaft, Jerome J. "South Carolina and the Slave Trade, 1783-1787." Master's thesis, University of Wisconsin, 1961.
Powell, William S. "John Pory: His Life, Letters and Work." Master's thesis, University of North Carolina, 1947.
Saladino, Gaspare J. "The Maryland and Virginia Wheat Trade from

Its Beginnings to the American Revolution." Master's thesis, University of Wisconsin, 1960.
Thomson, Robert P. "The Merchant in Virginia, 1700-1775." Ph.D. dissertation, University of Wisconsin, 1955.
Tilley, Nannie M. "Studies in the History of Colonial Granville County." Master's thesis, Duke University, 1931.
Wallace, Wesley H. "Advertising in Early North Carolina Newspapers, 1751-1778." Master's thesis, University of North Carolina, 1954.

III. MAPS AND PLANS

A. MANUSCRIPTS

Unless otherwise indicated, all of the following manuscript maps and plans are available, in the original or as photostat copies, in the North Carolina State Department of Archives and History, Raleigh, N.C. The scales specified are those of the original. All of the items are more fully described in William P. Cumming, *The Southeast in Early Maps* (Princeton, N.J., 1958).

A Map of Fourth Creek Congregation by William Sharpe, 1773. Scale: 1" equivalent to 1 mile.
    Photostat copy of the 1847 lithographed version. No known copies of the original map.
A New and Exact Plan of Cape Fear River from the Bar to Brunswick by Edward Hyrne, 1749. Scale: 1" equivalent to about 2 miles.
A Plan of part of the principal Roads in the province of N. Carolina. 177–. Scale: 1" equivalent to about 10 miles.
    William L. Clements Library, Ann Arbor, Michigan; Clinton Collection, No. 290.
A Plan of the Province Line from the Cherokee Line to Salisbury Road Between North and South Carolina. 1772. Scale: 1" equivalent to about 2½ miles.
A Plan of the Southern Boundary of Granville's District as marked out in 1746. . . . Scale: 1" equivalent to about 5 miles.
A Plan of the temporary Boundary Line between the Provinces of North and South Carolina . . . 24 Sept. 1764. Scale: 1" equivalent to 1 mile. 1806 copy.
C. J. Sauthier. Plans of the following towns: Hillsborough (1768), Bath (1769), Brunswick (1769), Edenton (1769), Halifax (1769), Newbern (1769), Wilmington (1769), Beaufort (1770), Cross Creek (1770), and Salisbury (1770).
    Various scales.
John Collet. . . . Accurate Map of the back Country of North Carolina. . . . 1768. Scale: 1" equivalent to about 8 miles.

Map of the Albemarle Sound Region: showing parts of several counties north of Albemarle Sound. Post-1770. Scale: 1" equivalent to 2 miles. William L. Clements Library, Ann Arbor, Michigan; Clinton Collection, No. 293.

B. EIGHTEENTH-CENTURY PRINTED MAPS

Collet, John. *A Compleat Map of North-Carolina from an actual survey.* Scale: 1" equivalent to about 14 miles. 1770.

Moseley, Edward. *A New and Correct Map of the Province of North Carolina.* . . . Scale: 1" equivalent to 5 miles. 1733.

Mouzon, Henry. *An Accurate Map of North and South Carolina . . . from Actual Surveys.* Scale: 1" equivalent to about 9 miles. 1775.
 (A reproduction of the North Carolina part of the map was published by the United States Sesquicentennial Committee, Washington, D.C., 1938.)

Wimble, James. . . . *Chart of his Majesties Province of North Carolina With a full & exact description of the Sea-coast, Latitudes, Capes.* . . . Scale: 1" equivalent to about 7½ miles. 1738.

C. TWENTIETH-CENTURY PRINTED MAPS

Lutz, J. F., and C. B. Williams. *Land Condition Map of North Carolina.* (Department of Soils, North Carolina State College.) Scale: 1:500,000. 1935.

N.C. Department of Conservation and Development, Division of Mineral Resources. *Geologic Map of North Carolina.* Scale: 1:500,000. 1958.

N.C. Wildlife Resources Commission in cooperation with U.S. Fish and Wildlife Service. *Wildlife Cover Map of North Carolina.* Scale: 1:500,000. Drawn 1946-50.

U.S. Department of the Interior, Geological Survey. *State of North Carolina.* Shaded relief map. Scale: 1:500,000. 1957.

INDEX

Albemarle region, early settlement of, 19-20, 23; comments on resources of, 33; population density in, 73, 177; slaveholdings in, 75, 81; exports of naval stores from, 90-92; shingle production in, 105-7; features of commercial agriculture in, 111-12, 115-16, 119-24 *passim*
Alexandria, Virginia, 116
Alston, John, 168
American Husbandry, 48-49, 136
Annapolis, Maryland, 11, 149
Anson County, establishment of, 27; Scottish Highlanders in, 57; slaveholdings in, 75; 1763 tax list for, 225
Ashe, John, 129
Auld, James, 62
Avery, Waightstill, 62

Baltimore, Maryland, function of, 11; role in wheat trade, 116
Bartram, John, 187
Bartram, William, 158
Bath, decline in importance of, 150; description of function of, 153-54
Beaufort, decline in importance of, 150; description of function of, 153-55
Beef. *See* Livestock
Beer, supply of in South Carolina, 13-14
Bertie County, data on slaveholding in, 76, 123, 225
Bladensburg, Maryland, role in wheat trade, 116
Blue Ridge, 11, 12, 20, 24, 31, 41, 47, 66
Boston, Massachusetts, description of function in 1750, 5-6
Bottomland, qualities of, in Coastal Plain and Piedmont, 43; utilization of vegetation cover of, 102-4; mentioned, 43, 87
Boundaries, of North Carolina, 30-31
Boundary, between Coastal plain and Piedmont, 39-41
Bread, made from corn, 108, 111; distinctiveness of Moravian attitudes towards, 113, 236
Brunswick, description of function of, 150-53; mentioned, 90, 91, 117, 130
Brunswick County, creation of, 29; map showing location of, 128; wealthy estates in, 129-30
Buchanans, Hastie, and Company, 168
Burgaw Savannah, 186-89
Burgwin, John, 198, 200
Burke, Edmund, 48
Burke, William, 48
Bute County, 27
Butter. *See* Livestock
Byrd, William, II, 34

Camden, South Carolina, role in wheat trade, 117
Campbelltown, origin and development of, 155, 160; in relation to break in navigability on river, 172
Cape Fear region, early settlement of, 20, 23; visited by Hugh Meredith, 21; large landholdings in, 27; slaveholdings in, 75, 81; commercial production of forest products in, 88-90, 96-100, 105-7; early surplus of Indian corn in, 109; characteristics of large estates in, 127-33, 175, 177; in relation to trade and urban centers, 151-53
Cape Fear River, use of for transporta-

tion, 90-91, 98, 116, 151; mentioned, 23, 27, 67, 100, 128, 129, 130, 150. *See also* Cape Fear region
Carolina Bays, map showing distribution of, 42; features of, 43, 216; vegetation cover of, 189-90; mentioned, 44
Carolina Charters, 18, 31
Cashie River, use of for transportation, 91-92, 116
Catawba River, 67, 234
Catesby, Mark, 36
Cattle. *See* Livestock
Charleston, South Carolina, description of in 1750, 13-14; trade ties with North Carolina, 127, 165; mentioned, 55, 117, 149, 179
Charlotte, function of, 162, 166; mentioned, 119, 180
Chatham County, 27
Cheese. *See* Livestock
Chowan County, slaveholding in, 76, 123, 225; mentioned, 147
Chowan River, tobacco production in vicinity of, 121-22; ferry across, 149
Climate, of South Carolina, 13; of North Carolina, 34, 44-46, 126, 185
Coastal Plain, 36, 37-41, 43, 46-48, 178, 185-93 *passim*
Colony, image of, 32-36
Connecticut, description of in 1750, 6
Counties, 29
County, boundaries, 27, 70-71; courts, 27, 29, 147; courthouses, 167, 169
Cowpens, 15, 140
Cows. *See* Livestock
Cross Creek, sawmills in vicinity of, 100; role in wheat trade, 116; growth and function as a trading center, 116, 137, 155, 157-60, 163 165-66, 171; store in, 153; Scottish merchants in, 164
Cumberland County, establishment of, 27; Scottish Highlanders in, 57, 100, 139; slaveholding in, 90; sawmills, 98, 100; production of naval stores in, 229
Currituck Sound, 95
Customs 16/1, 201-2, 226
Cypress (*Taxodium distichum*), 104-5

Dairy Products. *See* Livestock
Dan River, 34, 66
Decentralized trade, 167-72
Delaware, description of in 1750, 9
Dismal Swamp, 73, 105
Dobbs County, 27
Duplin County, 29

Eagle(s), Joseph, 128
Eastern part of North Carolina, 27, 29, 44-46, 73-74, 106-7, 159, 177, 180-81, 193
Edenton, tobacco warehouse in, 122; function of, 147-49, 171; mentioned, 91, 156-57
Edenton Bay, 91-92, 148
Edgecombe County, 161
Emigration, from Pennsylvania to North Carolina, 54
English settlers, 14, 21, 22, 23, 61-63, 65, 67-68, 106
Eno River, 62
Evans, David, 21
Evergreen shrub bogs, 47, 189-91
Exports, from New England, 5; from Philadelphia, 9; from New Jersey, 9; from Southern colonies, 11; from Virginia, 12; from South Carolina, 13; from Georgia, 14; of naval stores from North Carolina, 88, 90-91; of wood products from North Carolina, 93-96; of corn from North Carolina, 109-11; of wheat from North Carolina, 111-19 *passim*; of tobacco from North Carolina, 120-22, 124; of rice from North and South Carolina, 126-27; of indigo from North Carolina, 127; of livestock products from North Carolina, 134-36; data on, 201-2

Fall line, 40-41, 171-72, 177-79, 258-59
Fayetteville, 121, 157, 160. *See also* Cross Creek, Campbelltown
Few, William, 62, 163
Finlay, Hugh, 149
Fire, 47, 176, 185-93
Flatwoods, 38-39
Fox, George, 33
Franklin, Benjamin, 21, 54
Frederick, Maryland, 11
Free-range, 188, 249, 261. *See also* Open range
French settlers, 21
Frontier, 175-76, 181

Georgia, 14-15, 54, 60, 139-40
German settlers, 8, 12, 13-14, 21-22, 57-58, 59-61, 65-66, 67, 139, 165-66
Granville District, 24, 148, 200
Great Road, 12, 66, 67
Grist mills, 113, 159, 164, 166
Guilford County, 27

INDEX

Halifax, re-routing of road through, 149; growth and function of, 155-57; mentioned, 62, 124, 137, 168, 172
Halifax County, 29
Hazard, Ebenezer, 149
Headrights, 25
Hertford, 167
Hertford County, 29
Hillsboro, store trade in, 153; road link with Halifax, 156; growth and function of, 162-64; mentioned, 166
Hogg, James, 153
Hogg, Robert, 153
Hogg and Campbell, stores of, 153
Hogs. See Livestock
Holly Shelter Bay, 189
Hudson Valley, 7, 118
"Hunthill," 98-100, 104
Hurricanes, 45-46
Hyde County, 77
Hyrne, Henry, 129

Image of the land, 32-36
Immigration to North Carolina, 53-66 passim
Indian corn, 16, 108-11, 113, 134
Indians, 18, 20, 47, 60, 193
Indigo, 125-33, 180
Inner Coastal Plain, 38-39, 178
Interior portion of North Carolina, 35-36, 45
Interior portion of Seaboard, 35-36
Inventories of estates, 114, 136-37, 144, 174
Itinerant traders, 167, 169

James River, 54
John Hamilton and Company, 124, 167-68
Jones, Thomas, 129
Judicial districts, 29, 148, 157, 163

Lake Mattamuskeet, 214-15
Land, titles in New Jersey, 9; disposal of, 24, 148; grants, 25; survey, 25; image of, 32-36; prices, 63-64, 224
Landholdings, 26, 27, 89, 129
Lawson, John, 34, 35
Legend, about western part of North Carolina, 44, 48-49, 55, 63, 67
Leslie, James, 156
"Lilliput," 130
Livestock, raising in Southern colonies, 11; raising in Georgia, 14-15; regional contrasts in production, 137-40; mentioned, 134-40
Lloyds Meadows, 191
Loblolly pine (*Pinus taeda*), 47
Logan, William, 112
Longleaf pine (*Pinus palustris*), 47, 86-87, 89-91, 226-27
Lords Proprietors, 18, 24

McCulloh, Henry, 26, 89
Macknight, Thomas, 105
Maritime portion, of Seaboard, 35-36; of North Carolina, 48-49
Martin County, 29
Maryland, 10-11, 62-63, 118, 120, 124, 126
Massachusetts, description of in 1750, 5
Massy, Nicholas, 234
Meadows, 191
Mecklenburg County, 27
Meherrin River, 212
Merchants, 15, 149-50, 152-53, 155, 159, 160, 163-65
Meredith, Hugh, 21
Middle colonies, description of in 1750, 6-10
Midland towns, 155-66
Migration to North Carolina, 53-66 passim
Milk. See Livestock
Minot, George, 100, 129
Mohawk Valley, 7
Moor(e), Maurice, 129
Moor(e), William, 129
Moore family, 27, 100, 133, 246
Moravians, 8, 59-61, 67, 110, 112-15 passim, 118-19, 164-66, 169, 171, 175, 176
Moseley, Edward, 26, 35
Mosquitoes, 45-46
Murray, James, 64-65, 133

Narragansett area, 6
Naval stores, 85-92, 102-3, 106-7, 123, 129, 131, 151, 179
Navigability of rivers, 156, 161, 172
Negro, population, 3, 11, 20, 74-81 passim; taxables, 196. See also Taxables
Neuse River, 20, 22, 34, 138, 149-50
New Bern, founding of, 22; growth and function of, 149-50, 155, 171; mentioned, 148
Newcastle, Delaware, 9-10
New England, 3-7, 111

New Hampshire, description of in 1750, 6
New Hanover County, slaveholding in, 76, 78-79; sawmills in, 98; map showing location of, 128; wealthy estates in, 129-30; road system in, 152
New Jersey, 9, 135
New York City, 7-8
New York colony, description of in 1750, 7-8
Northeast Cape Fear River, 21, 97, 98, 100, 125, 128, 130, 151. See also Cape Fear region, Cape Fear River
Northwest Cape Fear River, 97, 128, 130, 151, 158. See also Cape Fear region, Cape Fear River

Oak-pine forest, 46-47
Onslow County, 54, 191
Open areas, 47, 185-93
Open range, 138-39
Orange County, 27, 62, 75-76, 162-63
Outer Banks, 167, 214, 249
Outer Coastal Plain, 38-39, 44, 45, 47-48, 104, 117, 178, 189, 191
Overseers, 140

Palatines, 22
Pamlico Sound, 21, 177
Patrol districts, 29-30
Peat soils, 37-38, 44, 185, 188-90, 192
Pennsylvania, 8-9, 55, 60, 135
Perquimans County, 225
Perquimans River, 167
Philadelphia, Pennsylvania, 8-9, 55, 116, 135
Piedmont, 36, 37, 39-42, 43, 46-48, 178, 180, 186, 191-92
Pine barrens, 139, 227-28
Pitch. See Naval stores
Pitt County, 29
Plantations, 100, 132-33, 179, 230
Pocosins, 190
Pollock, Thomas, 26
Pond pine (*Pinus rigida* var. *serotina*), 47, 189
Pond pine-pocosin, 190-91, 262
Pork. See Livestock
Port Bath Town, 90, 94-97, 101, 104, 109, 126-27, 138, 202
Port Beaufort, 88, 90, 94-97, 104, 109, 126-27, 138, 202
Port Brunswick, 88, 90, 94-97, 101, 104, 105-6, 109, 126-27, 177, 202
Port Currituck, 94-97, 101, 104, 109, 202

Port Roanoke, 90, 91, 94-97, 101-4, 105, 109-11, 116, 120, 126-27, 177, 202
Ports, definition of, 87-88, 202
Portsmouth, 167
Pory, John, 33
Potomac River, 11
Proclamation Line, 71
Promotional literature, 223

Quakers, 222
Queen's College, 166

Read, Charles, 135
Rhode Island, 6
Rice, 125-33, 180
Road districts, 29-30
Roads, 143-45, 146, 148-50 *passim*, 156, 159-60, 162-63, 168-69, 176
Roanoke River, 20, 115-16, 156, 235
"Rocky Point," 130
Rowan County, 27, 54, 70, 162-63
Rutherford, John, 98

St. John de Crèvecouer, 15
Salem, 162, 164-66
Salem, Massachusetts, 5
Salisbury, road through, 67; growth and function of, 162-64; mentioned, 119, 166
Sandhills, 39, 158, 178
Savannah, Georgia, 15
Savannah land, 47, 186-91 *passim*
Saw mills, 96-101, 159, 164
Sawn lumber, 93-95, 96-101, 107, 123, 128, 131, 151. See also Wood products
Scotch-Irish, settlers, 8, 12, 14, 22, 55-56, 65-66, 67, 139, 159; merchants, 152-53, 171
Scottish Highlanders, 14, 56-57, 65, 67, 100, 106, 137, 139-40, 153, 159, 175
Scottish Lowlanders, 57, 159
Scottish merchants, 124, 152-53, 164, 168, 171, 175
Seaports, 146-55
Seven Years' War, 54
Shenandoah Valley, 11, 12, 66
Shingles, 93-95, 101, 104-7. See also Wood products
Shortleaf pine (*Pinus echinata*), 47
Slaveholding, 12, 74-81 *passim*, 131-33, 177
Slavery, 13, 14, 89-90, 99, 104, 106, 123, 124, 128-33 *passim*
Source materials, 173-74
South Carolina, 13, 30, 55, 63, 81, 115-

INDEX

18, 125, 126, 131-33, 136-38, 152, 160, 162, 165-66, 169, 171, 179, 201
Southern colonies, description of in 1750, 10-15
Squatters, 9, 26
Starretts Meadows, 191
Staunton River, 66
Staves, 93-95, 101-4, 107. *See also* Wood products
Stock law, 188, 261
Stores, 159, 164-65, 167-69
Surry County, 27
Surveying, 179
Surveyors, 25
Swampland, 43
Swan, John, 129
Swiss settlers, 22

Tar. *See* Naval stores
Tarboro, 155, 160-62, 172
Tar River, 20, 161
Taxables, data on, 194-201
Taxation, system of, 194-95
Tax returns, 198-201
Tenant farming, 140
Tobacco, 10, 120-24, 168, 177, 180
Tobacco plantations, in Virginia, 12
Towns, function of in the thirteen colonies, 15
Townships, 5, 13-14, 179
Trent River, 20, 22, 149
Truck farming, 8, 147
Tryon County, 27
Turpentine. *See* Naval stores

Upland-grass sedge bog, 187-89. *See also* Savannah land
Urmstone, Reverend John, 32-33, 111-12

Venus's-flytrap, 260-61
Virginia, 12-13, 31, 34, 54, 55, 63, 66, 73, 81, 115-16, 118, 120, 122, 124, 126, 135, 136-38, 148, 156, 162, 163-64, 168-71 *passim,* 179-80, 201
Virginia pine (*Pinus virginiana*), 47
Von Graffenried, Christoph, 22, 34, 149

Wagons, 9, 10, 13, 54, 116, 144-45, 156, 159-60, 168, 176
Wake County, 27
Washington, George, 119, 121
Water transportation facilities, 90-92, 111, 116, 143, 145, 146, 150-52, 160-61, 176
Welsh, 14, 21
Western part of North Carolina, 27, 44-46, 54-55, 58, 73-74, 75, 81, 112-16 *passim,* 123, 159, 176-78, 180-81, 192
Western towns, 162-66
West Indies, 9, 23, 90, 91, 93-94, 97, 105, 126, 133, 147, 151
Wetland, 43, 44, 138-39
Wheat, 111-19, 159-60, 180
White cedar (*Chamaecyparis thyoides*), 104-5, 231-32
Williamsburg, Virginia, 149
Wilmington, intensive cultivation in vicinity of, 147; road through, 148; growth and function of, 150-53, 171; trade ties with Cross Creek, 160; merchants in, 164; trade ties with Moravians, 165; mentioned, 90-91, 117, 127-28
Wood products, 93-107, 179

Yadkin River, 12, 66-67
Young, Arthur, 48, 55

www.ingramcontent.com/pod-product-compliance
Lightning Source LLC
Chambersburg PA
CBHW021355290426
44108CB00010B/254